Pluralism on and off Course

Other titles of interest

AULIN
Cybernetic Laws of Social Progress

BAUM
Montesquieu and Social Theory

BLAZYNSKI
Flashpoint Poland

FITZGERALD
Comparing Political Thinkers

FOSTER
Comparative Public Policy and Citizen Participation

GEYER
Alienation Theories: A General Systems Approach

KOSHKISH
The Socio-Political Complex

LASZLO
The Inner Limits of Mankind

MAMAK
Colour, Culture and Conflict: A Study of Pluralism in Fiji

MOSLEY
Westminster Workshop, 4th Edition

SCHAFF
Alienation as a Social Phenomenon

SCHAFF
Political Participation in Communist Systems

SCHAFF
Structuralism and Marxism

TALMOR
Mind and Political Concepts

Journal of interest

HISTORY OF EUROPEAN IDEAS

Editor: Dr Ezra Talmor, Haifa University, Mount Carmel, Haifa, Israel

"History of European Ideas" is a multidisciplinary journal devoted to the study of the history of the cultural exchange between European nations and the influence of this exchange on the formation of European ideas and the emergence of the idea of Europe. The journal publishes regular review articles as well as a book review section; it also contains current information about European scholarly meetings and publications.
The journal will be of interest to scholars in European studies and literature, philosophers, political scientists, economists, historians, sociologists, linguists, educators, and military historians.

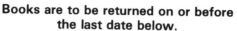

**Books are to be returned on or before
the last date below.**

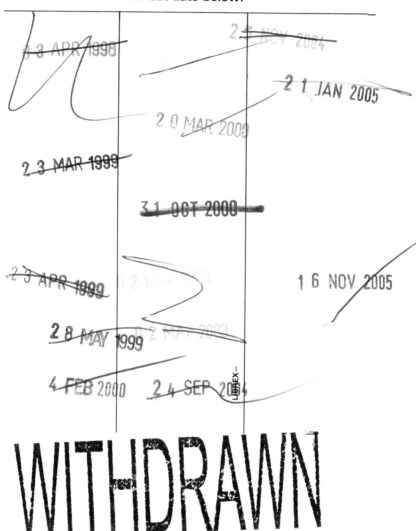

0 3 APR 1998

2 5 NOV 2004

2 1 JAN 2005

2 0 MAR 2000

2 3 MAR 1999

3 1 OCT 2000

2 3 APR 1999

1 6 NOV 2005

2 8 MAY 1999

4 FEB 2000   2 4 SEP 2004

LIBREX—

WITHDRAWN

Pluralism
on and off Course

by

STANISLAW EHRLICH

PERGAMON PRESS

OXFORD · NEW YORK · TORONTO · SYDNEY · PARIS · FRANKFURT

U.K.	Pergamon Press Ltd., Headington Hill Hall, Oxford OX3 0BW, England
U.S.A.	Pergamon Press Inc., Maxwell House, Fairview Park, Elmsford, New York 10523, U.S.A.
CANADA	Pergamon Press Canada Ltd., Suite 104, 150 Consumers Rd., Willowdale, Ontario M2J 1P9, Canada
AUSTRALIA	Pergamon Press (Aust.) Pty. Ltd., P.O. Box 544, Potts Point, N.S.W. 2011, Australia
FRANCE	Pergamon Press SARL, 24 rue des Ecoles, 75240 Paris, Cedex 05, France
FEDERAL REPUBLIC OF GERMANY	Pergamon Press GmbH, 6242 Kronberg-Taunus, Hammerweg 6, Federal Republic of Germany

First edition 1982

Library of Congress Cataloguing in Publication Data

Ehrlich, Stanisław.
Pluralism on and off course.
1. Pluralism (Social sciences)   I. Title.
HM73.E5 1982 303.4'82 82–11233

British Library Cataloguing in Publication Data

Ehrlich, Stanislaw
Pluralism on and off course.
1. Pluralism (Social sciences)
I. Title
321.8   JC325
ISBN 0–08–028114–1 (Hardcover)
ISBN 0–08–027936–8 (Flexicover)

Printed in Great Britain by A. Wheaton & Co. Ltd., Exeter

La multitude qui ne se réduit pas
à l'unité est confusion; l'unité
qui ne dépend pas de la multitude est tyrannie.

PASCAL

Foreword

THE PRESENT BOOK came into being slowly, and I had to toil over it as never before on my earlier publications. Preparatory work was done in the form of my *Pressure Groups. A Study in the Political Structure of the Capitalist System* (in Polish, 1962), whose later editions under the changed title of *Power and Interests* (in Polish, 1967, 1974) announced a continuation of the study of pluralism. It was also published in German: *Die Macht der Minuterheit.* (Europa Verlag), in French: *La pouvoir et les groupes de pression* (Mouton); and Italian, *Potere e gruppi di pressione* (Editori Riuniti).

Further steps were marked by my lectures on social and political pluralism, held abroad, namely at the Sorbonne (Ecole Pratique, VIème Section) in 1965/6, at the Catholic University in Louvain (at the then Flemish Section) for a semester in 1972, at the University of Toronto in 1973/4, and at the Foundation for Political Science in Paris for a semester in 1978.

Some parts of the book were published in Poland in 1977–8.

My heartfelt thanks are due to Professors Władysław Markiewicz and Jan Szczepański, who read the manuscript, and also to Dr Barbara Sobolewska and Professor Bogusław Leśnodorski for his help with part of Chapter 1. People of whose advice I could avail myself are unfortunately too numerous to list here. My gratitude is also due to all those who were my hosts at the above universities and who helped me organize my lectures.

And now the final message to the Reader: if he has grasped and assimilated Pascal's aphorism he can spare the time he has allotted for this book, for that on which a craftsman of science has to labour for years is elucidated by a single sentence that comes as a flash of genius.

STANISLAW EHRLICH
Warsaw

Contents

4 Pluralism in the United States

PART II

5 Pluralism and Marxism

6 Pluralistic Elements in the Socialist Reconstruction of Society

Preliminary Explanations

PLURALISM: a term which has given rise to many misunderstandings and has been assigned numerous meanings.

The current interpretation of pluralism in the Western world is linked to the idea that pluralism is a characteristic feature of democracy in a capitalist system, manifested by social and political differentiation and a supposed dispersal of power throughout its numerous centres. This scattering of power, whose various elements are to form a system of checks and balances, is considered to be the foundation of individual freedom. Pluralism interpreted in this way is opposed to socialist societies, which are seen as uniform and monolithic, marked by a lack of social and political differentiation, and accompanied by the centralization of power. This view is almost universally accepted, and pluralism is considered synonymous with Western democracy as its inherent attribute. In extreme cases socialist societies are labelled "totalitarian".

This version of pluralism has in turn evoked opposition and mistrust in socialist countries, where pluralism is usually seen (or was seen until recent times) as one of the many varieties of anti-communist ideology. This vulgarization of the issue which long preceded present-day controversies has resulted in an over-simplification of arguments and counter-arguments.

In this book, leaving the problem of ontological pluralism aside, we shall define pluralism as that trend which strives to restrict centralism (not justified in definite fields and in a given historical period). We shall class as pluralistic every trend which opposes uniformity, both in social and political structure and in the sphere of culture, the uniformity which centralism inevitably breeds. Pluralistic theories on the whole do not deny that there are vast areas of state administration and social life which are approved by all (*consensus omnium*) but consider it neither desirable nor possible that in a free country there should be a uniform common will that absorbs the diversified intentions of the various groups.[1] It is indifferent in this connection whether uniformity results from intentional action from the centre of power (i.e., the centre of decision-making in political matters) and hence is something artificial and imposed upon society, an entity duly institutionalized, i.e. comprised within a system of norms; or results from spontaneous, and hence uncontrolled, social development. All normative pluralism has social and political differentiation as its point of departure. And it is such differentiation which is the subject-matter of the reflections formulated in this book. Our knowledge of social history tells us that monism in the sphere of values, organizations, and normative systems is observable only in primitive and in totalitarian societies. So let us say that pluralism lies between monist and anarchist poles.[2]

By formulating the issue thus we avoid the simplification (which always arises if we are not concerned with a totalitarian system) inherent in any question about the presence or absence of pluralism in a given sociopolitical system; we can focus our attention on the problem of the *area* which will be the subject of contralist or pluralist decisions, and, later, on the degree of pluralism, its growth, and decline. We thus treat pluralism as a historical category, as a phenomenon which *manifests itself anew in every epoch*. Every epoch gives rise to a new structure of interests; hence the importance of the proper comprehension of the concept of interest when we reflect on pluralism.

Clarity in such matters is particularly important at the beginning of the period which requires a matter-of-fact dialogue not only among politicians, but also among representatives of the various social sciences, who work under different sociopolitical systems.

Pluralist thinking in the social sciences developed as early as the nineteenth century, the social and political aspects of differentiation being very closely intertwined, although we have to distinguish them all the time. Hence already at the turn of the nineteenth century we can trace three distinct currents: French, British and American pluralism, each of which was split into various trends and/or schools.

At this point the present writer could be accused of failing to single out German pluralism, and the pluralist elements to be found in Hegel's works (the more so as he has found them in Comte) and in the opinions of prominent present-day German pluralists. In Hegel's case, the glorification of the state and the principle which imposes the duty of absolute obedience practically annihilate the pluralist elements in his writings.[3] This is why an analysis of Hegel's pluralism is postponed—if time suffices—to be dealt with separately. In Western Germany, as has been pointed out by Fraenkel,[4] political sociologists have not shown interest in the revival of de Tocqueville's ideas, which in recent decades, have stimulated new research on pluralism. Those students of pluralism who have interesting theoretical achievements to their credit (Klaus von Beyme, U. Bermborch, R. Eisfeld, E. Fraenkel, W.D. Narr and others) have become active in the field during the last 10–15 years. I shall occasionally comment on their work; but their contribution means a continuation—independent, it is true—of certain existing opinions on pluralism. For a similar reason I have disregarded present-day French representatives of descriptive group pluralism (e.g., J. Meynaud). Thus, in the case of German sociopolitical thought I have not grasped (or perhaps I have failed to grasp) that relay race of theoretical ideas of pluralism which is specific to the said trends in France, Britain, and America.

The analysis of the various trends within pluralism naturally raises the question of the pluralist elements in Marxism. If they are not to be found in that doctrine, are we to assume that Marxism is an antithesis of those trends? If they are found, what is their content and in what do they differ from the other trends? In particular, what are the manifestations of the tendency to include pluralist elements in the practice of restructuring society on the socialist principles? And what are the obstacles encountered in that process?

Even these brief remarks show that the present writer's intention is to discuss various forms or examples of pluralism, its various ramifications, some of which ended in blind alleys, while the others contributed to our knowledge of society. This is why the book could also be given the title: "The Pluralism of Pluralisms".

But the author did not set out to discuss all forms of pluralism. He has therefore not taken up the issue of ontological pluralism, which would require entering into the old controversy over monism versus pluralism. Discussing the problems of philosophical pluralism would result in going back at least to Leibniz, and to trying to decide whether monism and pluralism are opposing or–for all their apparent opposition–only complementary concepts, etc. We would thus move away from the proper aim of this book, which would be even more unfortunate because there is no necessary link between philosophical pluralism, on the one hand, and social and political pluralism, on the other. This is why the philosophical issues had to be left to competent philosophers. In that respect I have only made two exceptions by pointing briefly to the connections between the philosophical views of James and Russell with their, or their followers', opinions on society and the state.

In the case of French pluralism, the elements of pluralism in Maritain's personalism have not been analysed either, even though his statement on the single Roman Catholic Church and the various Christian civilizations, orders, and systems encourages one to do that. Likewise, I had to disregard Mounier's acceptance of socialism on the basis of personalism, and his opposition to liberal individualism, although these aspects of his views suggest that much space should be given to a discussion of that trend. The same applies to the elements of pluralism in the decision of the Second Council of Vatican. Nor is it possible to analyse pluralism in post-colonial states, where age-old tribal differentiation clashed with the centralism introduced by the new machinery of the state and where at the same time a new pluralism of social and ethnic groups (at the supratribal or even national level) has been emerging. This overlapping of two processes: the class-making one, combined with the stratification of vocational groups, on the one hand, with the nation-making one, on the other, has bred tensions unprecedented in human history.[5]

It was not possible, either, to analyse the explosion of centrifugal forces in the form of the various ethnic groups in "old" states, groups which strive for their identity and autonomy, thus undermining the myth of the homogeneity of those states (Britain, France, Spain).

Finally, I have not taken up the issue of legal pluralism, by which is meant the plurality of normative systems binding in a given society.

All these important problems would require separate monographs, so the present writer had to impose limitations upon his work. But it seems relevant to reflect briefly, in these introductory paragraphs, on the concept of interest:

It was introduced by rationalist French materialists, such as Holbach, Helvetius, and Diderot, the first of whom had primarily individual interest in mind, while Diderot was also concerned with the various manifestations of social interest. Diderot treated interest as something which is advantageous for, or merely required by, the individual, the state, or the nation. And it was from Diderot that Marxism took over the distinction between individual and social interest, in its various forms, and raised it to the rank of a fundamental concept. Marx in his early writings had already declared himself in favour of a rationalization of social processes; he rationalized them by claiming that whatever man strives for is connected with his interests. And while Engels wrote in his *Housing Question* that although economic relations in a given society always take the form of interests, this is not to say that everything can be reduced to a kind of motivational monism. There is no reason why the concept of interests should be reduced to economic motivations alone. A believer, if he is a churchgoer, experiences the need to have a church at his disposal; a sportsman is interested in the construction of stadiums and swimming pools; museums come into being because of the interest of art-lovers, as do theatres and philharmonic halls. Interests occur in every sphere of human activity, and even at its forefront, in the sphere of experienced desires. John Plamenatz means by interest everything which is to the advantage of the individual or the group, and which gives him or them what they wish or consider gratifying.[6]

It must, however, be borne in mind that the philosophical, economic, sociological, political, and legal concept of interest does not appear in many schools of thought in modern psychology, either individual or social. In psychology, it has a fairly exact analogue in the concept of individual, group, or social need. T. Tomaszewski defines need as 'man's dependence on his environment in some respect'. This approach covers not only biological needs, but social and cultural as well, and also derivative ones, which Tomaszewski terms instrumental. They appear whenever we need something relative to something else.[7] It can easily be seen that semantically "interest" coincides with "need", or that in any case it would be very difficult to draw a demarcation line between them. This statement is, of course, not intended to claim preference for either of the two terms, which are used according to context and accepted linquistic convention; it is nevertheless useful to realize that such a semantic coincidence does take place.

When we consider the concept of interest (need) we are concerned with four relationships:

(1) A natural and/or social reality and the subject who strives to change or to preserve the existing state of things (relations). The subject who strives so to influence the surrounding world may be an individual or a group. The motivation of that striving need not be concerned with advantage (in the sense of a situation which results in participation in goods and values which are limited in amount and are unevenly distributed among men). But the fact that a situation is advantageous may also consist in that situation favouring participation in goods.[8] But it would probably be better to understand interest (need) more broadly as any factor which, as Bollhagen puts it, is significant for man, which results in a certain orientation of his personality.[9] The same applies to a group. This leads us to the conclusion that the very possibility of participating in social processes may be an additional value in that it satisfies the participant(s)' interest.

(2) The possibility of changing or preserving the existing state of things may or may not be realized by the subject. We can observe today how many people strive for something which is objectively detrimental to them, but which they consider advantageous; or, conversely, who abstain from taking measures which would end a situation detrimental to them because they consider the situation advantageous.

A physician may know what is good for a patient's health, although the latter may not realize it. Economists, sociologists, and political scientists may find that groups, strata, and classes do not set themselves the tasks which would favour the satisfaction of their interests. This also applies to the decision-makers within those groups. Leaders may fail to understand, or have no knowledge of, the interests of those groups whose behaviour is determined by the decisions they make. To make matters worse, they may fail to realize what is advantageous and what is detrimental to their remaining the leaders.

This relation between realized and non-realized interests, which is interwoven with that of subjective and objective interests, is of particular significance in the social sphere. The former was first discussed by Marx, who made a distinction between a "class in itself", which on the whole does not realize what its situation within society is, i.e., what are its relations towards the other social classes, and has accordingly not developed any organizational forms that would serve its interests, and a "class for itself", which consciously strives to satisfy its interests through the intermediary of the organizations it has developed. There is every reason to extend this Marxian distinction between two chronological stages (because the former must always precede the latter) to all those groups which have been or are going through an analogous process. It follows from the above that all interests must be treated as both subjective and objective,[10] and that the distinction must be made between those interests which are realized and those which are not. By objective interests some authors mean a certain disposition on the part of classes, strata, groups, and individuals which is oriented towards the goal adopted as a result of social development.[11]

(3) Variability of both individual and group interests is self-evident: some interests emerge, others vanish, but they are all the time shaped by changing reality. This is not to say that interests developed only in a spontaneous manner, having taken shape as requirements become the beginning (input) of a political process. The order of events may go in the reverse direction: the activity of political decision-makers does not only reflect incoming demands, but may in itself give rise to new interests or stimulate latent ones.[12] Social organizations are formed, disappear and change, following the fortunes of interests. In the flow of events we can single out those interests (needs) whose satisfaction does not require much time, and those which can be satisfied only in the long run.[13] Short-term needs are often instrumental relative to long-term ones. Grasping this relation between two categories of interests is important, because short-term interests may become autonomous with respect to those which can be satisfied only in a remote future.

In the case of this distinction the situations in which an individual can shape group interests also reflect an important problem. It seems legitimate to advance the hypothesis that a small group offers the greatest possibilities of such an individual influence. The larger and the more complex the organization, the smaller the possibilities and the greater the chances of an individual's alienation.

(4) The fourth relation is that between individual and social (group) interest. L. S. Rubinshtein says that individual ("psychological") interest assumes active behaviour; and that it is derivative with respect to social interest, and narrower; that it is a map or visualization of social interest. Rubinshtein in his formulation seems to exaggerate the otherwise obvious thesis that individual interest is closely connected with group interest (that obviousness being due to the fact that human personality is shaped in societal life).[14] "Psychological" interest may sometimes induce one to abstain from activity. Further most personal interests are not always deducible from social ones, they may be of no significance whatever for any social group, and as such will not reflect any social interest nor be its visualization.

All these intricate problems cannot be reduced to the dichotomy of individual and social interest, to which many authors refer in their comments on socialist society, and which assumes a lack or a gradual vanishing of conflicts among groups.[15] What is the source of this misunderstanding? Rousseau often referred to one and equal interest of all (in his *Discours sur l'inégalité*); he also wrote about the unity of interests and will (in *L'économie politique*), for he had a very strong dislike of particular interests (cf. *Contrat social*, livre 3, ch. 4), which he considered to be the principal social evil. But, first, these were his "organizational recommendations" for societies within small states, and secondly, Rousseau was in fact an enemy of heterogeneity and an admirer of homogeneity, but in the sense of ethical concepts.[16] And finally, this is not all Rousseau: as will be shown later (cf. section 5.1), his views included clear pluralistic elements. This is why–let this be said again–it is a gross misunderstanding to look, in the second half of the twentieth century, for inspiration in those semi-utopian recommendations striving for homogeneity.

The thesis on the dichotomy of interests is incompatible with the dialectic interpretation of social development. Nor can it be brought into agreement with the present state of sociological knowledge, which has dismissed the reduction of societal facts to individual psychology–the opinion shared, among others, by Homans.[17] And the adoption of that dichotomy does lead to such a reduction and to an atomistic model of society. Yet society is formed not of abstract individuals, but of persons connected with one another by definite links (persons-in-relations). It is they who form definite communities.[18]

Nor are there any grounds for the acceptance of the claim that "a small social group cannot determine the basic interests of those individuals who are its members because such a group does not represent the basic sphere of their social existence.[19] And if such a small group is a group formed on the professional basis (a group of electronic engineers, or immunologists, or sculptors, etc.), does it not determine the basic interests of these groups?

In a socialist society the interests of an individual, and those of society, interpreted not only as social interests in general, but interests of classes, strata, and formal and informal groups, form intricate systems of relations and this is why we have to speak about structures of individual and social interests.[20]

Confining oneself to a dichotomy of individual and social interests is an illegitimate simplification that prevents one from taking note of essential problems. In a socialist society, or non-capitalist, if you prefer, too, an individual belongs to various organizations and various informal groups, which may give rise to inner tensions and conflicts if the interests of those bodies are incompatible to some extent. Further, within formal groups there is a certain selection of individual interests in accordance with a system of norms produced by every organization,[21] which ultimately results in a *sui generis* organizational compromise.[21] This fact makes it possible for the members of an organization to accept its interests as their own and thus to internalize them. The cohesion of an organization depends on the degree to which individual interests are identified with those of the organization. It follows therefrom that we cannot speak about complete internalization: an individual as a rule–which has just been emphasized–is a member of various organizations, and this is why we can speak about limited internalization that can be graduated, and thus serve as a measure of the cohesion of a given group. The variability of interests, already mentioned above, also results in changes in the intensity of internalization. Diverse and conflicting interests in society are unavoidable but its survival and evolution depends on a minimum of consensus.[22] Both conflict and consensus are, of course, historical categories.

Finally, it is probably worth while to clarify a certain terminological misunderstanding, which makes a tentative distinction between "interest groups" and other groups, termed in various ways.[23] Now, people unite–in particular within organized groups (i.e. organizations)–because they share interests that consist in their attaining a more or less specified goal. One cannot think of any permanently functioning group that would not be guided by some interests, and which would not have any organizational framework. This is why we shall in future simply use the term *organization*.

One further point: the fact that class and group interests are complementary, and not opposing, concepts has been demonstrated by the present writer in his other work,[24] which makes the discussion of this issue superfluous here.

NOTES AND REFERENCES

1. E. Fraenkel, *Der Pluralismus als Strukturelement der freiheitlich-rechtsstaatlichen Demokratie* (München and Berlin, 1964).
2. J. Lively, Pluralism and Consensus. In: P. Birnbaum, J. Lively, and G. Parry (eds), *Democracy and Social Contract*. (London and Beverly Hills, 1978), p. 187.
3. In this connection see R. H. Bowen, *German Theories of the Corporative State* (New York, 1947).
4. *Ibid.*, p. 27.
5. C. Young; *The Politics of Cultural Pluralism* (Madison, Wisc., 1976). For a theoretical approach see R. A. LeVine and D. T. Campbell, *Ethnocentrism, Theories of Conflict, Ethnic Attitudes of Group Behaviour*, (New York and London, 1972).
6. J. P. Plamenatz, "Interest (Political Science)", in: J. Gould and W. Kolb (eds), *A Dictionary of the Social Sciences* (New York, 1964), p. 343.
7. Cf. T. Tomaszewski, in: M. Maruszewski, J. Reykowski, T. Tomaszewski (eds), *Psychologia jako nauka o człowieku /Psychology as the Science of Man* (Warszawa, 1967), pp. 222 ff.
8. W. Wesołowski, *Klasy, warstwy i władza /Classes, Strata, and Power* (Warszawa, 1966), p. 107.
9. P. Bollhagen, *Interesse und Gesellschaft* (Berlin, 1967), p. 18. See also I. Balbus, "The Concept of Interest in Pluralist and Marxian Analysis". *Politics and Society*, 1 (Feb. 1971), 151–78.

10. Concerning interest as an objective phenomenon, independent of whether it is, or is not, realized, see P. Bollhagen, *op. cit.*, p. 25.
11. P. Bollhagen, *op. cit.*, p. 41. P. Bachrach in the sphere of political interests makes a distinction between real and articulated interest; see his "Interest, Participation and Democratic Theory", in: J. R. Pennock and J.W. Chapman (eds), *Participation in Politics* (New York, 1975), p. 42.
12. Ch. Lindblom, *The Policy Making Process* (Englewood Cliffs, 1968), p. 102, S. Beer, *Modern Political Development* (New York, 1974), pp. 20 ff. The problem was discussed by the present writer in his *Le pouvoir et les groupes de pression* (Paris 1971) (first Polish edition 1962), ch. XII.
13. W. Wesołowski, *op sit.*, p. 117.
14. L. S. Rubinshtein, *Grundlagen der allgemeinen Psychologie* (Berlin, 1958), p. 774.
15. The advocates of this dichotomy should bear it in mind that a similar distinction between the state and the individual belongs to the heritage of the individualism that marked the bourgeois revolutions.
16. E. Fraenkel, *op. cit.*, p. 18.
17. G. Homans, *Social Behavior. Its Elementary Forms,* (New York and London), 1961, p. 30.
18. L. G. Bonin, Man and Society, in: J. R. Pennock and J. W. Chapman (eds.), *Voluntary Associations* (New York, 1969).
19. W. W. Lawrynienko, "Interest as a Sociological Category", *Problems of Philosophy* (Russ.), no. 10, 1966.
20. See also P. Bollhagen, *op cit.*, p. 80.
21. S. Ehrlich, *Wstęp do nauki o państwie i prawie/Introduction to the Theory of State and Law* (Warszawa, 1971), chap. XIV (On the pluralism of normative systems).
22. J. Lively, *op cit.*, pp. 188 ff.
23. On the terminological confusion in the Western literature of the subject cf. S. Ehrlich, *Władza i interesy,* chap. II, p. 2, for comments on terminology.
24. *Ibid.*, chap. I.

Part One

CHAPTER 1

Pluralism in France

1.1 THE SOURCES: DE TOCQUEVILLE

Democracy in America, by Alexis de Tocqueville, is of special significance for the issues connected with pluralism. De Tocqueville was the first to estimate properly the forces inherent in a diversified society that takes the form of numerous organized groups and of decentralization. He saw them as barriers against centralist despotism. He was a brilliant representative of the liberal trend that had been gaining in strength, from Locke and de Montesquieu onwards, and was to dominate bourgeois thought in the second half of the nineteenth century. His liberalism was signally different from that represented by Benjamin Constant, his senior contemporary, who had died in 1830, i.e. before de Tocqueville began his great tour of America.

Historians of political thought mention Constant and de Tocqueville in the same breath as founders of French liberalism; yet the opinions of these two authors show essential differences that many years later were to crystallize as the liberal progressive and the liberal conservative trends.

While Constant stood for a clearly individualistic liberalism,[1] de Tocqueville saw the prospects for individual development within different groups in a diversified society. De Tocqueville called himself a liberal of a new type. He stood for the individualism of a society-oriented person, individualism whose boundaries are marked by that person's moral consciousness. Individual interests are set in the organizational framework of freely emerging associations. This structure was to replace the formalized differentiation of feudal society crammed into rigorous provisions of the king's law.

These associations with their particular interests were expected to restrain the central authority, which in France at that time had age-old traditions going back to Cardinal Richelieu. The reining of the feudal monarchy began very early. It was marked by the expansion of the bureaucratic apparatus of the state, without which the absolute monarchy would not be in a position to function properly.[2] That heritage of centralized bureaucracy was taken over by the bourgeois revolution, modernized by Napoleon I, and then preserved by the Bourbon Restoration and the Orleans monarchy. De Tocqueville was one of the first to perceive that centralization had not been the work of the

French Revolution, and that succeeding systems were availing themselves of the experience of the absolute monarchy.[3]

Unlike Constant, who in his system of the separation of powers placed the royal power above the other three as the arbiter (which seems to be a signal modification of de Montesquieu's idea), de Tocqueville did not think that the sovereign power (that of the king or the people) could be restricted sufficiently by the legal guarantee of individual freedom. While in Constant's liberalism pluralistic elements take the form of empty declarations like "diversity means life, homogeneity means death", de Tocqueville's pluralist liberalism referred to American and French (*Ancient Régime* ...) realities and to their confrontation.

His contemporaries considered de Tocqueville to have been the greatest political thinker since de Montesquieu. Such was certainly the opinion of John Stuart Mill, who claimed that de Tocqueville had marked a new epoch in the study of politics. A similar opinion was held by Royer Collard, who paved for de Tocqueville the way to the French Academy. In our times, Ruggiero treats him as the greatest French political writer, and J. J. Chevallier calls him the de Montesquieu of the nineteenth century. The book on America written in his youth by de Tocqueville already included elements unequalled by other contemporaneous comments on American society (cf. M. Martineau, *De la société americaine*, 1838). But we are interested not so much in the enthusiastic assessment of de Tocqueville's writings as the fact that he was a disciple and a continuator of de Montesquieu. Contrary to the common belief, de Montesquieu saw the guarantee of individual freedom (interpreted as the antithesis of the arbitrariness of the despotic ruler) not only in a system of checks and balances associated with the separation of powers, but also in decentralization, in "intermediate bodies", and above all in the priority of moral principles before politics.[4] That priority was the basis of his toleration, expressed already in *Les lettres persanes* (1721), where he ranked religious pluralism in a state higher than the principle of a dominant religion and formulated his belief that those who profess religious tolerance are more useful to their individual countries. Are de Tocqueville's writings not marked by the same spirit of toleration? Like Constant and Guizot, de Tocqueville gave priority to moral principles before politics.

To come back to the issue of intermediate bodies, these were supposed to act as buffers between the state and the individual. But here a reservation must be made which brings out the difference between the idea of de Montesquieu and that of de Tocqueville. Everyone who has read *De l'esprit des lois* knows that de Montesquieu's intermediate bodies (or "authorities") cannot be interpreted as freely organized groups of citizens, which one century later came to attract de Tocqueville's attention. De Montesquieu referred to official bodies, subject to the monarch, and dependent upon him, but at the same time working to restrain the arbitrariness of an absolute ruler. He saw those bodies in the feudal estates: the nobility, the clergy and the third estate in the towns. Now the said elements intended by de Montesquieu to guarantee individual freedom were directed against absolutism.[5] The theory of separation of powers results from social differentiation, and may be interpreted only as a derivative of the latter, since otherwise it would be vulgarized as a recommendation of a separation of the prerogatives of state agencies.

No-one could have better prepared de Tocqueville for his famous American tour than de Montesquieu did.

Uniformity in societal life was hateful to both, and both saw the world as a diversified whole. Both constructed their normative political systems not on the basis of rationalistic speculation, typical of thinkers in the Age of Reason, but on the basis of a penetrating study of empirical social and political data. De Tocqueville once said about uniformity that it reduces people to the condition of a timorous and toiling flock of which the government (or the state) is the shepherd.[6] When it comes to de Montesquieu, his brilliant (but how fertile) mistake of ascribing to contemporaneous England the system of separation of powers, which did not exist there at that time (as it does not exist today), does not change the fact that his theoretical reflections started from empirical data. Both de Tocqueville and de Montesquieu may be considered forerunners of empirical research in the sphere of political and social phenomena.

Comte, in his *Cours de philosophie positive* (Lesson 47), paid homage to de Montesquieu's perspicacity, and Durkheim went even further by considering him, next to Rousseau, as the forerunner of sociology, as the man who laid the foundations of that discipline and outlined its distinctive features. In de Montesquieu, Durkheim wrote, social facts are not a subject matter of rationalistic speculation; he does not assess them on the basis of deduction which originates from human nature; they are for him the subject matter of observation which results in description and explanation. But this is not all. De Montesquieu has not only demonstrated that social facts can be a subject-matter of science, but also formulated fundamental concepts of sociology.[7]

When it comes to the consolidation and development of American democracy, which was being constructed as a system without the burden of feudal survivals, de Tocqueville's reflections were stimulated by two issues. The first–if we follow the order in which he discussed them–was the broad prerogatives of American local authorities, the system of local government on a scale unknown in Europe. When making that comparison he wrote that the strength of free peoples lay in the commune. If the commune is deprived of its strength and independence, one finds the inhabitants to be merely those who are governed, but not citizens. Communal institutions are for freedom what elementary schools are for education. They are independent bodies, and neither the federal nor the state authorities should interfere with them. While in France a state functionary collects local taxes, in America a communal functionary collects state and federal taxes.[8] Yet in the history of France, too, there was a brief period which made him think of American experience. That was the period of the revolution, during which the idea of *pouvoir municipal*, the idea of "the fourth power" was crystallized in the Act of December 1789. That Act defined the competences of the commune as distinct from those of the central authority. De Tocqueville spoke about that "communal spirit" as the major factor of public peace and order.[9]

De Tocqueville saw in decentralization a manifestation of freedom. The rulers never grant it themselves, and the people must rely on its own strength if it is to win and keep it. De Tocqueville saw local government as the fundamental school of freedom, because the national assembly is far away and involves only few persons, whereas many people are engaged in local government. He was struck by the fact that individuals identified themselves with the local community–a tradition going back to the colonial period, when the local authorities were considered "one's own", when mutual assistance was the natural order, and tax collectors and soldiers, representatives of the remote metropolis, were alien and hateful. Nor did he fail to notice that the various self-governing bodies, from the commune to the township to the county to the federal level, were not hierarchically subordinated to one another. He saw in it a guarantee of self-government.

When describing the differentiation of the local government de Tocqueville correctly noticed in it the temporal and systemic antecedent of the American federal system.

That federal system was interpreted by him as a guarantee of freedom in the sense of being an additional barrier to centralism, because he treated it as a variety of decentralization. All these three forms–the local government, the large number and popularity of large and small associations, and the federal system–promote an active attitude of the citizens and restrain the despotism typical of a centralized state.[10] These diversified elements can survive if they are cemented by common values.

The second problem which engaged de Tocqueville's attention was the freedom of association. He noticed that in America associations emerge in all spheres of life: public security, commerce and industry, morals, and religion. His general conclusion from these observations was that associations are particularly needed in democratic societies. He added that the right of association seemed to him almost as inalienable as individual freedom. He noted that in freely formed associations there was no relation of subordination and superordination, which contributed to variety as a permanent feature. He blamed the Europeans for treating associations as a kind of weapon which one uses in a hurry, and for an excessive interference on the part of the state. The very setting up of an association depends on the approval by the state authorities, which results in political interference with their internal business. Moreover, associations in Europe tended to become centralized, which gave the administrative power in them to the few.

It is to be noted here that de Tocqueville was right in connecting the broad range of associations with the differentiation of group interests. In one of his letters (published posthumously by A. Redier) de Tocqueville referred to interest as the mortar which keeps American society together, in spite of the fact that such interest is usually particular in nature. The doctrine of interest, he wrote, was commonly accepted in America. De Tocqueville meant by this the practice of revealing the genuine motivation instead of smoke-screening it by sublime phraseology, as was common in Europe. He concluded his reflections by stating that without the freedom of association democracy can change into equality in the face of tyranny. A despot can easily pardon those who are governed if they do not like him–so long as they do not like each other. As he shared with de Montesquieu the belief that morals must be given priority over politics de Tocqueville emphasized the particular role of "intellectual and moral" associations in America, associations which are no less important than political parties and industrial organizations.

We cannot disregard the fact that de Tocqueville subsumed under associations both political parties and business organizations, which even more emphasizes the distance which separates them from de Montesquieu's "intermediate bodies". When comparing the American party system with European systems, de Tocqueville pointed out that the lack of universal suffrage in Europe always enabled a given party to appear as the spokesman of non-represented interests and to attack the government as a usurper.

What is the relation between the revolutionary concept of the sovereignty of the people and de Tocqueville's pluralism? The sovereignty of the people is the foundation of the latter, but once the popular authority is established tendencies towards uniformity and centralization develop, and the idea of "secondary" bodies (which are analogues of de Montesquieu's "intermediate bodies") is blurred. Revolutionary practice destroys the feudal representative bodies, the mass of scattered individuals does not form new intermediate bodies, and the emergent vacuum is filled by a centralist state administration, which results in democratic absolutism, in uniformity, in taking up ever new tasks which the absolute monarchy did not set itself.

When drawing the picture of the paternalistic state de Tocqueville points to another process. In a society which is taking on new forms after having shed the shackles of feudalism, the tendency develops for individuals to isolate themselves from one another, to rely on their own enterprise and on the property acquired by that enterprise. They accordingly do not see any need to combine or to form associations, and they thus keep to their respective family circles. Such isolation constrains individual enterprise, limits the potential and the sense of independence in individuals, and morally impoverishes those individuals. A special role is played by the mesh of small associations. The state is not in a position to replace their diversified activities. De Tocqueville speaks in this connection of the immense scope of the central authority whose uniformity absorbs authorities and factors scattered among a mass of "secondary authorities". No similar power has been observed in the world since the fall of the Roman empire. De Tocqueville failed to foresee that that was not yet the limit of the expansion of the authority of the state. He was right in pointing to the fact that the dawn of democratic society is accompanied by a tendency on the part of the citizens to live in isolation, to close themselves up in their individualism, which he termed "the rust of society". That tendency toward isolation, which favoured despotism, was explained by him as due to the fact that those people who have just won independence were drunk with their newly-acquired power and imagined that they could do without the assistance of others.

In *Ancien Régime* he says that in such a situation people are inclined to be concerned with their own particular interests, to take into consideration primarily themselves and their families, to close themselves up "in a narrow individualism in which public virtues are smothered". J. Lively believes this opinion to be characteristic of de Tocqueville's description of democracy.

Individuals, once they have become citizens, notice first the shackles which are no longer there and their newly acquired autonomy which separates them from other "active" citizens, regarded by them as competitors. They come to realize the possibility of storming the social ladder; they are guided by motives recorded in the great psychological novels of Balzac, Stendhal, and Zola. The victory of bourgeois revolution, regardless of its course, meant a triumph of "possessive individualism", to use the title of a renowned book by C. B. Macpherson.[11] The new relationships of production do not encourage new social bonds. This applies to both "the rich" and "the poor"; and this so-called "possessive individualism" acts as a strong brake on association.

But the experience once acquired in associations is reproduced incessantly. Associations breed norms which prevent conflicts, or solve them if such conflicts arise. Associations pave the way to the socialization of individuals. This was the second form (after local government) of social self-regulation. This was the framework de Tocqueville assigned to individualism.[12]

De Tocqueville must be credited with having theoretically formulated the experience of the bourgeois revolution, of which the Jacobinic rule marked the peak. De Tocqueville makes us face the dilemma: the sovereignty of the people may give rise either to pluralism or to centralism and uniformism, and–not without a note of pessimism–he believed the latter course to be more probable. De Tocqueville saw the possibility of Europe's evolving toward democracy, but obviously not as a copy of the American system. Thus he did not recommend adopting the American institutions: he merely recommended a reflection on the American experience in the sphere of political system.

De Tocqueville was firm in declaring himself against socialism (on certain occasions he even approved of the anti-revolutionary reprisals in 1848).[13] He regarded private property as an unshakeable foundation of society, and hence as something unviolable, and revolution was for him a symptom of social malady. All that which the French revolution had achieved could have been attained without it. His pluralistic concept of an expanded system of local government, freedom of speech and freedom of association in social and political organizations, was to prevent new revolutionary upheavals and to ensure a conflict-free evolution.

His pluralistic conception of society did not take into account class stratification in Europe: it is on social classes that a student of history should focus his attention, since there is no doubt that they mark the basic caesura within society. Democracy gave rise to the industrial system, which split society into two opposing classes. In that respect, i.e. because of that opposition, Laski compared de Tocqueville to Marx. The analogy is, of course, extremely limited in scope. De Tocqueville's pluralistic conception was intended to overcome the antinomy of freedom and equality; it also comprised the state as a necessary factor which works upon society from the outside.

De Tocqueville gave American society a mirror at an opportune moment. Enlightened America accepted it enthusiastically, for many reasons. The American intellectual élite and its French guest possessed the writings of de Montesquieu as a basis for their understanding–de Montesquieu who had inspired first the state constitutions and then the Constitution of the United States of 1787, and to whom the founding fathers of the American federation afforded much respect. In *The Federalist* we read, in connection with the doctrine of separation of powers: "The oracle who is always consulted is the celebrated Montesquieu."[14]

La Fayette, hero of two revolutions, the American and the French, also was an adherent of de Montesquieu, whose ideas further reached the United States through the intermediary of Blackstone, his British disciple and admirer.

Secondly, no one had yet undertaken an analysis like De Tocqueville's. The United States had to wait a long time for an American author to analyse their society, because the next book on this subject, written half a century later (*The American Commonwealth*, 1888), was the work of an Englishman, James Bryce. The society which de Tocqueville wrote about covered the period of the presidency of Andrew Jackson. It was already a post-Jeffersonian America, agrarian rather than plebeian. In that period the original suspiciousness of "factions", typical of Washington and Madison, belonged to the dead past. By "factions" they meant–as also did other contributors to *The Federalist* who wrote under the collective pen name of Publius (in addition to Madison they were Hamilton and Jay)–not only political parties, but all organized groups whose activity threatens public, and hence republican, interest as it serves particular interests.[15] This suspiciousness, which reflected the conservative and individualistic ideology of those authors, had no chance of becoming a political and social guideline. On the contrary, the next period, studied by de Tocqueville, was that of the formation of the American two-party system and the free rise of various associations that were mushrooming before his eyes. They fitted the variety much better at the federal level (which de Tocqueville termed a society of societies) than did the uniformist individualism postulated by Washington and the Federalists.

Thirdly, it was not without significance that de Tocqueville to some extent idealized American society, for which he was later to be blamed by James Bryce, who claimed that de Tocqueville did not describe America, but put forward his own conception of the theory of democracy, illustrated by American experience.[16] De Tocqueville wrote of the communities in New England that on the whole they lived a happy life; that they were governed in a way which corresponded to the likings and choices of the citizens, and that in view of the peace and prosperity that prevailed in America, storms in American municipal life are rare. While he saw a diversity of interests in that society, he failed to notice the contradictions. It must be stated plainly that de Tocqueville's America is a picture of a society in which conflicts are unknown. In one of his letters he wrote that America was in a privileged position, because particular interests were never at variance there with general interest, which was not so in Europe. On another occasion he claimed that every American was ready to sacrifice his own particular interests to save the public ones. The German's usual comment is that such statements are too good to be true. Had de Tocqueville not been a member of an aristocratic family, and had he not studied middle-class America, we could say that the picture he painted was a court portrait.

While de Montesquieu was a man of compromise at the time of a transitional equilibrium of class forces and deliberately strove in his writings to ease revolutionary tensions and to avoid a revolution, de Tocqueville understood the regularity and irreversibility of events and even felt resigned to them. By studying a bourgeois democracy in its pure form, uncontaminated by survivals of feudalism, he comprehended the regularity of the changes which he considered definitive.[17] He saw in America that system to which France, and even the whole of Europe, would come close in the future.

Hence, as a progressive liberal, he found himself in conflict with the various shades of social reaction, and above all with Louis Napoleon, the Bonapartist usurper. He made his choice by declaring himself unambiguously in favour of bringing the bourgeois revolution to its conclusion. He realized that he witnessed the ultimate decline of aristocracy, but he regarded his nostalgia for aristocracy as his own personal problem. He used to say about himself that he was an aristocrat by instinct, but that reason told him to side with democratic institutions. It may be to the point to note in this connection that in France the strife between the two trends came to an end only with the proclamation of the Constitution of 1875, which opened the door for the Third Republic.

The approbation which accompanied the publication of de Tocqueville's first work was apparent rather than real. The British author J. P. Mayer wrote of him that he was applauded by the conservatives because he showed the dangers of democracy, and the democrats and socialists honoured him because he maintained that democracy was inevitable.[18]

In France he was admired more than he was understood, and, as Barbara Sobolewska says, he was in fact isolated. But that was understandable; France, involved in a conflict between the revolutionary and the reactionary forces (the latter having their support in the system under the Restoration) and looking for a compromise between these antagonistic factors, saw in that progressive aristocrat above all the author of *Ancien Régime*, who as it were screened the author of pushed aside study of American democracy. The traditions of the *ancien régime* survived long after the revolution in the minds, hearts, and attitudes of a whole, fully viable, social generation which still preserved in its memory the picture of old France–a generation linked to some at least of her symbols not only by resigned recollections, but by emotion and instinct. Thus the period of clashes of different epochs continued. This manifested itself in contacts between new institutions, established by the revolution, with some institutions that belonged to the traditional system; it manifested itself above all in contacts and clashes of different ideas, *Weltanschauungen*, and political programmes.[19] It seems that in a France contemporaneous with de Tocqueville it was believed that his panorama of American democracy referred to a totally alien society, and was thus irrelevant to the social processes of France. The perspicacity of his analysis was appreciated, but the theoretical conclusions it suggested were left unnoticed. Yet in fact *Democracy in America* and *Ancien Régime* were closely knit together and formed a veritable treatise of political praxiology.

That universal nature of de Tocqueville's work—universal, for it assumed that bourgeois democracy (*democracy* in his terminology) would drive out the feudal system (*aristocracy* in his terminology) everywhere–remained unnoticed for a long time. The scholarly world in both Europe and America was unprepared for the methodological and theoretical conclusions to be drawn from de Tocqueville's model. The pluralistic ideas contained in his work on America were simply not understood, and his *Ancien Régime* offered an analysis of a situation which no longer existed. The latter book Poggi classed correctly, from the methodological point of view, as a case study. De Tocqueville's penetrating generalizations did not reach his contemporaries. For all the upheavals France had gone through, there was still something which connected the different successive systems.

Centralism was the track which led from the *ancien régime* to the revolutionary France of the Jacobins, and after the collapse of the latter, to Napoleon's rule, to the Restoration, and to the systems that followed it.

Foundations for the future revival of de Tocqueville's work were laid only by pragmatic philosophy and the rise of Durkheim's school. The role assigned by de Tocqueville to associations found its continuation in Durkheim's 'professional corporations'. De Tocqueville was also close to Durkheim; the latter found in his works, in a nuclear form, the theory of *anomie*, which plays such an important role in Durkheim's system. This fact was stressed by both J. Lively and P. Birnbaum. P. Bastid regarded de Tocqueville rightly as a historian and sociologist.[20] But it was only the birth of modern empirical research of societal and political facts that fully paved the way for a proper understanding of de Tocqueville's work. And since the leading role in that empirical research was played by America, we had to wait for that type of research to be assimilated by European sociology and political science in order to witness the full reception of de Tocqueville in France– through the intermediary of the United States. Even as late as in 1925 A. Redier dedicated his book on de Tocqueville (*As M. de Tocqueville Used to Say*) to all those who did not know his works. But almost 40 years later R. Remond will say about him that he had foreseen the development of voluntary associations, thus becoming the sponsor of research on pressure groups.[21] Thus it was not by accident that France had to wait 100 years (counting from de Tocqueville's death) for a complete edition of his works. *Habent sua fata libelli*!

1.2 COMTE AND PROUDHON

At the time when de Tocqueville was writing his book on America, Auguste Comte, his elder by several years, was laying the foundations of positivist philosophy. In the writings of that founder of sociology there are few issues common to him and to de Tocqueville in the area which we are interested in. We should not be misled by Comte's anti-individualism. For Comte, that individualism which was preached by his contemporaneous economic and political authors was almost synonymous with egoism (Comte, for instance, opposed free competition). Yet Comte failed to notice the importance of social and political differentiation, if we disregard some of his normative statements projected into the very remote future (see below). In fact, society for him systemically preceded the individual, but we have to realize clearly what kind of society he meant. Comte saw the principal virtue in uniformity; yet his anti-individualism did not undermine private property, on which he was only willing to impose a "social" duty. Comte's thesis that positivism does not accord anyone any rights other than the right of performing one's duties, and that the concept of right (*droit subjectif*) should disappear from politics in the same way that the concept of cause should disappear from philosophy, was many years later to be decisive for the formulation of Duguit's theory (cf. section 1.3 below). This is why G. D. H. Cole is right in describing Comte as a radical anti-individualist,[22] who can imagine the real life of an individual only in a society in which the family is the most important and fundamental group. Comte in fact did idealize the institution of the family. A philosopher of industrial society and an admirer of the division of labour, Comte seems to have perceived neither the dangers which bourgeois industrialization meant for the family nor the other organizational forms which are necessary for the self-realization of the individual. He would rest satisfied with the triptych: the individual–the family–society, which he often identified with mankind. This conception had its companion in the idea of order and progress, which in Comte's system had their analogues in the statics and the dynamics of society.

But when we analyse Comte's various statements we can hardly resist the impression that it was order, social stability, which was for him the dominant factor. This contrasts sharply with Saint-Simon, who saw progress as the dominant factor.[23] This is also suggested by J. Lacroix, who says that Comte drew the sociology of order from de Bonald and de Maistre, and the idea of progress from de Montesquieu and Condorcet. The limits of progress are for him clearly marked and invariably determined by the institutions: Religion–Family–Property.[24]

Order was conceived by him in an abstract manner, and was to be guaranteed by a strong state. It was thus neither by chance nor in error that Comte, otherwise standing apart from current political events, enthusiastically greeted the coup of Louis Bonaparte, whereby he estranged many of his friends, including Littré, who left the Positivist Society.[25] Thus the state should be based on solidarity, harmony, and social consensus, which is a moral injunction. In that conflict-free society there was no place for the sovereignty of the people (Comte did not make any secret of his dislike of Rousseau and the Jacobins), which he referred to either as metaphysical dogma or as a depressing mystification. He treated equality as an ignoble lie.[26] In Comte's social order there is no longer any place for the rights of man and the citizen, the greatest achievement of the revolution. This was why the revolution filled him with abomination; he treated it as a pathological phenomenon, like de Tocqueville did. It was an idea that came to be assimilated by many a philosopher and sociologist at the turn of the nineteenth century.

Avoiding revolution was considered by Comte to be the principal goal of politics. Comte did not conceal his liking for de Bonald and de Maistre. This is not refuted by the fact that he corresponded for a long time with J. S. Mill: their letters concerned philosophical and scientific issues, and did not testify to any common language in the sphere of liberal politics. Politically, Comte was hostile to the parliament, which in his opinion exercised something like a dictatorship of ignorance. The only revolution he approved of was a revolution in philosophical thought. He assigned a very high stratum in society to thinkers (positivist-minded, of course). They should, following an almost Platonic pattern, if not govern society then at least wield moral power in it. This was no longer the requirement, formulated by de Montesquieu and de Tocqueville, of the priority of morals before politics, but a specific positivist "theory of two swords", which found its practical manifestation in letters, or rather advice–unsolicited, by the way–addressed to Napoleon III, Nicholas I, and Rashid Pasha. In these missives he persuaded the recipients to treat their power as provisional and to transform it, in a number of stages, into "preparatory governments" that should "invite" workers to join those governments as their members. This paternalistic approach was in accord with his political opinions as a whole.[27]

All this seems naive when we look back at it, but Comte was convinced that science, i.e. positivist philosophers, would take over power (*pouvoir spirituel*) in Europe freely and spontaneously. Spiritual power was supposed to co-operate with secular power. In Comte's schema of separation of powers the former should take charge of morals and education and thereby extend protection to the lower classes.

It is only in the normative stratum of Comte's reflections that we find elements of pluralism. When it comes to his political pluralism, it manifested itself in his proposal that France be split into smaller units, i.e. that the 17 *intendences* be transformed into republics. This division was to serve as an example to the whole world, because all states should reduce their respective territories. This would result in the emergence of 500 "sociocracies" which would, through peaceful co-operation, form the world republic that would know no wars.[28] These formulations strike us unfavourably by their lack of sense of reality and by their exaltation, but there is nevertheless a rational element in them: it is expressed today by regionalism in such countries as Britain, France, Italy and Spain, and in socialist countries as well. These recent trends call for large-scale self-government in regional units, whose size and number just correspond to Comte's "republics". Comte seems not to have realized that on this essential issue he was coming close to Rousseau, whom he opposed and who, as is known, preferred small states, or rather city-states, to big political entities.

When discussing elements of political pluralism in Comte's works we have to take note of the fact that the moral principles of positivist philosophy made Comte not only condemn colonialism as a crime, but also call for its elimination.[29]

In Comte's social views there are few pluralistic elements. One of them is an amended form of the trait mentioned above: Comte admitted that the collective organism consisted first of all of families, then of classes or castes which form their own groups, and finally of towns or communes. On another occasion we read that consumer associations should replace merchants; loan associations, bankers; and producer associations, industrialists.[30]

Such opinions must have been attractive to the positivist left, but had no major influence upon the masses.

These pluralistic elements did not form an integral part of positivist philosophy and sociology. They were foreign bodies in them, out of harmony with the positivist system of philosophy. The political order of that system was based on the hierarchical and centralized power of the state. Politically, the Positivist Society was a party that stood for autocratic order. In the sphere of religion, Comte was a monist, too. The positivist religion, an inseparable part of the system, was supposed, in the future, to become the religion of all mankind.

Comte abandoned liberal individualism, but did not embrace pluralism; this must have been due to two causes, each of them at a different level. One was the fact that in Comte's times organizations of entrepreneurs (industrialists and merchants) were practically non-existent, whereas France swarmed with freemasons' and workers' organizations, some of them revolutionary. This structure was at variance with the concept of order as understood by Comte. The other was his clearly defined and consistent political conservatism. The fact that his disciples included "reds", and even a few communards, should not mislead us.

We are faced with different problems when we analyse the case of Proudhon.

His heritage, together with the continuation of his work by disciples, both anarchists and anarcho-syndicalists, must also be classed as having a pluralistic trend. His anti-individualism (Proudhon on many occasions opposed "the strength of collective bodies" with "the strength of individuals", to whom societal life cannot be reduced), combined with the programme of maximum constraints on the state, must have led him to conclusions other than those drawn by other trends, which combined individualism with the acceptance of private property (as the foundation of society) and the political organization of the state.

Proudhon responded by a triple negation to his contemporaneous social order: he attacked private property, the state, and the Church. He saw inseparable connections between the exploitation of man by man and the government of men by men. He challenged both, because in his opinion they meant the same oppression. Both property and government were for him instruments of coercion. Protests against "the absolutism of the state" can be traced throughout many of his writings and pamphlets. Socialism meant for him a denial of both capital and power. It may also be said that Proudhon, by combating religion as authority and a system of subordination, and also as a justification of the reason of state, inspired French political anti-clericalism, so characteristic of the French left.[31] But we are here concerned with his pluralistic criticism of the bourgeois state. Proudhon, like Stirner and Bakunin (his junior), originally rejected the very *raison d'être* of the state, in which he saw an organization of centralized oppression. By stressing these elements we suggest that his views in that field were coherent, whereas in fact they were to become so only towards the close of his life. Coherence of views was alien to him if we consider his work as a whole. To simplify matters even more we disregard the zigzaggings of his career.

It may seem shocking that an anarchist allowed himself to be elected a deputy to parliament, because he used parliament to contrast the bourgeoisie with the proletariat (his famous speech delivered on 31 August 1848) and stated in writings that democracy meant constitutional arbitrariness, and did not spare criticism of universal suffrage and the representative system: the value of participation in political life for 48 hours, i.e. the time of each election, is practically nil. The president and the deputies, once elected, become masters, and others must obey them.[32] On the other hand, his brief support of General Cavaignac, who in June 1848 suppressed the French proletariat by bloodshed (the policy of choosing the lesser evil), and later–despite earlier crushing criticism–his ambiguous contacts with Louis Bonaparte,[33] who was later to become Napolean III, are astonishing; they suggest, quite wrongly, the convergence of his views with the conservatism of Auguste Comte. Nevertheless those facts provoked many contradictory comments and evaluations. If we add to this his occasional anti-Semitism (exacerbated by his controversy with Marx over *Philosophie de la Misère* , his consistent opposition to the emancipation of women (towards the close of his life he wrote a special study, *Pornocracy* ..., on the subject) and his approval of Negro slavery, we can see the amplitude of the oscillations in which Proudhon's life abounded.[34] His name evokes much dislike, unfortunately justified, and also much prejudice, especially in the international worker movement, on which a vulgarized assessment of anarchism is occasionally superimposed. People often failed to notice the fact that his programme was one of "positive anarchy", i.e. of an organized society, although a society outside the framework of the bourgeois state.

Proudhon's striking lack of sense of strategy and tactics in political conflicts can to some extent be explained by his socioeconomic assumptions. Being a dilettante in economics, he believed, after Saint-Simon and like Comte, in its primacy over politics, and thus reduced social relations to productive ones. The importance of economics seemed to him necessary at the time when the industrial revolution was beginning in France. This was at least how he understood the requirements of the industrial revolution. There was another reason why Proudhon underestimated the status of political problems. He was convinced that the attainments of the French revolution could not be restored by reforms of the electoral system, that socialism and parliamentary democracy were incompatible with one another, and that a political revolution would result in the reconstruction of the authoritarian system of power. The construction of socialism–to use the now current expression–would naturally and spontaneously be achieved by the industrial revolution, which would bring about far-reaching economic and social changes. This was not to say that the capitalist system would come to an end without conflict. This fact and the inevitability of the class struggle were accepted by Proudhon hesitantly and reluctantly.[35] It was not by accident that he spoke about the separation of classes, and in *Les Confessions d'un Révolutionnaire* we even find the statement that the revolution could triumph if it were embodied in the middle class. For all his ambivalent attitude towards the class struggle Proudhon engaged in it from the very beginning of his public activity. He thought that such a conflict could bring about a revolution of wealth producers, and although he considered it possible that such a revolution could stem from the working class, he did not exclude the taking over of that role by the middle class, which should, therefore, be won over to the cause.

Class differentiation must be taken as the foundation of his pluralistic reflection, but we have to realize clearly that in his interpretation class struggle did not mean political conflict and that an economic revolution did not have to be a political one. The illusions' of Bonapartist workers and craftsmen were well reflected in his slogan: social, but not a political revolution! In *Les Confessions d'un Révolutionnaire* he wrote that a revolution was legitimate only if it was spontaneous, peaceful, and tradition-oriented.

In his letter to Marx of 17 May 1846 (i.e. before he broke off with the latter), Proudhon agreed to co-operate with Marx in the international arena on condition that there should be no propaganda about revolution. He was consistent about this as he thought that "the epoch of revolutions was over once and for all". But there is very little point in talking about revolutions since in *Philosophie de la Misère* Proudhon stated that strikes were against the law. This followed not only from the penal code, but also from the economic system, which requires order.

In this connection it is worthwhile explaining what Proudhon meant by the "permanent revolution" (he was the first to use that term). His interpretation of permanent revolution did not, of course, have anything in common with that concept as understood by Marx and in the Bolshevik period of the worker movement. J. Garewicz is right in stating that for Proudhon it meant "a revolution which takes place gradually, almost imperceptibly, a revolution in which there are no big clashes among the classes".[36] His revolution was endless, because there are no final forms in societal life. Accustomed to distinguishing revolution from reform, we should be quite at a loss to make such a distinction within his system.

In *L'Idée Générale de la Révolution au XIXᵉ Siècle* that past master of the catchphrase wrote: the factory workshop will drive out the government. If a spontaneous social process leads from socioeconomic reforms to political ones, and not vice-versa, then a separate party of the working class is not necessary. This was the teaching that came later to be well assimilated by anarchist trends. The society of the future would be based on an agricultural and industrial federation which, once set up, would not be subject to dissolution. In present-day terminology, his federation would be an analogue of the alliance between workers and peasants. But in his last major work, published posthumously,[37] Proudhon foresaw the possibility of a conflict between town and country, between workers and peasants–a prediction which was to be tragically confirmed by the Paris Commune, when workers and members of the lower middle class clashed with peasants in military uniforms, commanded by officers from the nobility and the upper middle class.

But he saw in anarchy not just disorder (anarchism had for him nothing in common with nihilism), but an order which is not imposed from the top by a centralized state, an order which is built up "from bottom to top". The key to the comprehension of his ideas is to be found in one of his earlier works, *Principes d'Organisation Politique ou la Création de l'Ordre dans l'Humanité* (1843), order being the dominant concept in his system of anarchy. In one of his letters he wrote: while I am a great friend of order, I am an anarchist in the full sense of that term. And this is not to be treated as a spectacular paradox: Proudhon's concept of anarchy was aimed at all forms of hierarchic and centralized political power. In his opinion, anarchy was to play the co-ordinating role so as to exclude hierarchy and subordination.[38] He elaborated that in his later writings, but always excluded the possibility of a wilful imposition by the political power of its will so as to control society. This is how positive anarchy is to be understood. That new order, introduced by the proletariat and the middle classes, obviously differs from Comte's idea of order. Proudhon's order means an order which is differentiated, but not any uniformity under which "even an ape could give commands".[39]

Here we come to the heart of the matter. For all the said zigzaggings, Proudhon's writings show great coherence in the area with which this book is concerned. In the confusion of incessantly changing situations during the revolutionary period between 1828 and 1848, he succeeded in noticing essential trends, especially the emerging unions of workers, in which he saw the egalitarian and spontaneous organizations of the future.

Proudhon's activity coincided with the period of the struggle for the right of association, which was not listed among the rights of man and the citizen, and with the first tentative organization processes started by journeymen and apprentices in guilds. The first attempts at forming organizations of the proletariat in France go back to 1811, but the case of the silk factory workers in Lyon (1828) won most publicity. Proudhon was at that time 19 years old. The movement soon changed into a revolutionary struggle. The period in question was marked by a great number of spontaneously emerging worker organizations, with their own ethical and economic programmes. These organizations were cutting themselves off from bourgeois political parties, vacillating and poorly organized, and were firm in rejecting interference by, and the patronage of, the state. That spontaneity, readiness to co-operate, to help one another, and to fight, the spirit of solidarity and egalitarianism, and the ability to rise up again made a great impression upon Proudhon, who was inspired and attracted by the principle of self-government among those organizations. He saw in them the nucleus of the future economic and social order, and also took from them the programmatic term *mutualism* (*mutuellisme*).[40] The economic structure meant for him a plurality of groups and subgroups, organized on the principle of the division of labour. Their legal institutionalization was to ensure stability and to result in a correct functioning of social property.

While opposing political centralism, Proudhon declared himself in favour of the coexistence of small associations of producers, coexistent also with economic centralism, embodied in large producing associations (large industrial enterprises). On the other hand, he feared a "monopoly" by those large enterprises. His ambivalent attitude towards them can be explained, on the one hand by his intention to preserve the social values of small factories and craftsmen's workshops, and on the other by the lack of clarity concerning the prospects of capitalism. This ambivalence evoked strong criticism on the part of Engels (in the introduction to *The Civil War in France* by Karl Marx):

> Proudhon, a representative of the socialism of small peasants and craftsmen, just hated all association. He wrote about it that it had more evil than good in it, that it was by nature sterile, or even harmful, for it restrained the freedom of workers; association is a mere dogma, unproductive and onerous, in contradiction with both workers' freedom and the economy of manpower, and its defects grow much more quickly than do the advantages it brings; as contrasted with the former, competition, division of labour, private property are for him positive economic forces. It is only in exceptional cases, as Proudhon called them, in big industry and in big enterprises, such as railways, and it is proper for the workers to associate (see *L'Idée Générale de la Révolution au XIXe Siècle*, 3. étude).[41]

Hence Proudhon clearly gave preference to the medium-size property of workers' factories and to the small-scale property of craftsmen and peasants. To these the challenging formula about property as theft was not applicable.

This issue has evoked many controversies. Marx and his followers were not alone in regarding Proudhon as an ideologist of the petty bourgeoisie and a defender of small-scale property: a writer as remote from Marxism as M. Buber held a similar view.[42]

On the other hand, Guerin and A. Ritter brought out the significance Proudhon ascribed to large industrial enterprises under worker management.[43] True, he was naive in believing that the workers could directly manage factories under the capitalist system. As we shall see, that idea will later be taken up and developed by anarcho-syndicalists.

It seems that the criticism of Proudhon's view applies not so much to the dilemma mentioned above and the pluralism of organizations of producers as to something else. In Proudhon's opinion, the co-operation of worker associations of producers would breed solidarity that would mark competition that would be both vigorous and pursued in a moral atmosphere. As A. Ritter quite rightly noted, this was one of the few concepts Proudhon had taken over from those economists who stood for the *laissez-faire*.[44] Such an idea provoked Louis Blanc, a statist and centralist, who as a cabinet minister recommended and organized national workshops and considered himself a continuator of the Jacobinic tradition, to comment ironically about Proudhon that the state, as L. Blanc understood it, should be a "banker of the poor".

Proudhon replied by a series of vehement attacks (1851) in which he drew attention to the paternalistic policy of the state towards the workers. The organization of work by the state, he exclaimed, was nothing else than the last form of exploitation of man by man, and branded Louis Blanc as a socialist government follower (socialistes gouvernementalistes).[45] This critique was later expanded by him in *La Capacité Politique de la Classe Ouvrière* (1863) as a total assault upon state socialism which, in his opinion, was not the right way to put an end to capitalist property. To national (state-owned) workshops recommended by Blanc he opposed the idea of self-help of producers, i.e. their spontaneous and independent self-government. Producers' associations were to function on the principle of competition; but Proudhon realized that competition meant certain dangers and he accordingly wanted to humanize it, make it loyal, and to base exchange on the honesty which would be possible in a society of plenty. But there is a lack of clarity on one very important issue: whether he meant competition among socialized enterprises (as we would put it today), or between them and capitalist enterprises. The former would be a pioneering concept, in view of the fact that such a competition is now being considered, or practised, within specified limits, in many a socialist country; the latter would be Utopian in nature, because under capitalism such "workers' enterprises" would not have any chances of survival (with some exceptions in the co-operative field). Proudhon did not live long enough to see the beginnings of the concentration of capital, nor did he succeed in predicting it.[46]

But even in this sphere of his thought we can find some correct forecasts, such as those concerning the immense importance of negotiations between entrepreneurs and workers, which should lead to collective agreements. He would make that idea of his more general some years later by transferring it to the sphere of international relations, and recommending that these should increasingly be based on treaties.

In spite of assuming the primacy of economics, Proudhon rather early on took up the issue of political structure (cf. his idea of "positive anarchy" mentioned above), in particular that which would replace the centralized authority of the state. In the same study (*Du Principe Fédératif et de l'Unité en Italie*, 1863) in which he most broadly expanded his conception of a pluralistic economic revolution, we find the following ideas: no laws adopted by a majority vote or unanimously; every citizen, every commune, every federation should adopt his or their own laws; political power should be replaced by economic forces, economic categories, and specialized functions of agriculture, commerce, industry, etc.; the strength of the state should be replaced by that of the collectivity. On other occasions Proudhon called for "the disarmament and decentralization of the state", because the despotism of the government (*l'Etat gouvernementaliste*) deprives society of its autonomy and renders self-government impossible. The monopoly-oriented state puts an end to a pluralistic society which is thus deprived of all initiative. Democracy cannot be put into effect otherwise than by distributing authority (*distribution de l'autorité*), which for Proudhon is synonymous with state authority. As B. Voyenne wrote, his social contract was, unlike Rousseau's, based on groups,[47] but this statement requires a correction when it comes to Rousseau (see section 5.1 below).

Two issues strike us here: the call for the elimination of political power, or, to put it more precisely, for restricting it to a minimum, to the role of the arbitrator in exchanges among groups of producers; political power is to be replaced by "the social force" inherent in the community, a strong stress being laid on local authority. This means social order constructed from the bottom up.[48] Proudhon was in that respect obviously influenced by the idea of "municipal power" (*pouvoir municipal*), manifested in the Girondist-sponsored Communes Act of 1789, which assigned to the communes their own sphere of activity. In this way the communes rose to the rank of "the fourth power". De Tocqueville wrote about it thus: the communal spirit was a great factor of public peace and order. The idea of local power as the natural form of social organization would be developed by Proudhon in his later writings. Communes should associate, form federations, in order to be able to oppose centralistic tendencies. As in the case of the workers' associations of producers, the communes would develop bonds of solidarity through co-operation and on the basis of negotiated mutual guarantees (*mutuellisme*). This gives Proudhon an opportunity for emphasizing the legal aspect of the issue: the federation of the communes should be based on a contract, and the resulting mutual rights and obligations can serve as the foundation of a centralized authority, necessary for keeping the whole together.[49] It is evident that Proudhon wanted to replace the sovereignty of the state by that of the law.

Proudhon, as an advocate of the system under which economic activity would be co-ordinated by local authorities may reasonably be considered the originator of municipal socialism.[50] He did not see any need for a single centre of political decision-making; such a centre would be replaced by a network of local groups (communes or their federations), which he regarded as a barrier against the despotism of the state. This opinion showed his dislike of the Jacobins, which he used to emphasize as he believed that the freedom of the communes was incompatible with a uniform state. In a letter, written in 1861, he expressed his regret: "Oh, if I were Swiss"; in another letter, written one year later, he formulated the warning: "Beware of the Jacobins, true enemies of freedom and uniformists", and on still another occasion he said that the ideal of the Jacobins consisted in dictatorship with the underlying spirit of inquisition.[51] Proudhon's critique of Jacobinic centralism was ahistorical: feudal society could not be transformed into a bourgeois one with the decentralized structures, typical of feudalism, left intact. Jacobinic centralism was a necessity under the given historical conditions. By ascribing an absolute value to decentralization Proudhon condemned centralism under all historical circumstances. His typical exaggeration manifested itself in his study of revolutionary ideas in the nineteenth century, where he called for the replacement of the government by an industrial organization, and for the replacement of government-made laws by contracts in concluding which every citizen, commune, and federation of communes would participate, which would in turn replace voting in parliament. He thus demanded that political power be replaced by economic forces; traditional social classes, by vocational groups; standing armies, by industrial organizations; police, by identity of interests.[52]

Towards the close of his life Proudhon was concerned with a new problem, that of federal bonds among the states and the transformation of unitarian states into federal ones. He thought that expanding unitarian states were, in international relations, potential sources of war, while internally centralized bureaucracy ("functionarism") meant a lack of individual freedom. During the last period of his life he used to call himself a federalist rather than an anarchist.[53] This concept has also penetrated the international worker movement. The actual title of his work which significantly reflects that period of his activity pointed to a new, modified programme: *Du Principe Fédératif.* Those communards who referred to Proudhon also called themselves federalists. After the fall of the Paris Commune many communards learned the lesson of history and adopted the Marxist standpoint having understood that capitalist society cannot be transformed into a socialist one if the key problem of state authority and its taking over by the workers is left aside.

When demanding that large unitarian states be transformed into federations Proudhon did so not only for considerations of internal policy but also those of international relations, because in federations he saw a guarantee of peace, which was threatened by the constantly renascent rivalry of centralized unitarian states with their bureaucratic machineries and large armies that could be used against the people. "Whom then does the nation state serve?" he wrote in *Du Principe Fédératif* ..., "The people? No, the upper classes." This was why he consistently opposed the aspirations of the Italians, the Poles, and the Hungarians to political independence and unification, and he warned the Germans not to unite politically.[54] On the other hand, he defended the cause of the underprivileged Flemings in Belgium. Proudhon so much feared the dangers to peace that resulted from the rise of new unitarian and centralized states (one could say that he overstated such dangers) that he failed to notice the problem of national sovereignty and justifiable aspirations to political independence. He exaggerated the dangers of centralism without noticing the economic conditions which influence the aggressive tendencies of invading powers.

He expected that the twentieth century would be the epoch of federations as the dominant form of political organization of mankind,[55] and accordingly wrote in one of his letters about the mission of France in that respect (in which he strikingly resembles Comte): turn France into thirteen federated republics and she will be as young as she was in 1793.[56] He questioned national unity and stressed the importance of regional differences. In his idea of splitting large nation states into smaller units Proudhon came close to the ideal cherished by Rousseau: democracy in the form of small communities in which the general will can have its say directly.

When analysing the problems of federalism in Proudhon's works we have to realize that it is necessary to make two réservations which are lessons of history. First, we have to dismiss all superficial analogy with the constitutional conceptions of the Girondists, who advanced their federalist (or decentralist) theses to preserve, to some extent, the feudal order, whereas Proudhon's conceptions, outwardly similar to the former, expressed his criticism of the bourgeois order, a criticism which, inconsistent as it was, inspired his followers to fight on the barricades of the Paris Commune. Second, we have to beware of a modern interpretation of Proudhon's federalism.[57] He used the concept of federation in three senses:

(1) in the socioeconomic sense he meant organizations of producers, both in industry and in agriculture, which would form spontaneous "federations" restraining the authoritarian and centralistic interference of the state;
(2) in the sense of territorial administration, he meant communes that would combine to form "federations"; political federation was for him synonymous with decentralization, which marked transition to the modern concept of federation;
(3) in the sense of division of the political system of the state into autonomous, or, rather, sovereign subsystems (which Proudhon occasionally called "republics"), enjoying the full right of secession.

Transformation of unitarian states into federations would be of international significance as it would be aimed at centralistic expansion and pave the way for a confederation of states changed into federations. All these three meanings of the concept of federation were clearly anticentralistically oriented and, by forming a certain political or constitutional continuum, would guarantee individual freedom, social and international peace. The idea of this continuum was, perhaps, inspired by de Tocqueville (federalism at various levels), but Proudhon made one step further and saw in the principle of federation a possibility of international solutions once socialism would become dominant. At that time federalism (specifically interpreted by him) and socialism were synonymous for Proudhon. Whatever interpretation we adopt we have to admit, in view of the permanence of federations and their modern development, that de Tocqueville foresaw the trends inherent in political institutions.

We may conclude by saying that Proudhon treated every organizational form aimed at political centralism as a federation. His federalism was inseparably connected with mutual guarantees by members of a given federation (*garantisme, mutuellisme*). The underlying idea of his federalism was the belief in the values of social differentiation, which is to be analysed at various levels but which is organizationally coherent.[58] Differentiation in production: federated associations of workers in industry, in agriculture maintenance of peasant family holdings, to be brought into associations later; in post-political structures: federations of communes and division of unitarian states into smaller units; in international relations: federations of states.

1.3 ACADEMIC PLURALISM (DURKHEIM, DUGUIT)

Clearly pluralistic ideas are to be found in the writings of Durkheim. As the point of departure we have to take his dualistic conception of human nature with its individual, non-recurrent features, and its social features, universal and recurrent. This distinction has its analogy in the dichotomy between egoism and altruism, a dichotomy which has been raised in social thought many times (including the recent period) and which plays such an important role in Durkheim's monograph on suicide. The reader of that work may sometimes have the impression that the adjectives *altruistic* and *social* are used there as synonyms.

It was on the basis of this dichotomy that Durkheim constructed his theory, in which place is assigned to the critique of the liberal individualism of the utilitarians. In his major work (*De la division du travail social*, 1893) he argued much with the views of Herbert Spencer. Durkheim was disgusted by the "antisociological" conception of society advanced by the utilitarians, society conceived as a collection of individuals who strive for their egoistic goals, determined autonomously. He questioned the opinion that egoism was the starting point of the development of mankind and treated this as a manifestation of primitive social Darwinism. One cannot, as did Spencer, present social life as a simple resultant of the nature of individuals; on the contrary, it is rather the individuals who are the products of social forces.[59]

If it were that the only criteria for one's behaviour were individualistic, society would collapse and there would not be any durable contract. Durability of contracts emerges at a certain level of societal development, when egoistic interests are restrained by tradition, by moral rules developed by society, and by the authority which stands above the individuals. Durkheim in this way dismissed the illusionary idea of autonomous will in contractual relations, to which civil law theorists, brought up in the individualistic tradition of Roman law, were particularly attached.

Durkheim was convinced that social problems could not be reduced to physiological and psychological characteristics of individuals. Nor could they be deduced from individual behaviour, since the individual cannot be treated as prior to society.[60] He often referred to this idea in his later works.

> Society is not a simple sum of individuals; the system which comes into being through their association forms a specific reality, endowed with its own features. Certainly nothing can be done collectively if there is no individual consciousness; this condition is necessary, but not sufficient for the rise of society. The consciousness of the individuals must be associated, combined, and combined in a specified way at that. This combination produces social life which is the explanation of that combination.[61]

Durkheim, following the spirit of the Aristotelian tradition, saw in society a whole which is something more than the sum of the individuals. He elaborated this thesis in his works to state that all manifestations of social life originated in society. The individual is a social individual.[62]

The utilitarians did not draw proper conclusions from the data accumulated by anthropologists and historians and concerned with the role of social regulation, the role of social norm-setting, accepted by individuals for various reasons, and in recent times, with the incessantly expanding interference by the public authority. This was why Durkheim dedicated so much space in his writings not only to morals (differentiated according to social groups), but also to law and to other normative systems. There is no social life without certain restraints, especially moral ones.

All this makes the individual see society as something external and given. He has no chance of preserving his humanity outside society.[63] J. Szacki was right in stating that:

> if Durkheim says that society is external to the individual and if he emphasizes that society cannot be explained in terms of individuals, then he clearly means the individual as an abstract biological or psychological individual taken in complete isolation. ... The more an individual is socialized, i.e. the more he has internalized the ways of thinking, feeling, and acting, adopted in a given society, the less "external" society is to him.[64]

Speaking in present-day terms of systems theory we would say that society is an inseparable part of man's biological environment. Durkheim by treating social facts as "things" postulated that social facts be seen as something other than individual responses, as something supra-individual and external to individuals.[65]

His firm critique of individualism and liberalism resulted in many misunderstandings and even in Durkheim's being suspected of conservative and authoritarian leanings in his political opinions. This was understandable to a large extent because, as Lévi-Strauss says, the intellectual tradition links individualism to humanism.[66] But these suspicions are refuted by the whole of Durkheim career, all his writings, and the standpoint he took on the Dreyfus case.

Durkheim later extended his critique of utilitarian liberalism so as to include Tarde's individual psychology which so much magnified the individuals' tendency to imitation as the force which initiates and consolidates social bonds. Durkheim opposed Tarde's theory by stressing that the purely psychological process of imitation can develop among individuals without any social bonds among them.[67] Durkheim's sociology opposed not only social Darwinism, i.e. a mechanical transfer to sociology of the methods used and results obtained in biology, but also the transfer to sociology of individual psychology. He was a forerunner of social psychology.

Durable social bonds result only from the division of labour, which increases in proportion to the volume and density of society. The division of labour, which is universal and not limited to economics, can be either compulsory or spontaneous and voluntary, the latter case being that of higher organized societies. The division of labour is ensured and regulated by the law, which Durkheim, according to his adopted classification, classed into sets of repressive and co-operative norms. In view of the importance the division of labour has in social life the thesis that social facts are not reducible to individual behaviour acquires a different dimension. It is in this context that there are tangible differences between society and the individuals of whom it consists.

Durkheim attached particular importance to those vocational groups which emerge as a result of the division of labour. He called them corporations, which was synonymous with vocational groups and at the same time alluded to mediaeval forms of vocational organization, for Durkheim postulated the revival of such vocational organizations or groups which would unite both entrepreneurs and their employees. While corporations degenerated in the post-mediaeval period, driven out by individual enterprises, Durkheim believed that they should be reformed and modernized, and not doomed to irreversible destruction. He saw in them a fairly permanent form of organization, known also in ancient Rome, where *collegia* worked despite prohibitions, or were being tolerated, and hence functioned as it were *praeter legem*, before transforming themselves into agencies of state administration.

In the secondary groups (*groupes secondaires*), which were largely analogous to the intermediate bodies in the terminology used by de Montesquieu and de Tocqueville, Durkheim saw a permanent phenomenon, and hence also an organizational form that would function in the future.[68] They were, in his opinion, indispensable for the maintenance of moral solidarity in advanced societies. He accordingly wanted to set up a kind of new guild to replace those which had been destroyed successively by a regional division of labour, then by mercantilism under the absolute monarchies, and finally by both society and the state under the liberal bourgeoisie. In this connection it is worth mentioning that Durkheim in his historical enquiries consulted the works by Otto von Gierke, who inspired one of the trends in British pluralism (see section 3.2 below). These inspirations are, in a sense, natural because society based on organic solidarity is nothing other than one great community (*Gemeinschaft*), as has been noted appropriately by Nisbet.[69]

Durkheim's favourable attitude towards certain elements in syndicalist theories also deserves attention, because the future "corporations", supposed to be much more complex in structure than those existing in his times, would have other functions, which in Durkheim's times were performed by communes and private associations. He thus reduced the bodies which were intermediate between the individual and society to vocational groups; and if this formulation goes too far, it must be said in any case that he assigned the leading role to those groups.

The division of labour gives rise to social solidarity, the lower form of which–observable in primitive, little differentiated, societies–he termed mechanical, as opposed to organic solidarity which marks societies with advanced division of labour. The former type of solidarity means a very small autonomy of the individuals whose consciousness reflects collective consciousness; in such a society the division of labour is still very limited, the individual has no freedom of decision-making, the dominant norms are those with repressive sanctions. The latter type is marked by a specialization of activities undertaken by differentiated groups that develop their own consciousness, different from the consciousness of the whole society. Within such groups the individual has a greater freedom of decision-making, while in such societies social processes are controlled by norms with restitutive sanctions. In the process of history organic solidarity has been gradually replacing the mechanical.

Spencer, too, referred to the concept of solidarity–namely that of industrial solidarity, which is spontaneous, but to which all interference by the state can only be detrimental. Durkheim opposed the utilitarians, and in particular criticized their concept of negative solidarity, which consists in abstaining from infringing other people's rights, because he saw the necessity of state (public) control as an indispensable foundation of order (an idea he had taken over from Comte and later worked in greater detail). Hence the role of law, which Durkheim treated sometimes as the indicator and sometimes as the symbol of solidarity. That role is being played by law not independently, but jointly with morals and other normative systems, valid in vocational groups. He postulated that every vocational group should develop a normative system of its own.

Organic solidarity is kept together by the primacy of social duties, which express moral bonds in society. In his *Physics of Morals and Law* Durkheim says outright that discipline and authority are the foundations of morals. External sanctions merely reinforce morals. Durkheim's standpoint on the necessity–and not just interpretation–of authority for society does not differ much from that adopted by Engels in his polemics with the anarchists.

G. Poggi drew attention to the fact that organic solidarity was associated in Durkheim's writings with such concepts as integration, cohesion, harmony, order, discipline, and unity, but Durkheim neither described those ties with precision nor explained what he meant by solidarity.[70] One can reply to this that Durkheim–and this seems to result from the whole of his work–meant by solidarity just those social bonds which follow the division of labour and develop in the functioning of vocational groups, and not what we mean by solidarity today; hence we cannot ascribe solidaristic ideology to him. On the other hand, solidaristic trends certainly did draw inspiration from his interpretation of solidarity.

Social solidarity, the various bonds that develop spontaneously as a result of the division of labour within and among vocational groups, subsequently reinforced by societal control, are the only effective barrier against disorder and *anomie*. His theory of *anomie* was elaborated by him in *De la Division du Travail Social* and *Le Suicide, Étude de Sociologie*.[71] He treated *anomie* as a pathological phenomenon when viewed from the standpoint of solidarity resulting from a deliberate and organized division of labour. The breakdown of organic solidarity releases dysfunctional processes that yield disorder. It would thus, in a sense, correspond to the return to the state of nature as interpreted by Hobbes.

Anomie means such a dysfunction of behaviour which does not infringe merely a single rule or a single set of societal norms, but questions the very reason for the existence of societal norms. *Anomie* shows that the system of values previously adopted by society and the entire normative order of that society have broken down. This may be due to slow changes or to revolutionary ones, and such which destroy the traditional social structures. It seems that *anomie* is an inevitable result of all change, both that which points to degradation and that which marks progress.[72] Hence social stabilization is the desirable condition, because gradual changes, but not violent ones, could absorb the shocks that result in disorder. This was a novel approach which refuted Comte's "technocratic" optimism: Comte ascribed to technological progress positive consequences only, without foreseeing any negative ones, and thus failed to predict problems with which we are absorbed today.

The collapse of existing structures makes it impossible for both individuals and groups to satisfy the respective needs they have had so far, since there develops a hiatus between those needs and the possibilities of meeting them. This breeds *anomie* and adds intensity to suicide as a social phenomenon. When analysing the types of suicide Durkheim says: the suicide rate changes in inverse proportion to the degree of integration of political community.

The theory of *anomie* must have thus aimed at contemporaneous anarchist trends and at the revolutionary sense of Marxism; in the light of what has been said earlier it also questioned the doctrine of utilitarian liberalism, because the latter stood for individual egoism. While the theory of *anomie* complied with "the social demand" of its times, it was not devoid of great cognitive value, which explains its impact upon American sociology, especially upon R. K. Merton. The concept of *anomie* is related to that of alienation, introduced by Marx, but not identical with the latter. Reflection on how far these two concepts overlap and how far they differ from one another is otherwise essential, but the present writer will not engage in it in order not to deviate from the main issue of this book.[73]

Durkheim's theory of organic solidarity did, however, assume the possibility of a conflict-free society in which the harmony of interests would be the normal state. The French bourgeoisie, traumatized by three revolutionary upheavals sparked off by the revolution of 1789 strove to bring this harmony to completion. They noticed the political conclusions that could be drawn from the achievements of the founder of modern sociology. Durkheim's sociology of order and solidarity, which rejected class struggle, and *a fortiori* revolution, and its enlightened conservatism complied with the expectations of a social and political stabilization. But G. Poggi goes too far in his criticism when he claims that Durkheim's theory imposes upon us the dichotomy of the individual and society, that Durkheim's analysis was concerned only with the individual and society taken as a whole.[74] Poggi thus questions elements of pluralism in Durkheim's theory, whereas in fact Durkheim, when speaking about society, means by it–as can be seen from a given context–social groups and, contrary to Poggi's summary opinion, brings out the role of vocational groups ("corporations") in societal processes. But this is not the most important point. From the point of view of the problem under consideration in this book, in Durkheim's work his introduction to the second edition of *De la Division du Travail Social* is of particular significance. It is not simply editorial: Durkheim says that the book has its individual features which it should preserve, but when comparing its content with his later works he points, as early as the opening sentences, to the importance of the problem of vocational groups, a problem he has previously only alluded to, but intended to make the subject-matter of a special study. To fill that gap in his works he reverts to the problem and goes beyond the fundamental roles of vocational groups. He refers to the individuals' drive for association not only for the defence of their own interests, but for the very pleasure of co-operation, contacts, and mutual communication.

When criticizing the underdevelopment of forms of group life he says that society, consisting of the impenetrable dust of unorganized individuals, whom the hypertrophied state tries to define and to restrain, is a veritable social monster. Collective action is too complex to be expressed by only one agency, namely the state. Furthermore, the state is too far away from the individuals; it has only discontinuous contacts with them, and this is why it cannot socialize them.

Preserving the unity of the nation requires buffers in the form of secondary groups, which intervene between the state and the individual. They must stand sufficiently close to each individual to be able to get him involved in social life.[75]

These comments must be treated as a correction of the standpoint Durkheim had taken earlier. He says that the division of labour induces people to form groups and refers to the role of such groups in determining the behaviour of their members. His point thus is to expand and to give more precision to the idea formulated both in *De la Division du Travail Social* and *Les Règles de la Méthode Sociologique* where he wrote about those forms of association which determine social facts, and also on the last pages of *Le Suicide*, where he postulated restoration of the cohesion of social groups and the strengthening of their effect upon the individuals, who should feel bound with them and draw inspiration from them in their activity. Durkheim demanded that social life be controlled not by the state, but by "collective forces" other than the state, by intermediate bodies, to use once more the term introduced by de Montesquieu. In a word, he postulated restraints on the hypertrophied state whose power should be balanced by other social groups.

Durkheim's opinion on the relation between society as a whole and the various social groups, scattered in his writings, has been summed up by M. Włodyka as follows:

> Society of the political type, that is the state, was for Durkheim the most representative example of global society. It is not only individuals and individual consciousness, things that appear together with them, and social segments which are parts of society; social groups are parts of society as well. ... Social groups
> (i) are numerically smaller than what Durkheim means by a typical society;
> (ii) they are comprised by global society and form its separate parts;
> (iii) they are constant in nature, both in the sense of lasting longer than the life time of the individual, and in the sense of the scope of their functions and tasks;
> (iv) they are institutionalized, defined by the law ...
> (v) they are supraindividual in nature ... .[76]

It is only through the formation of self-governing groups which develop their own normative systems that *anomie* can be terminated or prevented.

J. Szczepański, when trying to explain the extent of Durkheim's influence, writes:

> In Durkheim's sociology one idea turns out to have been extraordinarily fertile: namely, that all spheres of human culture develop within definite social groups and are determined as to their origin and

evolution by the social forces working in those groups, and by the system and institutions of and in those groups.[77]

From the point of view of the problem we are concerned with, Durkheim continued the political ideas of de Montesquieu and de Tocqueville, and at the same time, and perhaps therefore, was a forerunner of group pluralism. This is why it is not the opinion of G. Poggi, mentioned above, which seems convincing, but that advanced by E. Wallwark, who ascribes to Durkheim the hypothesis that the development of individual personality (individualism) requires a pluralistic society, in which institutional differentiation prevents a social group from tyrannizing its members. His theoretical standpoint thus differs clearly from both the atomistic individualism advocated by Spencer, and Hegel's state with its elements of absolutism.

In such a pluralistic society a specified role is assigned to the state, which, by making use of law, preserves order, i.e. a dynamic equilibrium of the secondary groups.[78] This interaction between the state and the secondary groups increases individual freedom.

Durkheim's contribution to political sociology, usually underestimated by representatives of that subdiscipline, is not confined—unlike what E. Allardt thinks—to his book on the division of social labour, but should be interpreted in the light of all his writings. E. Barnes has rightly called his work a contribution to the reconstruction of political theory.[79]

After Durkheim's death, in the wake of his thought, matured the pluralist ideas of the great Belgian philosopher and sociologist E. Dupréel. Presenting his views he stressed the point that groups are the very basis of all *social* relations and political insitutions. Their diversity produces conflicts but both phenomena are the natural state of society. The main danger to this group pluralism is the irresistably growing power of the state. Dupréel, knowing from his own experience the totalitarian practice of the Nazi state, saw in the plurality of groups the only means to check this tendency inherent in any system. It was his conviction that this was also the way to check extreme individualistic liberalism.

He would have reduced the state to the role of an arbitrator who is trying to settle intergroup disputes, and ready to help forge principles of co-operation within the groups and among them.[80]

In the theory of law Léon Duguit has been probably the only author in whose works we can find elements of pluralism. Duguit himself emphasized that he was a disciple of Comte and Durkheim, and at the same time took over Proudhon's federalist views which were aimed at the sovereignty of the state.[81] His influence was not confined to France: the young Laski was strongly affected by it in the first period of his work (the issue will be discussed later).

Duguit took over from Comte and Durkheim the idea of social solidarity, which stresses the duties that reflect moral bonds in society, and dismisses the individual's rights resulting from the metaphysical authority which he claims to be relative to others. But he went further and accepted Durkheim's idea of the division of labour as the foundation on which organic social solidarity rests. Hence his famous formula: "The capitalist owner has been endowed with a definite societal function. I deny his right to property, but I approve his societal duty."[82]

In solidaristic society, as envisaged by Duguit, rights (*droits subjectifs*) vanish irreversibly; they came to be replaced by duties, which alone can cement social solidarity. These views found repercussions in *Solidarité* by L. Bourgeois (1912).

The right resulting from [private–St.E.] property is thus replaced by property as a societal function. The influence of Comte (who, in his *Système de Politique Positive*, saw in citizens public functionaries and treated property as "an indispensable societal function") is obvious here. Following Comte, Duguit qualified rights as survivals of the law of nature, as a metaphysical concept which assumes the existence of a supernatural power which grants them; he treated state sovereignty in the same way.

This opposition to rights and to individualism rooted in private property drew the attention of French academic circles.[83] But Duguit also noticed the role of other group bonds, based on the similarity of interests, customs, and aspirations, and hence showed society as a more differentiated whole.[84] This variety and complexity of social bonds makes individual personality richer. Yet it seems that ascribing to Duguit the discovery of a new democracy, of a mixed parliamentary system that includes representation of group interests, would go too far: it is denied by the syndicalist elements in his work (see below). The issue is linked to another one, new in the sphere of academic thinking: the critique of the sovereignty of the nation and of the state, such sovereignty being treated by Duguit as a dogma or, worse still, as a myth.

This endeavour to free the theory of the state from metaphysical contaminations was very much in the spirit of positivist philosophy. The state comes to be treated "not as an entity, but as something dynamic", as a flow of facts, which should be rigorously controlled by law in order to safeguard the interests of society as a whole. The idea of constraining the state by law is the guideline of Duguit's work. It appears in his first major study, *L'Etat* ..., and many years later he gives it the pride of place in his *Précis de Droit Constitutionnel*. Hence the idea of the supreme status of law or of the fundemental *règle de droit* (principle of law), by which he revalued the law of nature, which he opposed.[85]

The idea of restraining the state by the principle of law, accepted by the majority of individuals, was a return as M. Waline is right in pointing out, to that very individualism, opposition to which seemed to have been the characteristic feature of Duguit's theory.[86] Duguit's system starts, as has been said, from Durkheim's concept of organic solidarity, but while adopting this pluralistic approach Duguit failed to draw the proper conclusions in his theory of law, for his approach should have resulted in normative pluralism. Yet his changeless principle of law results in normative monism, which blurs the difference between law as a normative system produced by the state (or, to put it more precisely, by the machinery of the state) and the other normative systems that function within society. It is remarkable that the numerous critics and commentators of Duguit's work, who pointed to the lack of coherence of his ideas, failed to notice this basic inconsistence.

There is also another issue that deserves clarification. Gurvitch's "social law" seemingly resembles the conception of "the principle of law", because, like the latter, it is also law made by the state and, like in Duguit's system, it tends to restrict the sovereignty of the state. That would be achieved through the development of norms of self-government by "economic society" within the state, and without the sovereignty of the state would be restrained by international law. Gurvitch called this conception legal pluralism.[87] To avoid misunderstandings let us add that Gurvitch, like many other authors, and like the English convention, means by law every societal normative system except the moral system.

For all the accusations–exaggerated by the way–of anarchist leanings, Duguit was not alone in the academic milieu to criticize the sovereignty of the state. M. Hauriou, an eminent theorist of law and one of the founders of modern administrative law, also questioned the sovereignty of the state, although he did so from a somewhat different position since he treated the state as a set of institutions or the institution of institutions.[88] It is true that sovereignty had earlier been questioned by Saint-Simon and Comte, but Duguit on this issue consciously followed Proudhon and his syndicalist-minded disciples. He went so far as to separate the concept of public law from that of the sovereign state. Law is not imposed by the state, but is just a complex of rules for the organization of the public services or for defining the legal status of a given group. An administrative act always is an act of management.[89]

Duguit declared himself in favour of a far-reaching restriction of the omnipotence of the state authority on behalf of *syndicats* which would unite entrepreneurs and workers (Duguit's term is "corporate groups"). As seen by Duguit, this was not a recommendation, but the beginning of the process which consisted in the withering away of the bourgeois state (*l'état est en train de mourir*) and in the simultaneous emergence of the state of a new type. In syndicalism he saw the organizational form that would make it possible to turn the shapeless mass of individuals into a whole kept together by the feeling of solidarity owing to common vocational interests and a precise structure of the law.

Duguit did not hesitate to speak in this connection, after Proudhon, about a "federalist society" which would ensure more intense societal life than before, and he saw in it the only guarantee of freedom. Like the syndicalists, he attached special importance to unions of public functionaries, which were expected by him not only to protect those functionaries against the arbitrariness of the state, but also to participate in running state agencies and accordingly be responsible before the public.

Duguit closed his eyes to the existence of disputes among classes, and hence to the mechanism of class struggle. His conception of social development, like Durkheim's, was one of a conflict-free process. The new state, as he envisaged it, was not to be a socialist one.[90] In view of these assumptions it was natural that his attitude towards Marxism and towards anarcho-syndicalism, also called revolutionary syndicalism, was hostile.[91]

We have thus come to the next problem, namely that of pluralism in the workers' movement or, to put it more precisely, that of syndicalist pluralism.

1.4 PLURALISTIC THOUGHT IN THE WORKER MOVEMENT AFTER PROUDHON

In this section, we shall not dedicate much space to Nicholas Bakunin because his influence upon the French worker movement was limited, and also because we shall come back to his views in connection with his controversy with Marx, which resulted in the disruption of the First International.

Bakunin, who considered himself a disciple of Proudhon (which he emphasized in his writings dating from 1848 to 1851), was more radical than the latter on the issue of the state. He despised the existing representative system, and it would be hard to imagine him letting himself be elected to the National Assembly, as Proudhon did. He shared Proudhon's opinion that the state should be abolished at a stroke, or, rather, that this should be done with all the states, and was running about Europe to climb one revolutionary barricade after another. He was particularly suspicious of, and aggressively opposed to, the idea of setting up, following a revolution, a proletarian state, in which he saw a threat to individual freedom because such a state would also be a hierarchically organized and highly centralized body. In his opinion, every state was alien to society, a tumour which gradually sapped its forces, an artificial institution which was despotic by definition as it represented an authority imposed from the outside. His negative opinion of the state was formulated by him many times, in particular in *Le Catéchisme Révolutionnaire* (1866) and (most fully) in *L'Etat et Anarchie* (1873), where he wrote that every state is a dictatorship.

While in Stirner the solipsist individual was in conflict with society, in Proudhon and in Bakunin the individual was in conflict with the state as an entity which is alien to society.[92] The individual achieves his absolute freedom through the intermediacy of society and those collectives which he has joined of his own will. This was for him the substratum from which social solidarity was born. Like Proudhon, he saw the guarantee of liberty in the freedom of association. Social bonds should develop "from the bottom upwards", and from the peripheries to the centre, and not vice-versa. But Bakunin placed the stresses otherwise than Proudhan had done. He saw the centre of gravity in a federation of free, autonomous communes, each of which should organize and co-ordinate the productive activity of workers' associations (which should expropriate the means of production). Bakunin was also in favour of an intermediate body between communes and their federation at the national level, namely in favour of regional associations of communes (called by him provinces). Like Proudhon, he had a cult of spontaneity in societal development, of a free initiative of individuals and the masses, which would find its highest form of expression in a revolution emerging from grass roots, and not organized. This was inevitably linked with an attitude of mistrust of intellectuals, because the faith in the maturation of the masses in the course of their spontaneous activity precluded any other attitude on that issue. These views were to bring about a clash in the First International.

Between Proudhon's death and the birth of anarcho-syndicalism, writers and those anarchist leaders who sought understanding and compromise with the latter acted as the intermediary link. They included C. de Paepe, a Belgian who spoke in a conciliatory spirit at the congresses held by the First International in Brussels in 1868 and 1874,[93] and I. Guillaume, a disciple of Bakunin, advocate of a federation of productive associations that would have the collective ownership of the means of production.[94] F. Pelloutier must be classed in the same group. He recommended the abandonment of terrorist action aimed at individuals and the linking of anarchism with the masses through the intermediacy of labour unions, which would become the basic units of a future federalist society. Domination of the trade unions by the anarchist was supposed by him to guarantee the existence of an organization that would supervise production and be able to replace the machinery of the state. Pelloutier expounded his views most completely in *Histoire des Bourses du Travail* (1902), published after his death. Like Proudhon and Bakunin, he rejected the participation of political parties in the revolution, which was for him, too, societal and not political in nature. He considered corporate groups, which he identified with free unions (*syndicates*), to be the basic units of a future federalist society.[95]

Kropotkin worked in the same spirit, as he saw the future of anarchism in the labour union movement on a mass scale. His opinions concerning the role of mutual assistance originated directly from Proudhon's *mutuellisme*.[96]

Here, we should mention Paul Boncour, the prominent socialist leader, who was a syndicalist in his youth. The principal idea advanced by him in that period was the limitation of the sovereignty of the state in favour of the sovereignty of vocational groups. The state should perform the co-ordinating function, in which its sovereignty would manifest itself. Characteristic of his views was the demand that bureaucratic tendencies within the machinery of the state should be opposed by making public functionaries, organized in trade unions within their respective public services, totally independent of the state; i.e. of both the parliament and the government. Public functionaries should decide not only on all their vocational matters, but also–to a considerable extent–on the settling of official business. Paul Boncour thought that the appropriation to society itself of the means of production would result in an excessive expansion of the functions of the state. This would mean, the future French minister and premier claimed, entrusting gendarmerie officers with the management of factories, universities, museums, and libraries.[97]

In holding these opinions he was seconded by M. Leroy, when the latter spoke about the conception of the principle of societal organization which imposed itself upon all. It was to be decentralization–that is, syndicalist federalism–in which special importance was attached to the trade unions of public functionaries.[98]

Pointing to this intermediate link in political thought is important because the activity of the group described above concluded a certain stage in the evolution of anarchism in France: it meant the end of acts of terror directed against individuals (which were still to be continued in Russia, Italy, and Spain), and the transition to anarcho-syndicalism, also called revolutionary syndicalism. The latter trend is linked to the name of G. Sorel, the founder of "the new school", i.e. the group he and his co-workers, E. Berth and H. Lagardelle, led.

G. Sorel admired Proudhon,[99] but not uncritically. He accepted Proudhon's pluralistic analysis of society, and in particular the significance of bringing out the whole variety of interests and social aspirations, for he thought that it was necesary to oppose the pressure of societal unity, embodied by hierarchically organized authority that was imposing uniform rules of behaviour upon all citizens. Sorel stressed the fact that Proudhon had come better to understand the inevitability of the class struggle, as he had formulated it towards the close of his life in *De la Capacité*. He also noticed the consequences of *mutuellisme*, which–like the co-operative movement– could weaken the class struggle and incapacitate syndicalist groups by "the leprosy of social harmony".[100] Like Proudhon and other theorists and leaders of the anarchist trend, with Bakunin at the head, Sorel disliked–not to say was hostile to–political parties, worker parties not excluded, and was like them in favour of spontaneity in revolutionary action. He extended his dislike to political parties in the worker movement to the role in them of intellectuals, because it was they who were leaders of those parties. Trade unions, which represented the genuine trend in the worker movement, were free from that interference by intellectuals who imposed themselves as leaders. In his dislike of the intellectuals Sorel was seconded by E. Berth, who voiced the same opinion in his book *Les Méfaits des Intellectuels* (Misdeeds of Intellectuals).[101]

But "the new school" criticized the bourgeois state, and the state in general, more firmly in many respects than Proudhon had been doing. On essential issues they were closer to Bakunin. They rejected the idea that the bourgeois state be replaced by a socialist one. The state, Berth said, was "a bourgeois thing by its very essence and destination". State centralism was believed by them inevitably to give rise to bureaucracy. And Sorel said that statism was the ideal of the lower middle class and a contradiction of socialism. G. Goriely stressed that Durkheimian trend in his monograph on Sorel's pluralism.[102]

In this connection they rejected parliamentary socialism and all varieties of reformism, be it in the British (S. Webb) or in the German (Bernstein, Kautsky) version: they rejected the idea that the proletariat was to imitate the bourgeoisie.[103] But their most vehement attacks were levelled at French socialism, which at that time had Jules Guèsde as its leader. Berth accused "Guèsdism" of absolute statism and of endeavours to put socialism into effect within the framework of the contemporaneous bourgeois state by imparting to the latter "a working class sense" through the domination of the centralized apparatus of power. Berth called the French worker party (which was later to become the socialist party) the party of order; in his opinion Guèsde had the soul of the patriots of 1792, i.e. for Guèsde the citizen was, as it were, totally owned by the state. "The new school", when opposing the reformists, blamed them for militarism, chauvinism, statism, and misunderstanding of the role of the trade unions, which they would like to subordinate to the party and turn into something like "an elementary school" of socialism.[104] Incidentally, Guèsde was also criticized from the right by the reformists who used to write about "the corporate mentality" of Guèsdism.[105]

In conformity with the anarchist tradition, Sorel did not assign to the worker parties any role in the revolution to come and was in favour of a depolitized revolution to be carried out by trade unions alone. In his work that bore the telling title *La Décomposition du Marxisme* he explicitly disclaimed all intention to organize a new political party because in political parties in general he saw the inclination to have the workers serve under the command of party leaders recruited from among intellectuals. His dislike of intellectual leaders, who formed the party élite and believed it to be their mission "to think for the thoughtless masses", was shared with Sorel by Berth and Lagardelle. They thought that the working class would by itself mature enough to take power into its own hands. Lagardelle claimed that the division of labour into manual and mental favoured making the workers dependent upon the ruling class.[106] These opinions certainly echoed Proudhon's formulation that the working class was the creative centre of theories (cf. his *De la Capacité de la Classe Ouvrière*).

Sorel in this connection criticized the French and the German socialist parties. It was not by coincidence that both had a cult of the parliamentary system. Influenced by Proudhon, Sorel for the first time advanced in *L'Avenir Socialiste des Syndicats* the idea that the trade unions were the key organization of the class struggle and came to see in them the leading institutions of the working class. They should become the basic agencies of the society of free producers who would know no employers ("masters") and should absorb the machinery of the state.

Formation by Sorel of his pluralistic conceptions was to some extent influenced by James's pragmatism (it is noteworthy in this connection that Sorel wrote a study of the usefulness of pragmatism),[107] but the main factor was Durkheim's way of thinking, with its emphasis on the basic importance of vocational groups in society. This was emphasized by Sorel himself in his *Matériaux d'une Théorie du Proletariat*. We can also point to the fact that Sorel was greatly interested in the impact of the British trade unions upon unorganized masses which the unions often succeeded in activating as their supporters in conflict situations.[108] The influence of those trade unions far exceeded their membership. Sorel saw in them the cadre of the working class.

The traditional political activity would be replaced by entirely new tactics. The trade unions, forming "the class movement" as the only true worker organizations, would undertake a direct action (*action directe*) in which a distinction must be made between step-by-step action (*action partielle*) and a general strike that would be total in nature; i.e. would destroy the bourgeois state and society at a stroke. This was his reply to parliamentary socialism with its cult of elections (indirect action). Sorel, being against the parliamentary game, thought that a true parliamentary opposition could find expression only outside the then existing political system.[109]

The general strike was to be the uprising of the workers organized in trade unions on a mass scale. In the syndicalist movement, in the future syndicalist society the only organization that would unite the various trade unions would take on the form of their confederation, something like a clearing house of the initiatives undertaken independently by the various unions. The trade unions would owe their cohesion to a conscious and voluntary discipline of the workers, a discipline coming not from the outside, but from the inside, from the ranks of the workers themselves. This syndicalist revolution (the general strike) assumed its careful preparation in terms of a well-trained personnel. The general strike was to be the ultimate weapon of the workers and to put an end to the capitalist state which represented unproductive and parasitical society.

During the general strike recourse to violence would be inevitable, but the syndicalists had reasons to believe that the cruelties of the bourgeois revolution would not be repeated.

But that "indivisible whole" which the general strike as imagined by Sorel would be was merely a myth, a myth which would mobilize the workers to fight, an irrational element (we sense Bergson's influence here) indispensable in every great social movement.[110]

Yet any myth that affects attitudes only and does not immediately result in decisions made by a given group naturally shifts revolutionary solutions into an indefinite future, which has been fully confirmed by history. That, however, was not fully realized by the adherents of anarcho-syndicalism outside France, especially in pre-1917 Russia and in the first years after the October Revolution there (see below), in Britain (cf. Chap. 2 section B) and in Italy. Sorel strove to make a synthesis of the work of Proudhon and that of Marx–a mistake as great as it was instructive. In the present writer's opinion, the delay until the early twentieth century of the expansion on a mass scale of the socialist party in France can be explained by the blocking influence of anarcho-syndicalism. But at the time when the founders of "the new school" were crowning its edifice, Eastern Europe saw the victory of the proletarian revolution that undermined its foundations.

A digression into the future seems quite to the point here. Sorel, who died in 1922 and who called himself a disinterested servant of the proletariat, for all the diametrical differences between his own views and those of the Bolsheviks, responded to the October Revolution by expressing his admiration for the revolution itself and for Lenin personally. This he demonstrated particularly by adding to the third (1919) edition of his *Réflexions sur la Violence* a special appendix entitled *Pour Lénine*. He dissociated himself from the allegations that the Bolsheviks in their revolutionary tactics drew inspiration from his *Réflexions* and, expressing his hope that new Carthages would not triumph over the Rome of the proletariat, he concluded rhetorically: "Condemned be the plutocratic democracies which starve Russia ... before entering my grave may I live long enough to see the humiliation of bourgeois democracies which today are cynically triumphant". And in 1920, in Appendix II to *Les Illusions du Progrès*, he referred to the Soviet Republic which gives special encouragement to the advocates of socialist expansion in their struggle against the reformists.[111]

Berth wrote in the same spirit, and like his master used the sharpest words of criticism when writing about the European social democracy (he called Kautsky a petty bourgeois democrat) and concluded his book *Du "Capital" aux "Réflexions sur la Violence"*, which was a collection of articles, with the item *Lénine: Qui est-ce?* (Lenin: Who Is He?), which is an emotional defence of Bolshevism in the Western European worker movement and a condemnation of such "social traitors" as Gompers and Renner.[112]

This affection for Bolshevism was blurred in the minds of many people by the clamorous adoption by Mussolini of Sorel as a forerunner of Fascism, as if Fascist *sindicati* could have anything in common with the role assigned by

Sorel to the trade unions. The ideological provocation consisted here in obliterating the difference between the *syndicats* which "united" workers and entrepreneurs and the Fascist state.

Only the second generation of "the new school" abandoned solidarity with the proletarian revolution and the soviet state. S. Beracha saw in the syndicalist society the third path of development, different from both the bourgeois democracy and the communist-led society in the East.[113]

To revert to Sorel and his closest co-workers and adherents, we have to say that there could be no understanding between anarcho-syndicalism and communism despite such an important link between the two as the class struggle expected to result in a revolution. There were no grounds for any such understanding for three reasons.

(1) "The new school" rejected the role of political parties in the revolution-ary worker movement.
(2) "The new school" had a negative attitude towards the role played in political parties by intellectuals, and stressed "the working-class authen-ticity of the revolutionary trade unions". The Bolsheviks found it difficult to comprehend the constitution of a non-political revolution. We must leave aside also the paradox in the argument of "the new school" in view of the fact that anarcho-syndicalism was the work of intellectuals.
(3) The political revolution was to be replaced by the myth of a general strike, expected to bring about a revolutionary, but at the same time non-political, shaping of a new society, based on the structure of the trade unions.

Lenin, who did not value Sorel's philosophical views (he called them muddy), many years later replied with "ungrateful" silence to the advances made by French anarcho-syndicalists.[114]

Why did he do so? The struggle of the anarcho-syndicalists against social democracy and the leaders of the Second International foreshadowed the pro-Bolshevik attitudes of their leaders. This was certainly a fact of consequence to the worker movement in Western Europe, but the Bolsheviks at the time of encirclement in 1918–21 were too much engaged in their struggle against the Russian variety of anarcho-syndicalism ("the Worker Opposition") to be able to afford the luxury of long discussions and of formulating shades of opinion. The hot post-revolutionary period did not allow that; it required simplified non-ambiguity, it required "ungratefulness" on the part of those who were used to consistency in action, observance of principles and permanacy in attitudes.

It would be difficult to indicate any new pluralistic ideas in the French worker movement after World War I. Pluralism was hardly ever discussed, but opinions can be gauged from political practice, which informed the current trends. One could not fail to notice the continuing anarcho-syndicalist tendencies in which the communists opposed the autonomy of the trade unions under the general political guidance of the Communist Party, whilst the socialists, advocated the complete autonomy of the trade unions unrestricted by any political organization.[115]

New elements were contributed only by the Popular Front. Both the socialists and the communists declared their attitude by the very fact of participating in it, even though they did not make any formal declarations about being pluralists in politics and in culture. On that issue there were no essential differences between the communists and the remaining two parties that together formed the Popular Front. Toleration of different views in science and art and free expression of opinion on the various facts in public life were beyond discussion for the founders and members of the Front, since it was on toleration that their alliance of short duration, abolished by reactionary forces, was based. There was no discussion of a socialist system in France because the Front was absorbed by immediate goals: improvement of the living standards of the working class and the impoverished lower middle classes, and defence of democracy in France.

NOTES AND REFERENCES

1. This found expression in his idea of sovereignty. In 1819 he wrote that "The totality of citizens is sovereign in the sense that no individual, no group, and no association can appropriate sovereignty if this has not been delegated to it by the people." Cf. B. Constant, *Cours de politique constitutionnelle* (Bruxelles, 1839), pp. 64 ff. He shared with other liberals of the Restoration period the hatred of political parties and democracy. Cf. G. de Rugiero, *The History of European Liberalism* (Boston, 1959), p. 169.
2. Cf. H. H. Jacoby, *Die Biurokratisierung der Welt* (Neuwied, 1969), Part I.
3. P. Birnbaum, *Sociologie de Tocqueville* (Paris, 1979), p. 51; J. Lively, *The Social and Political Thought of Alexis de Tocqueville*, (Oxford and London, 1962), pp. 153 ff., 164.
4. This was pointedly indicated by J. Touchard *et al.* in: *Histoire des idées politiques*, vol. 2 (Paris, 1959), p. 396.
5. On de Montesquieu's intermediate bodies see K. Grzybowski, "Monteskiusz–kompromis feudalno-mieszczański" (De Montesquieu–A Compromise Between Feudalism and Burgherdom), *Państwo i Prawo*, 9–10, (1948), 10–11; J. J. Chevalier, *Les grandes oeuvres politiques* (De Machiavel à nos jours) (Paris, 1955), chap. II.
6. From de Tocqueville's correspondence quoted after Th. P. Neill, *The Rise and Decline of Liberalism* (Milwaukee, 1953), p. 254.
7. E. Durkheim, *Montesquieu et Rousseau (Precurseurs de la sociologie)* (Paris 1955), pp. 13 ff, 26 ff, 35 ff, 48 ff, 63 ff, 97.
8. Cf. G. Gojat, "Corps intermédiaires et décentralisation chez Tocqueville", in: G. Pelloux (ed.), *Libéralisme, traditionalisme, décentralisation* (Paris, 1952).
9. Attention to this fact was drawn by J. Lively, *op. cit.*, p. 141.
10. This debate in de Tocqueville's works was very penetratingly brought out by G. Poggi, *Images of Society*, Essays on the Sociological Theories of Tocqueville, Marx and Durkheim, (Stanford, 1972), pp. 34 ff.
11. C. B. Macpherson, *The Political Theory of Possessive Individualism (Hobbes to Locke* (Oxford and London), 1962.
12. On the various interpretations of individualism see L. Moulin, "On the Evolution of the Word 'Individualism'", in: *The International Social Science Bulletin*, 7, (1955), 781 ff.

13. From this point of view the Soviet historian M. A. Alpatov was right in claiming that de Tocqueville's views on democracy called for an alliance of the bourgeoisie and the aristocracy. See his *Les idée politiques de Tocqueville, Questions d'Histoire*, (Paris, 1954), vol. 2, p. 150. The reservation must be made, however, that this applies rather to de Tocqueville as an ideologist and politician than as a scholar.

14. *The Federalist*, A Commentary on the Constitution of the United States, New York (no date indicated), text No. 47 (by Madison), p. 313: "The oracle who is always consulted is the celebrated Montesquieu." For other references to de Montesquieu in *The Federalist* see pp. 49, 50, 53, 282, 285, 315, 504 of the same edition. See also P. Bastid, "Montesquieu et les Etats Unis," in: *La pensée politique et constitutionnelle de Montesquieu (Bicentenaire de l'Esprit des lois 1748–1948)* (Paris, 1952).

15. *The Federalist*, Nos. 9 and 10. See also S. Ehrlich, *Władza i interesy*, pp. 25 ff.

16. J. Bryce, The Predictions of Hamilton and Tocqueville, in: *Studies in History and Jurisprudence* (New York, 1901), p. 321 (quoted after P. Birnbaum, *op. cit.*, p. 31). De Tocqueville's correspondence points to the normative elements in his book on America. Cf. J. Lively, *op. cit.*, p. 29.

17. J. J. Chevalier, *op. cit.*, pp. 227 ff.

18. J. P. Mayer, *Alexis de Tocqueville* (Paris, 1948), p. 52.

19. B. Sobolewska, "Tocqueville pośród moralistów politycznych Francji pierwszej połowy XIX w." (De Tocqueville's Position Among French Political Moralists in the First Half of the 19th Century), *Czasopismo Historyczno-Prawne*, **XXII**, (1970), 61, 67, 69.

20. P. Bastid, "Tocqueville et la doctrine constitutionnelle", in: *Alexis de Tocqueville, Livre du Centenaire, 1859–1959* (Paris, 1960), pp. 45 ff.

21. "Tocqueville et la Démocratie en Amerique", *ibid.*, pp. 181 ff.

22. G. D. H. Cole, *Essays in Social Theory* (London, 1950), pp. k63 ff. See in particular A. Comte, *Cours de philosophie positive*, vols. 4 and 5.

23. J. Szczepański, *Socjologia. Rozwój problematyki i metod (Sociology. Development of Problems and Methods)* (Warszawa, 1961), pp. 51 ff. See also *Pozytywizm i sojologia Comte'a (Comte's Positivism and Sociology)* by the same author (Łódź, 1951).

24. J. Lacroix, *La sociologie d'Auguste Comte* (Paris, 1961), pp. 16, 20, 48, 89.

25. B. Skarga, *Comte* (Warszawa, 1966), p. 50.

26. Numerous statements by Comte on this subject can be found in his *Système de politique positive ou Traité de sociologie instituant la Réligion de l'Humanité*, vols. 1–4, 1851–4. See also B. Skarga, *op. cit.*, pp. 79 and 92.

27. Cf. A. Kremer-Marietti, *Auguste Comte* (Paris, 1970), p. 49.

28. A. Comte, *Système …*, Foreword to vols. 3 and 4, and vol. 4, p. 355.

29. Comte demanded that France restore freedom to Algeria and Corsica. On the basis of "brotherly help" he exhorted the English to return Gibraltar to Spain, and asked for justice for the Indians and the Negro slaves. Cf. *Système…*, vol. 4, pp. 417–519.

30. Kremer-Marietti, *op. cit.*, p. 93.

31. P. J. Proudhon, *Les Confessions d'un Révolutionnaire* (1st ed. 1849; Paris, 1929), chaps XIV, XVII, XX. See also J. Bancal, *Proudhon. Pluralisme et Autogestion*, vol. 1, *Les fondements*, (Paris, 1970), pp. 164 ff, 168 ff, 176, 243.

32. Cf. Proudhon, *op. cit.*, Idée générale de la révolution au dix-neuvième siècle (1st edn, 1851; Paris, 1923), and also *De la Justice dans la Révolution et dan l'Eglise* (Paris, 1958), by the same author.

33. P. J. Proudhon, *La révolution social demontrée par le coup d'Etat du 2 décembre 1851* (Paris, 1852). On Proudhon's attitude towards Louis Bonaparte see C. Cogiot, *Proudhon et la démagogie bonapartiste*, and also G. Gurvitch, *Proudhon* (Paris, 1965), pp. 7 ff.

34. A. Ritter, *The Political Thought of Pierre Joseph Proudhon*, (Princeton, N. J., 1969), p. 8. A good review of conflicting opinions on Proudhon is offered by P. Ansart, *Naissance de l'Anarchisme* (Paris, 1960), pp. 7 ff. On the contrary, the latest French studies try to minimize contradictions in Proudhon's writings by stressing the continuity of themes and the process of maturation of his theories. Cf. J. Bancal, *op. cit.*, and B. Voyenne, *Le Fédéralisme de P. J. Proudhon* (Paris–Nice, 1973), who gave the first chapter of his book the ostentatious title: "The unity of Proudhon's thought". This suggestion is made easy by the simple trick: the author begins his exposition of the subject by only presenting the latest and more mature writings of Proudhon.

35. Concerning Proudhon on the class struggle see P. Ansart, *Socialisme et Anarchisme* (Paris,

1969), pp. 169 ff, 191 ff.

36. Based on a Polish-language edition of Proudhon's selected works, vol. 1 (Warszawa, 1974).

37. *De la Capacité politique des classes ouvrières* (1st edn, 1865; Paris, 1924), pp. 67 ff.

38. P. J. Proudhon, *De la Création de l'ordre dans l'Humanité ou Principes d'Organisation politique* (1st edn, 1843; Paris, 1927), in particular p. 361; on the same subject see J. Voyenne, *op. cit.*, pp. 87 ff., 132 ff.

39. "Pour un pareil régime un singe suffirait au commandement", *De la Capacité...*, p. 205.

40. *De la Capacité...*, pp. 132 ff; *De la Justice...*, 4ᵉ étude.

41. F. Engels; *Introduction to the Civil War in France by K. Marx*, ... (Marx/Engels, *Selected Works* (Pol.), Warsaw, 1949, pp. 444 ff.

42. On the controversy between Marx and Proudhon see section 5.2 of this book. See also M. Buber, *Paths in Utopia* (Boston, 1958), p. 28.

43. D. Guérin, *L'Anarchisme* (Paris, 1965), pp. 54 and 65 and *passim*; A. Ritter, *op. cit.*, pp. 126–8; and G. Gurvitch, *op. cit.*, *passim*.

44. A. Ritter, *op. cit.*, p. 123; B. Voyenne, *op. cit.*, pp. 113, 121.

45. Quoted after J. Bancal, *op. cit.*, pp. 167 ff, 214. In fact L. Blanc was the first socialist to hold a cabinet post. Ch. Rapoport described him as the founder of reformist socialism. Quoted after L. Hamon, *Socialisme et pluralités* (Paris, 1976), pp. 85 ff.

46. The misunderstandings over the idea and practice of national workshops (atelier nationaux) were analysed by K. Marx in *The Class Struggles in France, 1848 to 1850.*

47. Cf. P. J. Proudhon, *Du Principe fédératif* (1st ed., 1863; Paris, 1959), chap. X; "Confessions d'un révolutionnaire ..." (1st edn, 1849; Paris, 1929), chap. XI. After Louis Bonaparte's coup d'état Proudhon exclaimed: "I make politics to kill it, to end with politics." See also B. Voyenne, *op. cit.*, pp. 31, 79, 82, 96; and J. Bancal, *op. cit.*, pp. 197 ff, 202 ff, 211 ff, 226, 233 ff, 250.

48. Cf. B. Baczko, *Rousseau: Samotność i wspólnota (Rousseau: Loneliness and Community* (Warszawa, 1964), pp. 676 ff.

49. *Idée générale ...*, cf. note 28 above. G. Gurvitch was right in blaming Proudhon for his excessive tendency to conceive of social relations in legal concepts. *Op. cit.*, pp. 38 and 45.

50. It is, however, Bakunin who is to be treated as the radical municipal socialist: he was in favour of expropriation of all the means of production on behalf of the communes.

51. Quoted after N. Bourgeois, *Les Théories du Droit International chez Proudhon* (Le Fédéralisme et la paix) (Paris, 1927), pp. 28, 51, 63–4.

52. *Idée générale...*

53. N. Bourgeois quotes a letter in which Proudhon writes that in 1840 he began with anarchy, and then ended in federation. *Op. cit.*, p. 65.

54. He dedicated a number of his works to that matter. In particular see *La Guerre et la paix* (1st edn, 1861; Paris, 1927).

55. *De la Justice...*, Part II (Petit catéchisme politique).

56. Quoted after Bourgeois, *op. cit.*, p. 54.

57. F. Neumann warned against that in *The Democratic and the Authoritarian State* (Glencoe, 1957), p. 218, but he went too far and in a sense distorted Proudhon's idea by claiming that it had nothing in common with a federal state and is even its denial.

58. *La guerre et la paix...*, pp. 313 ff; *De la Justice...*, Part II, p. 259; Part III, p. 249; Part IV, p. 263.

59. E. Durkheim, *De la Division du travail social* (Paris, 1973), pp. 173 and 341.

60. This is one of the fundamental ideas in *De la Division...* See also *Les Règles...* (cf. note 61 below): "La cause déterminante d'un fait social doit être cherchée parmi les faits sociaux antécédents, et non parmi les états de la conscience individuelle" (p. 109).

61. E. Durkheim, *Les Règles de la méthode sociologique* (1st edn, 1895; Paris, 1960), pp. 102–3.

62. On Aristotle's impact upon the development of the social sciences see P. Rybicki, *Arystotels–początki i podstawy nauki o społeczeństwie (Aristotle: the Beginnings and Foundations of the Science of Society)* (Wrocław-Warszawa-Kraków, 1963). But Maria Włodyka correctly pointed to the differences between Aristotle's interpretation of man as a being "social by his very nature" and the view of Durkheim; see her *Teoria faktu*

społecznego w systemie socjologicznym Emila Durkheima (The Theory of Social Fact in Emile Durkheim's Sociological System, (Wrocław-Warszawa-Kraków, 1974), pp. 135 ff.

63. E. Durkheim, *Sociologie et philosophie* (1st edn, 1924; Paris, 1963), p. 78.
64. J. Szacki, *Durkheim* (Warszawa, 1964), pp. 73–4.
65. This idea was most clearly formulated by him in *Les Règles...*
66. His anti-individualism and its sources are brought out by R. A. Nisbet in: *"Emile Durkheim" Selected Essays* (New Jersey, 1965), pp. 11 ff, 22 ff, and by R. K. Merton in his "Durkheim's Division of Labour in Society", in the same publication, p. 106. See also C. Lévi-Strauss, "La Sociologie française", in: G. Gurvitch (ed.), *La Sociologie au XX siècle*, vol. II (Paris, 1947), p. 537, and S. Lukes, "Durkheim's Individualism and the Intellectuals", *Political Studies*, 17 (1969).
67. E. Durkheim, *Le Suicide*, Étude Sociologique (Paris, 1897), pp. 107 ff. See also his criticism of Tarde's ideas in *Les Formes élémentaires de la vie réligieuse* (1st edn, 1912; Paris, 1960).
68. Durkheim also used the terms *groupes sociaux*, *groupes partiels*. To secondary groups he dedicated much space not only in *De la Division...* and *Le Suicide*, but in his other works as well. An interesting analysis of that pluralistic element in Durkheim's work is given by E. Wallwark in *Durkheim (Morality and Milieu)*, (Cambridge, Mass., 1972), chap. IV, "Moral Societies".
69. R. A. Nisbet, *op. cit.* Also A. Giddens: *Emile Durkheim*, (Harmondsworth, Middlesex, 1979).
70. G. Poggi, *Essays on Images of Society* (The Sociological Theories of Tocqueville, Marx and Durkheim) (Stanford, 1972), p. 180.
71. But R. K. Merton pointed to the fact that the concept of *anomie* had been used before Durkheim.
72. J. Duvigneau, *L'Anomie (hérésie et subversion)* (Paris, 1973), pp. 34 ff.
73. R. K. Merton published two studies on the theory of *anomie*: "Social Structure and Anomie", and "Continuities in the Theory of Social Structure and Anomie", both included in: *Social Theory and Social Structure* (Glencoe, Ill., 1957). In this connection it is to be noted that Durkheim and Merton differ in the interpretation of *anomie*, and that A. Schaff made a distinction between *anomie* and alienation in his *Entfremdung als soziales Phänomen* (Wien, 1977), pp. 190–210. See also H. McCloskey and J. H. Schaur, "Psychological Dimensions of Anomy", *The American Sociological Review*, 30 (1) (Feb. 1965). Neither Durkheim nor Merton took up that aspect of the problem, obviously for different reasons.
74. G. Poggi, *op. cit.*, p. 249.
75. E. Durkheim, *De la Division...* (Paris, 1973), pp. vi, xxxii ff.
76. M. Władyska, *op. cit.*, pp. 110–11.
77. J. Szczepański, *op. cit.*, p. 316.
78. E. Wallwark, *op. cit.*, pp. 104, 111. In the same spirit R. A. Nisbet, *op. cit.*, pp. 62 ff.
79. E. Allardt, "Emile Durkheim–ein Beitrag zur politischen Soziologie". *Kölnische Zeitschrift für Soziologie und soziale Psychologie*, 20 (1) (1968), pp. 1–16.
80. E. Dupréel: *Le pluralisme sociologique. Fondements scientifiques d'une revision des institutions* (Bruxelles, 1945), pp. 9, 18, 25, 29; *Essais pluralistes* (Paris 1949).
81. Cf. *Etudes de Droit Public I. L'Etat (Le Droit objectif et la loi positive* (Paris, 1901), pp. 23, 47, 80; *Le Droit social, le droit individuel et la transformation de l'Etat* (Paris, 1908), pp. 4, 8, 23 ff. 115 ff. 123–4, 149. A special importance to Proudhon's influence upon Duguit is attached by H. J. Laski in his introduction to L. Duguit, *Law in the Modern State* (London, 1921), Introduction, pp. xiii ff.
82. *Le droit social* (Paris, 1909), pp. 118, 148.
83. L. Duguit, *ibid.*, pp. 7 ff; see also *L'etat*, chaps IV and V. The subject was also taken up by him in *Les Transformations générales du droit privé*, (Paris, 1912). pp. 15 ff *et passim*. See also G. Davy, "Le Problème de l'obligation chez Duguit et Kelsen". *Archives de Philosophie du droit et de soziologie juridique*, 1–2 (1933); G. Pirou, "Léon Duguit et l'économie politique". *Revue d'Economie Politique*, I-II (1933).
   The opinion that law means the sum of duties has survived in France to our times; it suffices to point in this respect to *Initiation aux recherces de sociologie juridique* (Paris, 1947), pp. 4 ff, by H. Lévy-Bruhl, a sociologist of law.
84. See also P. Cinture, "La Pensée politique de Léon Duguit". *Revue juridique et*

Economique Sud-Ouest, **19** (1968).
85. Cf. J. Stone, *The Province and Function of Law* (London, 1947), chap. XII.
86. M. Waline, *L'Individualisme et le droit* (Paris, 1945). But it was probably F. Gény who was the first to draw attention to the fact that Duguit let the law of nature slip into the theory of law through the back door (cf. *Science et technique en droit privé positif* (Paris, 1924), vol. IV, p. xiii).
87. G. Gurvitch, *L'Expérience juridique et la philosophie du pluralisme en droit* (Paris, 1935).
88. M. Hauriou, *Droit administratif* (Paris, 1907), *passim.* Hauriou also sided with Duguit in demanding that the state be restrained by the law, and believed that to be the only issue in public law (cf. his *Principes de droit public* and also *Précis de droit constitutionnel*). On the parallel between Duguit and Hauriou see Ch. Esenmann, "Deux Théoriciens du droit, Duguit et Hauriou", *Revue Philosophique de la France et de l'Etranger,* no. 9–10 (1950).
89. L. Duguit, *Les Transformations du droit public* (Paris, 1913), p. 279.
90. L. Duguit, *Le Droit social...* (Paris, 1908), pp. 118, 121 ff, 138, 141.
91. *Op. cit.,* pp. 108 ff. See also "La Grève générale prolétarienne", *Mouvement Socialiste,* vol. XVIII (1906), by the same author.
92. This was pointed out by H. Temkinowa, *Bakunin i antynomia wolności (Bakunin and the Antinomy of Freedom),* Warszawa, 1964, pp. 122 ff.
93. D. Guérin, *L'Anarchisme* (Paris, 1956), pp. 56 and 74–5.
94. J. Guillaume, *Idées sur l'organisation sociale* (Paris, 1876).
95. F. Pelletier, *Histoire des bourses de travail* (Paris, 1902), p. 169. See also his earlier work, "L'Arnarchisme et les syndicats ouvriers", in *Les Temps Nouveaux* (Paris, 1895). In those views he was close to Fourier, who saw in associations the remedy against both revolution and the tyranny of the state (cf. *L'Individu, l'association et l'Etat* (Paris, 1906), p. 21).
96. P. Kropotkin, *Mutual Aid as a Factor of Development* (quoted after a Polish-language version (Łódź-Warszawa, 1946), chaps. VI–VIII).
97. P. Boncour expounded his views from the period in which he favoured anarchism most extensively in *Le Fédéralisme économique* (Paris, 1889).
98. M. Leroy, *Les Transformations de la puissance publique* (Paris, 1907), p. 265 *et passim.*
99. He dedicated to him his last major work, *Matériaux d'une théorie du prolétariat* (Paris, 1918). E. Berth, his closest co-worker, termed him the closest follower of Proudhon. On the formation of Sorel's views see J. M. Meisel, "The Genesis of Georges Sorel", *American Archives,* 1951.
100. G. Sorel, *Matériaux...* (Paris, 1918), pp. 154 ff, 372.
101. E. Berth, *Les Méfaits des intellectuels* (Paris, 1914).
102. E. Berth, *Les derniers Aspects du socialisme* (Paris, 1923), pp. 52 and 61: "L'étatisme c'est l'idéal du petit bourgeois, c'est l'inverse du socialisme". G. Sorel, "Les Théories de M. Durkheim", *Le Devenir Social* (1895). G. Goriely, *le Pluralisme dramatique de Georges Sorel* (Paris, 1962), p. 186.
103. G. Sorel, *Réflexions sur la violence* (1st edn, 1907; Paris, 1946), p. 266.
104. E. Berth, *Les derniers Aspects...* (Paris, 1914), the essay on Guesdisme et syndicalisme, *passim.*
105. See L. Hamon, *op. cit.,* pp. 100 ff, who points to Jaurès' foible to anarcho-syndicalists, paradoxical in the case of the leader of reformists.
106. H. Lagardelle, "Les Intellectuels et le socialisme ouvrier", *Le Mouvement Socialiste* (1907).
107. G. Sorel, *de l'Utilité du pragmatisme* (Paris, 1928).
108. G. Sorel, *Matériaux...* (Paris, 1918), pp. 115 ff.
109. D. Beetham, "Sorel and the Left", *Government and Opposition,* No. 4 (1969), pp. 308 ff.
110. The ideas presented by Sorel in *Réflexions...* were developed by E. Berth in *Les dernier Aspects...*
111. G. Sorel, *Les Illusions du progrès* (Paris, 1917), pp. 337 ff and in particular p. 383. On this turn in Sorel's views see M. Charzat, *Georges Sorel au XXᵉ siècle* (Paris, 1977).
112. E. Berth, *Du 'capital' aux 'Réflexions sur la violence'* (Paris, 1932), chap: "Lénine 'Qui est-ce?'", pp. 205 ff. See also *Guerre des Etats ou Guerre des Classes* (Paris, 1924), pp. 155 ff, 184 ff, 303 ff.
113. S. Beracha, *Le Marxisme après Marx* (Paris, 1937), chap. VII ("Sorel contre le marxisme politique") and chap. VIII ("Le néosyndicalisme"). See also *Rationalisation et Révolu-*

tion (Paris, 1931), by the same author.
114. Cf. V. I. Lenin, vol. 21, p. 335, of the 4th Russian-language edition of his collected works. See also section 6.1 below.
115. Léon Blum, when analysing the various relationships among European political parties and trade union organizations, wrote: "La thèse qui triompha sans conteste et qui constitua la solution purement française du mouvement syndical vis-à-vis de toute organisation politique." Cf. *L'Oeuvre de Léon Blum 1945–7;* (Paris, 1958), p. 258.

CHAPTER 2

Pluralism in Britain: The Fabians and Guild Socialists

A. The Fabians

Socialism in Britain developed as a result of a crisis in liberal political economy and a critical attitude towards the parliamentary system, and already in its early period established links with the labour movement. We shall accordingly discuss the Fabian Society and the rebellion in its ranks (the Fabian dissidents being known in the history of social and political ideas as guild socialists).

2.1 THE ORIGIN OF THE FABIAN MOVEMENT

The rise of the Fabian movement, which emerged from a club of people of good will, the Fellowship of the New Life, and strove for a moral revival and self-improvement, has been described many times and there is no need to repeat all that has been said elsewhere.[1] Let us just recall the "Fabians of the first hour", who had imprinted upon the Fabian Society those features which made it known in the history of Britain and that of sociopolitical ideas. They were Sidney Webb and George Bernard Shaw (who had studied the Marxist theory and acquired a fairly good knowledge of it, but later departed from it), Graham Wallas, Annie Besant, Hubert Bland, William Clarke, E. R. Pease, and Sydney Olivier. They were marked by a critical–in some respects at least–attitude towards utilitarianism and by personal connections and/or contacts with the various socialist groups.[2] Five years after the foundation of the Fabian Society and publication of several pamphlets (*The Fabian Tracts*) they wrote and published in 1889 *The Fabian Essays* (G. B. Shaw (ed.)),[3] which had a strong impact upon the development of socialist movement and thinking in Britain. The book, reprinted many times and read to this day, summed up the previous journalist activity of the Fabians. G. B. Shaw, who of all the Fabians had the most thorough knowledge of Marxist theory, was not the only member of the society who was inclined towards Marxism in the early period of Fabian activity. A. Besant and H. Bland (an ex-conservative) had clear Marxist leanings, and S. Webb had a critical interest in that theory.

When the said assays were being prepared one member of the group approached Engels, "as an accepted scholarly authority on socialism", with the suggestion that Engels write an essay on socialism, but Engels turned down the proposal. At that time there was even a special group formed to discuss Marxist theory. The departure from Marxism was due to a controversy over the theory of value. On that issue the Fabians ultimately adopted the theory advanced by Stanley Jevons, but they assimilated some elements of the Marxist theory and adjusted them to the conditions prevailing in Britain.[4] McBriar, the author of probably the best monograph of Fabian socialism, ascribed to the Marxist influence the overcoming by the Fabians of their original liberal radicalism and the consolidation of socialist views.[5] It is worth noting also that many years later the Marxist influence came to be reflected in the attitude of the leading Fabians towards Soviet Russia (the book by the Webbs on Soviet communism, many statements made by G. B. Shaw and recorded in Maysky's memoirs,[6] and visits by some Fabians to the Soviet Union).

Let us now return to the first programmatic action by the Fabians.

2.2   THE PROGRAMME: A GRADUAL TRANSFORMATION OF CAPITALISM

What did the Fabians strive for? Like the philosophers under enlightened absolutism, who wanted to win the kings for their ideas, they believed that British people were enlightened enough to understand that the capitalist system must gradually be transformed into a socialist one. The term *gradualism*, coined by Webb, was taken over by the Fabians to become one of the fundamental points in their programme.[7]

Gradual reforms were to cover primarily the socialization of the means of production (land and capital), which Sidney Webb considered to be inevitable, though in the distant future (inevitability of gradualness). The Fabians thought that they had to reckon with the resistance of tradition and the inertia of habits, and also to realize that certain sections of the national economy, such as small-scale production and some services, did not lend themselves well to socialization. Gradual socialization obviously assumed that the process would take place within the law. Evolution towards socialism was to be so gradual as to become almost imperceptible. This was an idea of the withering away of the capitalist system, and hence an idea of a process which is not spontaneous and has to be "pushed on" cautiously.

This pragmatic approach which assumed gradual transformations complied with the mentality of the middle class, from which the Fabians originated. It also suited that respectable (to use Marx's formulation) working class which had long ago lost the fighting spirit of the Chartists and in its mass was influenced by liberal ideology.[8]

As early as in 1854 Marx, when witnessing the numerical and organizational growth of the British working class (expansion of the trade unions), wrote that the working class was called more than any other group to lead that vast movement which was bound to bring about a final liberation of labour.[9] But the appearance of the Fabians on the political arena made people realize that the revolutionary aspirations of the British working class, manifest between the French revolution and the Chartist movement, had vanished completely and that the dominant ideology was now that of small producers.[10] Gradualism proved to be a catchy slogan, but later, before and after World War I, when the British labour movement was temporarily more radical, it came to be criticized vehemently.[11]

The Fabians did not doubt that capitalism (which they called an irrational anachronism) was bound to change, but they were programmatically reformers. They saw neither the need for, nor the possibility of, a revolution under the conditions prevailing in Britain. In their opinion there was no such need in a free country, and law was for them the mother of freedom.

In the original period of their activity they were to clash with another labour organization which had adopted the Marxist standpoint, namely with the Social-democratic Federation, but the working masses were won over by the Fabian programme and action. Transformations, as Sidney Webb wrote, should be (1) democratic, (2) gradual, (3) accepted by the masses as moral, (4) constitutional and peaceful.[12] Hence removal or destruction of the existing political organization of the state was out of the question. The point was to modify the parliament and the government and to make use of the various forms of social activity; the local government first of all. It is beyond dispute that the Fabians did fight vigorously to improve the communal economy. They succeeded in achieving that not only in the various provincial centres, but in London above all, and thus in reaching the masses and winning their respect. This was the political line later adopted by the Labour Party.[13] And Wells went further, beyond municipal reforms, and called for Britain being transformed so that all municipalities should have their autonomous local government (a new heptarchy).[14] This was an expanded plan of regional administration, which resembled the ideas advanced by Comte and Proudhon, and at the same time a forerunner of the present system of regional administration in Britain.

The emphasis placed by the Fabian Society on improving the living conditions dependent on the functioning of the local government resulted in their programme being identified with municipal socialism. They were ironically labelled "gas works and water mains socialists",[15] and their programmatically anti-revolutionary attitude provoked Lenin's well-known criticism, preceded by Engels' ironical comment on "the Fabian school", and G. B. Shaw personally, included in the Foreword to vol. 3 of *Capital*. That comment, however, referred to the economic views of the Fabians and was due to Shaw's departure from the Marxist standpoint.

As seen by the Fabians, and in particular by the Webbs, the municipaliza-tion of industry, i.e. the shifting of the centre of gravity from central to local government, should be the programme for socialist decentralization. This was why they envisaged only limited nationalization in the first period. Local government units, "democracies for citizens", were later extensively treated by them in the multi-volume monograph *The English Local Government* (vol. 1 appeared in 1906).

It is striking that the early programmatic declarations of the Fabian Society lacked emphasis on the role of the trade unions in a socialist sociopolitical system. Nothing like that can be found in the collective manifesto of 1889. They also failed to notice at that time the role of consumer co-operatives in the process of social reconstruction. It was only many years later that they admitted that failure of theirs.[16] To this we may add that they at first followed the beaten track of the dichotomy: the individual versus society, and saw in the state the representative and the trustee of the poeple. That "social organism" should be the owner and the manager of the wealth produced by the members of society.[17]

It is worth mentioning in this connection that those groups which were more radical than the Fabian Society (for instance, the Social Democratic Federation, founded in 1881 and for many years headed by H. M. Hyndman), treated the trade unions as a burden in the process of organization of the working class. Hyndman in his letter to Marx of 29 October 1881, substantiated that standpoint by arguing that the trade unions represented merely a small part of the working class and formed its aristocracy. But he was in favour of extending the political support for the demands set forth by the trade unions.[18]

Many years later Margaret Cole, an expert on the period under consideration, wrote that Sidney and Beatrice Webb imagined economic democracy only in the form of collective property owned by the state and the municipalities, and completely disregarded its functional aspect, the role which producer associations and other vocational organizations could play. They were also criticized for underestimating the role of the co-operative movement. In a word, their vision of non-capitalist future was that of "democratic *étatisme*".[19]

Many factors had contributed to the existence of those gaps in the programmes to be found in the early writings of the Fabians. Being active in discussion clubs attended mainly by intellectuals they were at first very loosely linked to the British labour movement. Fascinated by macrosocio-logical problems (economic and moral critiques of capitalism), and later by macropolitical issues (reorganization of the central political institutions), they either failed to notice certain problems or were unwilling to take them up without having analysed them thoroughly, the more so as at the time when they became active the trade unions were scattered and their total member-ship amounted to half a million only. Nor was there any political organization of the labour movement. The influence of the Social Democratic Federation was limited by the small number of its members, and the Socialist League, headed by W. Morris, soon came to be dominated by anarchists.[20] The workers were still not conscious of their distinct social status, and were on the whole influenced by liberal ideology.

In the workers' eyes the hated capitalists were represented by the Tories, while the liberals were considered advocates of social progress that would improve the living conditions of the working class. British workers still lacked class consciousness: the Chartist traditions had fallen into oblivion, and at the time when the Fabians became active publicly, the workers still formed "a class in itself", to use the term coined by Marx in *Misère de la Philosophie*. The trade unions rid themselves of the liberal influence and commited themselves to the socialist programme only during World War I.[21]

The programme of the Fabian Society was certainly affected by the personal careers of some of its members. Sidney Webb, certainly the most prominent of them next to G. B. Shaw, as a young man (like Olivier) held a high post in the Colonial Office, and later often worked as an expert on Royal Commissions. It was only later that he changed from a government expert into a labour politician. Under such conditions the Webbs quite understandably ascribed to experts a special role in the long period of transition from capitalism to socialism and *a fortiori* in the future socialist system (this applied above all to industrial management). The Webbs, it seems, had an unshakeable faith in the possibilities and ingenuity of enlightened civil servants.[22] They were not exceptions in that respect, for both Graham Wallas and J. A. Hobson saw in experts the crucial figures in the process of social transformations. Naturally enough, Sidney Webb, when he happened to have the financial possibility to do so, became the principal organizer of the famous London School of Economics, later to be incorporated in the University of London.[23] He can reasonably be treated as a forerunner of those who believe experts to be necessary elements of political processes, and perhaps even a forerunner of technocratic tendencies.

2.3 ADDITIONS TO THE PROGRAMME

The Webbs nevertheless came to fill the gaps in the Fabian programme: 1891 saw the appearance of *The Co-operative Movement in Great Britain (1891)* by Beatrice Webb. In the country which had seen the Rochdale pioneers of 1844 and in which consumer co-operatives (contrary to producer co-operatives) were expanding briskly in the second half of the nineteenth century, social reformers could not disregard that issue. The Fabians, like other right-wing socialists (Bernstein, Vandervelde) and theorists of the co-operative movement (e.g. the economist Ch. Gide), had a negative attitude towards producer co-operatives.

Beatrice Webb also engaged in field work concerned with the working conditions in industry, which made her familiar with trade union problems and opened her eyes to the opportunities offered by social organizations, and among these by consumer organizations.[24]

The latter, being the core of the co-operative movement, were to form the analogy to the trade unions: the democracy of producers was to be complemented and balanced by that of consumers. Relationships between the trade unions and the co-operatives should be as harmonious as those prevailing "in an ideal married couple".

It must be emphasized, however, that the Fabian conception of the co-operative movement should not be identified with the co-operative movement programme advanced by Ch. Gide, nor should it be interpreted as an analogue of the former. Gide was not a critic of the capitalist system, for him the co-operative movement was expected to mitigate the defects of that system. The Fabians, on the contrary, complemented the acute critique of capitalism with a programme of reforms, gradual and moderate, as they wanted them to be, but in any case moving towards a socialist system. Seen in this way, consumer co-operatives were one of the organizational forms of the future socialist system. Beside the socialist sectors of the national economy, namely the state-owned and the co-operative, they saw a place in that system for small private businesses and non-organized craftsmen.

McBriar was right when stating that recognition of the importance of trade unionism and the co-operative movement was the foundation of all subsequent recommendations made by the Fabians.[29]

The standpoint adopted by A. D. Lindsay was close to that of the Fabians. A labour adherent, but influenced by Fabian ideas, he distinguished three kinds of associations: those having economic goals in view, those with other statutory goals, and those which have broader goals while pursuing their particular activity. All of them function as intermediate bodies between the individual and the state.[26]

The research interests of Beatrice Webb did not fail to affect the views of Sidney Webb, who several years later published two fundamental monographs, *The History of Trade Unionism* (1894) and *Industrial Democracy* (1897).

In this way the Webbs signally modified the original Fabian programme, and we have to make a distinction between the two periods of their activity if we want to avoid distorting simplifications. The Webbs were not the only ones to engage in practical activity among organized workers. They were followed by G. B. Shaw and other Fabians, among them Annie Besant, who organized the famous strike of the women workers in a match factory (1888), an event of much import for the further development of the trade union movement in Britain.

The Fabians did not adopt any particular attitude towards the various social orgnizations at that time active in Britain, nor did they assess their work. They thought that such organizations formed a natural social tissue, which under the socialist system would adjust itself to the new order and develop within its framework. But it is to be stressed that in Graham Wallas's opinion society can become "great" only owing to a variety of social organizations active in it. He saw in that variety the only remedy to the centralization of power and depersonalization of public life. In particular he declared himself in favour of co-existence of public and private property, and thus stood for economic pluralism.[27]

There are reasons to treat the Fabians as both social and political pluralists. They were social pluralists, for all idea of uniformization and reduction of organizational forms within society was alien to them. Decentralization based on the expansion of the local government, recommended by them, was programmatically pluralistic, and hence the Fabians firmly rejected the criticism that they were centralists who wanted to see "a single employer".[28] They used to work not only on general problems, but also on local programmes for London, Bristol, etc., and when their society expanded and had its provincial Branches founded the head office strove not to interfere with their work, thus practising advanced decentralization in their own sphere.

When it comes to political pluralism, the starting point of the constitutional reform advocated by the Fabians (most completely formulated by the Webbs in *A Constitution for the Socialist Commonwealth*, 1920) was the distinction between groups with economic interests (in the sphere of production, services and consumption), groups with social interests (in the sphere of education, culture, religion, etc.), and groups with interests in the sphere which unites all, i.e. in that in which the individuals function as citizens. Hence the formula of social democracy as distinct from political democracy, and the recommendation that the Parliament be split into two: Social Parliament and Political Parliament. Self-evidently, the House of Lords would have to be abolished, and the reform would apply to the House of Commons. Social Parliament would not only reflect the advanced differentiation of British society, but would directly interfere in the socioeconomic sphere. The nationalized branches of industry would be supervised by standing committees of Social Parliament, and current management would be passed to national boards consisting of representatives of managers, workers, and consumers.

Municipalized industries and agencies would be managed similarly. Political Parliament would handle defence, international relations, and public order. This was obviously an endeavour to bring into agreement functional representation (representation of organized interests) with local representation, the latter modified considerably. These ideas reflected elements of federalism, advanced by Webb not for the first time. The proposals reveal concessions made in the controversy with the guildists and also the influence of the new Weimar Constitution, adopted in Germany in 1919, with the *Reichswirtschaftsrat* as the second house of the Parliament.

Reorganization suggested in this way would result in increasing the prerogatives of Parliament and of experts in the civil service, whose role had been stressed by the Webbs already in *Industrial Democracy*. Their conception strikes us by advocating a tentative but artificial separation of the socioeconomic sphere from the political one. The difficulty of such a separation was noticed by their critics rather early (this was done, e.g., by H. J. Laski). We have to agree with A. Ulam, who wrote that nothing could be more naive that the endeavour, with its underlying assumptions, that economics could be separated from politics.[29]

2.4 THE POLITICAL PRACTICE: PERMEATION

Fabian pluralism was also manifested in their political tactics, which they termed *permeation* of other political and social organizations. Permeation as tactics meant–which was the most important point–renunciation of the aspirations to set up a separate working class party in the near future. This was opposed by some members of the groups, namely by A. Besant, who at one time parted with the Fabians and joined the Social Democratic Federation, and by H. Bland; G. B. Shaw's standpoint on the issue was one of vacillation. But the Webbs' opinion, for whom permeation simply resulted from the Fabian idea of socialism introduced step by step, came to prevail for many years. Permeation had nothing to do with the later tactics, used by some political leaders, of planting their agents in the various political parties. The double allegiance of such planted agents was always apparent only. In fact they remained loyal to their respective leaders only, and would unmask themselves at the appropriate moment, working like time-fuse bombs. It was in this way that adherents of Piłsudski and de Gaulle acted within the various political parties until they formed their own political parties, totally dedicated to the charismatic leader.

Nor would it be correct to look for analogies with lobbying, because the latter is confined to Congress and to state legislatures in the United States, and besides it consists in confidential influence (sometimes at the borderline of legality) by paid representatives.[30]

Fabian permeation is not to be interpreted in terms of planting agents who worked clandestinely. It was an open action, intended, as Shaw put it, to convey socialist ideas to new converts and to those who did not agree with the Fabians.[31] Members of the Fabian society were openly joining the various organizations to canvass there with eagerness that marks people conscious of their mission.[32] This tactic was used by the Fabians with respect to other socialist political organizations, to trade unions (at that time dominated on the whole by liberal ideology), and primarily to the Liberal Party itself, and even to some progressive-minded conservatives. The Liberal Party included many MPs who enjoyed support by trade union (the so-called Lib–Lab formula).

As applied to the Liberal Party, this tactic was to be used as long as there were no sufficient social and political conditions for setting up a separate socialist party. In the transition period this tactic was intended to win for the liberals a programme that would comply with the interests of the working masses. It was made easier by the lively contacts between Fabians and radical liberals. The policy of permeation had its peak in the Newcastle Programme (1891), upon the formulation of which, as far as social reforms were concerned, the Fabians seem to have had the decisive influence. It can be supposed that without the Fabian contribution the liberals would not have won the elections. But when the liberal cabinet did not hurry to put that programme into effect, the Fabians attacked, their battle-cry being an article with the jocular headline: *To the Tents, O Israel!*

Even if it were not known who had written it, it would be easy to guess that it came from the mocking pen of G. B. Shaw. When the liberals lost the next elections, the road was open for the setting up of a workers' party.[33] In the course of many years the Fabian Society changed into a group of disciplined and experienced agitators. Their habit of co-operating in some fields with people who held quite different opinions, or advocates of a different ideology, helped the Fabians acquire vast political experience, which made it possible for them to extend their activity all over the country. This led to the emergence of provincial branches of the society. Pierson pointedly stresses openness and toleration and the dislike of all sectarianism as the characteristic feature of the Fabians. This obviously assumed—or, should anyone put it so, resulted in—a certain ideological pluralism.[34] All this did not prevent the Fabians from presenting their views in the political journal whose foundation they had inspired, i.e. in *The New Statesman.*[35] What then were their views? Were they utilitarians?[36] This is not quite certain. We have to agree with such an opinion when it comes to their philosophy and ethics, but when we discuss their sociological and political views the answer must be probably in the negative.

2.5 FABIANS' SHARE IN THE FORMATION OF THE BRITISH WORKING CLASS PARTY

Permeation, as has been seen, was not any programmatic principle, but just merely tactics. After many years of hesitations and controversies the Fabians came to the conclusion that this tactic had to be modified, and that they should be active in organizing a separate and independent socialist party.[37] When such an opportunity offered itself the Fabians did not miss it. They thus played an important role in founding the Independent Labour Party (ILP), set up in 1893 and based on individual membership. Its programme was to the left of that of the trade unions.[38] The party came to be headed by Keir Hardie, an experienced working class leader, who had been a Fabian for some time. But then, too, the Fabians (represented at the ILP founding conference by G. B. Shaw), defended the possibility of keeping double allegiance so that they could resort to their permeation tactics in socialist organizations and to submit their own independent viewpoint.

Thus the British labour movement was at that time the arena of four forces: the social democrats, the Fabians, the ILP, and the trade unions (the latter still scattered and influenced by the Liberal Party). The ILP was consistently internationalistic and anti-imperialistic in its attitude and formed the left wing of the British labour movement;[39] it was significant that it left the Second International twice.

But the ILP did not represent the broad masses, its members being mainly skilled workers. The trade unions also remained outside its organizational framework. This was why when the Labour Representation Committee was formed in 1900, and in 1906 was transformed into the Labour Party, the Fabians were also active in that process. The Labour Party drew its main strength from the group membership of trade unions, while individual membership was possible through the local ILP organization or through the Fabian Society.[40] The Fabian influence can explain the unique pluralistic structure of the Labour Party, which has remained to this day a coalition of left-wing, centre-of-the-road and right-wing labour organizations. Outside Britain the only analogy can be found in the structure of the Swedish social democratic party. It seems doubtful whether Michels' "iron law of oligarchy", which developed from the Continental, primarily German, tradition is applicable to the federalist organization of the Labour Party.

Finally, it was none other than the Fabian Sidney Webb who, together with A. Henderson, turned the Labour Party into a modern political organization.[41] It was also the Fabians who laid the ideological foundations of the Labour Party. From the adoption of the new statute and the new programme (*Labour and the New Social Order*) in 1918 the Labour Party must be treated as a socialist one. All those events in which the Fabians had taken such an important role were soon to bring about the decline of the Liberal Party. As can be seen in the current political practice of the Labour Party, the Fabian influence (gradualism) is noticeable to this day.

B.   The Fronde of the Guild Movement

While the Fabian philosophy of the state and society had its roots in rationalist and optimistic utilitarianism it was opposed to the individualism that marked the latter trend. This ambivalent attitude of theirs was to breed many controversies over the interpretation of the Fabian principles. The Fabians did not expect insurmountable conflicts among social groups, conflicts which would replace those among the individuals active in the market.

They did see the differentiation within British society, but in their opinion social groups as it were by themselves tended to bring their respective interests into harmony. Gradual and "almost imperceptible" development did not assume conflicts among those groups.

The Marxist standpoint adopted by G. B. Shaw marked merely a brief episode in his intellectual evolution. The tactics of "permeation" did not assume vehement clashes of interests nor the destruction of those organizations which would be permeated. This tactic was based on the belief in the effectiveness of persuasion and the propaganda which must work ahead of societal development and speed it up because it has grasped its trend. The great transformation of the parliamentary system they planned did not take into account a conflict between Social Parliament and Political Parliament.

Yet in view of the class conflicts which were intensifying both before World War I and later the optimistic faith of the Fabians in "harmony in diversity" became a glaring anachronism. While earlier endeavours on the part of more radical leaders, such as H. M. Hyndman, who in principle accepted the Marxist theory, had ended in failure,[42] now the rebellion developed within the very Fabian ranks and took on the form of guild socialists. The rebellion had been preceded by the secession of Graham Wallas, who left the executive of the Fabian Society in 1895, and the Society itself in 1904. His friend H. G. Wells did not stay long in the Fabian Society, either. The former feared excessive centralism, which seemed to result in particular from the ideas advanced by the Webbs, and the latter blamed them for narrow bureaucratism which wanted to see the world as something "flat and metallic".[43] But both Wallas and Wells remained at a distance from guild socialism.

2.6 THE BEGINNING OF THE REBELLION

Guild socialism was originated by *The Restoration of the Guild System* by A. J. Penty (1906); the ideas formulated in that book found a good response in the political situation prevailing in Britain at that time.

Many adherents of the guild movement were not only writers, but also labour leaders active in trade unions, yet the principal role was played by the Oxford branch of the Fabian Society, headed by G. D. H. Cole. Others included S. G. Hobson (*National Guilds*; *Guilds Principles in War and Peace*; *National Guilds and the State*), in Eastern Europe better known for his study of *Imperialism* (1902), valued by Lenin, and in Western Europe respected as the author of books on economic theory which had influenced Keynes, as the latter himself admitted (this did not suffice to make him lecture at any university: for that his views were too radical at that time); A. R. Orage, editor of *New Age*; and the said A. J. Penty, whose books *The Restoration...*, *Old World for New*, and *A Guildsman Interpretation of History* won much response. Nor could we disregard R. H. Tawney, whose book *The Sickness of*

an Acquisitive Society (1920) was not without popularity either. These were
the main leaders of the anti-Fabian rebellion, who wanted to make the proper
use of the Society's name: the explanatory note to the title page of the first
pamphlet of the Fabian Society states that one has to wait patiently for the
proper moment to come, as had been done by Fabius Cunctator, but when
the time comes, one has to strike forcefully, as Fabius did, because further
delay would be pointless. The guild leaders concluded that their time had
come, and they attacked. Their National Guilds League was the most
intensely active in the years 1915–25.

Members of the guilds movement differed visibly among themselves in
their attitude toward the Fabians, but if we are interested in their great
controversy with the Fabians we have to reduce the description of those
differences to a minimum in order to show clearly what they had in common
with the Fabians, and what was the subject-matter of the controversy.
Drawing such a balance sheet is made easier by G. D. H. Cole's *Guild
Socialism Restated* (1920), a *sui generis* codification of the opinions prevailing
in the guilds movement,[44] and in particular of Cole's own, but rapidly
changing, views.

2.7 SIMILARITIES AND DIFFERENCES BETWEEN FABIAN AND GUILD VIEWS

Despite a vehement controversy that went on for years guild socialists
shared with the Fabians the same opinion on many issues. The main point in
common was the essential critique of the capitalist system, which they too
believed to be definitively obsolete. They differed from the Fabians on the
issue of the integrating or co-ordinating role of the state.[45] The guildsmen
assigned the state a much more modest role. A. J. Penty with his longing for
feudal guilds went even further and recommended referring to mediaeval
institutions not only because it would otherwise be impossible to regain
control of economic forces, but also because it was imperative to return to
simpler forms of social life.[46]

The progressives in the guild movement saw in the guilds merely an
inspiration for reshaping society so as to protect it against excessive and
bureaucratic interference by the state. This was to be made possible through
individual initiatives within social organizations. But the guildsmen–except
for Penty and his adherents–did not intend to revive the mediaeval structure
of the guilds.[47] It must be emphasized again that when it comes to the
acceptance of the role of the state, agreement between the Fabians and the
guild socialists was very general in character, whereas the differences of
opinion on the issue of central political institutions and their relationship to
social organizations were strongly marked.

Like the Fabians, the guild socialists made a very sharp distinction between economics and politics, which they believed to be independent of one another, but they drew from that assumption further-reaching conclusions than the Fabians had done. Hobson thought that separation of economic and political functions would give the state stability and equilibrium.[48] Hence the social system should be divided into two, each having its own organizational structure, different from that of the other. When we come to the organizational consequences of that separation we notice considerable differences between the guild socialists and the Fabians.

While the main trend of the changes suggested by the Fabians focused on local government, which was closely connected with their idea of municipalization (which was also the sphere of their practical activity: see the role played by Sidney Webb in the London City Council), the social programme of the anti-Fabian rebellion had the guilds as its cornerstone. These organizations of producers were to be something much more comprehensive than the trade unions: they were to be confined to the defence of the economic interests of the workers. That merely defensive role of the trade unions made them a foreign body in the system of industrial administration.[49] The guilds were expected to organize production and sales, and also to take over the social welfare of producers. This broad sphere of their activity required revision of the traditional idea of the sovereignty of the state: every guild was to be sovereign in its own field. The guild socialists thought that the state was unable to cope with the task of economic management and economic development, and they even questioned the role of the state as the institution which co-ordinates social processes.[50]

The theorists of guild socialism assumed that their system would not only put an end to the "absurd" egalitarianism of wages, but would ultimately abolish the wage system, which saps the creative forces of the workers.[51] On the contrary, the Webbs did not believe that it would be possible to abolish the wage system and to rely on a type of worker self-government that would do without a source of authority in the factory. The guilds were expected to bring about a restructuring of the whole social system. In the transition period the guilds would absorb the white-collar workers, and systematically take over the control of production in factories; this would put an end to individual relations between the employer and the worker and replace them by collective agreements. Strongly decentralized, the guilds would form a flexible confederation with the apex in the form of a Congress of Industrial Guilds, conceived as the successor of the Trade Union Congress. That topmost part of the organization of producers would accordingly participate in organizing society as a whole, which was the essential idea underlying industrial self-government or industrial democracy, as conceived by the guild socialists.

A. J. Penty was the only one to stick to the idea of small guilds, not linked to any more comprehensive and stratified organization.[52] In practice this would amount to replacing the anarchy of individuals active under the capitalist system by an anarchy of small groups of producers. G. D. H. Cole thought that small guilds could function on a limited scale: they could remain outside the framework of large ones, because the guild system did not strive to monopolize any branch of industry. Craftsmen and small-scale industry would retain their economic autonomy. The guildsmen's programme was a reply to Fabian municipalism, which Cole called unrealistic. Even the Webbs and other members of the Fabian society realized that existing local government was in many regions not adjusted to provide management of services on a large scale under the conditions which involved the use of modern technology. The guild system was not to be confined to industry: a separate Collective Utility Council would be in charge of the services, an Educational Guild, in charge of the school system, there would also be a Health Guild, etc. All of them would be structured along similar lines by being decentralized national organizations. Agriculture would be included in the guild system on principles similar to those governing the other branches of production.

This gives rise to two questions: What would be the relation between the producers, organized in the various guilds, and the consumers? And what would be the relation between the producers and the machinery of the state? There is no producer in general, there are only producers of specified products or services, who function within definite organizations. Likewise, there is no consumer in general, but specified categories of consumers. Cole at first treated consumers as an undifferentiated mass of people, but his standpoint changed in 1920, which saw the appearance of his two books, *Social Theory* and *Guild Socialism Restated*. His approach to the protection of consumers' interests became more diversified. The role of the state also came to be treated differently. Cole made a distinction between personal consumption, which of necessity must be greatly differentiated, and collective consumption, whose needs would be met by public utilities of various kinds and by public means of transportation. Who, then, should represent consumers' interests: the state, local government, or co-operative organizations?

Cole barred the state and local government, *qua* political institutions, from representing economic interests, and declared himself in favour of protection of collective consumption by a special Collective Utilities Council. Its consultation with the guilds would eliminate conflicts between producers and consumers. The guild socialists, like the Fabians, were extremely optimistic in their belief that a Joint Council of producers and consumers would solve all the conflict that might arise between the two groups. Hobhouse remarked pointedly that consumer co-operatives had the same defect as producer organizations: the one would not do anything for the other. He accordingly suggested that the bodies charged with supervision of the various industries should consist, in equal numbers, of representatives of consumers, representatives of the managerial board and technologists, and representatives of the workers.[53]

The differences between the Fabians and the guild socialists can be seen very clearly in this connection. The former stood aloof from the trade unions: they treated them as organizations of employees charged with the defence of the economic interests of their members, which made it possible to draw a demarcation line between the tasks of the trade unions and those of the Labour Party. In the Fabians' opinion industrial management could not be a sphere of activity for trade unions, because that would be the domain of state agencies, assisted by experts, and of municipalities.[54]

The guild socialists, while mistrustful of the trade unions, believed that only extended prerogatives of producers' unions could block the rule of bureaucrats and the Fabian "servile state". To stress the difference between their vision of those unions and existing trade unions they called the former *guilds*, using a term drawn from the mediaeval tradition. Thus they were opposed to the reformed territorial representation, advocated by the Fabians, a functional representation, based on the principle of industrial democracy.[55] This brings us to the other differences between the two trends on the issue of the role of the state.

The guildist conception questioned territorial representation as an integrated one, for the guild socialists thought that man cannot be represented as such, as a certain whole: he can only be represented in definite spheres.[56] This idea was derived from the distinction made between economics and politics. By being opposed to the functional representation of producers in a political, territorial representation, that is to the state, they did not place these two types of representation on an equal footing: priority was given to guild-based representation. Only the guilds were held by them to be capable of ensuring individual freedom, individual enterprise and free activity. Political (territorial) representation was believed by them undemocratic as it left those represented at the mercy of their representative. Changing the representative through elections was irrelevant, because a personal change did not affect the system of representation, and those who were represented would remain (politically) incapacitated as before. Unlike the Fabian "collectivists", the guild socialists favoured industrial, i.e. syndicalist, democracy and belittled the role of the local government.

The guild socialists levelled all their criticism at "the sovereignty of Parliament", as did the young Laski, and earlier Figgis. In Parliament the representatives eclipsed those whom they represented, and were themselves eclipsed by the executives. The guild socialists thought that the political organization of the country was beyond repair, they as it were tacitly assumed that the process of political degradation was inevitable. This was the idea to be continued for years by political writers of various opinions, the idea of the decline of the parliamentary system. Cole even placed the word *state* in quotation marks, and to make matters clear he replaced it by the term *commune*. But this opposition to the omnipotence of the state (Cole spoke about its painless destruction) and the striving for a maximum restriction of its prerogatives was inconsistent, because a political organization of the state was being reintroduced through the back door in the role of the co-ordinator or even the arbitrator, who would replace the old capitalist state.[57] In this respect Cole differed from his contemporary pluralists.[58] But, here, Cole made the reservation that what he had in mind was not to be a Leninist proletarian state. On the other hand, the state would plan on the national scale what would be left for consumption and what would be spent on investments. Hsiao points to the inconsistencies in the guildist programme: their vehement attack on the "sovereignty of the state" ultimately results in their assigning the state the key role in social organization.[59] Moreover, it was not clear how far the new state–commune would have the prerogative of resorting to coercion, which the guild socialists believed to be an evil, regardless of its form, whenever used against an individual, not to mention state-exercised coercion used against a social group, in particular a producers' guild.

Nationalization, advocated by the guild socialists, could give rise to doubts, but it would be erroneous to conclude that they wanted in this way to let the state run industry. Nationalization was to be a brief transition stage during which ownership was to be snatched from the capitalists in order to be passed on to the guilds. Nationalized industry was to be run by the guilds, and not by any Fabian-conceived state boards, headed by experts. But the latter category of people was to be made use of by the guilds.

Without going into detail, suffice it to say that the idea of restricting the role of the state as the factor which interferes with social processes was much more radical than the Fabian conception of two Parliaments, the social and the political one. Guildist conceptions show the influence of French anarcho-syndicalism, but without any revolutionary rhetoric on the issue of the state. This assumption is supported by the fact that guildist writings make no reference to political parties. This is no coincidence, because there was no place for them in the guild system; it is legitimate to believe that they considered political parties a product of the capitalist system, which would vanish together with that system.

The Fabians, on the contrary, as co-founders of the ILP and later of the Labour Party–the period of "permeation" being over–combined their programmatic declarations with the political activity of their party.[60] The Labour Party was to be one of the principal instruments of the gradual restructuring of society. The guild socialists, who did not approve of the Fabian step-by-step evolution, were aiming further. Their evolution could easily change into a revolution, which they did not exclude even in Britain. This was consistent in view of the fact that they approved of the class struggle.

2.8 GUILD SOCIALISTS AND THE OCTOBER REVOLUTION

References to the snatching by the workers of control of industry, to be found in guildist writings, are very significant in that respect. They clearly reflect the actions by Russian workers between the two revolutions in 1917, actions which prepared the first decrees on nationalization in Russia. Neither Hobson nor Cole thought that transition to socialism should be hindered by Parliamentary procedures and the bourgeois rule of law. Cole wrote in 1919 that society which tolerates exploitation has no rights relative to those workers who rise against it, and that the state has no prerogative to intervene as an impartial third party.[61] He did not exclude the possibility of resorting to revolutionary measures.

This attitude of the guild socialists can be explained by the conditions prevailing in the period in which they were active. It was a period of great social and political unrest; fascination with two revolutions in Russia in 1917; revolutionary upheavals in Central Europe in 1918 to 1920; the revolution in Germany; and the rise, in 1919, of a Soviet republic in Bavaria and a Soviet republic in Hungary. All this resulted in a radicalization of the British working masses, in the formation of action committees as a form of revolutionary protest against the imperialist intervention in Soviet Russia.[62] At that time the guildists were very influential in many trade unions.

The guild socialists also opposed the defence of the British Empire, spread by the Fabians from the Boer War on, for they were consistent anti-imperialists and pacifists.

Finally, a few words about the last difference between the two trends to be mentioned here. The Fabians considered their programme of social changes to be specifically British; for all their contacts with representatives of the international reformist worker movement who were active in Britain (e.g. Edward Bernstein), they were not interested in the applicability of their ideas outside Britain, even if they did attend international meetings of socialists.[63] They were not only preoccupied with the future of Britain, but in their early period they attributed a certain progressive role to the British Empire. G. B. Shaw was not against the abolition of the Boer republics by military action. In his opinion the process would just resemble absorption of small firms by giant ones. Other Fabians did not go to such extremes, but they were tolerant of the Empire, and none of them raised his voice against British colonialism.

On the other hand the guild socialists, who were one generation younger, were growing up to become theorists and politicians during World War I, i.e. at the time when the colonial system broke down for the first time and the idea of self-determination of nations was heard speaking with full voice.

On the international arena, both within the worker movement and outside of it, the Fabians were classed as members of its right wing. The name of Sidney Webb was mentioned in the same breath as those of Millerand and Bernstein. Yet, on the Continent Bernstein was considered the principal representative of revisionism, whilst in fact the roots of revisionism must be sought in Fabian socialism. The young Bernstein was influenced by it when he stayed in Britain as an émigré. But he was not alone in accepting the influence of gradualism, that is, socialism without revolution: This became the declaration of faith of French reformists, including Jaurès, despite his anarcho-syndicalist leanings, and others, except Guèsde and his followers.[64]

Guild socialists, on the contrary, used to maintain international contacts and followed the guild-like trends in the international worker movement; they accordingly were being stimulated by anarcho-syndicalist circles.

2.9 THE DECLINE OF THE GUILD MOVEMENT

Guild socialists were being criticized not by Fabian leaders alone. Graham Wallas, an eminent ex-Fabian, claimed in 1920 that the guilds would hinder technological progress and drive wages up, which would result in diverting funds needed for public use.[65] On the other hand, Bertrand Russell was in some respects quite close to guild socialists, which can be explained by his dislike of the "omnipotence" of the state (even though he accepted the state as an instrument of preserving social order) and his liking for anarchism in the Kropotkin version.[66] This brought him particularly close to G. D. H. Cole. Guild socialism would best guarantee creative development of individuals, and should replace capitalism, which Russell used to criticize severely.[67] Russell was linked to both guild socialists and Fabians (the Webbs and G. B. Shaw) by his objective interest in the Soviet experience (cf. his *Theory and Practice of Bolshevism*, 1920); he was in favour of strong autonomous social organizations, namely trade unions, churches, cultural associations, as he saw in them guarantees of freedom, working against the capitalist state.[68] Some differences of opinion between Russell and guild socialists pertained to minor questions, such as protection of consumer interests which, he thought, should be entrusted to organizations established *ad hoc*, and the specific balance between the guilds and workers' self-government, which he recommended. He also believed that state interference on a limited scale was indispensable; he treated the state as a necessary evil.[69]

A brief digression is worth while here. As has been said, there is no necessary junction between ontological pluralism and social and political pluralism, with which we are concerned in this book. But in Russell's case his revision of views is due to his dislike for the logical foundations of monism (he himself claimed to have been a logical atomist), and his adoption of the viewpoint of "absolute pluralism"[70] was in harmony with his social and political pluralism and—at one time—with his version of guild socialism.

To go back to our principal topic, we have to say that the guild socialists were bound to lose: they had assailed the basic political institutions without which no-one was able to imagine public life in Britain, namely Parliament, political parties, and local government. For all that they paved the way to the idea of worker self-government in Britain. The great controversy between the Fabians as political pragmatists and eclectics and doctrinaire theorists of the guild movement is long over and pointless today, but it did make an indelible impression on the British labour movement and the evolution of socio-political thinking in Britain. Its protagonists after many years modified their views quite considerably and in different ways, and all found themselves in the Labour Party. They met there with another political thinker, Harold Laski, a radical in his young age.[71] The growing importance of the Labour Party in British public life and its strong position in the working masses accelerated the end of the guild movement.[72] The great clashes between the guild socialists and the Fabians ultimately resulted in the revival of the Fabian Society and the modernization of the ideology of the Labour Party as one of the main forces in international social democracy. The return of guild socialists to the Labour Party and the renewal of their activity in the Fabian Society meant a strengthening of the left wing of the British labour movement and also a stabilization of social democratic ideology.

NOTES AND REFERENCES

1. The club was founded by Thomas Davidson, an American eccentric. Its rules stated that its goal was the attainment of perfect character by all members and every member severally.
2. On this evolution see W. Wolff, *From Radicalism to Socialism* (*Men and Ideas in the Formation of Fabian Socialist Doctrines, 1881–1889*) (New Haven, 1975).
3. Shaw was the author of the basic Fabian pamphlet, *A Manifesto* (1884). *Facts for Socialists* by S. Webb, which made Fabian leaders popular and paved the way for further activity, appeared 3 years later. The influence of *Capital* upon that pamphlet seems obvious. On Engels' contacts with the Fabians see also S. Bünger, *Friedrich Engels und die deutsche sozialistische Bewegung, 1881–1895* (Berlin, 1962).
4. On this subject see G. Wallas, "Socialism and the Fabian Society", in: M. Wallas (ed.), *Men and Ideas* (London, 1940); and S. Pierson, *Marxism and the Origin of British Socialism* (*The Struggle for a New Consciousness*) (Ithaca and London, 1973), pp. 120 ff.
5. E. H. Pease, *The History of the Fabian Society* (London, 1916), pp. 24 ff; A. M. McBriar, *Fabian Socialism and English Politics (1884–1918)* (Cambridge and London, 1966), pp. 8 ff, 30, 62 ff.
6. S. and B. Webb, *Soviet Communism–a New Civilization*, 2 vols, (London, 1935); see also Mayski's reminiscences about G. B. Shaw.
7. There is a notable formulation by S. Webb that history shows us nothing except for constant, gradual evolution. Cf. *Socialism in England* (London, 1890), p. 5.
8. Marx often used to ridicule that compromise-proneness and respectability of British workers.
9. It was Marx' "Letter to the Labour Parliament" (1854), p. 402.
10. E. Thompson, *The Making of the English Working Class* (London, 1963), p. 759.
11. Cf. T. P. Mador: *Padiom rabotchevo dvishenia v Anglii 1910–1913y* (Moscow, 1966).
12. *Fabian Essays in Socialism* (1st edn, 1889), G. B. Shaw (ed.) (London, 1948), p. 32.
13. Cf. S. Webb, *Facts for Londoners* (Tract No. 8) (London, 1889); W. J. Hartman, *Facts for Bristol* (Tract No. 18) (London, 1890); S. Webb, *The London Programme* (London, 1891); see also various pamphlets by many authors, primarily by Webb.
14. A. M. McBriar, *op. cit.*, p. 232.

15. G. D. H. Cole, *British Working Class Politics, 1832-1914*, (London, 1946), p. 122; M. Cole, *Makers of the Labour Movement* (London, 1948), p. 235. See also G. K. Lewis, "Fabian Socialism: Some Aspects of Theory and Practice", *The Journal of Politics*, 14 August 1952, p. 459.

16. Cf. D. Grinberg, "Towarzystwo Fabiańskie 1884–1914" (The Fabian Society, 1884–1914), unpublished doctoral dissertation deposited at the Warsaw University Institute of History, 1977, pp. 329 ff.

17. S. Webb, "The Historical Basis of Socialism", in: *Fabian Essays, ed. cit.*, p. 53; G. B. Shaw, "The Transition to Social Democracy", in: *Fabian Essays*, p. 168. See also E. Barker, *Political Thought in England, 1848–1914* (London, 1928), p. 192.

18. S. Pierson, *op. cit.*, pp. 67 ff.

19. E. R. Pease, *op. cit.*, p. 114; M. Cole, *Beatrice Webb* (New York, 1946), pp. 54 ff; M. Cole, *Makers ...*, p. 236; S. Pierson, *op. cit.*, p. 124.

20. G. D. H. Cole, *op. cit.*, chap. X, "The Trade Union Awakening", pp. 126 ff.

21. S. H. Beer, *British Politics in the Collectivist Age* (New York, 1965), pp. 167 ff.

22. M. Cole, "Labour Research", in: M. Cole (ed.), *The Webbs and Their Work* (London, 1949), p. 156. These opinions of the Fabians evoke associations with Max Weber's concept of rational bureaucracy.

23. Cf. Sir Sidney Caine, *The History of the Formation of the London School of Economics and Political Science* (London, 1963).

24. G. D. H. Cole, "B. Webb as an Economist", in: M. Cole (ed.), *op. cit.*, pp. 270 ff. Some years later the Webbs reverted to problems of the co-operative movement: see Sidney and Beatrice Webb, "The Co-operative Movement", *New Statesman*, 30 May 1914, Supplement.

25. A. M. McBriar, *op. cit.*, p. 53. See also R. H. Tawney, *The Acquisitive Society* (London, 1922), chap. XI.

26. A. D. Lindsay, *The Modern Democratic State* (London, 1943), and *The Essentials of Democracy* (Philadelphia, 1943).

27. See his "Property Under Socialism", in: *Fabian Essays*, and *The Great Society*, 1914 (also published in New York, 1940). When the book appeared Wallas was no longer a member of the Fabian Society, but he had written it in the Fabian spirit. Wallas was connected with the Labour Party and was professor at the London School of Economics. See also M. J. Wiedner, *Between Two Worlds (The Political Thought of G. Wallas)* (Oxford, 1971).

28. A. M. McBriar, *op. cit.*, p. 109.

29. A. B. Ulam, *Philosophical Foundations of English Socialism*, (New York (1st edn, 1951), 1964), p. 132. See also Kung Chuan Hsiao, *Political Pluralism (A Study in Contemporary Political Theory)* (London, 1927), pp. 69 ff.

30. S. Ehrlich, *Le pouvoir et les groupes de pression* (Paris/Hague, 1971).

31. *Fabian Essays* ..., p. xxvi. See also H. Bland, "The Outlook", *ibid.*, p. 199.

32. D. Grinberg, *op. cit.*, pp. 46 ff. For this reason the parallel with the methods of action of the physiocrats and the encyclopaedists seems to the point.

33. M. Cole (ed.), *The Webbs and Their Work* (statement by G. B. Shaw), p. 12; R. C. K. Ensor, "*Permeation*", and J. S. Middleton, *Webb and the Labour Party*, in the same book. McBriar, *op. cit.*, p. 238, doubts whether the Fabians should be assigned such an important role in those events. McBriar dedicated four chapters in his book to the tactics of permeation.

34. S. Pierson, *op. cit.*, p. 138.

35. S. K. Ratcliffe, *The New Statesman* (1913), quoted in: M. Cole (ed.), *op. cit.*

36. McBriar, *op. cit.*, pp. 149 ff.

37. H. Bland, *op. cit.*, pp. 202–3.

38. Cf. the monograph of ILP by R. E. Dowse, *Left in the Centre* (London, 1966).

39. The ILP merged with the Labour Party in the early 1930s, but the Labour Party left wing draws from the traditions of the ILP.

40. R. E. Dowse, *op. cit.*, chap. 2, pp. 51–2, 191.

41. M. Cole (ed.), *op. cit.*, pp. 210, 214 ff, 227.

42. Concerning Hyndman's Marxist views see his *The Record of an Adventurous Life* (London, 1911), and H. W. Lee and R. Archbold, *Social Democracy in England* (London, 1935).

43. Before leaving the Fabian Society H. G. Wells criticized the Fabians sharply in *The Faults of the Fabians* (London, 1906).

44. This mature exposition of guild socialism was preceded by other works, the major ones being: *The World of Labour* (London, 1913); *Self-Government in Industry* (London, 1918); *Social Theory* (London, 1920).
45. But the difference is visible when a comparison with the mature Fabian movement is made. In the first period they represented vulgar economism (incorrectly assigned to the influence of Marxism: one should rather say, to the influence of undigested Marxism), marked by an underestimation of the role of central political institutions. It was G. B. Shaw, who excelled in that economism, and used to give vent to his mistrust of the parliament and the political parties. This economic deviation, typical of the first period of Fabianism, is admitted by E. Pease (cf. *op. cit.*, p. 132), who speaks about a clear line between socialism and politics. He says that the Fabians claimed that socialism was an economic doctrine and had nothing to do with other problems, and were only later to comprehend that the form of government was no less important than economics, and that economics and politics were difficult to separate from one another.
46. A. J. Penty, *Guilds and the Social Crisis* (London, 1919), pp. 46 ff; see also *Old World for New* (London, 1917), and *Guilds, Trade and Agriculture* (London, 1921), chap. VII, *Guilds and the Just Price*, by the same author. Those opinions came to be assessed as reactionary or even obscurantist (A. Ulam, *op, cit.*, p. 93).
47. G. D. H. Cole, *Guild Socialism Restated* ..., p. 46.
48. S. G. Hobson, *National Guilds* (London, 1919), p. 258.
49. G. D. H. Cole, *Guild Socialism Restated*, p. 19.
50. G. D. H. Cole, *Social Theory* ..., p. 97.
51. S. G. Hobson, *op. cit.*, pp. 134 ff, 154.
52. A. J. Penty, *Old World for New*.
53. L. T. Hobhouse, *The Elements of Social Justice* (London, 1922), p. 180 ff.
54. The Webbs criticized the guild socialists in that spirit (cf. *A Constitution for the Socialist Commonwealth* (London, 1920, pp. 148 ff., 156 ff.). But their social parliament was a concession to the demands of the guild socialists, as was correctly pointed out by S. H. Beer, *(British Politics in the Collectivist Age*, p. 75). The very idea of a parliamentary reform had been earlier advanced by A. J. Penty, who envisaged a Lower House, elected by universal suffrage, and an Upper House, whose members would be appointed by the guilds, which was to secure a balance of interests (*Restoration of the Guild System* (London, 1906), pp. 70 ff.).
55. See G. D. H. Cole, *Self-Government in Industry* (London, 1917).
56. G. D. H. Cole, *Social Theory* ..., chap. 3.
57. S. G. Hobson, *op. cit.*, p. 133.
58. See D. Nicholls, *Three Varieties of Pluralism* (London, 1974), p. 12; and *idem.*, *The Pluralist State* (London, 1975), p. 48.
59. Hsiao, *op. cit.*, p. 120.
60. But the Fabian Society has remained autonomous within the Labour Party to this day.
61. G. D. H. Cole, *The World of Labour* (London, 1919), p. 228 and chap. "Social Peace and Social War"; also pp. 19 and 392.
62. P. W. Gorovitch: *Padiom rabotchevo dvishenia v Anglii w 1918–1921 yy.* (Moskow, 1965).
63. Cf. G. D. H. Cole, *The Second International, 1889–1914* (London, 1963).
64. Léo Hamon, *Socialisme et pluralités* (Paris, 1976), Part I, chap. V, and Part II, chaps VI and VII. He calls the French socialists (with some limitations formulated in the text) both before and after World War I, just gradualists, and says they were strongly influenced by the Fabians and Bernstein.
65. G. Wallas, *Our Social Heritage* (London, 1921); see also the criticism of the guild system in G. C. Field, *Guild Socialism* (London, 1918), and his *Democracy and Direct Action* (London, 1919).
66. B. Russell, *Roads to Freedom* (London, 1918); and *Democracy and Direct Action* (London, 1919).
67. See also his *Principles of Social Reconstruction* (London, 1916), and *Prospects of Industrial Civilization* (London, 1923).
68. B. Russell, *Political Ideas* (New York, 1917), pp. 11 ff.
69. For a criticism of Russell's view see Th. H. Griffiths, *Politischer Pluralismus in der zeitgenossischen Philosophie Englands* (Giessen, 1933), pp. 23 ff.
70. This is what he wrote about monism in *The Scientific Outlook*, New York, 1931, p. 98:

"... the fundamental of my intellectual beliefs is that this is rubbish. I think the universum is all spots and jumps, without continuity, without coherence or orderliness".
71. On the differences of opinion between H. Laski and G. D. H. Cole, see Th. Griffiths, *op. cit.*, pp. 69 ff.
72. For a retrospective view of the Fabians and the guild socialists in the development of British socialism consult also (in addition to the items already cited): J. N. Clayton, *The Rise and Decline of Socialism in Great Britain, 1884–1924* (London, 1926); M. Cole, *The Story of Fabian Socialism* (London, 1961); E. Reichel, *Der Sozialismus der Fabier* (Heidelberg, 1947); M. Beer, *A History of British Socialism* (London, 1948); J. H. S. Reid, *The Origins of the Labour Party* (Minnesota, 1955); M. McCarran, *Fabianism in Political Life of Britain, 1919–31* (Chicago, 1957); Z. Bauman, *Klasa–ruch–elita (The Class–the Movement–the Elite), A Study in the history of the British labour movement* (Warszawa, 1960). S. Glass, *The Responsible Society* (London, 1966).

CHAPTER 3

Academic Pluralism in Germany and in Britain

... Otto von Gierke, whose monumental researches into the history of intermediate association remain even yet the finest of their kind (R. A. Nisbet, *The Sociology of Emile Durkheim* (London, 1975), p. 141.

3.1 PRELIMINARY REMARKS

The trend to be discussed in this chapter can be termed academic. It is associated primarily with the names of such prominent scholars as Otto von Gierke, F. W. Maitland, E. Barker, and H. Laski. The last name on the short list given above requires a comment: he drew least, and mainly indirectly, from von Gierke, and his views were shaped by other thinkers as well; further, Harold Laski became a prominent leader of the British labour movement and of the Labour Party, without abandoning, however, his academic activity.[1] F. W. Maitland and Ernest Barker were almost at the same time influenced by Otto von Gierke, an eminent German jurist who on the Continent is treated by many primarily as a historian of German law and the leading representative of the Germanicist school that grouped adherents of the historical school of law. He was known for his campaign for a Germanicist reinterpretation of the German civil code, which he believed to have been too much permeated with Romanist ideas. In that capacity he is considered to have continued the work of G. Beseler,[2] and also to have been the last "Germanicist" (*Das alte und das neue deutsche Reich* (1874); *Das neue Genossenschaftsrecht*, 4 vols. (1868–1913); *Die historische Rechtsschule und die Germanisten* (1903); *Johannes Althusius und die Entwicklung der naturrechtlichen Staatstheorien*, (1880)) and an eminent expert on civil law, the main founder of the real theory of legal (juridical) persons (cf. his fundamental treatise on civil law, *Deutsches Privatrecht*, 3 vols. (1895)). In fact, von Gierke's theories reached far beyond that sphere of problems and covered primarily the basic issues of society and the state.[3] It was in these elements of his work that Maitland and Barker came to be interested. This is why it seems necessary to begin the description of one of the trends in British pluralism with a brief presentation of von Gierke's opinions on those matters, without confining oneself to what has been done by his translators and popularizers. Maitland published *Political Theories of the Middle Ages* (1900), which is a translation of part of vol. 3 of *Das deutsche Genossenschaftsrecht*, preceded by Maitland's comprehensive introduction, while Barker edited *Natural Law and the Theory of Society, 1500 to 1800* (1934), which consists of large fragments of vol. 4 of the same treatise by von Gierke.[4]

In Germany itself von Gierke's work was not interpreted in the same way as it was in Britain, and did not bring about the rise of pluralism as a separate trend. The ground was not ready for that; there was no continuity between the past and von Gierke's theory. Hegel's philosophy did include pluralistic elements, his civil society–an intermediate link between the family and the state–was differentiated in the sense of being composed of associations, and thus opposed to the idea of individualistic atomism.[5] In the German literature on the subject attention was often drawn to the connections between Hegel's philosophy of society and von Gierke's theory of associations,[6] but these ideas were not continued. What did catch on was Hegel's exaltation of the state and the sharp distinction he had drawn between society and the state; this applies not only to Germany, but to Britain as well, where the Neo-Hegelian Bosanquet was the favourite target of attacks by pluralists.

It seems that there were two other factors which did not favour the emergence of the pluralist trend in Germany. One of them was the lack of coherence in von Gierke's views. Next to pluralistic elements his theory included organicism as an important component, combined with the magnification of the role of the German state (which especially marked the later period of his activity), the latter being in harmony with his conservative and chauvinistic political ideas.[7] This, of course, could not have any response in Britain. The other factor, quite natural in post-1871 Germany, was that the broad response which von Gierke's writings had found abroad as an inspiration of pluralism, was of little interest to anyone in his own country.[8] His two most prominent disciples, Erich Kaufmann and Hugo Preuss, can hardly be considered to have continued that trend in von Gierke's work in which we are especially interested here.

Preuss was at first perhaps even more radical than von Gierke himself, for he treated sovereignty–which was characteristic of the pluralistic trends at that time–as a cobweb which enmeshes political theory: the concept of sovereignty should be *definitively* removed from political theory.[9] But following World War I and the revolution in Germany he changed his views and adopted a middle-of-the-road standpoint.

The only German author who grasped the importance of pluralism was not connected with academic circles; it is even to be doubted whether he knew von Gierke's works at all–in any case he never referred to him. He was Walther Rathenau, a German statesman and captain of industry, who drew inspiration from observation of societal processes and his own professional experience. The controversies between the Germanicists and the Romanists were alien to him, but as a businessman and politician he was looking for an attractive alternative to the idea of the soviets, which the October Revolution made popular in Germany. Today we are witnessing a revival of interest in the pluralistic elements in von Gierke's work, but the German literature on the subject still lacks a comprehensive study of his influence upon pluralists in Britain.

3.2   OTTO VON GIERKE AND HIS INFLUENCE UPON PLURALISTS IN BRITAIN

When interpreting feudal institutions and mediaeval political and legal thought von Gierke drew attention to the fact that the postulated political (the Empire) and spiritual (the Church of Rome) unity of the world did not in the least mean any striving to eliminate the inner differentiation of feudal society and to make that society uniform, because that postulated unity reflected merely the unity of the goals of mankind. Between the individual and the governing bodies there were various intermediate bodies (von Gierke, by the way, did not use this term, introduced by de Montesquieu), such as communes, guilds, leagues of towns, merchant associations, and a great number of other organizations. Diversity and autonomy also marked the inner life of the Church of Rome after a brief period of papal supremacy over the secular authority.

Von Gierke was convinced that Germanic peoples had had a special gift of association (the faculty of organizing themselves in associations) and that they excelled other peoples in that respect in his times, too. The basic idea of his great work was expounded by von Gierke in the introduction to vol. 1 of *Das deutsche Genossenschaftsrecht*. It was a diversified unity, such as that which emerges from having a simple basis, and increases in scope with a view to attaining bigger and bigger goals. That diversity is a permanent feature. Social life is not reducible to any single form of association, and is manifested in a wealth of forms. The rights and the independence of those smaller unities, which are basically identical with individuals, are the essence of freedom. Conflicts between these two great principles, unity and diversity, determined the most important movements in human history. They reflected the struggle between the popular sense of freedom, manifested in free associations, and the principle of authority (*Herrschaft*), a struggle which in the course of time took on the form of a conflict between the free commune and the feudal lord.

We shall leave aside the issue of the stages in the development of German associations, which von Gierke discussed in great detail. The essential point is the result of that development and the conclusions which he drew from his thorough historical research.[10] Before the centralized state had time to emerge the towns had developed the conception of their distinct personality, which found its formal manifestation in their winning the acceptance of the institution of free towns. Their personality existed independently of the original membership. The idea of corporation, i.e. collective personality, was taken over from towns by craftsmen's and merchant's guilds.

The scope of control by the superior authority, to which autonomous associations were subjected, was increasing gradually. The dominance of the superior authority over free associations marked the consolidation of the power of kings and princes, and the consolidation of territorial sovereignty (*Landeshcheit*) marked the end of a cycle in evolution, during which the former free associations were degraded to the level of dependent legal persons, even if privileged as corporations.[11] Their status came to be regulated by civil law. The loosely hierarchical structure of autonomous groups, which mediaeval thought drew from the organizational experience of the Church, was becoming more and more rigid as their autonomy was shrinking to give place to centralized interference by the nascent absolute state.

In this way the mediaeval conception of organic structure was changed: organic unity came to correspond to a different structure of social relations.[12] This was due not only to sociopolitical changes in Germany, but also to the reception of Roman law, the work of glossators, postglossators, and legists, which favoured consolidation of royal sovereignty and simultaneous weakening of the status of free association. Reception of Roman law became an historical necessity. Normative systems established by associations and contracts they used to conclude with one another, based on popular law (*Volksrecht*), were markedly restricted by the law imposed by legal experts. The abstract concept of the state absorbed the living practice represented by communes and corporations. Von Gierke was right in describing the authoritarian idea of the state as something alien to the people. The authority represented the abstract conception of the state, and outside the state the place was left for individuals only.[13]

In individualistic Roman law the individual's freedom of action was confined to the sphere of private law, while in public law, von Gierke wrote, all rights were inherent in the Roman state, which under the Republic was identified with the people of Rome, and in the imperial period, with the divine caesar. Roman corporations were bodies functioning under public law, they were derivative of the state and it was in the state that they had their reason for existence.[14]

Germanic associations thus had no room for action either under the public law or under the individual-oriented private law. Roman private law reduced the rights and obligations of associations to the rights and obligations of their respective members. Associations enjoyed no rights, whether under the public or the private law.[15]

The task von Gierke had set himself was to revive the role of free associations within the framework of modern society. He was a firm advocate of restricting the functions of the state and, as has been emphasized by O. Brunner, he did not conceal his dislike of excessive regulatory activity of the state, and of 'absolutism'.[16] In methodology, he naturally had to rise against legal formalism, represented in Germany by Bergbohm, Gerber, and Laband, whose methodological attitude boiled down to making "legal constructions" within the framework of the normative stratum of the law, but in a philosophical and social vacuum. He was especially critical of what was called "legal thinking" and the formal–logical conception of the law. R. Pound held von Gierke's analysis to have been the strongest critique of jurisprudence in the nineteenth century, and some 40 years later J. Stone referred to von Gierke as the man who pointed to the importance of groups, neglected by jurisprudence, even though legal practice had had to do with them for a long time.[17] Yet a reservation must be made in this connection: in his works on civil law, especially those concerned with the then new German civil code (*Bürgerliches Gesetzbuch*, usually abbreviated as *BGB*), von Gierke was a legal "dogmatist", because the normative elements in the law cannot be explained without the "dogmatic" approach. Those studies by him had legal practice in view, legislation above all,[18] and there is no legal practice without the "dogmatic" approach. But his studies were based on an incredibly vast historical and social knowledge, equalled by his knowledge of political philosophy, which enabled him to avoid the one-sidedness characteristic of "the jurisprudence of concepts" (*Begriffsjurisprudencz*).

The federalist construction, which von Gierke applied to feudal society, was subjected to the pressure of centralism, rooted in the idea of the sovereignty of the monarch, the idea which obviously referred to the omnipotence of Roman emperors and in the Middle Ages began to take shape slowly, probably from the twelfth century on.

Von Gierke, as it seems, was especially interested in the clash of the idea of association (*Genossenschaft*) and that of authority (*Herrschaft*), in which he saw the sources of the feudal system. He thought that the freedom of German urban communes had developed from free associations. While he did not postulate the sovereignty of associations, he called for their greater independence: local administration should be on an equal footing with the state (the principle of *Ebenbürtigkeit*).[19]

This struggle for sovereignty was being waged as it were on two fronts. The emperors at first, and later the Christian kings and the independent princes, had to wage it against the secular claims of papal sovereignty, and against the never-extinct idea of the sovereignty of the people (the latter being understood in a broad or in a narrow sense), which in Germany was reinforced by the old Germanic tradition of association (*Genossenschaftsidee*) or that of associations as free bodies which had definite goals in view, mainly in the vocational sphere (crafts and trade). Those associations also met the religious, social, private-law and political needs of their respective members. This trend to cover all the interests of the members and to lay the main stress on vocational division, noticeable already in corporations active in the thirteenth and fourteenth centuries, resulted in their fall, because by becoming states within a state they had to clash with the supreme authority (*Landesobrigkeit*), if the latter was not to become merely symbolic.

The idea of association had its analogues in the feudal institutions such as guilds, secular charitable organizations, Church-sponsored organizations, and the various para-ecclesiastic associations. Von Gierke's principal thesis[20] was that sovereignty was not an attribute of any part of the state (or any state agency), but of the entire organized community (*Gesamtperson*). Hence the conclusion which is probably the key to the understanding of von Gierke's theory of the state and the corporations: both the state and the corporations are species of the same kind. His theory of the state (*Staatslehre*) was based on the theory of associations (*Genossenschaftstheorie*); he did not, however, deny that the state had existed in the Middle Ages.[21]

The old German term *Genossenschaft* (association) corresponds, as Maitland claims, to the equally old English term *fellowship*,[22] and does not denote associations that have legal personality. *Genossenschaften*, as understood by von Gierke, were commonly existing bodies that come into being without the interference of the state. They are groups with the various vocational, religious, and educational goals, developed directly by society. Their activity at the moment of birth did not depend on their being endowed with the status of legal persons by the state; they were not legal fictions, but really existing autonomous bodies, which relative to the state were capable of self-government and were self-governing in fact. But in the course of the drive intended to strengthen the status of the monarch the theory of fiction was used, according to which the secular authority establishes artificial persons by endowing them with legal personality or by accepting their status of legal persons. This prerogative to establish fictive social bodies (legal persons) was accepted as one of the prerogatives of the monarch. Von Gierke quoted in this connection the opinion of the legist Lucas de la Pena: *Solus princeps fingit quod in rei veritat non est.*[23]

Interference by the state in the form of imposition of a legal form of organization could not put an end to the differentiation of feudal society: resistance to that process was due to the differentiation into estates (status groups), within which further diversity could be found.[24] It seems that von Gierke, while noticing the scale of *horizontal* pluralism, failed to assign sufficient significance to *vertical* pluralism, namely to the dysfunctional role of expanded hierarchization. W. Kornhauser opposes the thesis that mediaeval states were pluralistic in nature and points to the fact that the individual was being supervised in every respect by the associations and corporations of which he was a member.[25] If we keep the term *pluralism* reserved for the bourgeois democracy based on the system of representation, then we have to admit that Kornhauser is consistent in his views. But if we accept the fundamental thesis adopted in the present book, namely that we have to do with a "pluralism of pluralisms", then we have to be less categorical in our opinions of society and the state in the Middle Ages. It might be described by the formula of pluralism of groups of unequal status, within which their members also held positions unequal in terms of law and fact. Supervision of the individual was many-sided but paternalistic, and hence could be evaded. It is not to be confused with much more oppressive police supervision in absolutist, caesarist, and totalitarian states.

Society, as von Gierke saw it, is the sum and the totality of the various groups. We shall disregard here the biological, organicist aspect of his theory, often distorted by his critics. Von Gierke was himself a founder of the organic theory, but he did not apply the concept of organism in its empirical sense drawn from natural science. On the contrary, he thought it absurd to apply the natural-science concept of organism in jurisprudence.[26] Organism was for him a kind of metaphor used with reference to a diversified whole consisting of interconnected parts. The important point is that groups, whatever their organization, and hence legal persons, too, were treated by him as real entities in which he saw a sphere of freedom other than that which can be obtained within the framework of the state. It was a reasoning quite different from that which traditionally referred to the ideas characteristic of the founders of Roman jurisprudence, with their rigorous division into public and private law, a division which ultimately resulted–as von Gierke claimed, in which opinion he was followed by Maitland–in an absolutist public law and in individualistic private law.

The struggle within the Church between the opposing tendencies relative to the vision of the universal Church was similar and parallel to what has been described above. The absolute authority of the pope found opposition in the ideas of the Church as a congregation of the faithful (*congregatio fidelium*), with their doctrine of the sovereignty of the ecclesiastic community, which was of special importance at the time of the controversy over the rank of the councils. The victory of the institutionalized Church, with the dominant power of the pope, must have also been a blow to the idea of free associations, an idea revived later only by the Reformation.

All these controversies were directly or indirectly related to the mediaeval idea of representation. Old or even obsolete as they were–including von Gierke's interpretations of the views of Althusius, John of Salisbury, Marsilius of Padua, and Occam–they nevertheless shed new light upon issues which are of topical interest even today. Marsilius' opinion that the Church was one of the voluntary associations and the state was a community the unity of which was not imposed by any superior authority, must have been particularly close to von Gierke. The unity of the said community was ensured by its very members.[27] Maitland as a historian was struck by the fact that the conception of associations made it possible to see the otherwise known historical processes in a new way, and even opened one's eyes to the controversies which were contemporaneously taking place in Britain. Whilst Maitland was considering von Gierke's work, the discussion was going on with the Fabians concerning their centralistic ideas which, if put into effect, could mean the end of autonomous organizations. Excessive centralization was considered one of the main threats to a new society.

Maitland, who had assimilated von Gierke's work, not only made his methodological apparatus more comprehensive, but by popularizing von Gierke's writings pointed to new aspects of pluralism. Some authors claim that Maitland under the influence of von Gierke's work changed, in the second edition, the conception of his monumental study in the history of English law. He was not alone in his interest in group pluralism (to use the now current term); H. Maine also thought that groups are those basic social units of which the body politic is formed.[28]

Maitland, followed in that respect by Barker, took up primarily von Gierke's essential thesis which questions the monopoly of sovereignty on the part of any single agency of the state. Plurality of forms in sociopolitical life could not be eliminated by interference by the state with its resulting imposition of a unitary legal form of organization. Maitland shared Gierke's view that society is the sum and the totality of the various groups.

Ernest Barker, one of the founders of modern political science in Britain, came to be influenced by von Gierke, inspired in that respect by Maitland. Neither a Fabian nor a guild socialist, Barker was one of those radical pluralists who criticized the omnipotence of the "discredited" state.[29] He manifested that opinion of his, and accepted (though not without reservations) von Gierke's views, in his comprehensive introduction to the translation of another part of the same opus which had attracted Maitland's attention, that is, *Das Genossenschaftsrecht.*[30] Barker must have been struck by the fact that von Gierke's erudite analysis of the trends concerned with the idea of natural law unexpectedly proved fertile. Von Gierke himself owed much to the historical school of law, associated primarily with Savigny, and interpreted by Barker as a reaction to the rationalism, universalism, and individualism of the school of natural law.[31] Von Gierke, of course, did not mean any primitive imitation of the past (for which Penty came to be criticized); his idea was to look in perspective at the fundamental problems of society and the state, and to find inspiration to a revaluation of certain firmly established values. Von Gierke's analysis was pertinent primarily because he brought out the rationalistic ahistoricism and consistent individualism of the school of natural law.

In every version of the school of natural law the individual precedes society; if not historically then at least ideally (Kant). The sovereign individual plays the leading part in each of those trends. Hence every social body is nothing else but a set of individuals. In the general trend we can single out two different, and even in a sense, opposing, currents that marked the individualism of the school of natural law, each of these currents having, of course, its own various ramifications. It would be difficult to discuss them here, the more so as there is no need to, and we shall accordingly confine ourselves to bringing out their main characteristics. The differences between these two currents focus on the issue of social contract.

In one case the idea was that by concluding a social contract the individuals renounced their freedom on behalf of the state (the ruler). Once a social contract is concluded the state guarantees the former freedom of the individual. The irrevocability of that renunciation resulted in centralism, because there were no reasons why the autonomy of any social entities except the family, be it the commune or any other association, should be protected. Thus, the state and the family are the only entities originating from the law of nature. This must have led to absolutism, advocated by the extremist representatives of that trend, including Hobbes. His law of nature was, in fact, a denial of the doctrine of natural law as it deprived the individual, once and for all, of all his "natural rights" and the possibility of setting up self-governing bodies.[32] Atomized society (the dispersed crowd) was thus squeezed into the framework of the absolutist state.

Hence, associations can function only if the state permits, their prerogatives being merely derivative; such bodies are treated as agencies of the state. Thus, "the intermediate bodies" between the individual and the state vanish. The social contract that had the establishment of the state in view binds the individuals, but no social contract binds the ruler, who embodies the state, in relation to the individuals. The ruler is bound only by the less circumspect divine law, whose infringement gives the individuals "the right to resist" (but note that such a resistance must not be organized). The defenceless individuals are thus confronted with the insuperable power of the state. The dichotomy between the state and the individual was thus pushed to the extreme; it reminds one of the maxim of the Roman emperors: *princeps legibus solutus*. Louis XIV in his *Institutions pour le Dauphin* wrote that within the state the king represented the nation, and the private man represented, in relation to the king, only the individual.[33] The idea of absolutism could hardly be worded in a more forcible manner.

This approach came very close to that of Hobbes, as formulated in his *Leviathan*, a *sui generis* anticipation of totalitarian regimes.

On the other hand, the individualistic assumptions led to the conclusion that a number of social contracts gave rise to the various intermediate bodies, and not to the state alone. Those bodies thus had an equally respectable origin–or were based on an equally respectable idea, if the "contract" is not treated genetically–as the state, and could effectively protect the individual against the omnipotence of the state.

The other trend was termed by von Gierke the federalist theory of natural law. The idea of self-governing associations, little dependent on the state, had been extremely strong in Germany. The League of Rhenian Towns had a particularly firm position in the thirteenth century, and the sovereign associations of merchants, known as the Hanseatic League, were active for centuries. The idea that the communes and other associations were independent of the state as were the individuals (their rights being not derived from the state) and were of the same nature as the state, was deeply rooted.[34]

In discussing the second trend we cannot overlook Althusius, to whom von Gierke dedicated a separate monograph, thereby saving him from oblivion.[35] Althusius formulated the theoretical foundations of a differentiated society, in which associations, whether secular or religious, were formed by the intention of free individuals. This idea was based on the assumption that natural law was oriented towards the individual; the consequences were not confined by Althusius to the state, but extended so as to cover the intermediate bodies; he thus created a theory of society based on natural law. Althusius assumed the various forms of association to be the fundamental element of the state. He accordingly singled out, within society, the family, the association, the commune, the province, and the state. Individuals formed associations and communes (local communities), which in the same way set up more complex social bodies, and these in turn the state. Thus a ramified hierarchy of intermediate groups intervened between the individual and the state.

Althusius' theory could be termed a specific theory of vertical federalism. A similar idea was to be advanced by Proudhon two centuries later. Federalism conceived in this way was based on the mutual obligations of groups. Althusius' federalism meant a union of groups and subgroups at various levels. He viewed the state as an articulated whole and saw the proper carriers of sovereignty in the elements of that whole. Such a federalism has, of course, little in common with the modern federal state.[36] The idea outlined above leads to that of popular sovereignty, obviously opposed to the centralist and absolute sovereignty of the monarch, the latter being associated with the name of Bodin. Althusius' opinions recall those of John Locke, and–if we look for more radical trends–those of Calvinism, in which Althusius' views were rooted. He saw in the people the origin of spiritual and secular sovereignty, and his *homo symbioticus*, born to live in a community, self-evidently can be traced back to Aristotle's *zoon politikon*. C. J. Friedrich says in his monograph on Althusius that there is only a small step from acceptance of the emotional bonds that link people who live in groups, to collectivist treatment of the community. This approach must lead to the conclusion that power comes from the community, which alone has the *potestas constituens*.[37]

If one is of the opinion that in order properly to comprehend macrosocial processes it is necessary to overcome the dichotomy between the state and the individual, then one has to say that the ideas typical of the second trend have not become obsolete. We are particularly interested here in the fact that von Gierke stressed the importance of the individual, who simultaneously acts as a member of these various bodies. He can thus be treated as a forerunner of the sociological theory of social roles.

Barker presented von Gierke to his British readers critically. He pointed to some shortcomings in his scholarship, and in particular dedicated much space to the idea of real legal persons, which Barker thought to be highly metaphysical.[38] This could be expected, because Barker reduced group pluralism to the pluralism of systems of ideas. This approach could easily result in a misunderstanding when von Gierke's theory was analysed, the more so as Barker had not assimilated the whole of von Gierke's work; the latter not only opposed the individualistic approach of the doctrine of natural law, but above all, as a Germanist, opposed the individualism typical of Roman law.[39] In Roman law the individuals were isolated carriers of rights (cf. the conception of *pater familias*), each encased in himself and only externally restricted in his intentions. The concept of real legal persons, and hence that of the legal personality of associations, was introduced by von Gierke with a view to abolishing that juridical monism. By the complete reality of the legal personality of associations (*die vollgültige Realität der Verbandspersönlichkeit*) von Gierke meant their complete equality before the law, their status equal to that of the individuals. Von Gierke's point was to treat associations not as collectivities of individuals, but as independent social wholes.[40] Associations, as seen by von Gierke, were real wholes analogous to groups in the sociological sense of the term (organized groups at that). While he did not use the term *group*, his views were not metaphysical in nature, the more so as he opposed the theory of legal fiction, which went back to Roman jurists and was later supported by such authorities as Pope Innocentius IV and later Savigny, a theory which was dominant in the nineteenth century and was further reinforced by English judicial law.

Von Gierke treated this theory as a failed endeavour to substantiate the functioning of legal persons. He considered his opposition to the fiction theory as the basis of his theory of associations. It is worth while mentioning the opinion formulated by S. N. Bratus, a Soviet civil law expert, on some aspects of Von Gierke's realist theory of legal persons: he credits von Gierke with the recognition of the real existence of legal persons as real collectivities which are reducible neither to the arithmetical sum of their respective members, nor to functions, nor to any device in jurisprudential technique. He goes on to say that the formula on inseparable bonds between the personality of an association as a whole and its members and on the existence of, and penetration into, a collectivity is free from Germanist scholasticism and includes elements of the correct interpretation of the concept of a legal person. The formula includes the correct idea that the whole is not reducible to the sum of its parts and that it does not exist outside of its parts. Von Gierke did not overlook those human beings who in their unity form a legal person.[41]

Barker also pointed to von Gierke's inconsistency of including in his theory the concept of "a higher whole", which comprises smaller wholes as its parts and limbs. Von Gierke was criticized by L. Duguit on the same point.[42] Von

Gierke's pluralistic reasoning broke down probably as a result of adopting the concept of the state as the social entity which rises above all other groups. He was also blamed for that by J. D. Lewis, who, while pointing to the fact that von Gierke always strove to preserve the balance between the principle of association and that of authority (planning), denied all pluralism in his work and saw him simply to be a loyal Prussian.[43]

S. Mogi also thought that von Gierke had been attaching great importance to the idea of a balance between unity and plurality in every group and in relation to higher-level groups,[44] but he did not draw such a conclusion as J. D. Lewis did when ironically questioning the pluralistic character of his views.

Barker went even further than Lewis and claimed that von Gierke's ideas had been put into effect by Fascism.[45] It is true that von Gierke's theory could have been assimilated by Nazism in a distorted form by disregarding his views of the role of freely organized associations and at the same time by separating such views from his conception of the state and civil law. One should not jump to conclusions in this connection.[46] This would be as groundless as linking Nietzsche's artistic idea of superman to the *Führerprinzip*, used as an instrument of Nazi policy.

3.3   A TENTATIVE SYNTHETIC EVALUATION OF THE ISSUE

As the present writer sees it, von Gierke deserves a more balanced appraisal, free from admixtures of political evaluation. It is true that his views lacked coherence (but how many eminent thinkers can stand that test?), and that his chauvinistic and conservative views, anachronistic even at the times he propounded them, could hardly be likeable; it is true that his endeavour to save constitutional monarchy in Germany by reviving the old German form of self-government was based on wrong assumptions and politically naive; it is also true that one can shrug one's shoulders when studying his attempts to prevent the acceptance of Roman law, and that he idealized both the old Germanic *Markgemeinde* and *Genossenschaften*, which he treated as specific temples of liberty. But if we separate the analytical and descriptive elements in his writings from the normative ones, as was done by Maitland and Barker, then we have to admit that he saw in old forms of self-government values which should not be lost and which serve as a source of inspiration even now. The parallel drawn by him between absolute individualism and the absolutist state and the related statement that the centralization of power, if pushed too far, inevitably results in the atomization of society[47] because all authoritarian power tends to suppress all autonomous associations, have a permanent heuristic value. S. Mogi, an expert on von Gierke's work, says that his pluralism manifested itself in his treating the state as a social organism next to which others are necessary too. Mogi believed that he strove to bring into harmony the supreme authority (of the state) with communities of associations, and that his theory of associations could become the foundation of modern pluralism and federalism, the point of departure being in constructing a modern theory of decentralization of political power. As Mogi puts it, von Gierke's theory of associations was pluralistic in its meaning, juridical in its manner of exposition, and rationalistic in the philosophy on which he had based it.[48]

We have to see in von Gierke a forerunner of group pluralism in social life and in politics, a forerunner of the theory of social groups. The emphasis he used to lay on the statement that a community (a group) is not merely the sum of its individual members, and his dogged striving to find a suitable formula for unity in diversity, shed the proper light upon the basic elements of his theory. Those merits cannot be cancelled by otherwise justified criticisms of his ideas in other fields.

Maitland and Barker came to be profoundly interested in von Gierke's theory for reasons we can easily understand. While for him associations were to serve as those instruments which, owing to their autonomy, guaranteed the individual's freedom of action, in Britain it was the flexible institution of trusteeship that functioned as that instrument and protected the individual against the ubiquitous interference by the state; it offered ample opportunity for individual enterprise and grouped people interested in the attainment of various goals. In von Gierke's theory Maitland found confirmation of the view that social groups are real entities, not reducible to, nor confineable within the framework of, juridical entities (*entia iuridica*); group personality was thus claimed not to be a purely juridical phenomenon. His study in moral and legal personality is of especial importance for following the path of his reasoning. He says there that if the personality status of corporations is a legal fiction, then it is the gift of the ruler, and he refers in this connection to the decision made by Charles II, who sentenced all Londoners to imprisonment for having acted as a corporation. He also wrote that the guiding principle of modern absolutism was: the absolutist state versus the absolute individual.[49] Both British authors mentioned here came easily to realize that they shared the same interests with the eminent German jurist. Barker wrote that every national community is a unity, but every society also means diversity; it is a rich tissue that includes religious and educational groups, professions and trades, formed for pleasure or for profit, some of them based on neighbourhood or some other sense of proximity.[50]

Like Maitland and Barker, J. N. Figgis and A. D. Lindsay came under von Gierke's influence, too. All of them were inclined to think that the state should be treated as one of the many social organizations. Yet the shaping of that trend cannot be ascribed to von Gierke alone. As has been shown by D. Nicholls, the authority of Lord Acton, whose impact upon British pluralists should not be underestimated, worked in the same direction.[51] His formula for freedom, which breeds diversity and preserves it by providing the means in the form of organization, could be used as the motto of the studies written by pluralists. Figgis, who had investigated relationships between Church and State, came closest to Acton in that respect.[52] He stood for the freedom of religious life within the Church, which is a corporation that is autonomous relative to the state. He thus wanted to exclude the interference by the state with the inner issues of the Church, By extending that thesis upon trade unions and other social organizations Figgis advanced the idea that society consists of many communities, large and small, which have the right to develop independently. It was not the state which established the family, the Churches, the clubs, the trade unions, and—in the Middle Ages—the guilds and the university colleges. All those bodies to which, like von Gierke, he ascribed group personality, were called into being by the instinct of association. This was why Figgis firmly opposed Austin's idea of sovereignty. He thought that groups' freedom of action was a condition of individual development, being the only effective barrier against the state uniting as society. Free society must have as its foundation not an autarchic individual, but an individual who manifests his personality in the plurality of organized groups. An isolated individual cannot exist, man always is a member of some community. Individuals are not grains of sand, similar to one another and undifferentiated, linked only to the state. It is small associations, and not the state, which shape human personality.[53] The state was treated by Figgis as the community of communities (A. D. Lindsay defined it as the organization of organizations). The government supervises and controls smaller associations, but does so within the limits of justice and respects their autonomy. The individual is in the state only through being a member of smaller organized groups.

Figgis in this way opposed "the orgy of state autocracy", which began during the Renaissance.[54] It follows therefrom that he did not reject the idea of sovereignty, worked out by generations of British jurists, the idea embodied in Parliament, but, like A. D. Lindsay, he strove *to restrict it essentially*.[55] This is why Nicholls goes too far (inadvertently contradicting what he wrote earlier) when he concludes that their philosophy of pluralism rejected the notion of state sovereignty.[56] This could apply *only* to G. D. H. Cole and to the early opinions of Harold Laski.

It is a specific paradox that a co-founder and at the same time an epigone of the Germanist school of law, a student of German feudalism, a political conservative and German chauvinist came to inspire a trend in British pluralism. But the paradox is merely apparent: the work of that Germanist looked attractive to the country which had opposed reception of Roman law and succeeded in preserving the tradition of the various feudal communities with their distinctive features. Von Gierke's theory of the essential homogeneity of associations was termed by Hsiao as the first shot fired in the pluralist rebellion.[57] Further, von Gierke's consistent search for plurality in unity must have been attractive to all those who were estranged from

Neo-Hegelian influence in Britain (Bosanquet and his school), and also to those who thought that the Church of England was too much linked to the state; they feared that under favourable circumstances that pattern could be extended so as to cover other social organizations.

British historians must have responded intellectually to the fact that the first page of von Gierke's work on associations carried the statement that not only did the possibility of setting up associations increase the strength of a given generation, but associations, by being able to outlive individuals, linked past generations with those to come. They must have also been attracted by the liberal elements in von Gierke's theory of associations as free unions of individuals, a theory to which organicist interpretations of social groups did not put an end.[58] This was a vision of development of mankind, and hence a vision of the ways in which we could shape our own history. These elements also explain the present revival of interest in von Gierke's opus in Germany.

3.4   THE VIEWS OF WALTHER RATHENAU

The trend now under consideration includes the views of Walther Rathenau, who became active during the final period of von Gierke's life. Rathenau, a prominent organizer of German industry and a leading politician under the Second Reich and after 1918, was not himself an academic man.[59]

Even in his pre-1914 publications he criticized the uniformity of contemporary German society. His last two books, *Der neue Staat* (1919) and *Die neue Gesellschaft* (1923), contributed new elements. Rathenau criticized the idea of sovereignty and brought out the importance of numberless self-governing bodies, unions, associations, etc., whose network was increasing in density. There are the connecting links between those organizations and the political centre, which would never vanish, but would lose its dominance over other unions. There can be no true and full democracy if each group does not have its due influence guaranteed within the state. He wanted to modify existing organizations by linking them to bodies that would represent both territorial and vocational groups. He conceived of a structure consisting of functional bodies, crowned by a "functional" parliament and also linked to the political structure of the country. "Functional" ministries would be headed by political ministers. Rathenau termed his system *organocracy*. This functional conclusion separated him from von Gierke, and showed a close affinity to British guild socialism; but Rathenau differed from Cole in the latter's later period of activity by cutting himself off firmly from Marxist theory.[60]

Rathenau was not guided by research aspirations alone: he wanted his theory to counterbalance the idea of the soviets, which after 1918 looked attractive not only to the workers, but also to the broad masses of the people. The appearance of Rathenau's book in 1919 was preceded by a year of spontaneous emergence of soviets in Central Germany, followed by the establishment of the Bavarian Soviet Republic. Rathenau rejected the system of soviets as a form of the dictatorship of the working class and condemned it as a system which was "one-sided and mechanical".[61]

While the period of the world war and the revolution pushed von Gierke towards the political right, Rathenau sought a solution in a deep-reaching transformation of the social and political structure of the country. He understood that an irreversible historical process had taken place, which required a democratization of the capitalist system.

3.5 HAROLD LASKI: THE FIRST PERIOD OF ACTIVITY

Harold J. Laski was shaped as a "radical" pluralist primarily under the influence of Figgis. He expressed his ideas at the very beginning of his academic career in three books: *Studies in the Problem of Sovereignty* (1917), *Authority in the Modern State* (1919), and *The Foundations of Sovereignty* (1921), and in a number of papers in various periodicals.[62]

No other author, perhaps except G. D. H. Cole, dedicated to pluralism so much space as did Harold Laski. The vast body of his works includes items which differ from one another in value; he is, or may be, not among the greatest authors discussed in the present book (he is blamed for eclecticism by some[63]), but his rank must also be measured by his impact upon his contemporaries, and this is why his work cannot be treated cursorily.

It was only many years later that Laski played down the radical elements in his pluralistic views and came to take part in the British labour movement by becoming active in the Fabian Society and in the Executive Committee of the Labour Party. That turn in his political thinking was marked by the appearance of one of his major works, *A Grammar of Politics*.[64]

In the earliest period he was influenced in his political thinking by Maitland, through whom he came to study von Gierke's writings; by Barker, under whom he studied at Oxford; and also by Figgis. As he shared to some extent Figgis's interest in the freedom of the Church and the history of religions, he used Figgis's arguments to defend the autonomy of trade unions.[65]

During his stay in the United States Laski was influenced by James's pragmatic philosophy, and especially by its pluralistic elements to be found in *A Pluralistic Universe* (1912). The echoes of James's pragmatism can be heard in many of Laski's writings, for example when he says that man cannot be described merely as a member of the political organization of the state for he is not reducible to a single factor, he is not only a member of a state; his ability to associate cannot be confined to that.[66] His claim that other groups are as real as the state, and their impact is incomparably stronger than the state's because group membership rests on a voluntary basis, resembles von Gierke's ideas very strikingly. Any group of which an individual is a member makes his personality richer and enables him to be active in a way in which he would not otherwise have engaged. According to Laski, man is a builder of communities.[67]

Note, by way of digression, that Laski, like G. D. H. Cole, after some years abandoned the conception that groups are real entities and have personalities of their own. He changed his standpoint under the influence of M. R. Cohen, the American philosopher of jurisprudence, whom he publicly admitted to be right.[68] This controversy gave rise to many misunderstandings, which it would be difficult to clarify here. To put it briefly, Laski abandoned the idea of the plurality of sovereignties (i.e. the assumption that there are many co-existing centres of decision-making), that is, the idea which had no counterpart in political facts and was not being used by anyone except for anarchists. But this should not have led to his abandoning the idea that groups are real entities: there is no link between the two ideas, and the sociology of groups, as has been said, has recently declared itself in its favour, though in a different language and by substantiating that conception in a different way.

Laski wrote about pluralism not only in his books and articles, but also in his private letters. The following significant statement was made by Laski in his letter to Justice Holmes: he wrote that barriers between things were more obvious than their unity. Holmes even blamed him for being uncritical of W. James's terminology.[69] Yet pragmatism was in tune with the utilitarian tradition of Bentham and Mill, in which Laski had been brought up.

Laski also drew pluralistic inspiration from other sources, such as Leon Duguit, whom he extolled, with youthful exaltation, as the most eminent contemporary political thinker. He had much in common with him, pride of place going to their attempt at undermining, or even discarding, the sovereignty of the state. To simplify matters, one could say that Duguit degraded the boundless power of the state and placed it at the same level as that of the individual; that is he subordinated it, like the power of ordinary citizens, to the supreme principle of law. Laski translated, prefaced and published *Les Transformations du Droit Public*, and also wrote a separate essay on Duguit.[70] But later he dissociated himself from Duguit's solidarism treated as the remedy for all practical social problems. This was due to his critique of capitalism growing more radical (cf. section 3.6 below).[71] Now Laski drew inspiration from these three sources: German and British pluralism in its form we have conventionally labelled academic; James's pragmatism; and French pluralism, which—as we shall see—was not confined to Duguit's influence.

Laski's views can best be understood when we start from his critique of sovereignty, critique of the monism of the state and law, represented by Bosanquet and Austin. Laski often criticized Bosanquet for exaggerating the role of the state in society. He was estranged by the monistic conception of the state, with its hierarchical structure of institutions and a single centre for making decisions on social issues. Bosanquet in fact treated the state in the spirit of the Hobbesian tradition as the supreme authority and the only cohesive element in society. In his polemic with Austin (especially with his *Lectures on Jurisprudence*, 1869) Laski blamed the latter for legal formalism whose one-sidedness prevented him from grasping the political aspects of the state and the pluralism of social groups and forces. Laski opposed the idealism which preferred the study of forms typical of *Staatslehre* to the hard facts of politics:[72] the truth had to be sought in events. On another occasion Laski advanced the methodological principle of empirical verification of the value of the rules in force, because mankind cannot be governed by principles of formal logic.[73]

Laski's controversy with Austin was largely over the interpretation of the law, but the controversy itself and the related issue of the state's responsibility for its officials requires some comment. Laski exemplified the claims resulting from unrestricted sovereignty by court decisions inspired by the mediaeval principle of the king's not being responsible, because "the King can do no wrong: in him there is neither sin nor weakness"; the said decisions extended the principle of the king's not being responsible to the king's officials, that is, the civil servants, and denied indemnity to those who had incurred damages. Such persons could claim indemnity from the direct perpetrators only, but not from the Treasury. Laski saw in this lack of the state's responsibility for its servants an excess of sovereignty which was incompatible with the rule of law, for the ruler's prerogative (*imperium*) should not be claimed when the state acts as a party on the market.[74]

As can be seen, the controversy over the interpretation and the scope of sovereignty had its purely practical consequences.

Laski was convinced that the modern state had taken over the unrestricted power enjoyed by the Papacy in the Middle Ages. The monistic state did not leave any margin of freedom from its interference, and yet, as Laski wrote in his *Studies* ... (p. 17), all social issues could not be viewed in the context of the state. This opinion was stubbornly worked out by him in his numerous writings.[75]

In his criticism of the supporters of the Hegelian *Rechtsphilosophie* in Britain, Laski was supported by L. T. Hobhouse (cf. *The Metaphysical Theory of the State*, 1918).

Laski focused his critique on the sovereignty of Parliament. Austin's analytic jurisprudence granted that sovereignty a status free from all restriction. If that principle were to cover the state as a whole, this would result in the lack of responsibility on the part of the citizens, because the state tended to absorb all forms of societal activity.[76] The state, Laski claimed, cannot be granted such centralized infallibility.[77] In his critique of the sovereignty of the state Laski came close to Duguit's *anti-étatisme*. But the defect in Laski's analysis was that he often blurred the difference btween the state, on the one hand, and its machinery and the government, on the other.

It seems that Deane was right in his monograph of Laski when he blamed Laski for this.[78] While he criticized the monistic conception of the state Laski was always aware of the fact that the context of the state and our living in the state could not be disregarded. In the second period of his activity he considerably modified his pluralism he had stood for in his early period. As he wrote in *Liberty in the Modern State* (1930), one can break away from one's family, one's club, and one's Church, but one cannot evade the state. Today the only effective opposition to the state and its bureaucracy is a pluralistic social order.

That critique of the sovereignty of the state had its positive counterpart, which Laski saw in social differentiation, in organized groups to which he would assign sovereignty that could vie with that of the state, provided such groups occupied an important place in society. The division of sovereignty, which strongly resembled the idea of the dispersion of power, later to be found in American political science, was the cornerstone of Laski's pluralism. Laski described the state as a kind of fortress that had to be demolished if the pluralistic state was to be built on its ruins. The division of sovereignty must have led to the conclusion, typical also of other British pluralists, that the state was one of many social organizations, and that the sovereignty of the state in fact did not differ from the power of the Church or a trade union.[79] The state should substantiate its position within society by definite achievements as any other social organization should do.

W. Y. Elliott, when analysing the work done by Laski and other pluralists, wrote that pluralism meant transforming the sovereign state into a sovereign group. The pluralistic theory rested on the polyarchy of sovereign groups. But, in Elliott's opinion, Laski, by treating the state as the prime organization among other groups deprived it of its independent functional significance.[80]

While thus "degrading" the state Laski was careful not to give preference to any group before others. During the first period of his polemic with the advocates of the monistic theory of the state, Laski was visibly influenced by Maitland and von Gierke, and through the latter by Althusius as well. He accordingly came to the conclusion that sovereignty did not have to mean omnipotence, but could be an attribute of various organizations and differ from the sovereignty of the state by degree only.[81] Laski accepted groups as necessary elements of social reality, as real persons (entities). The individual, with his diversified and manifold interests, is accordingly a member of many organizations and is bound by various allegiances. Laski was thus one of the first scholars to notice the necessity of studying the problem of social roles.

He took over from von Gierke and Figgis the conception that groups are real entities, but abandoned it later, influenced in that respect by M. Cohen.[82] He thought that the individual, by being active within various groups, has greater possibilities to act, and that his individual responsibility is thereby increased, and not reduced.[83]

The recommendation of the division of power led Laski to the idea of social federalism, which in some respects resembled Proudhon's concept of federalism; by the way, Laski did not conceal his positive interest in Proudhon's views. While he did not deny the importance of decentralization and the necessity of increasing the prerogatives of the local government (territorial federalism),[84] certainly under the influence of the American political system, both at the federal and the local level, he nevertheless believed the functional, vocational representation, the polyarchy of sovereign vocational groups, to be the key issue of federalism. This, of course, brought to the fore the problem of the workers' share in industrial management. True political democracy in his opinion results from industrial democracy, under which the workers should have an important say in choosing the managers.[85] If put into effect, this would result in the emergence of a federal organization of producers, representing the interests of the workers employed in the various industries. Such a council of producers would have to have an executive body of its own.[86] Under the impact of French syndicalism, Laski extended industrial democracy so that it should cover even civil servants.[87]

Such a functional or vocational federalism would bring about a reform of Parliament, whose "sovereignty" would be restricted by its new division into two houses; a House based on territorial representation and a vocational House. This would separate the political function of Parliament from its socioeconomic one.[88] Zylstra is right in this connection when he writes (*op. cit.*, p. 77) that functional federalism was the core of Laski's political pluralism.

In that period of "radical pluralism" Laski was, of course, far away from the standpoint at one time held by the Fabians, whom he blamed for their governmental paternalism.[89] This was due to his anarchist leanings, in particular, especially his fondness of Proudhon's views and of French syndicalism. He thought that the latter had undermined the very principle of the authority of the state, which was tantamount to the conception of the citizens being subjects (cf. *Authority* ..., pp. 36 ff.). In his introduction to Duguit's book Laski wrote about the significance of "going back to Proudhon", to the latter's idea of a federal organization of society. At that time he valued Proudhon higher than Marx. In a letter to Holmes he wrote that Proudhon's theory of the state complied with all his, Laski's, "anarchist prejudices".[90] The influence of anarchist thought can also be traced in the idea that the individual is, in the last analysis, the centre of political sovereignty. On the basis of Laski's writings from that period we can classify him as an extremist among those pluralists whose views we have discussed in this chapter.

But Laski was not uncritical of anarchists and syndicalists, and used to cut himself off from their opinions quite firmly. While Laski "degraded" the state, the anarchists dismissed it. He blamed French syndicalists and British guild socialists for obliterating the difference between the economic and the political functions of the state.[91] In *The Foundations* ... he wrote (pp. 52 ff.) that it was necessary to single out those interests which resulted from geographical neighbourhood, and also to study consumers' interests.

Local groups, he claimed, live their own life. The modern state needs territorial federalism, i.e. far-reaching decentralization, whose advantage would consist in taking local interests into consideration. Laski thus was decades ahead of the standpoint represented by contemporary regionalism, and did not let himself follow the views of Comte and Proudhon, who were radical on this issue. He thereby also rejected the standpoint of Dicey, who considered federalism to be a path towards a centralized state. We can conclude, accordingly, that Laski saw merely a quantitative difference between federation and decentralization. He thought that it would be a misunderstanding to try to link, or to subordinate, deeply rooted local and regional trends to the interests of the producers.

3.6 HAROLD LASKI IN HIS MATURE PERIOD OF ACTIVITY

Laski's pluralism was inseparable from his critique of the capitalist system. In all his writings from the period marked by his pluralist views we can easily trace that critique which unmasked the capitalist nature of the state. While he did not use the term class struggle, there is no doubt as to what his position was. As early as in 1916 he wrote to Justice Holmes that the interests of capital are incompatible on fundamental issues with those of labour.[92] In *Authority* ... he wrote that it was of little importance how the institutions of the state be organized: they would in practice reflect the dominant economic system and protect it. In the same year (1919) he wrote in one of his much-publicized articles about conflicts of interests in modern society; some of these interests were incompatible with some others.[93] In *Foundations* he says that those who wield economic power are the real source of power in every state.[94] Such being the case Laski saw only one solution: to neutralize the state through the division of power.[95] This is why he consistently criticized G. Jellinek's theory of self-restriction of the state,[96] because the state can really be restricted only by concessions made by the class which has at its disposal the means of production on behalf of its opponents.

This leftist trend became stronger in Laski's later works, in which he described the basic antagonism between capital and labour and gave a picture of the society in which profit is the ultimate motive power, which results in anarchy in production.

Nothing, however, indicates that Laski considered revolution as the way in which the workers would take over the economic power.

In the 1920s, Laski considerably revised the radical elements in his pluralist views, which found manifestation in his popular essay on Marx and in *A Grammar of Politics*, which marked a turning point in his views. In his preface to the latter work he made a signal assessment of his past.[97] There can be no doubt as to the trend in the evolution of his opinions. He came to see the weak points of his pluralism primarily in the fact that he had not realized the necessity of preserving the state and its class-based nature. Hence the pluralist should have a classless society as his goal only at a later stage. It would then be possible to make the appropriate institutions reflect the federal nature of society. But to attain that it is necessary to destroy the class structure of society, because the state is simply the instrument of that class which owns the means of production. Many years later he would say, in *The State in Theory and in Practice* (pp. 173 ff.), that the legal concepts and the administration of justice were imbued with the spirit of the class struggle. And *A Grammar of Politics* ends with the significant conclusion: once the class society is destroyed there is no need for the state as the sovereign apparatus of coercion; in Marx's interpretation, the state "withers away".

In the said preface Laski also formulated with more precision what he considered valid in his writings from the previous, pluralistic, period:

(i) The purely legal conception of the state is untenable; he rejected it as it offered a merely technical description of prerogatives, regardless of the real prerogatives. Note that in his second period of activity, opened by *A Grammar of Politics*, Laski consistently criticized analytical jurisprudence, which offered merely a skeleton of the legal system and disregarded its moral and political aspects.[98]

(ii) Nothing can substantiate the state's claim to stronger allegiance that can be claimed by any other association. No ethical and political considerations can be adduced to support that claim.

(iii) Sovereignty is morally neutral as a conception of real power.

(iv) *Society, as a complex whole, is pluralistic* [italics–S.E.].

At that time Laski was close to the Fabians and connected with the Labour Party, but it seems an exaggeration to call *A Grammer of Politics* a Fabian book, as K. Martin did.[99] It suffices to point in this connection not only to the said preface, but also to the critique levelled by him at the Webbs because of their idea of separating Parliament into a social and political one.[100] As has been pertinently emphasized by Elliott,[101] Laski in his controversy with the Webbs acted as a supporter of the British parliament as an instrument of social change; he thought the idea of the Webbs to be unrealistic, even in a federal state, because in his opinion it infringed the principle of the uniform functioning of power (cf. *A Grammar of Politics*, pp. 190 ff.). Division of power does not in the least mean the balance of power. In his opinion, the executive body would be nothing other than the executive committee of the parliamentary party. When it comes to protecting the interests of producers and consumers, he believed that instead of turning Parliament into a two-headed body it would be necessary to surround it with consultative bodies that would represent the various industries and the various vocations and professions. It would be obligatory for Parliament to consult those bodies when preparing its acts. Yet the final decision should rest with Parliament (*A Grammar of Politics*, pp. 52, 177).

Laski also criticized the guild socialists for their intention to entrust with power those organizations which protected vocational interests (functional bodies), and raised four objections on this issue:

(i) Their theory makes it possible to establish which organizations would be consultative bodies, but it is difficult to say which one would govern.

(ii) Nothing speaks in favour of the supposition that the guild system would be more effective in controlling industry than is the House of Commons.

(iii) It is impossible to draw a demarcation line between the guilds' congress and the territorial representation.

(iv) If the drawing of that demarcation line were left to interpretation by the judges, then power in society would be left with them.

In the light of these principles and in the light of this reconsideration of his former views, opinions sometimes expressed that Laski "abandoned pluralism", obviously miss the point.[102]

On another occasion, also in *A Grammar* ..., Laski in his polemic with the guild socialists openly postulated that final decisions be left to the state. He also criticized the Economic Council of the Reich, an institution established in Germany by the Weimar Constitution.[103]

But Laski in his later period of activity remained suspicious of the state, which cannot take charge of man's personality *in toto*.[104] Allegiance to the state depends on whether the state performs its duties;[105] Laski thus modified "the right to resist", an idea developed in the various versions of the doctrine of natural law. On another occasion he wrote jocularly that a modicum of anarchism was always necessary if one was not to deliver oneself unconditionally to the authority.

This intertwining of rights and duties resembles strongly Proudhon's idea of *mutuellisme*. The special position of the state is not due to its being the supreme body, but to the fact that, being a territorial organization, it performs functions which neither the individual nor any other organization can perform: it protects the citizens' interests and acts as the co-ordinating agency.[106]

Laski singled out three levels of interests: those of individuals, those of groups which provide for the specific needs which an individual cannot satisfy if acting in isolation, and those which are common to all. The last category can be satisfied neither by individuals nor by groups of individuals, but by the state alone.[107]

Armand Hoog ascribed this toning down of extremist pluralism that marked the young Laski's creed to the impact which the failure of the general strike had had upon Laski, who could see how the coercive power of the state had prevailed over the trade unions.[108]

Years later Laski would write in *The State in Theory and Practice* that every society revealed that within its national limits there were not only individuals, but also associations which group people for the attainment of their various religious, cultural, and political goals. Such a society makes the state. This toned-down formula sheds light upon the distance covered by Laski from the time of his first formulations of pluralistic ideas.

Fourest brought out the pluralistic elements to be found in *A Grammar of Politics* and in *The State in Theory and Practice*, but blurred the difference between the two stages in the evolution of Laski's opinions; on the other hand, Hsiao's claim that in the later period Laski turned towards Bentham-like individualism seems groundless.[109] *A Grammar of Politics* opened the second period in Laski's activity; that of moderate pluralism.

Laski's abandonment of radical pluralism should not affect the assessment of his political standpoint. When he was active as a politician he was in the left wing of the Labour Party. These comments on him could not be concluded without mentioning his letter to Justice F. Frankfurter, in which he wrote that his standpoint was clearly defined: he was in the left wing of the Labour Party and, if necessary, he would move to the extreme left.[110] One should note also that in *The State in Theory and Practice* he declared himself to be a firm advocate of the nationalization of the means of production (cf. p. 328).

Laski certainly did not see any contradiction between pluralism in the modified form and true Marxism, or rather Marxism as he interpreted it. No less essential is the fact that he wanted to see the capitalist state replaced by a social-democratic pluralist state. Did he not say that if the state is to be considered as an instrument of the ruling class the pluralist's aim should be a classless society? Such opinions and the consistency which marked them linked the young Laski with Laski in his mature period.

NOTES AND REFERENCES

1. For a general characteristic of this version of British pluralism see F. Coker, "Pluralistic Theories and the Attack upon State Sovereignty", in: Ch. E. Merriam and H. E. Barnes (eds), *Political Theories. Recent Times* (New York, 1924); consult also A. M. Flagiol, *English Political Pluralism* (London, 1941); and M. Y. Polak, "Pluralistische Staatsleer", in: *Staatswetenschapelijke apstellen ...*, *(Alphen a.d. Rijn, 1948)* (quoted after B. Zylstra, cf. note 63 below).

2. See his *Volksrecht und Juristenrecht* (Leipzig, 1843). Von Gierke dedicated vol. I of *Genossenschaftsrecht* to Beseler.

3. Note the interesting study by G. Gurwitsch, who saw certain pluralistic elements in von Gierke's work, but assigned them much less importance than the British authors used to do. Cf. G. Gurwitsch, "Otto von Gierke als Rechtsphilosoph", *Logos*, **XI** (1922/3), 86–132.

4. Interest in von Gierke's work was not confined to the English-speaking world. Cf. F. W. Coker, "Organismic Theories of the State", *Collective Studies in History, Economics and Public Law* (New York), **38** (1910); E. D. Ellis, "The Pluralistic State", *American Political Science Review*, **XIV** (1920); R. Emerson, *State and Sovereignty in Modern Germany* (New Haven, 1928); S. Mogi, Otto von Gierke (*His Political Teaching and Jurisprudence*) (London, 1932); J. D. Lewis, *The Genossenschafts-Theory of Otto von Gierke* (*A Study in Political Thought*) (Madison, 1935).
5. This is brought out by D. Nicholls, *The Pluralist State* (London, 1975), p. 77.
6. Cf. K. Lårenz, "Hegels Dialektik des Willens und das Problem der juristischen Persönlichkeit", *Logos*, **20** (1931), 240; E. W. Boeckenforde, *Die deutsche verfassungsgeschichtliche Forschung im 19. Jahrhundert* (Berlin, 1931), p. 153.
7. This is reflected, e.g., in vol. IV of *Genossenschaftsrecht*, entitled *Die Staats- und Korporationslehre der Neuzeit* (Berlin, 1913), and in the minor works from the last period of his life. Cf. "Der germanische Staatsgedanke", in: *Staat, Recht und Volk*, no. 5 (1919). Von Gierke's chauvinistic and conservative standpoint developed under the impact of World War I and its consequences.
8. Despite the fact that in his later works he reverted to pluralistic elements. Cf. his rector's speech, *Das Wesen der menschlichen Verbände* (Leipzig, 1902).
9. Among H. Preuss' works the one that comes closest to von Gierke's ideas is *Gemeinde, Staat, Reich* (Berlin, 1889). S. Mogi notes that in that period he was a sociologist rather than a jurist. (Cf. his *Otto von Gierke: His Political Teaching and Jurisprudence* (London, 1932), p. 234.) For the change on Preuss' opinions see his *Obrigkeitsstaat und Grossdeutsche Gedanke* (Jena, 1921), and *Staat, Recht und Freiheit* (Töbingen, 1926).
10. *Das Deutsche Genossenschaftsrecht*, vol. II, *Geschichte des deutschen Körperschaftsbegriff* (Berlin, 1873), pp. 820 ff.
11. *Ibid.*, vol. III, *Die Staats- und Korporationslehre des Altertums und des Mittelalters und ihre Aufnahme in Deutschland* (Berlin, 1881), pp. 512 ff.
12. *Ibid.*, vol. II, pp. 15 ff.
13. *Ibid.*, vol. I, p. 643.
14. *Ibid.*, vol. I, *Rechtsgeschichte der deutschen Genossenschaft* (Berlin, 1868), pp. 164 ff.; vol. III, pp. 38 ff.
15. Cf. J. D. Lewis, *op. cit.*, p. 46.
16. O. Brunner, *Land und Herrschaft* (Brünn, 1943), p. 151.
17. Cf. O. von Gierke, "Die Grundbegriffe des Staatsrechts und die neunsten Staatsrechtstheorien", *Zeitschfit für die gesammte Staatswissenschaft*, **XXX** (1874), and Laband's "Staatsrecht und die deutsche Rechtswissenschaft", *Schmollars Jahrbuch, 1883*, Heft 4; R. Pound, "The Scope and Purpose of Sociological Jurisprudence", *Harvard Law Review*, 1910–2 (quoted after M. P. Follett, *The New State. Group Organisation. The Solution of Popular Government* (New York–London, 1926) (first published in 1908)); J. Stone, *The Province and Function of Law* (London, 1947), p. 667.
18. *Der Entwurf eines bürgerlichen Gesetzbuchs und das deutsche Recht* Leipzig, 1889); *Deutsches Privatrecht*, vol. 1 (*Allgemeiner Teil und Personenrecht*) (München, 1895); *Das bürgerliche Gesetzbuch und der deutsche Reichstag* (Berlin, 1896); *Deutsches Privatrecht*, vol. 2 (*Sachenrecht*) (Leipzig, 1905); and a series of minor works on civil, commercial, and labour law. On von Gierke as a "dogmatist" see A. Janssen, *Otto von Gierkes Methode der geschichtlichen Rechtswissenschaft, Musterschmiedt*, (1974), pp. 53.
19. *Genossenschaftsrecht*, vol. I, pp. 714 ff, 759 ff, 843 ff.
20. *Ibid.*, vol. I, pp. 296 ff, 577 ff.
21. On that controversy, which divided German experts in mediaeval history, see O. Brunner, *op. cit.*, pp. 124 ff, 165 ff.
22. W. M. Maitland, *Introduction to O. von Gierke, Political Theories of the Middle Ages* (London, 1958), p. xliii.
23. *Genossenschaftsrecht*, vol. III, p. 371. Also quoted in Maitland's Introduction, *op. cit.*, p. xxx.
24. On this issue see E. Lousse, *La Société d'Ancien Régime (Organisation et Représentation Corporatives)* (Paris, 1952), *passim*.
25. W. Kornhauser, *The Politics of Mass Society* (London, 1960), pp. 79 ff.
26. G. Gurwitsch, *op. cit.*, p. 87 ff.

27. W. Ullmann, *Individuum und Gesellschaft im Mittelalter* (Göttingen, 1967), p. 96.
28. H. Maine, *Lectures on the Early History of Institutions* (London, 1893), and also *Popular Government* (London, 1893).
29. The Discredited State, *Political Quarterly*, **II** (1915).
30. E. Barker presented von Gierke for the first time only 34 years after Maitland. Cf. *O. von Gierke, Natural Law and the Theory of Society 1500 to 1800* (Boston, 1957).
31. E. Barker, *op. cit.*, Introduction, p. 1.
32. *Leviathan*, chap. 19.
33. Quoted after O. Brunner, *op. cit.*, p. 410.
34. *Genossenschaftsrecht*, vol. 1, pp. 832 ff.
35. O. von Gierke, *Johannes Althusius und die Entwicklung der naturrechtlichen Staatstheorien* (1st edn, 1902; Breslau, 1929); W. Voisé, *Początki nowżytnych nauk społecznych (The Beginnings of Modern Social Science)* (Warszawa, 1962), pp. 292 ff.
36. Cf. *Johannes Althusius ...*, p. 226; *Genossenschaftsrecht*, vol. I, p. 299, vol. III, pp. 544 ff; C. J. Friedrich, *Johannes Althusius und sein Werk im Rahmen der Entwicklung der Theorie von der Politik* (Berlin, 1975), pp. 68, 88, 120 ff. G. Gurwitsch indicates that von Gierke was markedly influenced by the mediaeval federalistic idea of law; *op. cit.*, p. 131.
37. C. J. Friedrich, *op. cit.*, pp. 77, 86 ff, 120.
38. E. Barker, *op. cit.*, Introduction, p. lxii.
39. E. Barker, *The Discredited State...*
40. O. von Gierke, *Deutsches Privatrecht* (1895), vol. I, p. 406, quoted after G. Gurwitsch, *op. cit.*, p. 116. See also *Das Wesen der menschlichen Verbände* (Berlin. 1902).
41. O. von Gierke, *Die Genossenschaftstheorie und die deutsche Rechtssprechung* (Berlin, 1887), p. 5; *Genossenschaftsrecht*, vol. III, pp. 43 ff, 103 ff, 128 ff; S. N. Bratuś, *Osoby prawne w radzieckim prawie cywilnym (Juridical Persons in the Soviet Civil Law)* (Warszawa, 1950), p. 119.
42. E. Barker, *Natural Law ...*, Introduction, p. lxxxiii; L. Duguit, *L'Etat, le droit objectif et la loi positive* (Paris, 1901), pp. 131 ff.
43. J. D. Lewis, *op. cit.*, p. 50.
44. S. Mogi, *op. cit.*, p. 216.
45. E. Barker, *Natural Law*, Introduction, p. lxxxiv.
46. A. Janssen, *op. cit.*, p. 4.
47. O. von Gierke, *Genossenschaftsrecht*, vol. I, pp. 648 ff.
48. S. Mogi, *op. cit.*, pp. 60, 64, 164, 216, 230, 263.
49. *Moral Personality and Legal Responsibility, Collected Papers* (Cambridge, 1911), vol. III.
50. E. Barker, *Natural Law*, Introduction, pp. xxii ff.
51. D. Nicholls, *op. cit.*, p. 26; Lord Acton, *Essays on Freedom and Power* (Boston, 1956), p. 160.
52. J. N. Figgis, *Churches in the Modern State* (London, 1913), *passim*.
53. *Ibid.*, pp. 47 ff, 87 ff.
54. *Ibid.*, p. 101.
55. A. D. Lindsay, "The State in Recent Political Theory", *The Political Quarterly*, **I** (1914).
56. D. Nicholls, *op. cit.*, p. 53.
57. Kung Chuan Hsiao, *Political Pluralism* (London, 1927), p. 32.
58. O. Brunner, *op. cit.*, p. 180.
59. W. Rathenau headed the AEG and was adviser on war-time economics. One of the most enlightened economic leaders, he was also a renowned political writer of his generation. His most important books written before and during the war were: *Zur Kritik der Zeit* (1912); *Zur Mechanik des Geistes* (1913); *Von kommenden Dingen* (1917).
60. On Rathenau's theory see G. Raphael, *W. Rathenau, ses idées et ses projets d'organisation économique* (Paris, 1919). The similarity of opinions of Rathenau and guild socialists was indicated by S. Mogi, *op. cit.*, p. 239.
61. *Der neue Staat* (Berlin, 1919), pp. 35 ff, 42 ff.
62. The most important ones were: "The Personality of the State", *The Nation*, **VII** (July 1915); "The Apotheosis of the State", *The New Republic*, 22 July 1916.
63. B. Zylstra, *From Pluralism to Collectivism (The Development of Harold Laski's Political Thought)* (Assen, 1968), p. 26. On the turn towards pluralism in British socio-political thought see H. M. Magid, *English Political Pluralism* (New York, 1941).
64. The edition to be quoted henceforth will be that of 1948 (the fifth).

65. This was pointed out by H. F. Deane, *The Political Ideas of H. J. Laski* (New York, 1955), p. 29.
66. *Authority...* pp. 313 ff.
67. *Foundations...*, and also *Studies...*
68. H. J. Laski, "Morris Cohen's Approach to Legal Philosophy", *Chicago Law Review*, 5, 575 ff. On the same subject see E. Fraenkel, "Der Pluralismus–Strukturelement der freiheitlich-rechtsstaatlichen Demokratie", *Verhandlungen des 45. Deutschen Juristentages*, vol. **II/B**, (München and Berlin, 1964), pp. 11 ff.
69. Letter of 16 September 1916, quoted after B. Zylstra, *op. cit.*, pp. 26 and pp. 68 ff. Holmes and Pollock moreover deplored the influence Figgis had had upon Laski. Quoted after D. Nicholls, *op. cit.*, p. 50.
70. The English-language title of *Transformations...* was: *Law in the Modern State* (New York, 1919); A Note on Duguit appeared in the *Harvard Law Review*, **XXXI** (1917–18), 181–92.
71. H. J. Laski, "Duguit's Conception of the State", in: W. J. Jennings (ed.), *Modern Theories of Law* (London, 1933).
72. Cf. *Studies...*, pp. 4 ff, 23; *Foundations...*, pp. 232 ff.
73. *Authority...*, p. 61; *Foundations...*, pp. 232 ff.
74. H. J. Laski, "The Responsibility of the State in England", *Harvard Law Review*, **XXXII** (1918–19) (later included in *Foundations...*).
75. See also The Apotheosis of the State, *The New Republic*, 7 July 1916.
76. This idea is especially stressed in *Studies...*, pp. 3 ff.
77. *Authority...*, p. 312.
78. H. F. Deane, *op. cit.*, p. 16. On the contrary, this is not noticed by M. Fourest, Laski's uncritical admirer (*Les Théories du professeur Harold J. Laski* (Paris, 1943), p. 39).
79. *Studies...*, pp. 27, 270, 273: "We prefer a country where sovereignty is distributed." Cf. K. C. Hsiao, *Political Pluralism, A Study in Comparative Political Thought* (London, 1927), pp. 12–13.
80. W. Y. Elliott, *The Pragmatic Revolt in Politics* (New York, 1928), pp. 90, 153, 162.
81. *Studies...*, p. 270.
82. B. Zylstra, *op. cit.*, p. 35.
83. *Authority...*, p. 313. Cf. also *ibid.*, p. 61: "The life of politics as the law, lies in its functioning."
84. *Studies...*, pp. 271–84.
85. Cf. *Authority...*, pp. 87 f: "True political democracy is ... the offspring of the true industrial democracy", and *Foundations...*, p. 84.
86. *Foundations...*, pp. 43–72.
87. *Authority...*, chapter on "Administrative Syndicalism in France".
88. H. J. Laski, "Parliament and Revolution", *The New Republic*, **XXII** (19 May 1920).
89. H. J. Laski, "Democracy at the Crossroads", *Yale Review*, 9, (1921), 798, 800 ff.
90. See Laski's introduction to the translation of Duguit's book *Law in the Modern State*, and also Holmer/Laski Letters, 1916–35 (Cambridge 1953), quoted after B. Zylstra, *op. cit.*, pp. 48 ff.
91. *Democracy...*, p. 799.
92. Letter of 16 September, quoted after B. Zylstra, *op. cit.* p. 90.
93. H. J. Laski, "The Pluralistic State," *The Philosophical Review*, 28, 566.
94. *Authority...*, p. 81.
95. *Ibid.*, p. 374.
96. G. Jellinek, *System des subjektiven öffentlichen Rechts* (Berlin, 1892), pp. 12 ff, 201 ff. See also *Allgemeine Staatslehre* (Berlin, 1912), pp. 386 ff.
97. Fifth edn. (London, 1948), pp. xii-xiii.
98. See also H. J. Laski, "Law and the State", *Economica* (1929), pp. 267 ff.
99. K. Martin, *Harold Laski (1893–1950). A Biographical Memoir* (London, 1953), p. 74.
100. *A Grammar...*, pp. 335–8.
101. W. Y. Elliott, *op. cit.*, p. 167.
102. G. D. Carson, *Group Theories of Politics* (London–Beverley Hills, 1978), p. 20.
103. *A Grammar...*, pp. 82–3, 444 ff, 454 ff.
104. *Ibid.*, p. 62.
105. *Ibid.*, pp. 27–8.
106. *Ibid.*, pp. 69–70.

107. *Ibid.*, p. 141.
108. A. Hoog, "Les Théories d'Harold Laski et le pluralisme démocratique", quoted after M. Fourest, *op. cit.*, p. 36.
109. Hsiao, *op. cit.*, p. 163.
110. K. Martin, *op. cit.*

CHAPTER 4

Pluralism in the United States

4.1 FROM ONTOLOGICAL TO GROUP (SOCIAL AND POLITICAL) PLURALISM

De Tocqueville, admired as he was in America, did not directly inspire empirical studies in politics. The period necessary for the philosophical and sociological preparation of such studies must have elapsed before de Tocqueville found his way into American handbooks of sociology, political science and monographs devoted to interest groups. The foundations for such studies were laid by W. James, T. H. Cooley, and A. Bentley.

When it comes to James, we have to warn the reader against superficial associations based on terminology, and due to the fact that James himself often called himself a pluralist. Following G. W. Allen we can single out three aspects of James's scholarly and philosophical work: pragmatism, pluralism, and radical empiricism.[1] It is, of course, risky to try to compartmentalize the intellectual output of such a rich personality as James, the more so owing to the fact that James identified pluralism with radical empiricism. To make matters worse, James's pluralism was not of a kind with which the present book is concerned: his comments on pluralism were philosophical and ontological, whereas we are interested here in the social and political elements of pluralism. However, it is useful to bear in mind the fact that James's writings, his teaching work at many universities, and his personal contacts with eminent thinkers on both sides of the Atlantic paved the way for empirical research on those aspects of pluralism which interest us in this study. It was James and Peirce who influenced Oliver Wendel Holmes, members of the Metaphysics Club at Harvard University in the 1870s, and founders of the realist school in the theory of law, the school which came to play an essential role in overcoming the tradition of formalism in jurisprudence.

Parallel elements are to be found in Bergson (the stream of consciousness, to be discussed below). Sorel, too, was interested in pragmatism, perhaps because of the anti-intellectualism of that trend, and so was Durkheim, because of those elements which were close to sociological issues.[2] Harold Laski and the American economist A. A. Berle also sought inspiration in

James's work, and all of them only stand at the top of the long list of names that could be produced in this connection.[3]

If we have said about James's having merely paved the way for social and political pluralism, we have used that formula because of the highly abstract nature of James's reflections and because of the fact that his pluralism was aimed at idealistic monism.

James expounded his pluralist views in a number of minor writings, the most important of which are concerned with the dilemma of determinism, dated from 1884. James, it is true, made the reservation that we should not let ourselves be involved in such a controversy, because, as he put it, facts practically have nothing in common with our becoming determinists or indeterminists. Pluralism means such an interpretation of the world in which the various parts of the universe affect one another. It means seeing the universe as changing incessantly, a view which is difficult to accept for those who seek unity in the universe. In that diversity chance plays an enormous role. "I know that pluralism means chance and nothing more."[4]

A systematized argument against the monistic world view is to be found only in one of James's last works, namely in a series of lectures at Oxford University, published in 1909 as *The Pluralistic Universe*. The very close links between James's psychological views and his pluralism are beyond doubt, even though–unlike in the case of radical empiricism–the two cannot be identified.[5] His pluralistic antithesis of the monistic world was rooted in individual psychology, to which he contributed much through his laboratory research. In that field he must have been struck by a great variety of perceptions and individual responses, conditioned by different records of what had been experienced by a given individual. His pluralism assumes a plurality of individual worlds: every empirical subject creates his own world by guiding his own will.

These inner interconnections within James's pragmatic system are of essential significance, because they explain both the voluntaristic and deterministic nature of his pluralism and his use of the concept of stream of consciousness (cf. his *Principles of Psychology*, 1890), which corresponds to the stream of human experience. As James says in *The Meaning of Truth* (1909), pluralism reduces to the belief that the world is still being created.[6]

This dynamic concept will be used later, when the sociology of groups and political sociology adopt the concept of process and utilize it as an instrument in research.

James saw a parallel between the monistic vision of the world and the concept of state sovereignty. To the former he opposed the plurality of worlds, and to the latter, "polyarchy". However we imagine the all-comprising whole, something is always left outside to provide its environment. Things bear various relations to one another; they penetrate one another and combine with one another, but there is nothing that could comprise or dominate everything. Every sentence seems to have *and* behind it, and something always evades us. The pluralistic world resembles a federal republic rather than an empire or a kingdom. However great the concentration in an efficiently functioning centre of consciousness, something self-governing will always be left. The world cannot be reduced to unity.[7]

James's perspicacity, so far ahead of his times, is remarkable. The statement that every whole, if it is to function, must have an environment that can never be completely eliminated, complies with the present-day ideas of the systemic approach.

In political sociology and in the theory of the state James's formulations give no chance to totalitarian monism, whose endeavours to annihilate the social environment have been encountering impassable barriers.

It is also worth noting that the pluralistic element in James's pragmatism was in harmony with the pluralism of American society, which had never been cramped by political despotism. John Dewey, whose instrumentalism was a critical continuation of pragmatism, also took up the pluralist ideas. As a philosopher he criticized exuberant individualism (cf. his *Individualism Old and New*, 1932), and his theory of education, as has been pertinently noted by B. Crick, could not fail to influence political theory, because it advanced the idea of the individual as a product of groups functioning within society, those groups being treated by him as interest groups.[8] His pluralistic views were formulated in an expanded version in *The Public and Its Problems*, which was a study in political science. He says there that a human being, whom we treat as an individual, acts in co-operation with others, his activity is regulated by the group, and his experience cannot be sensibly described if he be taken in isolation. There is also an extremely significant formulation which refers to James's onotological pluralism: there is no single public, there is a universe of many publics, and hence there is no uniform society, but a society in which there are many social groups.[9] But an individual is never totally absorbed by any single group, since such a group reflects only one of that individual's many attitudes. In this way Dewey became one of those students of group sociology who paved the way for research on social roles.

Dewey singled out three levels of organizations of which an individual is a member: those which are closest to him; those with which his contacts may be infrequent and occasional because of the distance separating them from that individual (in the present-day sociological terminology they are called complex organizations); and the state. The public is a result of the activity of associated individuals; it becomes a state owing to its officials and their prerogatives. But it must be borne in mind that if there is no state without its highest authorities, there is likewise no state without the public. The state is a derivative of the social tissue, a form other than, but derived from, social associations. In agreement with his philosophical views Dewey treated the state not as a goal in itself, but as an instrument for supporting and promoting other voluntary social organizations. The state is to control groups, and not to form them. This instrumental function of the state led him to the conclusion that the state on an increasing scale would be replaced by groups that do not resort to coercion.[10] While stating that he was a pluralist Dewey cut himself off from more radical pluralists who, like Laski or–to a lesser extent–Bentley, reduced the role of the state to the level of other social organizations. Dewey thought that the plurality of human groups did not by itself mark specified boundaries of the activity of the state. The state could not be treated as merely an arbiter called upon to settle disputes among groups. Like MacIver,[11] Dewey assigned to the state a much more important role than did his contemporary pluralists; he saw in the state the conductor of an orchestra who by co-ordinating the movements of its members turns it into a whole.[12]

Dewey used to take up pluralistic ideas in his writings on educational issues, too. In one of his papers he demanded that individuals' participation in societal life be not confined to the highest authorities of the state, but cover the family, the school, and the world of business as well. Such a social democracy is necessary if we are interested in the all-round development of the individual. Barring the individual from participation in social life is in itself a subtle form of oppression.[13] This is a very important observation, since depriving the individual of the possibility of *actively* taking part in social life, blocking the paths along which individual enterprise can manifest itself, must effectively result in the alienation of individuals, so typical of totalitarian systems.

Process and group interests were conceived by Dewey as an aspect of structure: a structure means a slowed-down and controlled process, and a process, conversely, means a structure in action, so that they are two phases of the same reality, a static and a dynamic one. There is a certain analogy here with the work of Bentley. Dewey must have influence on both Bentley himself and his followers. Bentley used to attend Dewey's seminar, and later they corresponded extensively with one another on scholarly issues,[14] which yielded a book written jointly by them (*The Knowing and the Known*, 1949). But it must be borne in mind that Bentley's fundamental work on the subject appeared almost 20 years earlier than the book dedicated by Dewey to group pluralism. Dewey attracted Bentley by his neo-pragmatic instrumentalism, but, on the other hand, Dewey's group pluralism easily reveals Bentley's influence.

When seen in the perspective of over 50 years the work of Ch. H. Cooley seems a necessary bridge between James's ontological pluralism and the pluralism to be found in political sociology. At the turn of the nineteenth century the methods of individual psychology ceased to suffice, and those of social psychology became necessary. We disregard here his interesting conception of looking-glass self; that is, the social nature of the idea one has about oneself, advanced by Cooley in *Human Nature* (1902). In Cooley's work, it is the elimination of the opposition between the individual and society which is of special importance for the issues discussed in this book. An individual is an abstraction unknown in the empirical world, and the same holds for society analysed in separation from individuals. It is human life which is the real object; it can be treated both individually and societally, but in fact it is always both individual and general.[15]

But the priority of the group, which Cooley did not state explicitly, follows from the fact that the individual is shaped in social groups and as such forms an integral part of social processes. Social processes are essential for comprehension of society as a whole, and for interaction among groups. While the concept of social process was used by A. W. Small and E. Ross either before or simultaneously with Cooley, and although Ross treated process as the basic unit of sociological research,[16] it seems that Cooley and A. F. Bentley played a more important role in shaping the dynamic approach to social issues. This led to the study of that specific variety of social process which is political process. Interaction breeds various forms of consciousness: both self-consciousness and social consciousness; by the latter, when referred to the individual, Cooley meant what one thinks about others, and finally public consciousness, i.e. the collective view of the events taking place within the group; public consciousness reflects the communication processes within the group (discussions, interpenetration of ideas).[17] Public consciousness on the whole corresponds to the present-day interpretation of social consciousness, and recent research has confirmed the correctness of Cooley's viewpoint.

Cooley's analysis of primary, informal groups, within which people communicate with one another "face to face", has had a great cognitive value as it has opened various vistas and proved extremely fertile in practice. These are the groups in which the individual grows (the family), learns or studies (the school), works (vocational groups), engages in civic activity (committees, the jury, discussion groups), and rests (clubs).[18] They are an indispensable link between the individual and organizations.

G. H. Mead wrote in the conclusion of his paper on Cooley that the latter's great contribution consisted in placing the individual and those with whom he communicates on the same level of the reality which is being studied, and in treating society as derivative from associations and co-operation of primary groups.[19]

4.2. THE WORK OF A. F. BENTLEY

A. F. Bentley, an economist by training, had a very wide range of intellectual interests: the imprint of his thinking can be found in philosophy, logic, and political sociology. When it comes to group pluralism, it is mainly *The Process of Government* (1908) that counts. His later writings carry only additions to that synthesis, which was quite novel at the time of publication.

The responsibility for using the term *synthesis* rests with the present writer, because Bentley himself treated his book much more modestly as an attempt to fashion a tool. This meant a departure from the normative sociology characteristic of the preceding period and pointing to the necessity for an empirical study of facts, in particular the behaviour of social groups.[20]

Three concepts are essential for the proper comprehension of Bentley's ideas: process, group, interest.

Many references have been made to those philosophers and sociologists who happened to use the concept of process in a novel way: one could go back to Heraclitus when it comes to the dialectic values of this concept. In this case, however, it suffices to say that Bentley's inspiration is due to Darwin, whose theory of evolution made it possible to link the natural disciplines with the social ones. As we shall see, Bentley's work includes elements of social Darwinism, and his system has been termed by one of the authors as socio-cosmological dialectic.[21]

While P. F. Kress is right in stressing that Bentley was not the only one to use the concept of process in research on political sociology,[22] we have to add that no-one had before him applied the concept to an analysis of social groups.

H. Arendt points to the great role played by the idea of process in sociopolitical thought in the nineteenth and twentieth centuries; the idea became a kind of a common denominator of the natural and the social sciences (Arendt primarily means historiography). The idea of process assumes an end of the gap between the particular and the general, a single thing or event and the general meaning. It is only the concept of process that imparts meaning to events. We view everything in terms of a process and we are not interested in the isolated whole nor individual events and the particular course they take.[23]

The concept of process is of a special significance for the explanation of the chain of successive events in time, that continuum of occurrences from a given particular initiative taken by a group to the political decision in the form of a normative legal act or transaction (if it comes to that), which is general in nature. This is what a political process means, and not just some procedure, even though a segment of that continuum can be, and very often is, a procedure regulated strictly by law or by other social norms. The characteristic feature of Bentley's conception of political process was that such a process was interpreted as a conscious activity of groups, activity in the course of which negotiations are of essential significance.

Bentley thought that the raw material of the social sciences reduces to action, which he interpreted very broadly and emphasized that all action is goal-oriented and can be defined only by reference to some other action.[24] But in his writings process occasionally is identified with progress, which clearly means transformation of the Darwinian description of the evolution of species into an ordinary value-judgement.

A contemporary German author draws attention to the similarity between Bentley's idea, on the one hand, and Max Weber's interpretation of the concept of action, which he always referred to the behaviour of others, and Simmel's standpoint that we have to do with society whenever human co-operation yields temporary or permanent unity, on the other.[25] Bentley also made a distinction between action as external behaviour and tendency to act or potential action.

The idea of action as a process, which Bentley later expanded in his monograph *Behavior, Knowledge, Fact,* inspired those trends which are called political behaviourism and the theory of groups. Under Bentley's influence, politics came to be treated not as a manifestation of a societal crisis and the mutual adjustment of rival ideas and scattered institutions, but as a functional relationship between inseperable parts of the societal whole.[26]

Bentley included the written law ("law in books") in the social process, but he emphasized that he who wants to know what the process of government is cannot confine himself to the study of legal norms.

The process of government is neither in law books nor in the proceedings of the legislative assembly, but in the very process of law-making, administration, jurisdication, and that stream of human action which moves in that field. This anti-formalist approach was in Bentley's case combined with the growing influence of behaviourism in social psychology, manifested also in the views of Graham Wallas (cf. his *Human Nature in Politics*).[27] Bentley thus tried to remove the bonds of formalism, in particular those of legal formalism, since the formalist approach meant a static analysis of institutions and blocked empirical research on both the process of law-making and the functioning of the legal system. His opposition to formalism coincided with the new trend in American legal philosophy, represented by realists (O. W. Holmes, R. Pound, J. Frank, and others), and in economics, where a similar standpoint was taken by Ch. A. Beard (cf. his *Economic Interpretation of the Constitution,* 1913), who had been clearly influenced by Bentley; it also converged with the ideas to be found in the writings of Th. Veblen. It was the period termed by an American author as a revolt against formalism.[28]

When we pass to the concept of social group, we have to point out that Bentley identified the group with action in the sense of ascribing activity to groups only. By treating the social group as the basic subject-matter of research Bentley was not tilling a barren land. We have mentioned Simmel and Ross. The former, praised by Bentley for his clarity,[29] drew Bentley's attention to social psychology, reflected in the study of the forms of social action, and also in the analysis of interaction among groups. Such interaction among numerous groups shapes the personality of the individual.

Bentley studied Gumplowicz and Ratzenhofer as well. The former attracted his attention by the statement that the social process results from the very contact between two different groups which mutually penetrate their spheres of action. Group interaction underlies all social movements. Such an interpretation of a social process reduces the individual to a random factor.

Ratzenhofer's treatment of society as a mass of people[30] could not please Bentley, who nevertheless considered it important that Ratzenhofer analysed social life from the point of view of interests (some authors even believe that he was the first to have adopted this approach), among which he singled out particular interests, and that by social process he meant interaction among individuals not *qua* individuals but *qua* members of social groups.[31]

Bentley was fond of Durkheim because the latter explained social facts (treated as if these were "things") by reference to other social facts, and not to facts in the sphere of individual psychology, which assumed opposition between the individual and society. Like Durkheim, Bentley was looking for regularities and trends in social processes; like Durkheim, too, he treated law and legal customs as social facts. But Bentley went further than Durkheim had done because he did not accept the idea that social facts are external.[32] Bentley's approach can be formulated as the reduction of social facts to interaction among individuals within groups and, through the intermediary of the latter, among groups. The process of interaction makes the group differ from a crowd. As we have seen, Bentley identified group and action. The goal which a given group strives to attain may be to change the existing state of things or to maintain it by eliciting an appropriate political decision. Bentley's continuum of social process ranged from man to society.

S. Ratner[33] saw one of the principal merits of Bentley's book in the fact that he stressed the objective nature of the process of group differentiation, whereby the group is not reducible to individuals, that he did not treat groups as more or less closed wholes, and that he rejected the idea of man as a societal atom independent of any group.

The group was for Bentley the key for comprehending societal processes and thereby the fundamental unit object of research. He claimed that if we properly define groups, we define everything. And he added: "If I say 'everything', I mean everything." In that respect he differed antipodally from Homans, whose methodological guideline was to explain social behaviour in terms of individual behaviour.[34] This was why Bentley was consistent in reducing the process of law-making to a game in which interest groups engage. This left no room for the action of other factors, such as law experts, without whom legislation is inconceivable. On another occasion Bentley wrote that interest groups establish the government and act through its intermediary.

Yet he was blamed by his critics for not having explained the sense in which he used the term *group*.[35] It is worth noting that Bentley was interested solely in interaction among groups, but not in relationships within the group which made his concept of political process less comprehensive. On the other hand, it has been often stated pointedly that Bentley exaggerated the role of organized groups, which he claimed to be the only ones that reflect social ideas,[36] as if he failed to notice national interests, ideas and values that integrate the various groups, and that he accordingly was unable to draw a complete picture of the process of government. This was due to his specific neutrality: he failed to notice any hierarchy of interests, all interests were equally justified in his eyes, and all seemed to work in a political vacuum.

What was novel in his contribution to political sociology was his relating group action to political institutions. While he did make a distinction between informal and formal groups, he focused his attention upon the latter (voluntary associations) because of the role they play directly in the process of politics. Following Simmel,[37] he pointed to the importance of the fact– disregarded by Gumplowicz and others–that the individual is simultaneously a member of various groups (overlapping membership). Such a membership may cause tension in the individual if it exerts cross-pressures upon him, and may reduce his allegiance to one of the groups of which he is a member in favour of his allegiance to another. This is so because every group produces its own values and the individual often faces the necessity of choosing among them; he may accordingly have to do something which the present writer would term an *allegiance shift*.

Inspired in that respect by Ratzenhofer, Bentley linked the concept of group not only to that of action, but also to that of interest, interest manifesting itself in group behaviour. He started from the correct assumption that people form groups because they are led to do so by some interest of theirs; they would not co-operate in the long run if they did not see any interest in doing so. Group and interest are inseparable concepts. In *The Process of Government* he wrote that there is no group without interest, and that nothing is left if we try to analyse the group in isolation from interest.[38] While identifying group with interest he did not describe the latter concept clearly.

Bentley seems to have opposed traditional liberalism which knew individual interest only, but at the same time he cut himself off from the concept of objective interest. He was satisfied with the compromise statement that group interest means the common interests of those individuals who form a given group. But this is not all. The equation: group = interest, is complemented by another one: interest = action, as he says that *group* and *group action* are equivalent terms. This gives rise to serious objections, because the latter equation deprives the former of its heuristic value (it follows from the first equation that the individual does not explain social processes, in particular those which result in decisions made by state authorities; this is so because there are no isolated individuals, but there are individuals who are organized in social groups with a view of making their interests good).

This was penetratingly criticized by I. Balbus[39] who pointed out that Bentley by identifying group interest with group behaviour, produced a purely descriptive concept instead of linking the problem of group formation to "objective" factors in social structure. If interest means action, then obviously interest cannot explain action. If groups are everything, and if groups mean action, then all a researcher can do is to confine himself to *watching* group action.[40] In this way the process of group formation, which begins with an increase in social consciousness, is eliminated as a subject-matter of research. And while Bentley shifted the problem from the sphere of valuation to that of behaviour, and while he treated interest as group interest and not as individual interest, his reasoning in fact was parallel to that of representatives of classical liberalism: he treated interest as something accidental, not shaped by the social organization as a whole. It is, therefore, almost self-understood that he did not use the concept of global society.[41]

Bentley's reflection on the concept of interest made him criticize the conception of interest advanced by R. Ihering, the German theorist of law, whom Bentley otherwise valued highly. Bentley did admit that Ihering's approach was novel in his opposing both those theories which saw the origin of law in the will of the ruler and those which saw it in coercion. In Ihering's opinion, the utility of law is crucial for our comprehension of the very concept of law, because the concept of interest is the core of every right. But Bentley blamed Ihering for not having gone beyond the individualistic and static interpretation of interest. To make matters worse, Ihering later replaced the concept of interest by that of goal, without explaining the relationship between the two despite the fact that next to *goal* he used synonymously such terms as *motives, motive power, levers,* and *means*.[42]

While Ihering interpreted the individual from the societal point of view, he nevertheless preserved the opposition between the individual and society, or, to put it strictly, between a given individual and a given society. In that respect the order in which Ihering listed the goal-oriented actors: (1) the individual, (2) the state, (3) the Church, (4) associations, (5) society. It is obvious that although Ihering and Bentley jumped from the same spring-board of the concept of interest, they swam in different directions....

Much space was dedicated by Bentley to conflicts among group interests, whereby he paved the way for the modern theory of conflicts. He wrote that compromise is the essence of the activity of those groups whose interests clash: when conflicts become too drastic, the built-in tendency to strive for a compromise begins to work within society, and a stronger group emerges which interferes in order to eliminate the most radical approach that marked the original conflicts. *Adjustment, compromise,* and *balance* are nearly synonymous terms. The essential point is that balance, when established, prevents the using of the machinery of the state for the domination of one group by another.[43]

Lindblom was right in blaming Bentley for not having explained in what balance consists and why it is meaningful, and also for a lack of clarity in the formulation of the differences between balance and imbalance, adjustment and maladjustment.[44] Note also that Bentley, while he dissociated himself from the individualism of classical liberalism by his conception of balance, nevertheless retained ideological bonds with liberalism, and his ideas were in harmony with Adam Smith's theory of self-regulating market processes.

Without belittling the novel elements in Bentley's approach and the importance of dialectical elements in his theory we cannot confine ourselves to the criticisms outlined above and have to consider other weak points of his group pluralism.

Like Simmel,[45] Bentley dismissed class differentiation, in particular the theory of class struggle. The dynamics of social differentiation manifests itself in the process of politics. He treated classes as loose conglomerates of antagonistic groups. He accordingly thought that the concept of class was less useful as a research tool than group is, because classes lack unity.[46] The adoption of this view must have led him to false conclusions, the more so as he thought that in modern society there were no clearly outlined classes. Moreover, as has been noted by W. Hirsch-Weber, he used the terms *class* and *group* interchangeably.[47] Bentley knew the Marxist theory only super-ficially, and he thus reduced social differentiation to group differentiation. Yet the conceptions of class differentiation and group differentiation are not mutually exclusive, but one necessarily complements the other.[48]

Further, Bentley treated political parties as groups whose task was to discuss problems and to engage in organizational activity within the state.[49] This standpoint, which meant a confusion of the structure of interests with political structure (which includes political parties), had far-reaching con-sequences as it was adopted by many authors. The present writer will comment on this cardinal error, in which Bentley was not in isolation, later and at this point will confine himself to stating that Bentley extrapolated his shallow reflections on American political parties so as to cover all parties, because he assigned to his *Process of Government* the status of universality.

Third, Bentley was often criticized for his ahistoricism, and rightly so. In his interpretation, the free play of interests takes place without any historical conditioning and has no roots in the past.[50] Such ahistoricism is naturally concordant with the anti-Marxist standpoint in his theory and with his dislike of historical materialism.

Fourth, in analysing the various aspects of the process of politics Bentley reduced the government to one of the elements of that process. The state as a whole was, as it were, dismantled by him into the various government agencies, and ceased to form a political unity. Those agencies function as recorders of compromise solutions or, at best, as arbitrators in conflicts among groups, which are terminated by a compromise. Politics meant for him just trade. He was not interested in the state as a whole, because he saw in it a sum of those actions which can be subsumed under government. Government bodies sometimes act as spokesmen of potential groups, i.e. such which are not yet organized. Conceived in this way the process of

politics is a one-way process: it does not provide for the initiative of the
machinery of the state that could initiate a process in the reverse direction.
There is no place for the machinery of the state as a definite whole. In his
Relativity in Man and Society Bentley even placed the term *state* in quotation
marks and said that this term points to a vast complex of converging and
mutually reinforcing actions, which become representative enough to ensure
stability.[51]

What in the Marxist theory of the state, and in other trends as well, is
treated as parts of the machinery of the state is treated by Bentley as separate
interest groups; he fails to comprehend that they can occasionally be vehicles
of those interests, but that it does not follow therefrom that it is legitimate to
identify the two. In his theory there is no place for the autonomy of the centre
of political decisions and for its organizing function, because Bentley fails to
notice the integrating role of the state.[52] This led him to interpret the process
of government as a simple function of freely competing and co-operating
interest groups, as a result of the compromise solution they arrive at. This
viewpoint does not leave any place for an autonomous action of the political
structure, which is assigned a passive role.[53]

Obviously, problems of oligopolies and autonomous interference of the
state with economic and societal life were then not so clearly outlined as they
are now, but even in Bentley's times they were clear enough not to
substantiate his idealization of American democracy by the liberalism of
interest groups, an idealization which is largely to be found in *The Process of
Government*.

Classical liberalism atomized society at the individual level; Bentley
atomized it at the level of freely acting groups that enjoy equal rights.

Some of the critical remarks raised here should perhaps be modified if we
knew Bentley's book *Makers, Users and Masters in America*, with its criticism
of American capitalism; we can only guess that Bentley, a supporter of La
Follette's party, was not a benign critic. Unfortunately, the book has never
found a publisher, and its manuscript is still deposited in the archives of one
of the American universities.

4.3   MARY PARKER FOLLETT

These reflections cannot be concluded without mentioning the views of
Mary Parker Follett, a prominent personality, even though less known and
less renowned than Bentley. She started writing on industrial organization
and was probably the first to realize that management was the focal issue.
Later, she turned to problems of social and political structure. Her
fundamental work, *The New State*, appeared in the same year as *The Process
of Government* by Bentley, and she was also the first to go beyond the
framework of purely American experience; by confronting American and

British conditions she tried to formulate a general theory of social and political pluralism.[54]

Like Bentley, she adopted "the group principle" as the basis of political processes, which meant that she did not start from isolated individuals supposed "later" to organize themselves into complex wholes. Co-operation develops within and among groups. Unlike Bentley, she paid much attention to the integration of diverse group aspirations, as translated into the language of rational collective policies (especially in *Creative Experience*). Of all groups M. P. Follett attached special importance to neighbourhood groups, even though she was aware of the great role played by vocational groups.

On this point we notice another difference between her ideas and Bentley's conception, the latter having been attracted mainly, not to say only, by formal groups, and among them by the various vocational groups, while Follett emphasized the role of informal groups, which neighbourhood groups as a rule are. Those small groups were also to become the basis of political activity and of a non-partisan organization of voters. M. P. Follett's demands had a strong impact upon the study of local communities and local authorities in America. She assigned neighbourhood groups a really gigantic task: local communities were supposed to rise to the status of the principal "intermediate body" between the citizens and the government. They were expected to shape new citizens and new democracy, and to deal the "mortal blow" to political parties by (i) replacing the apparent unity of a given party with the genuine unity owing to the formation of genuine public opinion; (ii) making genuine leaders replace corrupt party bosses; (iii) bringing about the formation of a responsible government in lieu of irresponsible parties. A politician is the leader of the crowd, and not of the group. The state was thus supposed to consist of hierarchically organized representations of neighbourhood groups.

M. P. Follett did not take into account the growing migration movements that were intensifying as a result of rapid urbanization. The development trend in American society did not confirm her forecasts. Vance Packard in *The Nation of Strangers* described American society as ultra-mobile: one-fifth of the population changes residence at least once a year, and in some towns this applies to one-third of the inhabitants. M. P. Follett postulated that in the system she had envisaged neighbourhood democracy should be assisted by experts from the top downward, but the basic neighbourhood unit should preserve its own activeness and should not delegate its responsibility to the group.[55] While some of her ideas were obscure and even utopian, her critique of the capitalist system, combined with the tendency–which marked the difference between her views and the other pluralistic trends–to preserve the active role of the state, were quite remarkable. There were solidaristic and populistic overtones in her demand that all groups be equal and that none should dominate any other. On the other hand, she failed to notice the danger of conflicts between the state and the group,[56] conflicts which could make individuals face a difficult choice. This element of her views, and also her faith in the experts, made her work come close to the opinions of the Fabians, and especially of the Webbs.

Small groups, together with vocational organizations, were also to become the basis of the political activity of a non-partisan organization of voters (which was an idea that showed some similarity to the opinions of guild socialists). Such groups, she hoped, would develop in their members the sense of common goals (an idea totally alien to Bentley) and of mutual trust–features characteristic of new federalism.

H. S. Kariel, when describing M. P. Follett's views, stressed her attachment to values inherent in a pluralistic community, which for all its inner tensions can ultimately arrive at an equilibrium between interests and values. Follett identified individual freedom with a fully functional social order.[57]

Disciples of the pluralistic trend in America did not set themselves such far-reaching tasks. By carrying on Bentley's principal work they studied the inner life of pressure groups and the course of the process of history, as a result of which we have at our disposal comprehensive empirical data, traditionally, however, confined to America (S. Beer, La Palombara and some others being the few exceptions in this respect).

M. P. Follett's influence was not so wide as Bentley's but she may be classed, next to Veblen, as a critic of the American system. The said H. S. Kariel comments favourably on her writings. In this connection the present writer interprets *The New Federalism* by S. Seabury as an expansion, to some extent, of M. P. Follett's views. Seabury wants industrial management to be based on self-government and, to remain outside the interference of the state, it should be manifest in voluntary associations of workers, capitalists, and consumers active under the system of the new federalism based on functional representation.[58]

4.4 PLURALISM AFTER BENTLEY: THE FIRST CLASH BETWEEN ELITISTS AND NEO-PLURALISTS

Bentley's work, having encountered the barrier of academic traditionalism, formed of the various kinds of formalism and normative sociology, found no response for all its originality–or just because of it. Occasional positive evaluations, like E. Barnes's, included in the book on the then recent political thought, with Ch. E. Merriam as its editor,[59] were exceptional. Much time had to elapse before Bentley came to be accepted as the founder of modern pluralistic thinking in America, the first to show the role of organized groups in public life and to inspire empirical studies on that subject. The second edition of *The Process of Government* (1935) made only a small impression and things changed only much later as a result of two facts: the third edition of the book in 1954, and–more important still–the taking up of the first studies of organized groups. This applies primarily to P. H. Odegard's work on the prohibition campaign[60] and to E. P. Herring's book, *Group Representation Before Congress* (1929), where his idea of the process of politics was developed (to be followed by *The Politics of Democracy*, 1940). It is to be noted that Herring was among those pluralists who combined the study of group pluralism with stressing the role of the state: he emphasized that the very existence of the state proves that the goal is basically the same.[61] Other eminent pluralists included E. E. Schattschneider and O. V. Key, Jr.[62] and above all D. B. Truman. The latter's fundamental monograph drew inspiration from Bentley, which was indicated in the title: *The Governmental Process* (1951). It was only in 1950 that B. Gross's review of Bentley's opus appeared in *The American Political Science Review* and showed it in a more balanced way. It also came to be treated favourably by Earl Latham (*The Group Basis of Politics*, 1952), D. Easton (*The Political System*, 1954), and others.

On the other hand, in a UNESCO publication on political science B. E. Lippincot mentions Bentley among numerous American authors, but distorts his ideas and treats him as the author of a signal book on pressure groups, which *effectively influence political parties* (italics–S.E.); this groundlessly reduces the range of the problems raised in *The Process of Government*. In the same publication M. Faisod clearly alludes to Bentley by writing that the analysis of interest groups is an example of the typical trend in American political thought.[63]

D. B. Truman considered himself a disciple of Bentley's,[64] which is not to say that he lacked originality. While Bentley's starting point was the group identified with interests, in Truman's case it was the attitudes which the group members shared (shared-attitude groups). This idea of potential groups can also be found in Bentley (the tendency to act), but since Truman–unlike his master–did not identify action, interest, and group, he assumed correctly that while there is no group without interests, there can be interests without action, which means that interest is nothing other than potential action, or, in other words, an attitude shared by members of a given group.[65]

But the value of this novelty introduced by Truman is dubious, because it identifies groups with interest groups, and the latter with potential groups. But if an attitude means a state of readiness or possibility to act, then such an identification is groundless, because transition to action (to interaction) may be blocked by various factors, not to say that if it comes to action, then we no longer have to do with potential groups: we have to do with groups-in-action whether informal or formal, i.e. with organizations. I. D. Balbus blamed Truman for one further inconsistency; namely that Truman started not from potential groups, but from organized ones.[66]

On the other hand, Truman was very close to Bentley's views (which he elaborated in detail) on the issue of one and the same individual being a member of different groups. He started from the observation that in contemporary societies no group can satisfy all the needs of the personality of an individual, who as a rule is a member of more than one group.[67]

This assumes that the group must be treated not as a set of individuals, but as people who behave in accordance with a certain pattern of co-operation, or, as a jurist or a student of ethics would say, in accordance with a certain normative system. The statement that social disturbances end in a return to the previous equilibrium is in the Bentleyan spirit, too. And if such disturbances are intense or of a long duration, they give rise to new groups whose specialized function consists in bringing about a new equilibrium and a new adjustment of individuals in their customary interaction.

Truman's opinion has had many analogies in American political sociology, and we accordingly have to return to this issue; the same applies to the problem of public interest, whose existence is denied by Truman after Bentley.

As the Bentley–Truman school was gaining approval, naturally criticism was being voiced. W. Y. Elliott was one of the first critics, 2 years before the appearance of Truman's book.[68] But the turning point came with the advent of those authors who represented the American theory of élites. They strove to put an end to the prevalence of the school of group pluralism. The way for the new approach had been paved by both general studies, such as *Business as a System of Power* by R. A. Brady (1943), *The Managerial Revolution* by J. Burnham (1941), etc., and studies of local communities, such as *Middletown* (1929) and *Middletown in Transition* (1937) by the Lynds, *Street Corner Society* by W. F. Whyte (1943), *Plainville, USA* by J. West (1945), *Democracy in Jonesville* by W. L. Warner et al. (1949). All these studies strove towards the construction of a model of the social structures of local communities.

But the long controversy between the élitists and pluralists, a controversy not extinct to this day, has been typified by the works of C. W. Mills and Floyd Hunter.[69] In the synthetic overview of pluralism, attempted in the present book, there is, unfortunately, no possibility of considering all the aspects of that interesting polemic.

The said two leading élitists drew inspiration from Mosca, Michels, Pareto, and doubtless Burnham too, and accordingly advanced the claim that in the United States the ruling groups, at both the federal and the state and local level, consist of the most influential people, connected primarily with the large corporations and the world of the big business, who form the power élite. Mills singled out three categories: the corporate élite and the military élite, closely intertwined and in a sense dominant above the third, that of professional politicians. While we have to stress the importance of that distinction of the said three categories we have to bear it in mind that in Mills's theory the power élite forms a connected hierarchical whole, opposed to the inert masses. In his interpretation, this is a result of the trend which brought about the concentration of capital. In the nineteenth century, in de Tocqueville's America, the élite was still pluralistic in character and consisted of a number of loosely acting groups. As Mills put it, it was the period of "Romantic pluralism".

This statement follows from the picture of American society, which Mills saw as passive and apathetic, and alienated from public life in the sense of participation in the process of politics.

In the opinion of M. A. Rose, Mills in his appraisal of American society adopted at his starting point both the Marxian concept of false consciousness and Durkheim's *anomie*.[70] This "political neutralization" of a large part of society accounts for the fact that the power élite is incapable of rational and goal-oriented decisions, a conclusion advanced by Mills in the spirit of M. Weber and K. Mannheim.[71]

A. Hacker, who expanded Mills's thesis on the dominant position of the corporate élite in American society, emphasized that the said élite determined the prices, co-determined negotiations with trade unions about the wages, and had the exclusive say in the investments policy–that is, in the number of new jobs and in the economic development and stagnation of the various parts of the country.[72] There is, accordingly, no place for the idea of social equilibrium, one of the important theoretical principles of group pluralism, an idea drawn from the free play of economic forces on the market. A great role is also played in that system by the mechanism of negotiations, which helps restore the equilibrium once it has been disturbed. Nor is there any place for the state as the arbitrator, because the state functions as such in controversies between groups which carry more or less the same weight, but not in a situation where on the one hand there is a mass of scattered individuals and on the other three vertically integrated groups represented by the said three categories of élites.

Mills deliberately and consistently rejected group pluralism as an instrument of explaining the basic political processes in American society. The issue of interest groups is practically disregarded by him in *The Power Elite*, where A. F. Bentley is not mentioned even once. The theses advanced by Mills proved extremely catchy, and his book immediately became the subject of lively discussions. The book was translated into many languages, and published in socialist countries, too. His views even inspired President Eisenhower, who in his farewell message warned against "the military–industrial complex".[73]

Mills's book was certainly an answer to the apology of the system, suggested by the pluralist approach of the Bentley–Truman school. *The Power Elite* was the sharpest critique of the capitalist system based on the assumptions of that system, if we disregard the earlier works by Thorsten Veblen and M. P. Follett. As W. E. Connolly put it, the book gave vent to the disappointment caused by the hiatus between practice and promise in American politics.

Decisions made by a small élitist group keep large sections of society away from politics; this applies primarily to such non-organized groups as poor

Negroes, seasonal workers, and lower categories of white-collar workers. People who are barred from participation must naturally feel disappointed and discouraged; this is the case of the said sections of society who, as Connolly put it, have no say and thus cannot voice their protest.[74]

Floyd Hunter is another prominent personality in the élitist trend. His study in the structure of local authorities covered a new and important area of facts by the élitist critique. His standpoint can be reduced to the claim that in all local communities the centre of decision-making ("the hierarchy of power" in Hunter's terminology) is in the hands of businessmen. He focuses his attention on the structure of power and belittles the weight of group and individual interests as not essential for the problem with which he is concerned. Such interests are just absorbed by the institutions which form the structure of power.

It was only later that Hunter applied this idea to his analysis of the structure of political power at the federal level. Like in Mills, Hunter's panorama of American society strikes us by the emphasis on the domination of the monolithic world of big business. We can also mention R. O. Schulze as one of the many adherents of Mills and Hunter.[75]

In his studies of the structure of local power Hunter was probably one of the first to make use of the reputational method, which consists in finding, following a two-stage selection, which people are reputed in their local community to be influential and to have the final say on the major issues. The method has been used by many other authors and its application has almost become the identification mark of membership of the élitist school.[76]

The pluralistic critics of this method claimed that it assumes the existence of an élite regardless of whether it does exist in fact in a given case, and in particular regardless of whether the reputation of being influential is a good indicator of the real distribution of power or influence. In this connection it is worth noting the balanced opinion formulated by Wolfinger, who wrote that the reputational method could at best be treated as the first step in research on local politics.[77] We disregard the issue here because reflections on the legitimacy of the reputational method are beyond the sphere of the basic subject-matter of this book.

The writings of the élitists were criticized by the new generation of pluralists, who considerably modified the theoretical assumptions of the Bentley–Truman school. These modifications pertained above all to a better understanding of the role of the interference by the state, which is linked to a correction of the model of the state as the arbitrator. They also covered a more differentiated treatment of groups, among which the influence of complex organizations, such as large corporations and top bodies of trade unions, upon political decisions could hardly be questioned. There is also another characteristic which makes that trend, which we might term neo-pluralism, differ from the older version of pluralism. While the latter opposed formalism both in sociology and in jurisprudence and sought inspiration in pragmatic philosophy, neo-pluralism levelled its criticism at the neo-élitist theory of Mills and Hunter, but that criticism was not linked to any definite preferences in the philosophical approach.

In the opinion of the present writer, the main protagonists of neo-pluralism were R. A. Dahl, N. Polsby, and A. M. Rose.

The controversy with the Mills–Hunter school was opened by a critical paper by R. A. Dahl on the model of the governing élite, which found a wide response among both sociologists and political scientists.[78] Dahl excluded from the ruling élite the group in control which had been set up formally, i.e., as a result of the functioning of binding norms, Dahl raised the following objections:

(1) The ruling élite should not be confused with a group which has a considerable control potential. There may be many such groups which have a considerable control potential. Without questioning Mills's claim that the leading businessmen together with the leaders of both political parties have a great control potential, Dahl pointed to the fact that this may be accompanied by a low potential for unity of the two groups. A political effectiveness is just a function of both potentials.

(2) From the fact that a community lacks the political equality of its members it does not follow that there is a ruling élite in that community.

(3) From the fact that a group is influential in one field it does not follow that it is also influential in other fields, and only such a conclusion would confirm the hypothesis that an integrated élite exists and is at work.

(4) The principal objection raised against Mills and Hunter was that they had not investigated any series of definite decisions, and only such investigations could confirm the hypothesis on the existence of an integrated ruling élite. We have accordingly to assume (although Dahl did not state that explicitly) that the theory of élites is based on certain assumptions made *a priori*.

N. W. Polsby, closely connected with Dahl (through their studies of the community of New Haven), also criticized several times the studies of local communities carried out by the élitist school, and proposed in its stead the pluralistic approach.[79] Polsby introduced new elements by treating the élitists as advocates of a theory of social stratification, a theory which sees politics as just a simple consequence of such stratification. Hence the conclusion, assumed in advance, that the upper strata produced a definite and always active group, i.e., the power élite. The power élite may abstain from settling an issue only if that issue is of no great significance for it. But the pluralists claim that nothing can be said with precision on the élite, because it is unlikely that the same pattern of the process of decision-making would be repeated in another sphere in which a decision is to be made. Patterns of decision-making in a local community are almost the opposite of what the élitists claim them to be, and are rather of short duration. Instead of sticking to the idea of power élites it would be better to study the roles of leaders. They are varied and varying in a given sphere of social life, in which important decisions are made, and in a given time interval.

The papers with these statements were expanded into a book which came to play a special role in the controversy under consideration. It was Dahl's monography *Who Governs?* (1961), concerned with the structure of power in the city of New Haven. The answer given by Dahl to the question posed in the title was quite unambiguous: it proved impossible to find any definite group of people who could be said *always* (italics–S.E.) to make decisions on the key issues of the city (Dahl selected several kinds of such issues).

Issues are settled according to the sphere to which they belong. This is the most one could say about the various élites; their composition varies, because social life constantly produces new kinds of problems to be solved and/or issues to be settled. The answer to the question posed in the title of the book can accordingly be that of questioning the existence of a single power élite as a definite group. This answer has universal validity and is thus applicable not to New Haven alone, but to other local communities and to metropolitan cities, to the state level, and to the federal level as well. Whenever the question about who governs arises, the answer should be that suggested by Dahl. To sum up: power is exercised by little differentiated groups of "actors", which vary in their composition, and affect or settle specified kinds of issues.

It is striking that Dahl extrapolated the results of his research in New Haven upon the whole country, and also that he minimized the importance of the scope of participation in government and the resulting issue of the political apathy of the masses. He claimed that even if the majority was politically inactive and its (direct) impact weak, its indirect collective influence *was strong* (italics–S.E.)[80]

The social system interpreted as a highly differentiated and hence complex whole required permanent negotiations or "bargaining" if it was to function smoothly. The mechanism of that bargaining was analysed by Dahl in the study he wrote jointly with Ch. Lindblom.[81] He meant by it a form of the mutual supervision by the leaders who, as it were, mutually restricted the scope of decision-making. Dahl and Lindblom claimed that this technique in some form is to be found in every society, because conflicts resulting from differences of goals are accompanied by interdependence of groups in the implementation of their respective goals.

Ten years later, Lindblom reverted to this problem in a book of his own, where he advanced the hypothesis that decentralized power was under a constant pressure of the procedure of solving conflicts step by step and on the basis of compromise.[82]

These arguments were corroborated by N. Polsby, who linked the issues of local power to a general theory of politics. The book he wrote on the subject expanded his earlier paper discussed above, and also was intended to sum up the controversy that had been going on for years. Polsby stressed the role of numberless *small* (italics–S.E.) interest groups which are centres of power and thus affect other individuals, whereby they form an exceedingly complex whole which the American sociopolitical system in fact is. This self-evidently accounts for the incessant variability of the system. It is, therefore, not to be wondered that Polsby opposed the stratification theory, which assumed a relatively constant system of power relations. Like Dahl, he linked power relations to social issues which needed solution and which in turn could be either transient or more or less permanent (i.e. recurrent).[83]

Dahl's and Polsby's opinions were supported by McFarland, who blamed the élitists for having excessively simplified their model of power, which accordingly distorted social processes in a complex system; this was why such processes were better reflected by a pluralistic model, marked by a decentralized structure of power and by the functioning of what might be termed split causality.[84]

J. K. Galbraith, the noted economist, also is in favour of the pluralistic model; in *The New Industrial State* he writes (p. 397 in the London edition of 1967) that private associations make decisions on issues which concern them and this leads to a dispersion of power and thus the tyranny of the centralized state is being restricted. Unfortunately, we are not told how this occurs.

A. M. Rose, when referring to the leading American representatives of the pluralistic doctrine, does not deny the élitist claim that the undifferentiated masses form the social reality, but says that the core of society, its non-integrated groups, wield power whose scope and reach vary from case to case. To the élite theory he opposes the hypothesis on the plurality of influences, which questions the basic thesis in the élite theory, namely that on the dominance of the economic élite. In this connection Rose attaches much importance to the role played in American society by voluntary associations. In his opinion, the very existence of such organizations counterbalances the shortcomings of the mass society; it is in them that he sees a remedy against the danger of *anomie*. Without engaging in his analysis of voluntary associations we have to say that he introduced a new and important element of the discussion. He points to the fact that only few people from classes in low income brackets are members of the great many organizations that wield informal power. In 1935 those people started joining trade unions, but their influence upon the union policies is very small which results in their apathy and a dislike of being politically active.[85]

While he stands midway on many issues, his viewpoint could be summarized thus:

In many cases a small group of individuals wields the greatest power in the city, but such a group cannot be termed a power élite, because those influential individuals may disagree with one another and because their power is specialized and depends on the range of the issues to which it is applicable. The combined strength of those whose influence in the community is more limited may nevertheless prevail, and it occurs that the decisions made by those who are the most influential may be of "routine or trivial consequence to the community".[86]

If we disregard the last point, which is rather obscure and looks unconvincing, we can conclude that Rose's standpoint is not far from those of Dahl and Polsby. When it comes to the federal level, he adopts the opinion which is a continuation of what he said about local communities. He rejects Mills's and Hunter's claim that there is a hierarchical and uniform structure of power in which the decisive role is being played by the economic élite and which operates from behind the screens. Like Dahl, Rose places higher the political élite, which is not subordinated to the economic élite and has the upper hand.[87] While there are structures of power in every society, they are not uniform whether it comes to the economic or the political élites. Wherever there are elections the masses can to some extent restrict and modify the decisions made by the élite. Every élite can work only within its own sphere; in particular, in the case of the economic and the political élite one can affect the domain of the other. In view of the emergence of new "popular pressure groups" and their increasing consciousness Rose is optimistic about the issue of political apathy and the low level of the participation of the masses in public life. There is little evidence to prove that the world of business plays any major role in public life. He also advances the hypothesis that society as a whole is influenced by many different élites.

4.5 CONTROVERSY BETWEEN ÉLITISTS AND PLURALISTS (CONTINUED)

Neo-pluralism came to be strongly criticized by P. Bachrach and M. S. Baratz; in their paper on "Two Faces of Power",[88] which had a wide response, they blamed the neo-pluralists for what the élitists had been blamed by the pluralists, namely that they were making assumptions which predetermined the conclusions. They claimed that pluralists arbitrarily dismissed the problems of the social sources of power and concentrated on its functioning, the latter being manifest solely in definite decisions made on key issues. This linking of power with specified kinds of issues to be settled, the varying composition of the groups of decision-makers (which loosely resemble élites formed *ad hoc*), adjusted to the changes in the subject-matter of the decision to be made, are claimed to lead us to the conclusion that there is no constant group that would control the city. The other objection pertains to the possibility of blocking public discussions of certain issues, and also the possible influence of other (obviously weaker) groups. He who can block a public discussion of something wields real power. To support their standpoint they quoted E. E. Schattschneider, who claimed that every political organization tends to make a biased use of some conflicts and to put an end to others. For "Organization is the mobilization of bias. Some issues are organised into politics while others are organised out".[89]

It is, therefore, not legitimate to disregard the values and trends that are built into a political system and to begin with an analysis of decisions made. The dynamics of non-decision-making (the other aspect of power, to which the authors point) is no less important than the process of decision-making. In what does non-decision-making manifest itself? On the one hand, it is inherent in the veiled control of the process of making political decisions, control which consists in not responding to demands that come from below and pertain to allocation of means on behalf of the local community, with the resulting advantages for the various groups. Such demands can be blocked in a veiled manner or else can be suppressed before they are formulated or set forth. On the other, non-decision-making can take the form of activating the tendencies that are not favourable to demands from below, the great role being played by making use of existing systems of legal and social norms.

Bachrach and Baratz say that non-decision-making is the principal method preserving existing tendencies. The process of non-decision-making can take on various forms: next to the veiled ones it can consist in outright coercion intended to prevent change, in denying the legitimacy in the principles of the system, in appointing a committee that would discuss the demands made, or in strangulating the whole with red tape. Finally, co-opting the opponents is also an effective method of evading the necessity of change. Note that the last-named measure is also a tested technique of corrupting public life outside the United States.

All these tricks, the authors say, tend to preserve the social consensus on the basis of the *status quo*. Obviously, as seen by Bachrach and Baratz, the concept of decision is narrowed down to decisions that bring about a change in existing social reality. A social decision is one which results in a change in the group's behaviour.[90]

In a later work of his Bachrach wrote that the American political system failed to develop channels and institutions which would encourage people from the lower strata to formulate statements about what their interests are, and would make such formulations easy. Democratic co-participation is treated by him as a continuous process during which people formulate their demands, discuss them, and also make decisions on public issues which concern them. In his opinion, none of the existing forms of co-participation offers an opportunity to take part in the process of decision-making "on a regular face-to-face basis". It is common knowledge, he continues, that the overwhelming majority of the lower socioeconomic strata is apathetic and ignorant when it comes to politics, and that there is a (statistically) positive correlation between social status and participation in political life. People who are crushed by the toil of everyday life and locked, as E. Fromm put it, "in the prison of their loneliness", have neither vigour nor opportunity for transforming their bitterness and disappointment into articulate demands, for which fact the social system must be blamed. This refutes, Bachrach says, the assumption by the advocates of the pluralistic doctrine that the American political system is an open one. It is a fact that those who are not organized, who are poor and weak, are to a greater or lesser extent excluded from the political system. Their political protests usually do not give rise to conflicts big enough to influence those who make political decisions. This is the evidence of the powerlessness of the said lower strata.[91]

Bachrach and Baratz were not isolated in their opinion. They were supported in developing their idea of "non-decision-making" by such authors as Th. Anton, M. Parenti, and M. A. Crenson; the last-named writer produced a book based on empirical studies carried out in two cities and concerned with the mechanism of non-decision-making on the issue of air pollution.[92]

This standpoint was criticized (e.g. by G. Debnam) for making use of the concept of "non-decision-making" which lacks practical value and, to make matters worse, blurs the difference between the veiled control of societal processes and the blocking of demands by means of mobilizing those who are opposed to change.[93]

As seen by the present writer, the controversy over whether a "non-decision" is, or is not, a decision in itself is basically verbal. It is a matter of convention whether we adopt the narrower conception advanced by Bachrach and Baratz, or include in the process of decision-making both the fundamental decisions intended to preserve the existing state of things and all those subsequent decisions which derive from the former ones.

The essential point seems to be that Bachrach and Baratz are among those authors who question the claim that American society is marked by the pluralism of equal opportunities. That claim is undermined by polarization in the sphere of social status, in wealth, in the various forms of enjoying special privileges or benefits, in access to political decision-making, and in participation in public life.

There is no possibility of analysing all the subtleties of that most interesting discussion, but the reader's attention must be drawn to a striking evolution of opinions.

The fairly conciliatory standpoint adopted by Rose, on the one hand, and the radical critique of neo-pluralism by Bachrach and Baratz, on the other, raise the problem of whether the élite theory and neo-pluralism are in fact so strongly opposed to one another as it would appear from the duration and vehemence of that controversy. Mutual criticism has resulted in modifications of the original theoretical formulations, which is particularly striking in the case of Dahl's latest works[94] and in those by the second generation of American representatives of the élite theory (R. Agger, R. Presthus). Dahl, one of the most prominent theorists of neo-pluralism, denounced the term and turned to James to re-label it as "polyarchy", which in his case means a class of definite democratic systems drawing attention to the obvious antipathy between costs of tolerance and costs of repression. He symbolizes this antipathy in Figure 1. Polyarchy is interpreted as a mixture of élite rule and democracy (cf. his *Democracy in the United States...*, chap. 6), while the term *democracy* is reserved by Dahl to denote an ideal system. In this interpretation, the term *polyarchy* occurred sporadically in Dahl's earlier works, parallel with the term *pluralism*.

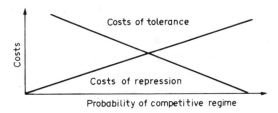

FIGURE 1.

Polyarchy can thus asymptotically approach the ideal of democracy and include some elements of the latter. In this way Dahl replaces the dichotomy of oligarchy and/or power élite versus democracy and/or polyarchy by a certain continuum, and suggests that polyarchy be interpreted as a certain set of points in that continuum (see above). This idea, which he stressed emphatically several times, illustrates the evolution of his views. But he is not consistent in that evolution of his: in the concluding part of his latest book (cf. note 94) we find a rather apodictic statement that the American political system is evolving at an astonishing pace towards polyarchy rather than towards any narrow oligarchy, while the latter is supposed to be dominant in Britain over the next few generations.

A renewed analysis of the data on socioeconomic conditions in the United States was not without effect upon the evolution of Dahl's views. He pointed in this connection to the broad scope of self-government in America (38,000 local communities apart from other forms of self-government) and took it to be one of the signal features of American polyarchy which has the Supreme Court as its guardian on the national scale. His reasoning also shows elements not to be found in his earlier works: in particular, he pointed to a lack of protection of special interests of those minority groups which are underrepresented or not represented at all. He also stressed the fact that voters do not take into consideration the political standpoints of candidates to Congress because they simply do not know what these standpoints are. It is significant, he wrote, that according to the latest data not less than 25 per cent and not more than 50 per cent of Americans are totally apolitical.[96]

These undertones of increased criticism recur in Dahl's *After the Revolution?* and other later writings: in them he discussed corporations as political oligarchies which owing to their vast power and negligible restraints working from the outside had become a destructive force within the democratic system.[97]

G. Parry, who presents an excellent analysis of the pluralist–élitist controversy, characterizes "poligarchy" in the following way: "Equal political participation does not exist but neither is there a single élite. Minorities and their leaders will tend to be specialists in their own issue areas. The politicians who aim at the positions which will give them the overall view of the battle are themselves dependent on the support of the many authorities."[98] Parry rightly points out that the counterpart of the élite in all these theories is the mass, with its characteristic feature–inertia.[99]

From the fact that pluralists exclude the possibility of social and political emotions being controlled, in periods of tension, by any single group, it does not follow that no élites emerge from the privileged groups and strata. It is in this spirit that neo-pluralists are criticized by Agger and W. Domhoff.[100] The latter blames neo-pluralists for disregarding the fact that 1 per cent of the population has excessive wealth and income, holds key posts in industrial and financial corporations, in government, in the largest universities and foundations, and in the mass media.

Agger and other authors point to the fact that the poorest categories of the people do not participate in voluntary organizations and have little influence upon the decisions made in the communities in which they live.[101] A similar conclusion has been reached by W. E. Connolly, who criticizes the illusion that pluralism ensures development of personality, protects the rights and freedom of individuals, enables them to formulate their demands and have them satisfied, and favours gradual change on the basis of a long-term stabilization, supported by the common acceptance of the system (in this connection see the opinion of D. B. Truman). This illusion is refuted by the fact, which everyone can notice, that only a small number of people, members of upper socioeconomic groups, participate in the life of political parties and interest groups.

Yet Connolly does concede that the policy of equilibrium is a characteristic feature of the American process of politics, and that pluralist principles must be included in the ideal of contemporary society.[102]

Note that all this is linked to the fact that the lower strata have little contact with members of the upper classes. These invisible but effective barriers restrict the opportunities for taking part in the process of politics.

H. Kariel even earlier drew attention to the fact that the authorities (boards, etc.) of large national organizations that represent certain particular interests, which owing to their power had won an officially recognized status, in fact represent the interests of a small section of the members, namely, the most influential ones, so that such large national organizations work for organized élites. The state authorities, by accepting the élites in those organizations as spokesmen of certain particular interests, in fact freeze the existing state of things and thus paralyse the opposition that may develop within any such organization.[103] Kariel quoted two cases: that of the International Brotherhood of Teamsters, which was being controlled in a dictatorial manner by the ex-convict Hoffa, and the American Medical Association, in both of which those who opposed the authorities of the Brotherhood or the Association had no chance in the struggle for their demands.

The authors quoted above have confirmed, with their American data, Michel's pessimistic appraisal of the situation, namely that organization means oligarchy. This critique of unidimensional pluralistic policy was also supported by H. Marcuse.[104]

Th. Lowi's criticism of pluralism came from different quarters: he questioned the very foundations of that trend as formulated by Bentley and Truman, he ascribed to them, and to the pluralist doctrine in general, the focusing of attention on social equilibrium that emerges spontaneously as interest groups co-operate. His criticism was levelled mainly at the new liberalism of interest groups, that new trend being an amalgam of capitalism, statism, and pluralism, the last-named element being treated by him as the intellectual centre of new liberalism. He saw the way out in liberating American society from that element and in revaluing the position of the citizen, who has been driven out by representatives of the various group interests.[105]

If we disregard the fact (analysed thoroughly by G. Tournon[106]) that Lowi distorted Bentley's and Truman's views we have to say that his criticism applies not so much to the theory of pluralism as to its underlying ideology. It is that philosophy which is blamed for all the undesirable aspects of contemporary American society, in particular for the elimination from the process of politics of entire sections of that society, participation in that process being one-sided and warped in favour of privileged groups. It is those privileged groups which, by availing themselves of their more efficient organization and the various means of influencing the masses (not financial means alone), bar the "expropriated" members of society from access to the making of political decisions.

Lowi thinks that the dominance of organized interests, consolidated under the New Deal, has resulted in the hierarchization and petrification of society.[107] He sees the remedy in restoring the law to its due rank and in clipping the practice of delegating legislative prerogatives to the various executive bodies, which would mean increasing the role of Congress in the system of the highest authorities in the country. A special role in modifying existing political practice is assigned by him to the Supreme Court, which should see to it that all delegation of prerogatives to administrative bodies be rigorously controlled so as to exclude any further expansion of the prerogatives of those bodies as a result of the prerogatives accorded to them originally.[108]

Lowi's book is the most radical criticism of pluralism, because it negates all tradition in that sphere, a tradition whose cornerstone was a scattering of power due to the functioning of interest groups. His criticism, often superficial and idealistically naive, meant, as has been stressed by Tournon,[109] a return to Rousseau and to the glorification of majority rule. It is to be borne in mind that the ruthlessness of such majority rule has recently brought about a revolt of black Americans. For all these shortcomings Lowi's book has the undertones of the critical passion of Veblen, which also marked the writings of C. Wright Mills. It seems, nevertheless, that the work of Robert Presthus is much more balanced, and it accordingly deserves our attention.

Like some other American experts in political sociology, Presthus began by studying local élites (cf. his *Men at the Top. A Study in Community Power*, 1964), to pass to a comprehensive comparative study of the élites in Canada and in the United States, a study based on extensive empirical research.[110] While in *The Power Elite* by C. W. Mills the problem of interest groups does not appear as an element of the political system, Presthus studies relations between interest groups and the élite. Among the interest groups he singles out those which are politically active; those which have access to some elements of the political system and can influence them; and those which form subélites. All of them are included in the general political élites of the United States and Canada, respectively.

Presthus notices in interest groups mechanisms that link a non-organized individual to the formal political machinery as a social subsystem.[111] Interest groups thus synthesize diverse and often mutually incompatible individual demands. By doing so they make it easier for the highest agencies in the state to fix social goals, to distribute means, and to resolve conflicts. This formula, advanced by Presthus, clearly indicates that he cuts himself off from exaggerating the role of pressure groups, which was typical of both Bentley and Truman and neo-pluralists. The essential feature of the functioning of those groups is manifest in the fact that their leaders are, on account of their competence, asked to take part in running federal programmes. Trying to do without such expert opinion would be risky for the system as a whole. At the same time interest groups broaden, in principle or in theory, the opportunity for a democratic participation of citizens both in group actions and in a given political subsystem, which does not exclude the possibility of such participation often being merely symbolic in view of the distance that separates rank-and-file members of the group from the centres of decision-making. This would confirm the universal validity of Michel's "iron law of obligarchy" in complex organizations. This is just one of the causes of political apathy and lack of adequate information about the process of government.

The role of interest groups also consists in their supporting the political subsystem ideologically, which reinforces the social legitimacy of that subsystem. The basic techniques of that liaison function are those of negotiation and consultation. In Presthus' opinion, the role of the élite of interest groups in defining national goals and the means whereby to attain such goals is no less than that of the political élite. The latter cannot work in a vacuum, and to perform its role it must constantly interact with those organizations which represent major interests within society. Those interactions have been termed by Presthus *élite accommodation*; he has written a book devoted to the issue.[112]

Unlike the neo-pluralists, Presthus does notice the fact that when it comes to the intensity of contacts with, and the effectiveness of influence upon, the government agencies the pride of place among interest groups goes to organizations of industrialists, whereas trade unions hold one of the last places, behind consumer co-operatives, farmer organizations and organizations representing liberal professions.[113] This is understandable, because organizations of industrialists exceed other groups not only by the means they have at their disposal, but by prestige as well. Hence the greater frequency not only of their contacts with federal agencies, but also of statements made by their representatives at hearings by Congress committees and state legislatures.[114]

Élite accommodation develops bonds among the élites involved, bonds based on exchange of information and on common values. The most natural bonds are those between leaders of given interest groups and officials in government agencies, which is due to the functional basis of the process of government and conditioned by the division of prerogatives within the federal administration. All this produces a common substratum of interests. This socioeconomic homogeneity and the common professional base (there is no need to mention the large role played by lawyers both in the world of business and in the governing élite) favours accommodation and the emergence of an ideological poltical and social cohesion of those subélites which co-operate with one another. Presthus' opinions on the issue come fairly close to what Ch. Lindblom wrote in *The Intelligence of Democracy*.[115] Co-operation among those subélites ensures the continuity of contacts, the more so as the subélites in question consist of members of the middle and the upper class. Bonds are easily consolidated through frequent social contacts, be it alone in more or less exclusive clubs.[116]

The question arises quite naturally as to what is the difference between the subélite of an interest group and the governing subélite. Presthus answers that he sees the essential difference in the fact that managers from interest groups never formally assume political power, nor assume responsibility for the ways in which the country is governed.[117] When it comes to interest groups, only one-quarter to one-third of their members take part in the process of politics, and it is only they who count. Other groups are excluded from it because they have no access to the political élite, or their access to it is limited. The issue becomes significant in the light of the studies carried out within organizations (Presthus examined 1400 groups);[118] now four-fifths of members of those organizations have to be classed as middle class or upper middle class people, the average for the United States being 44 per cent. The persons in question are usually educated and fairly rich and hold high positions in their respective professions. That regularity is even more manifest when we consider individuals who are members of more than one organization or association: this testifies to a high level of education, considerable political involvement, and a socioeconomic status which is above the average.

All this accounts for the fact that the import of groups of industrialists is greater than that of other interest groups; this in turn marks the boundaries of genuine participation in politics (one-quarter to one-third of all organized groups). Large groups of manufacturers are indispensible elements of the American political system. It may thus be said that the comprehensive process of accommodation covers three subélites: legislators (at the federal and the state level), high officials in central federal agencies, and about one-quarter of the politically active members of interest groups (managers, lobbyists, etc.). These three categories yield, as a result of contacts of long duration, a coherent whole, namely the political élite. This may be treated as an answer to Dahl's question: who governs?

Presthus' reasoning enables us easily to trace the evolution of American political thinking on the matter in which we are interested here. Both Agger and Presthus abandoned Mills's rigid division of the élite into three vertical groups, with the role of the political élite belittled in a marked way. They recognized the role of interest groups and the élite that emerges from those groups as an indispensable element of the American political system, but they also pointed to the fact that this situation gave only limited opportunity for participation in the process of politics.

The standpoint adopted by S. Verba and N. H. Nie is close to that of Presthus; they emphasize that individuals at lower social levels are less likely to be active members of social organizations, such organizations being only potential instruments of reducing the hiatus between the involvement of the privileged and the non-privileged in society.[119] In fact, categories of those individuals who are socioeconomically privileged and make the appropriate use of their means, become active members of the various associations and political parties and thereby increase the said hiatus where participation in public life is concerned. This obviously reduces the opportunities for supervision by fellow-citizens. To put it briefly, it follows from Verba and Nie's studies that those who are richer are more active. This is so because people whose acute personal needs remain unsatisfied are less involved in the various kinds of social activity than those who do not face such problems. Those people whose social status is high make up more than one-half of those with the highest indicator of participation in public life. The said authors sum up their reasoning in the form of the schema shown in Figure 2.[120]

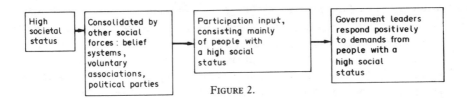

FIGURE 2.

Unfortunately, the said authors prove inconsistent when they claim that institutions which promote participation in public life are *politically neutral* (italics–S.E.), even though there is no equality in making use of them. Further, they state that participation in public life is a powerful force which increases or reduces inequality. But that depends on who avails himself of that participation.[121] Would that be a matter of free choice? In any case, the book suggests that the American political system has a kind of brake built in to it, which bars the masses from participating in public life.

If we disregard the various modifications of the standpoints adopted by the various authors, the controversy between the élitists and the pluralists can be summarized thus (the formula being necessarily simplified): the former are quite critical of the capitalist system, especially in its American version, but they do not suggest any solutions; the latter reveal an apologetical inclination (tempered in the later period), so typical of group liberalism initiated by Bentley.

D. Nicholls is ironical about the philosophy of American conformism and quotes Shils who said that a large number of groups would be tolerated as long as their demands were moderate and members of the groups would not be too strongly or radically attached to their respective particular values. Pluralistic society consists of those who lead and those who are led, and its élites must feel that they belong to each other. Rockefeller, greatly experienced in politics, says openly that there is no better system of government than the American one, based on a flexible political structure of democracy, on individual enterprise and on responsible citizens, a system that could more effectively improve the quality of human life.

When commenting on these statements Nicholls says that pluralism is American and hence it is good.[122] While his book has appeared recently, his irony is somewhat obsolete. We have assigned so much place to the controversy between the élitists and the pluralists to draw the reader's attention to the fact that American sociopolitical thinking is in a state of 're-evaluating its values'.

One could add to the Nicholls analysis that the pluralist equilibrium with its "rules of the game" was in practice overruled during the Vietnam war by outbursts of student and black revolt, overt and latent. The facts challenge the assumption of an equilibrium due to overall consensus. The view here expressed is not quite alien to D. Apter's opinion when he wrote that "pluralism drew directly on the inheritance of institutionalism and it was itself interpretable as a form of élite theory".[123]

Some statements made by élitists could easily be replaced by the well-known formulations which say that the superstructure serves those classes and strata which have the means of production at their disposal. But using the Marxist terminology is not an indispensable condition of engaging in a dialogue on scholarly issues between the West and the East. The important point is that this discussion between the different types of élitists and pluralists shows their fascination with egalitarian American pluralism, so marked in de Tocqueville, is now a thing of the past. It is true that Americans have been brought up in a mesh of diverse organizations and voluntary associations, but the polarization of wealth and of the possibility of deciding what the other people's behaviour should be, the monopolization of broad participation in public life by the upper and middle classes, combined with the sense of powerlessness on the part of the lower classes, provide probably the best explanation of the apathy in American political life, apathy which has become permanent. Having compared the present-day conditions with the picture of American political life drawn by de Tocqueville we must say that the observable rapprochement between the standpoint of the pluralists and that of the élitists suggests the conclusion that pluralism has been greatly narrowed down in present-day social life in the United States; this, obviously, is not the final verdict.

Next to the authors discussed above we could indicate those who point to the ambiguity of the term *pluralism* and claim that it cannot be identified with American democracy,[124] and those who, while continuing the criticism of the capitalist system to be found in the writings of Thorsten Veblen, emphasize that America is governed by a "hierarchically structured, bureaucratically managed organization", which Galbraith terms technostructure, that the power is wielded by supercorporations and that this "corporate state" is marked by a symbiosis with the executives. The United States has thus come to be controlled by largely autonomous élites which rest on a narrow social base.[125]

American pluralists often ignored the fact that some associations could be more burdensome for their respective members, as S. A. Lakoff has pointed out, than the state whose agencies are bound to observe the law.

We have intentionally confined the discussion of pluralism in America to the controversy between two schools and their followers. But pluralistic elements in American sociology and political science originate from other assumptions, too. Thus, when concluding this chapter we have to mention the trend which bases its theoretical reflections on research in the applications of mathematics and systems theory to social and political issues. Here we are thinking above all of the two Seminal works by K. W. Deutsch (*The Nerves of Government*) and D. Easton (*A Systems Analysis of Political Life*). To Easton we owe the formulation that the systemic feedback turns heterogeneity into homogeneity.[126]

A few remarks may be useful before closing Part I. In the last few years a new trend has come to our attention. It was, if not antipluralist, certainly very critical of the pluralist concept. The conviction grew up that pluralist trends were undermining sovereignty–to be precise, undermining the role of the political decision-making centre as an arbitrator and co-ordinator–that they were playing down the indispensable limits to pluralism, and underestimating the necessity to co-ordinate the interests of the public and private sectors.

These views of the neocorporatists (put above into a nutshell and therefore simplified) very carefully stressed the deep differences between the new and the old corporatism which was shaped–as we remember–by Italian Fascism. However, neocorporatism quickly gained new ground, because it seemed to be confirmed by the inexorable process developing in the West of aggregating the fundamental social interests within the framework of political structure (D. Bell, G. D. Carson, P. C. Schmitter). This trend was not without influence on West European thought (G. Lehmbrusch, R. J. Harrison, C. Offe, H. Wiesenthal, L. Panitch).[127] The latter of those authors regards corporatism "as a political trend within advanced capitalism which integrates organized socioeconomic producer groups through a system of representation and co-operative mutual interaction at the leadership level and mobilization and social control at the mass level".[128]

The limits to pluralism are one of the main problems put forward by the neocorporatists.

Without going into detail, what kind of comments could a researcher from the East make? From this vantage point, it is striking that none of the many pluralist trends in the social and political sciences could be considered as dominant. If one were, all attempts to refute it would be futile.

NOTES AND REFERENCES

1. G. W. Allen, *William James. A. Biography* (New York, 1967). See also E. C. Moote, *William James*, (New York, 1965).
2. E. Durkheim, *Pragmatisme et sociologie* (Paris, 1955).
3. On the interpretation of two Anglo-Saxon pluralisms see J. Wahl, *Pluralist Philosophies in England and America* (London, 1925).
4. W. James's paper, "The Dilemma of Determinism", was reprinted in collected papers, *Essays on Faith and Morals* (London, 1949).
5. See A. J. Reck, *Introduction to William James* (Bloomington, 1967).
6. W. James, *The Meaning of Truth* (New York, 1909), p. 226. See also H. Schmidt, *Der Begriff der Erfahrungskontinuität bei W. James und seine Bedeutung für den amerikanischen Pragmatismus* (Heidelberg, 1959).
7. W. James, *The Pluralistic Universe* (New York, 1909), especially the chapter on "The

Continuity of Experience", and "Conclusions".

8. B. Crick, *The American Science of Politics* (London, 1959), Chap. 4, "The Circularities of Pragmatism".
9. J. Dewey, *The Public and Its Problems* (New York, 1927), pp. 8, 188.
10. J. Dewey, *Reconstruction in Philosophy* (New York, 1920), pp. 202 ff.
11. R. M. MacIver, *The Web of Government* (New York, 1947), p. 56.
12. J. Dewey, *The Public* ..., p. 73 ff.
13. J. Dewey, "Democracy and Educational Administration" in: *School and Society*, vol. IV (1937), pp. 457 ff.
14. D. G. Smith, "Pragmatism and the Group Theory of Politics", *American Political Science Quarterly*, vol. 58 (1964), no. 3. See also D. B. Truman, *The Governmental Process* (New York, 1951), p. 14, and B. Crick, *op. cit.*, pp. 91 ff. An essay in interpretation of Dewey's thought can be found in S. R. Peters (ed.), *John Dewey Reconsidered* (London, 1977).
15. Th. N. Newcomb, *Social Psychology* (quoted after a Polish-language version, Warszawa, 1970. See also two books by Ch. H. Cooley, *Social Organization* (1909), and *Social Process* (1918).
16. J. Szczepański, *Socjologia (Sociology)*, (Warszawa, 1961), p. 12.
17. Ch. H. Cooley, *Social Organization* (New York, 1909), p. 10.
18. S. Verba, *Small Groups and Political Behaviour* (Princeton, 1961), p. 17.
19. G. H. Mead, *On Social Psychology. Selected Papers* (Chicago and London, 1956), p. 307.
20. Cf. A. Leibson, "Problems of Methodology in Political Research", in: H. Eulau *et al.*, *Political Behavior. A Reader in Theory and Research* (Glencoe, 1956), pp. 53 ff.
21. M. O. Hale, "The Cosmology of A. F. Bentley", in: W. E. Connolly, *The Bias of Pluralism* (New York, 1969); see also S. Ratner, in: W. Taylor (ed.), *Essays in Honor of A. F. Bentley*, (Yellowstone Springs, 1957), p. 53.
22. P. F. Kress, *Social Science and the Idea of Process. The Ambiguous Legacy of A. F. Bentley* (Urbana, 1970), p. 11.
23. H. Arendt, *The Human Condition* (Garden City, 1959), and in particular *Between Past and Future* (New York, 1961), by the same author, pp. 61 ff, 64.
24. A. F. Bentley, *The Process* ..., pp. 176, 275, 328.
25. *Ibid.*, pp. 177, 213, 217. See also W. Hirsch-Weber, *Politik als Interessenkonflikt* (Stuttgart, 1969), pp. 40 ff; G. Simmel, "Die Selbstverwaltung der sozialen Gruppen, Soziologische Studien" *Jahrbuch für Gesetzgebung und Volkswirtschaft*, Jahrgang 22, Heft 2, quoted after W. Hirsch-Weber, *op. cit.*, p. 26. Simmel's influence upon Bentley is also discussed by S. Ratner in his introduction to S. Ratner and J. Altman (eds), *John Dewey and A. F. Bentley. A. Philosophical Correspondence 1932–51*, (New Brunswick, 1964).
26. On this issue see H. S. Kariel, *The Decline of American Pluralism* (Stanford, 1961), p. 131; L. Weinstein, "The Group Approach: A. F. Bentley", in: H. Storing (ed.), *Essays on the Scientific Study of Politics*, (New York, 1962).
27. This convergence of the views of Bentley and Wallas, which favoured the expansion of behaviourist opinions, was demonstrated by E. M. Kirkpatrick (see "The Impact of the Behavioural Approach on Traditional Political Science", in: A Ranney (ed.), *Essays on the Behavioral Study of Politics* (Urbana, 1962).
28. K. Opalek, and J. Wróblewski, *Współczesna teoria i socjologia prawa w Stanach Zjednoczonych (Present-day Theory and Sociology of Law in the United States)*, (Warszawa 1963). See also M. White, *Social Thought in America. The Revolt Against Formalism* (Boston, 1959). On Beard cf. Th. I. Cook. "Les Méthodes de la science politique notamment aux Etats Unis", in: *La Science Politique contemporaine* (Unesco, Paris, 1950), p. 83.
29. He paid much attention to Simmel in his later work, *Relativity in Man and Society* (New York, 1926), chap. XX, "Simmel, Durkheim, Ratzenhofer".
30. G. Ratzenhofer, *Wesen und Zweck der Politik. Als Teil der Soziologie der Staatswissenschaften* (Leipzig, 1893).
31. A. F. Bentley, *Relativity* ..., pp. 158 ff.
32. *Ibid.*
33. S. Ratner, "Introduction to A. F. Bentley", *Relativity* ..., p. 8.
34. G. C. Homans, *Social Behavior. Its Elementary Forms* (New York and London, 1961), p. 30: "... we need no new propositions to describe and explain the social. With social

behavior nothing unique emerges to be analyzed in its own terms. Rather from the laws of individual behavior ... follow the laws of social behaviour ... ."

35. A. F. Bentley, *The Process* ..., pp. 208 ff., 224 ff., 230; P. H. Odegard, "A Group Basis of Politics: A New Name or an Ancient Myth", *Western Political Science Quarterly* (1958), **XI** (3).
36. Ch. Londblom, *The Intelligence of Democracy. Decision Making Through Mutual Adjustment* (New York, 1965), p. 13.
37. G. Simmel, *Ueber soziale Differenzierung* (Leipzig, 1890), Kap. 5, "Ueber die Kreuzung sozialer Kreise", pp. 103 ff.
38. Cf. *The Process* ..., p. 21 *et passim*.
39. I. D. Balbus, "The Concept of Interest in Pluralist and Marxian Analysis", *Politics and Society* (1971), **I** (2), 158.
40. W. Hirsch-Weber points to the fact that Bentley programmatically used the word *description*. See *Politik* ..., p. 29.
41. In this connection R. M. MacIver's statement that Bentley rejected the integrating function of the state, seems well grounded. Cf. *The Web* ... p. 56.
42. A. F. Bentley, *The Process* ..., chap. I.
43. *Ibid.*, pp. 208, 372.
44. Ch. Lindblom, *The Intelligence* ..., p. 24, in connection with A. F. Bentley, *The Process* ..., pp. 264 ff.
45. To put it precisely, in the book referred to above he ignored the problem of class struggle.
46. A. F. Bentley, *The Process* ..., pp. 304, 465 ff.
47. *Ibid.*, pp. 319, 362 ff.; W. Hirsch-Weber, *Politik* ..., p. 134.
48. Bentley openly admitted he was not competent on the issue of the Marxist theory. Cf. *Relativity* ..., chap XX. On the indispensable complementarity of class and group differentiation see S. Ehrlich, *Le pouvoire et les groupes de pression* (Paris, 1971).
49. A. F. Bentley, *The Process* ..., pp. 400 ff.
50. B. Crick, *The American* ..., pp. 128–9; W. Hirsch-Weber, *Politik* ..., pp. 27, 61, 202.
51. A. F. Bentley, *Relativity* ..., p. 49.
52. A. F. Bentley, *The Process* ..., *passim*; R. M. MacIver, *The Web* ..., p. 56.
53. S. Ehrlich, *op. cit.*, pp. 429–30.
54. Her major works were: *Creative Experience* (London, 1924); *The New State. Group Organization, the Solution of Popular Government* (New York and London, 1926) (1st edn, 1908); *Dynamic Administration* (New York, 1942) (collected papers published posthumously).
55. M. P. Follett, *The New State*, pp. 237 ff., 339 ff. If Mary P. Follett was only partly right to consider neighbourhood as an important element of society's pluralist tissue, one cannot miss drawing attention to the rebirth of research interest in this field in recent times. J. Thorpe (ed.), *Decentralist Trends in Western Democracies* (London and Beverly Hills, 1980) and particularly in this volume: F. Kjellberg: *Neighbourhood Democracy in Oslo and Bologna*; W. Magnusson: *The New Neighbourhood Democracy: Anglo-American Experience in Historical Perspective*.
56. *Ibid.*, p. 312.
57. H. S. Kariel, *The Decline of American Pluralism* (Stanford, 1961), p. 163.
58. S. Seabury, *The New Federalism* (New York, 1950), pp. 21, 302 ff.
59. E. Barnes, "Some Contributions of Sociology to Modern Political Theory", in: Ch. E. Merriam (ed.), *A History of Political Theories in Recent Times* (New York, 1924).
60. P. H. Odegard, *Pressure Politics. The Story of the Anti-Saloon League* (New York, 1928).
61. E. P. Herring, *Public Administration and the Public Interest* (New York, 1936), p. 397. See also *Presidential Leadership* (New York, 1940), by the same author.
62. E. E. Schattenschneider, *Politics, Pressures and the Tariff*, (New York, 1935); V. O. Key, Jr, *Politics, Parties and Pressure Groups* (New York, 1958) (first published in 1942).
63. *La Science politique contemporaine*, ed. cit., pp. 221, 490.
64. D. B. Truman, *op. cit.*, p. ix.
65. *Ibid.*, pp. 34 ff.
66. I. D. Balbus, *op. cit.*, p. 159.
67. D. B. Truman, *op. cit.*, chap, 6, "Cohesion and Overlapping Membership", pp. 157 ff.

68. W. Y. Elliott, *Western Political Heritage* (New York, 1949). Other authors criticized the excessive importance attached to the theory of groups and the claim that it can explain all political behaviour. Cf. P. H. Odegard, "The Group Basis of Politics: a New Name for an Ancient Myth", *Western Political Quarterly*, 10 (Sept. 1958); R. Golembiewski, "The Group Basis of Politics", *American Political Science Review*, 34 (Dec. 1950).
69. C. W. Mills, *The Power Elite* (New York (1st. Ed., 1951), 1956); preceded by his lesser known work, *The Men of Power: America's Labor Leaders* (New York, 1948); F. Hunter, *Community Power Structure* (Chapel Hill, 1958), and *idem.*, *Top Leadership USA* (Chapel Hill, 1959). Among many other papers on this subject mention is due to R. A. Agger, "Power Attributions in the Local Community", *Social Forces*, 34 (May 1956), 322 ff.
70. M. A. Rose, *The Power Structure. Political Process in American Society* (New York, 1967), p. 20.
71. This is emphasized by D. Kettler, "The Politics of Social Change: The Relevance of Democratic Approaches", in: W. E. Connolly (ed.), *The Bias of Pluralism* (New York, 1969), p. 213.
72. A. Hacker, "Power to Do What?" in: I. L. Horowitz (ed.), *The New Sociology* (New York, 1964), pp. 134 ff.
73. Cf. M. Pilisuk and Th. Hayden, "Is There a Military–Industrial Complex which Prevents Peace?" in: W. E. Connolly (ed.), *op. cit.*, pp. 125 ff.
74. Cf. W. E. Connolly, "The Challenge to Pluralist Theory", in: *The Bias of Pluralism, ed. cit.*
75. R. O. Schulze, "The Role of Economic Dominance in Community Power Structure", *American Sociological Review*, 23 (1) (1958).
76. In one of his later works Hunter admitted that better-organized groups had a say in local communities. See his "The Organizational Community and the Individual", in: R. L. Warren (ed.), *Perspectives on the American Community* (Chicago, 1963), p. 519.
77. R. E. Wolfinger, "Reputation and Reality in the Study of Community Power", *American Sociological Review*, 25 (Oct. 1960), 636 ff. See also L. J. Herson, "In the Footsteps of Community Power", *American Political Science Review*, 55 (Dec. 1961), 817 ff.; S. Fisher, "Community Power Studies: A Critique", *Social Research*, (Winter 1962); J. Walton, "Substance and Artifact: The Current Studies of Research on Community Power Structure", *American Journal of Sociology*, LXXXI (Jan. 1966), 430 ff.; and *idem.*, "Discipline, Method and Community Power", *American Sociological Review*, 31 (Oct. 1966), 684 ff.
78. R. A. Dahl, "A Critique of the Ruling Elite Model", *American Political Science Review*, 25, (June 1958), 463 ff. See also *idem.*, "The Concept of Power", *Behavioral Science*, 2 (July 1957), 201 ff.; and *idem.*, "Further Reflections on the Elitist Theory of Democracy", *American Political Science Review*, 60 (June 1966).
79. N. W. Polsby, "How to Study Community Power: The Pluralist Alternative", *Journal of Politics*, 22 (Aug. 1960), 474 ff.; among the major earlier publications mention is due to H. Kaufman and V. Jones, "The Mystery of Power", *Public Administration Review*, 14 (Summer 1954), 205 ff., and N. W. Polsby, "The Sociology of Community Power: a Reassessment", *Social Forces*, 37 (Mar. 1959), 232 ff.
80. R. A. Dahl, *Who Governs? Democracy and Power in an American Community* (New Haven, 1961), pp. 233, 311 ff.
81. R. A. Dahl and Ch. Lindblom, *Politics, Economics and Welfare* (New York, 1953), Chapter "Bargaining: Control Among Leaders".
82. Ch. Lindblom, *The Intelligence of Democracy* (New York, 1965). A similar standpoint is adopted by J. Lowi, *The End of Liberalism* (New York, 1969), and by many other authors.
83. N. W. Polsby, *Community Power and Political Theory* (New Haven, 1963), pp. 115 ff.
84. A. S. MacFarland, *Power and Leadership in Pluralist Systems* (Stanford, 1969), p.23, where he writes: "A pluralist power structure is a complex power structure. ... An elitist power structure is a simple power structure ...", and Chap. 3, "Pluralism: an Explanation", where complexity is identified with pluralism. But some authors, when speaking about American Society, resort to its outright apology (see, e.g., A. S. Kaufman, "Participatory Democracy Ten Years Later", in: W. N. Connolly (ed.), *The Bias ...*, ed. cit.)
85. A. M. Rose, *The Power Structure. Political Process in American Society* (New York, 1967), p. 245.
86. *Ibid.*, pp. 282 ff.
87. *Ibid.*, chap. XIV, "Conclusion", pp. 483 ff.

88. P. Bachrach and M. S. Baratz, "Two Faces of Power", *American Political Science Review*, **46**, (Dec. 1962), 947 ff.; *idem.*, "Decisions and Non-Decisions: An Analytical Framework", *American Political Science Review*, 57 (Sept. 1963), 632 ff.
89. E. E. Schattschneider, *The Semi-Sovereign People* (New York, 1960), p. 71: "... organisation is the mobilisation of bias. Some issues are organised into politics while others are organised out."
90. Bachrach's and Baratz' papers quoted above were included by them in the book complemented with the results of empirical studies in Baltimore: *Power and Poverty. Theory and Practice* (New York, 1970). A pithy formulation of their standpoint is to be found in their polemical paper "Power and Its Two Faces Revisited", *American Political Science Review*, **69** (Sept. 1975).
91. P. Bachrach, "Interest, Participation and Democratic Theory", in: J. R. Pennock and J. W. Chapman (eds), *Participation in Politics* (New York, 1975), pp. 40 ff. A similar standpoint was adopted by the present writer in the earlier (1962) version, published under a different title, of *Władza i interesy* (1967, 2nd edn, 1974).
92. Cf. Th. Anton, "Power, Pluralism and Local Politics", *Administrative Science Quarterly*, 7 (Mar. 1973); M. Parenti, "Power and Pluralism: A View from the Bottom", *Journal of Politics*, **32** (Aug. 1970); M. A. Crenson, *The Un-politics of Air Pollution: A Study of Non-Decision-Making in Two Cities* (Baltimore, 1971).
93. G. Debman, "Nondecisions and Power", *American Political Science Review*, **69** (Sept. 1975). The new version of élitism was criticized also by R. A. Dahl, "Reply to Anton's Power, Pluralism and Politics", *Administrative Science Quarterly*, 7(Sept. 1963); R. Merelman, "On the Neo-elitist Critique of Community Power", *American Political Science Review*, **62** (June 1968); E. Wolfinger, "Nondecisions and the Study of Local Politics", *American Political Science Review* 65 (Dec. 1971).
94. See in particular *A Modern Political Analysis* (New Haven, 1969), *passim*, and *Democracy in the United States. Promise and Performance* (Chicago, 1972), *passim*.
95. R. A. Dahl, *Polyarchy: Participation and Opposition* (New Haven and London, 1971), pp 15–16.
96. R. A. Dahl, *Democracy ...*, p. 301.
97. R. A. Dahl, *After the Revolution?* (New Haven, 1970), pp. 12 ff.
98. G. Parris *Political Elites* (London, 1969), p. 113.
99. *Ibid.*, pp. 58 ff.
100. W. Domhoff, *Who Rules America?* (Englewood Cliffs, 1967), *passim*, and also his monograph: *The Higher Circles* (New York, 1970).
101. R. Agger, G. Goldrich and B. B. Swanson, *The Rulers and the Ruled* (Belmont, 1972), pp. 60, 124, and Conclusions.
102. W. E. Connolly, "The Challenge to Pluralist Theory", in the same author's *The Bias ...*, pp. 4 ff., 13 ff.
103. H. Kariel, *The Decline of American Pluralism* (Stanford, 1961), pp. 61 ff., and 110 ff., and *passim*.
104. H. Marcuse, *One-Dimensional Man* (Boston, 1964).
105. Th. J. Lowi, *The End of Liberalism* (New York, 1969), chap. 2: "Pluralism and the Transformation of Capitalist Ideology".
106. J. Tournon, "Le Pluralisme: une mise à mort ratée", *Canadian Journal of Political Science*, **IV**, (2) (1971), 365 ff.
107. Th. J. Lowi, *op. cit.*, pp. 58 ff., 88 ff.
108. *Ibid.*, pp. 297 ff.
109. *Ibid.*, pp. 276 ff.
110. R. Presthus, *Elites in the Political Process* (London, 1974).
111. *Ibid.*, pp. 54 ff.
112. *Ibid.*, pp. 119 ff. On élite accommodation in Canada see R. Presthus, *Elite Accommodation in Canadian Politics* (London, 1973). On that subject see A. Lijphart, *The Politics of Accommodation* (Berkeley, 1966), and his *Politics in Europe* (Englewood Cliffs, 1969). In the latter book Lijphart claims that mutual accommodation within the political élite is necessary in those societies which include various conflicting ethnic and religious subcultures.
113. R. Presthus, *op. cit.*, p. 221.
114. *Ibid.*, chap. 8.

115. The book's subtitle, "Decision Making Through Mutual Adjustment", is characteristic enough. See in particular pp. 93 ff., Part 5 ("Comparative Analysis of Central Coordination and Mutual Adjustment") and Part 6 ("Policy Toward Mutual Adjustment").

116. It is notable that one-fifth of managers of Canadian corporations are members of four or five exclusive clubs. Cf. Presthus, *op. cit.*, p. 349.

117. *Ibid.*, pp. 65 ff.

118. *Ibid.*, pp. 116 ff.

119. S. Verba and N. H. Nie, *Participation in America, Political Democracy and Social Equity* (New York, 1972), chap 11 ("The Organisation Context of Political Participation"), pp. 191 ff, and chap. 14 ("Participation: the Record of the Past Two Decades").

120. *Ibid.*, schema on p. 336; see also chap. 20 ("Participation and Equality: Who Gets What and How?").

121. *Ibid.*, pp. 335 ff., 342 ff.

122. D. Nicholls, *The Pluralist State* (London, 1975), pp. 115–16. Both E. Shils *The Torment of Secrecy* (Glencoe, 1956), pp. 225 ff., 231, and N. D. Rockefeller are quoted after that source.

123. D. Apter, *Introduction to Political Analysis* (Cambridge, Mass., 1977), pp. 377 ff. An insight into the complex debate on pluralism *v* élitism. See also W. A. Kelso, *American Democratic Theory* (Westport, 1978).

124. Cf. G. McConnell, "The Public Values of the Private Associations, in: J. R. Pennock and J. W. Chapman (eds), *Voluntary Associations* (New York, 1969), p. 147.

125. A. S. Miller "The Constitution and the Voluntary Associations; Notes Toward a Theory", in: J. R. Pennock and J. W. Chapman (eds), *op. cit.*, pp. 242–58; in the same book, S. A. Lakoff, "Private Government in the Moneyed Society", pp. 176 ff. The opinions expressed in that book largely coincide with what the present author wrote in 1961 in "Państwo monopoli (Monopoly State)", in: *Spór o istotę państwa (The Controversy over the Essence of the State)*, Warszawa.

126. D. Easton, *A Systems Analysis of Political Life ...*, (New York, 1965), p. 376.

127. D. Bell: *The Coming of Post-Industrial Society, A Venture in Social Forecasting* (New York, 1976); G. D. Carson: *Group Theories of Politics* (London and Beverly Hills, 1978), chap. 2, "Pluralist, Statist and Corporatist Elements in the Emergence of Group Theories"; P. C. Schmitter and G. Lehmbruch (eds), *Trends toward Corporatist Intermediation* (London and Beverly Hills, 1980); R. J. Harrison: *Pluralism and Corporatism: The Political Evolution of Modern Democracies* (London, 1980); C. Offe and H. Wiesenthal "Two Logics of Collective Action", in: *Political Power and Social Theory*, 1 (1979); C. Offe: "The Attribution of Political Status to Interest Groups in Western Europe", in: S. Berger (ed.), *Interest Groups in Western Europe* (Cambridge, 1980).

128. L. Panitch "The Trade Unions and the Capitalist State", *New Left Review* (Jan.–Feb. 1981), p. 24.

Part Two

CHAPTER 5

Pluralism and Marxism

INTRODUCTION

When discussing the problem of pluralism both in the labour movement and in the Marxist theory one cannot disregard–if one follows the course of events–the attitude of Marx and Engels towards the Jacobins and later the anarchists, and also the Bolshevik attitude towards both groups. An assessment of the attitude of the Marxist doctrine towards pluralism is possible only in that perspective. Analysing that attitude is necessary for comprehending how far the Bolsheviks were centralists and how far they had taken over the Jacobinic heritage. Many authors treated the Bolsheviks as disciples of the Jacobins and accordingly reduced the problem to the continuation of the centralist tradition in the organization of the state based on the masses. Those authors saw in this the end of the process which originated from Rousseau, but whose dangerous utopia led in practice to the political terror resorted to by the Jacobins, then by the Communards, and later under war, communism and Stalinism. If we adopt this interpretation we would have to assume that the adjective *democratic* as delimiting the noun *centralism* was purely ornamental and was later taken over by popular democracies as an indispensable element of propaganda-oriented liturgy. Under such assumptions, qualifying socialist systems as totalitarian (the issue to be discussed later) required that the said periods be treated as characteristic of the socialist system and its ideology. This in turn suggested an inherent impossibility of that system to overcome bureaucratic centralism and led to the said periods being presented not as harmful political deviations, but as the only possible course of development based on the Marxist ideology. The Stalinist idea of monolithism, closely linked to the claim that the class struggle was growing in intensity all the time, was used in the West as a convenient basis for criticism.

But before we proceed to analyse the Jacobinic element in Marxism we have to explain the origin of that long series of misunderstandings. Blaming Rousseau for having laid the foundations of modern totalitarianism is one of the paradoxes of Western political thinking. These accusations feed on his alleged hostility towards the intermediate bodies, which would make scattered individuals powerlessly face the omnipotent state.[1] This false belief was the result of some of Rousseau's statements in *Du Contrat Social* being given absolute validity, regardless of the fact that they were accompanied by reservations made by Rousseau himself. In fact, his dislike was confined to parties, factions, and sects, and in this sense many years late, he was close to sharing the views of the makers of the American Constitution. Other social organizations were treated by him as useful, which he expressed, for example, in *Emile*. This also applied to such small states as Geneva. If one disregards his basic distinction between those social organizations which are harmful because they paralyse the common will, and those which are functional, one must essentially distort Rousseau's views.

Furthermore, Rousseau in fact was fond of the city-state, but he often mentioned the ways whereby the problems of large states might be cured. As his remedy, he recommended federal institutions, regionalization, and decentralization. It is sufficient to mention in this connection his *Considérations sur le Gouvernment de Pologne*, an outline of a constitution for Corsica, and his letters to d'Alembert. His aversion for the feudal intermediate bodies should not be confused with his normative statements on improving the contemporary existing political systems, and on such systems in the future.

This penetrating re-interpretation of Rousseau's ideas has been taken by the present writer from a paper by M. L. Goldschmidt, with whose opinion[2] he has agreed without reservation, having consulted the appropriate texts written by Rousseau. This writer has thus modified his opinion formulated earlier in *Władza i interesy* (Power and *Interests*).

Detecting pluralistic elements in Rousseau's works is essential for further research. But let us now revert to the assessment of Jacobinism by Marx and Engels and to the elements of pluralism to be found in the works of these two authors, primarily in their writings on historical subjects.

5.1   MARX AND ENGELS ON JACOBINISM

Under the growing revolutionary tension in Germany, Marx and Engels showed interest in the history of the French revolution, and in particular in Jacobinism, already prevalent in the 1840s. At that time their attention was attracted by the class stratification of bourgeois society, and also the stratification of the masses which had not yet emerged as a class. In the masses, they singled out owners of small workshops, petty traders, and hired labourers whom they termed *preproletariat*. They analysed the budding alliance, temporary of course, between the plebeians and the revolutionary-minded peasantry which struggled to rid itself of the feudal bonds.[3]

The issue of that alliance–interpreted as the convergent striving of classes, strata, and groups, for a common goal (or for fairly similar goals)–will also be seen in later popular and socialist revolutions. It will also attract Lenin's attention (see below). Attaining that goal which consisted in the final appropriation of the land by the peasants marked the end of that alliance and the beginning of the bourgeois influence upon the peasants. Marx and Engels were attracted by the problem of radicalization of the revolution, in particular by the pressure exerted by the masses upon the Jacobins–the problem which recently has been labelled "revolution within a revolution" (Debray) and which is linked to, although not identical with, the problem of diarchy.[4]

The sansculottes introduced an organized form of that diarchy by setting up the Commune (after 10 August 1792). Engels praised Saint-Simon for having noticed a transformation of one revolution into another, that is, the turning of the bourgeois revolution against itself. When commenting on Saint-Simon's *Lettres d'un habitant de Genève à ses contemporains* he wrote in *The Development of Socialism from Utopia to Science* that interpreting the French revolution as a class struggle, and that not only between the nobility and the bourgoisie but also between the nobility and the *non-propertied classes* (italics–S.E.), was–in 1802–a brilliant innovation.

It is worth noting in this connection that one of the present-day authors writes about the revolution as an extremely complex phenomenon: there is no single revolution, there are *many* of them (italics–S.E.).[5]

These processes made it possible to bring the revolution to an end contrary to the intentions of the bourgeoisie–a specific paradox of history as the plebeian masses gave the revolution a different sense and a different form. The bourgeoisie in fact just wanted to transform the absolute monarchy into a constitutional one, and to do so without any revolution by means of peaceful reforms.[6]

Marx and Engels admired the determination and courage of the Jacobins, who kept the bourgeoisie in check between 31 May and 26 July 1794, so effectively that the latter did not dare to rise. Both authors studied the problem of terror, and considered the latter as the plebeian way of fighting the enemies of the bourgeoisie: absolutism, feudalism, and the rich burghers.[7]

Yet in their writings concerned with that period we cannot find any normative statement which would treat the Jacobinic centralism as the principle whereby the popular state should be governed. No such statement can be found because the Jacobins themselves had never made any declaration of it. On the contrary, they treated the dictatorial centralist government as a temporary measure, useful at the time when the popular rule was threatened by a military intervention and by a counterrevolution, but one to be followed by a return to "constitutionalism".[8] If they opposed the "federalism" of the Gironde, they did not do so because of federalism as such, but because it was linked with a conservative social programme, and in many cases with the intention of weakening the republic internationally, including negotiations with the armies of intervention.

The political programme of basing the system on a network of communes in which the authorities were to function on the electoral principle and on direct democracy is telling enough. Saint-Just said, on 15 June, 1793, that the sovereignty of the nation was based on the communes.[9] As we may judge, that was more significant than the tactical retreat from such principles by the Jacobins, a retreat forced upon them by the historical necessity, which in Robespierre's opinion required the unification of the people if the bourgeoisie was to be defeated.

In his speech of 10 October, 1793 Saint-Just spoke about the necessity of making the declaration that the revolutionary government would stay only until a peace treaty is concluded, and that under the condition under which the republic functioned at the moment no constitution could be promulgated, because that would pave the way for attacks against liberty. Robespierre spoke in the same spirit in his report submitted at that time to the Comité de Salut Public.[10] There is thus no doubt–in view of the formulations to be found in the 1793 Constitution, and especially the subordination of the deputies to their electors, provisions for a broad use of the referendum, and the acceptance of "the right to resist"–that the dictatorial concentration of power and the domination of the Comité de Salut Public over the Convention were treated by the Jacobins as temporary, to be followed by the return of the power to the masses. During the revolution numberless clubs, people's associations, etc., cropped up and they formed, in their totality, the prototype of a society governed by the people.

Analysis of that revolutionary pluralism is of primary importance for comprehending the essence of the issue, because all democratic tendencies in socialism have drawn directly or indirectly from this source. Robespierre was the one who castigated all endeavours of the people's representatives to become independent of their electorate. He stigmatized that as oppression of the people. Those popular organizations used deliberately to stress the right to associate as the foundation of liberty.[11]

Marx thought that after 10 August 1792, the point of gravity had shifted towards popular associations, municipalities, and improvised centres of power which were "emanations of anarchy". Such also was the character of the sections in Paris, which changed from ordinary electoral districts into organizations of popular power.[12] When describing the Jacobinic dictatorship Marx wrote that it had included political centralization combined with a broad development of the local government, based on democratic elections, and he treated those factors as the strongest levers of the revolution.[13] The final assessment submitted by the present writer will thus differ diametrically from the opinions circulated by Western scholars: *it was not the Jacobins, but the conservative bourgeoisie which was anti-pluralistically-minded.* The bourgeoisie was hostile to organized groups. The first capitalists–factory owners, big merchants and bankers, who grew from early manufactories, overseas trade, and Bourse speculations–did not feel any need to organize; they usually acted individually as capitalists, guided, to quote Adam Smith, by the "invisible hand" of the market. Success strengthened their belief that they did not need to organize. The Robinson myth was still vivid, and continued to stimulate the imagination of entrepreneurs. The time when capitalists would organize did not come yet, and what threatened them was the clubs and associations spontaneously set up by the people. This was why the Le Chapelier Act forbade them. Marx called it pointedly a bourgeois *coup d'état*.[14]

5.2 THE CONTROVERSY WITH THE ANARCHISTS (PLURALISTIC ELEMENTS IN MARX'S AND ENGELS' HISTORICAL WRITINGS)

The controversy between Marx and Engels, on the one hand, and the anarchists (Proudhon first, and Bakunin next), on the other, was distorted in a similar way as was the two authors' attitude towards the Jacobins. The distortion consisted in the claim that Marx and Engels had totally rejected the achievements of their opponents, in presenting Marx and Engels as centralists without explaining in what their centralism consisted; that is, in what sense they were centralists. But their controversy with the anarchists was not focused on the opposition between centralism and pluralism. Let us begin with Proudhon.

One of the points in that controversy was Proudhon's competence *qua* economist. The quarrel became particularly acute when to Proudhon's *Systèmes des Contradictions Economiques ou Philosophie de la Misère* (1846) Marx replied with his *Misère de la Philosophie* (1847). In the heated atmosphere that preceded the revolution of 1848 Marx claimed that Proudhon had "a schoolboy knowledge of political economy" and treated political processes idealistically, which damped the revolutionary aspirations of the working class. Since Proudhon even maintained that the epoch of revolutions had passed once and for all, Marx blamed him for adopting a standpoint between those of capital and labour, and assessed that standpoint as the code of petty bourgeois socialism. Echoes of that anti-Proudhonian diatribe can be found, many years later, in vol. 1 of *Capital*. Marx also criticized Proudhon for the latter's lack of comprehension of the importance of national strivings for independence (he referred to the Poles in particular).

That criticism levelled at Proudhon by Marx was later supported by Engels in *The Housing Question* (1872–3), the latter author's intention being to block the Proudhonian influence in the German labour movement. Engels also criticized Proudhon's economic views from a new angle, in that he discussed Proudhon's escape from a serious analysis of the conditions under which social production takes place into the sphere of reflections on law and "eternal justice", reflections which prevented him from seeing properly the concept of interest, i.e., the basic concept in economics. Proudhon thus interpreted economic relations in legal terms, and even explained the interest rate from a legal point of view. Engels blamed him for a lack of comprehension of the regularities of industrial development and a dislike of the industrial revolution, which introduced a reactionary element into his views, and finally repeated after Marx the charge of petty bourgeois attitude.[15]

But this criticism of Proudhon, outlined here in a summary way, makes up only part of the picture. Not only did Marx not overlook the values of other parts of Proudhon's works, but he did not conceal his admiration for them. Probably, had he known Proudhon's last opus, *De la Capacité de la Classe Ouvrière*, his final opinion of Proudhon would have been modified. After Proudhon's death Marx even intended to write a paper on him, and but for a lack of time wrote to Schweitzer a long letter (dated 24 January 1865) intended for publication, a letter which was in fact an essay on the scholarly production of his great opponent. In it he praised Proudhon's first work, *Qu'est-ce que la Propriété?*, about which he wrote that it was his best work, an epoch-making work that described Proudhon's own discoveries. When comparing Proudhon with N. Linguet he justified this by stating that the latter's *Théorie des Droits Civils* was an inspired work. In his introduction to the second edition of *Le Dix-huitième Brumaire de Louis Bonaparte* he made it a point to stress that there were only two studies on the subject which were worth mentioning, one of them being *La Révolution Sociale Démontrée par le Coup d'Etat* by Proudhon.[16] If we draw the reader's attention to the fact that Marx's opinion of Proudhon was more balanced than it is generally believed, we do so in order to emphasize that *not a single word of criticism was levelled at Proudhon's communalistic pluralism, conceived as a broad programme of the socialist system*. Even more important still, we find a pluralist approach to the analysis of social and political facts in Marx's historical writings of the period 1850–71.

In the appeal by the Central Committee to the Union of Communists (March 1850) Marx and Engels analysed the social stratification of the petty bourgeois democratic party, and spoke of the possibility of independent political action by workers. They also considered the indispensability, scope, and temporal framework of centralism. The appeal states that in a country like Germany, where it is still necessary to remove numerous remnants of the Middle Ages and to put an end to so many provincial and local whims, it is not possible to let every village, every town, and every province raise *new barriers to revolutionary activity* (italics–S.E.), which can develop vigorously only if it is guided centrally. Like in 1793 France, in 1850 Germany rigorous centralization was the task of any really revolutionary party.[17]

While the goal of centralization and its temporal framework (the revolutionary period and the subsequent period of the struggle for staying in power) were clearly formulated in the appeal and did not admit of assigning them any absolute sense, Engels added in 1895 a comment which disperses all doubts. He wrote that due to Bonapartist and liberal forgers of history it had previously been taken for granted that the French centralized machinery of public administration was introduced by the revolution of 1789 and that the Convention was using it as an indispensable and decisive weapon in defeating both royalist and federalist reactionary forces and foreign enemies. But at his (Engel's) writing it was already common knowledge that throughout the revolution, until the 18th Brumaire, the entire administration of departments, districts, and communes consisted of authorities elected by those who were governed by it and that it enjoyed complete freedom of action within the limits of the law. *That provincial and local government*, similar to the American one, *had given the strongest impetus to the revolution* (italics–S.E.), so that Napoleon immediately after the coup of the 18th Brumaire hurriedly replaced it by prefects, who remained up to the time when Engels wrote his comment and who since the very beginning had been instruments of reaction. But to the same extent to which local and provincial government was not in contradiction with political and national centralization it was not inevitably linked with the narrow cantonal and communal egoism.[18]

Thus the said appeal first mentions democratic centralism as the principle along which the revolutionary worker movement, and later the socialist system, is to be organized. By democratic centralism Marx and Engels meant centralism originating from, and based on, *the various levels of local and self-government*.

Concern for bringing out social and political differentiation can also clearly be seen in Marx's *Class Struggles in France from 1848 to 1850*. He singled out within the bourgeoisie its strata with conflicting interests: the financial aristocracy, the industrial bourgeoisie, and the petty bourgeoisie (split into various groups), and also the ideological representatives of the bourgeoisie and the spokesman of its interests, who form a separate group.[19] We find there also an in-depth analysis of the various strata of the working class: Marx focuses his attention on the industrial workers, on the one hand, and on the *Lumpenproletariat*, which the reactionary forces had been using against the revolutionary ones, on the other. This was the basis of a proper understanding of the process of politics and the party system in the period in question. Characteristically enough, when discussing the process of politics Marx points to the bill aimed at the freedom of association, whose text opened with the provision stating that clubs were prohibited.[20] This was accordingly intended as a revival of the Le Chapelier Act.

Apart from the fact that this meant a violation of the constitution, which Marx emphasized, the bill was intended to be a weapon against the proletariat, because the clubs were the places where members of the revolutionary proletariat could gather and conspire. The National Assembly thus prohibited coalitions of workers against capitalists. The constitution, Marx pointed out, could, of course, mean by the freedom of associations only the functioning of those associations which were in harmony with the rule of the bourgeoisie, that is, with the bourgeois system. Tracing all manifestations of social differentiation (not reduced to class differentiation only) and of political differentiation is the significant feature of these studies by Marx.

Pluralistic elements can also be found in *The 18th Brumaire of Louis Bonaparte*, the text of which is marked by the same path of non-schematic reasoning which leads from an analysis of social stratification to a correct interpretation of political differentiation. In this study Marx increased the range of the issues he was interested in by describing three rival monarchist trends: the Orleanists, the legitimists, and the Bonapartists.[21] When it comes to the peasantry's support of the Bonaparte dynasty, that support was given by the conservative peasantry, but not by the revolutionary peasants. They did not represent those peasants who wanted to free themselves from the tethers of the social conditions in which they lived, the tethers of their plots; it represented those who wanted to strengthen their grips on their respective plots; they were not the rural population which, in alliance with the towns, wanted to abolish the old order by its own efforts, but they were groups which stubbornly cocooned themselves in the old order and saw salvation and privileges for both themselves and for their land.[22]

Marx also analysed and justified the alliance of the petty bourgeoisie and the workers, an alliance which had the social-democratic party as its organizational framework; he at the same time declared himself against the delusion that the petty bourgeoisie adopted a supra-class standpoint. He paid particular attention to the political role of the December 10th Society, the allegedly charitable organization used by Louis Napoleon to mislead the masses, to promote Bonapartist attitudes, and to terrorize his political opponents.

Before we discuss the last work in that series, namely *The Civil War in France*, it seems necessary to draw the reader's attention to the last paragraph of vol. 3 of *Capital*, where Marx refers to "the infinite fragmentation of interest and rank into which the division of social labour splits labourers as well as capitalists and landlords".[23]

The texts quoted above show how much vulgarized the presentation of Marx's views is when these are claimed to be a theory that opposes a class to another class, as a theory of the conflict between two monolithic blocs, as the theory that starts from the identity of class and group interests.

The Civil War in France, concerned with the Paris Commune, reflects the great controversy between Marx and Bakunin. That controversy can probably be better understood if its discussion be preceded by reference to certain ideas included in Marx's analysis of the Paris Commune. He saw clearly that the goal of the Commune was "to expropriate the expropriators". He also realized that its social programme initiated "the economic liberation of labour". In the programme of the Commune he attached special importance to the socialization of the means of production and to the transferring to worker's associations of all those workshops and factories that had been closed. He wrote that if production based on associations is not to be an empty sound and juggling, if it is to drive out the capitalist system, if the totality of associations is to control the national production in accordance with a common plan, and hence to guide it itself and to put an end to incessant anarchy and periodically recurrent convulsions which are an inevitable share of capitalist production,[24] this will mean communism. Engels, when commenting on Marx's standpoint, formulated in the introduction to *The Civil War in France*, wrote that undoubtedly the most important decree issued by the Commune ordered such an organization of large-scale industry and even crafts which would not only be based on an *association of workers within each factory, but would also combine all those associations into one union* (italics–S.E.).[25]

This would be a pluralistic organization of industry, opposed to the authoritarian organization of production under the capitalist system, which differed from Proudhon's anarchistic idea by the unification of the associations into a single union that would operate according to a common plan. This was thus an idea of democratic centralism in the organization of production, which inevitably must have been linked to the same organizational principle in politics. What was then the attitude of Marx and Engels toward political pluralism revealed in practice in the political actions undertaken by the Commune? The relevant texts do not give rise to any doubts.

As Marx wrote, the *variety of interests* (italics–S.E.) reflected in the Commune prove that the Commune was a thoroughly flexible political form, whereas all the previous forms of government were oppressive by their very nature. Its true secret consisted in its being by its very nature a *government exercised by the working class* (italics–K.M.), a result of the struggle between the class of producers and that of appropriators, it was that newly invented political form under which the economic liberation of labour could take place.[26]

In what was that political form to consist? The Paris Commune was of course to serve as the model for all large industrial centres in France. If the communal system had been introduced both in Paris and in secondary provincial centres, the old centralized government would have ceded to the self-government of producers in the provinces, too. The Commune was to become the political form of even the tiniest village. The communal system was not to disrupt, but, on the contrary, to organize the unity of the nation, while that unity was to be achieved through the destruction of that state authority which wants to be the embodiment of that unity, but at the same time wants to be independent and to dominate the nation on whose body it is a parasitic excrescence.[27] This pluralistic look at the political form was completed by an analysis of the political groups active within the Commune. Before the uprising Marx and Engels warned the workers against such an act of despair, but they were above petty considerations and knew how to notice the merits of Proudhonists and Blanquists (of whom the latter formed the majority), the main groups in the Paris uprising, also assisted by the Union Républicaine, the party which represented the middle class (shopkeepers, craftsmen and traders, except for big capitalists).[28] Note that freemasons were also active in the Commune, which became known only after *The Civil War in France* had been written.

The criticism formulated by Marx and Engels in the introduction to the last-named study did not question the pluralistic nature of the Commune, but primarily pertained to tactical issues, the blameworthy vacillations on the part of the leaders of the Commune, which ultimately resulted in the military and political isolation of the movement. Marx wrote that three months of free communication between Paris and the provinces would have led to a general uprising of the peasants. Abandoning the idea of nationalizing the Bank of France was a grave mistake, too, because such a step would immediately increase the organizational swing of the Commune.[29]

A digression seems appropriate at this point.

Marx's pluralistic approach to social and political facts was preceded by Engels' important study on *The Peasant War in Germany* (1850), in which he analysed the stratification of the peasantry. This study became the starting point for further Marxist investigations. It is obvious that the materialistic interpretation of history would not be possible without a pluralistic approach to social facts.

Let us now return to the controversy with Bakunin, whose views, as his great antagonists claimed, were a mixture of Proudhonism and communism. The conflict took place at two levels: that of political practice (the struggle for the working-out of the principles of the First International), and that of political theory (primarily the goals of the revolution), both levels being closely interconnected.

In the conflict within the First International,[30] the controversy focused–if we disregard personal antagonism (Marx and Engels accused Bakunin of disloyalty and intrigues, inadmissible in relations among revolutionaries)– around the issue of whether the International, the first revolutionary party of the proletariat in history, a party which was international in nature, was to be loosely structured, confederation-like, and hence lacking a guiding centre.

Such a party, by renouncing co-ordination and the authority of its leaders, would have to act spontaneously, according to the opinion of local, loosely organized groups. Marx and Engels maintained that a guiding centre, based on democratic principles (i.e. leaving a broad autonomy to local revolution-ary centres) but endowed with the task of co-ordinating revolutionary activities, was indispensable.

Marx took up the issue again in his *Critique of the Gotha Programme*, where he wrote that the International Association of Workers was the first endeavour to set up a central agency for the working class movement; Engels in a letter to Bebel firmly protested against the insinuation that the

Association intended to bully the workers.[31] He wrote there that they had almost never interfered with the internal problems of the party, and if they had done so occasionally, then it was only in order to correct the mistakes made, *and only theoretical mistakes at that* (the italics are Engels'). Otherwise the proletariat would have no chance to abolish the centralized bourgeois state which had a powerful apparatus of coercion at its disposal. In a civil war it is necessary that the proletariat set up a uniform centre of decision-making. This meant that the principles of democratic centralism, indispensable–in Marx's and Engels' opinion–in a revolutionary struggle, had to be opposed to what Bakunin's communists suggested.[32]

The controversy over the state formed another axis of the conflict. Bakunin, who opposed all forms of the state, declared himself in favour of abolishing the state immediately, in the very course of revolution; he was hostile to all authority, which should disappear after the revolution in the process of a spontaneous self-organization. In *Statehood and Anarchism* (1873), he accused both Marx and Engels (contrary to their texts which he had at his disposal) of the fact that they wanted to preserve the state for an indefinitely long time. It is interesting and rather little known that Bakunin, like Marx, had in 1871, already given his own assessment of the Paris Commune, and in this connection also attacked "authoritarian communists", by whom he meant the adherents of Marx and Engels, and opposed revolutionary socialists to them. Bakunin noticed in the Paris Commune something else than that which Marx and Engels did. Having classed most of the participants in the Commune (that is, the Blanquists) as Jacobins, he reserved his friendly feeling for the minority (i.e. the Proudhonists), without perceiving the fact that the latter had in their political practice departed from Proudhon's theoretical assumptions. When it comes to Blanquist émigrés, it is to be noted that after the fall of the Paris Commune they shifted to Marxist positions. Bakunin also failed to note that both the Blanquists and the Proudhonists had been active in organizing the first dictatorship of the proletariat in human history, and merely saw a spontaneous construction of the communal system, but one that would be free from the superior and protective activity of the state. He thought that in the Paris Commune "revolutionary socialism" (which in Bakunin's terminology meant anarchism) challenged authoritarian communism; he also believed it to have been an historic event that the "denial of the state" which the Paris Commune was, had taken place in France, and that a non-political revolution had been made there.[33] As Lenin noted in *The State and the Revolution*, this was an unmistakable attempt to "appropriate" the Paris Commune.

In Bakunin's article we find the significant statement that the communists were adherents of authoritarianism, both in principle and in practice, while the revolutionary socialists had confidence in liberty alone; the former strive to impose their system by force, the latter try to propagate it so that groups of those who become convinced could organize and federate spontaneously and freely from the bottom upwards in a self-activated movement that complies with their interests, but never according to a preconceived plan imposed by a higher intelligence upon *unconscious masses* (italics by Bakunin).[34]

On the contrary, Marx and Engels held that the path indicated by Bakunin would lead nowhere. Once the power is seized by the proletariat it is necessary to transform the conditions under which the state was born; the problem of putting an end to "oppressive power" would be handled later. As Engels wrote in a letter of his, dated 24 January 1872, if the principal evil is seen in the state, then one loses sight of capital as the principal evil, capital of which the state is a servant. Bakunin's approach meant *abstaining completely from all politics* (italics–F.E.). In Bakunin's society there is no *authority* at all, because authority = the state = absolute evil. Every individual and every commune is autonomous, but Bakunin is silent on the issue of how a society, consisting be it of two persons only, can function if neither person renounces at least some of his autonomy.[35]

The state cannot be abolished, it can wither away at most, but if that is to take place, a state specific to the transition period, a "provisional state" is necessary; such a state would still preserve class stratification and would be, being a state of the dictatorship of the proletariat, more democratic than the earlier bourgeois state was. In a confidential circular letter of the International, entitled *Alleged Splits in the International*,[36] Marx wrote that the state authority can cease to exist only when the objective of the proletarian movement has been attained, that is, when classes have been abolished. Engels, in his letter to K. Terzaghi, written in early January 1872, stressed that the revolutionary struggle required concentration of all efforts, and that if a person says that authority and centralization deserve condemnation under all circumstances, he does not know what a revolution means.[37]

Marx replied to Bakunin's adherents in his article *Political Indifferentism* (1873), where he criticized their dismissal of politics and stressed the necessity of preserving the revolutionary and transitional form of the state as a weapon in the struggle against the bourgeoisie.

Engels reverted to the controversy with Bakunin in early 1873, in his article *On the Principle of Authority*, where he criticized the utopian nature of the anarchists' struggle and protest against authority in social life; this was aimed at both Proudhonists and Bakuninists, for authority implies subordination, which is indispensable in all combined action: there is no organization without authority. It would, therefore, be nonsensical to claim that the principle of authority is absolutely evil, and the principle of autonomy, absolutely good. Authority and autonomy are relative concepts, and the range of their application changes from stage to stage in social development.[38] The conflict with Bakunin was a replica–enlarged by increased revolutionary experience–of the great controversy, marked by *The German Ideology*, with Stirner's utopian individualism, which also postulated the necessity of abolishing all forms of the state.

To conclude one may say that in the controversy between Marx and Engels, on the one hand, and Bakunin, on the other, the limits of that controversy were clearly outlined: the controversy did not cover the communal system; both parties declared themselves in its favour, the difference being that Bakunin wanted a communal system *without the state*, while Marx and Engels *assumed that the state had to exist during the transition period, but wanted to base it on a communal, and hence highly decentralized, system;* they wanted to bring into harmony the state with its centre of decision-making and the communal organization–a solution in which they saw a guarantee of democracy during the transition period. To anarchistic pluralism they opposed organized pluralism covered by the formula of democratic centralism.

5.3 MARX'S AND ENGELS' PROGRAMMATIC STUDIES AND KAUTSKY'S ATTITUDE TOWARDS PLURALISM

Marx and Engels elaborated this stand point in their later statements. In his letter to A. Bebel (18 to 28 March 1875) Engels wrote that since the state was only a transitional institution, to be used in struggle and in revolution in order to keep the adversaries in check, to speak of a free popular state does not make any sense. As long as the proletariat makes use of the state, it does so not to protect freedom but to keep its enemies in check, and when one can reasonably speak of freedom, the state as such ceases to exist. They accordingly suggested that the term *state* (italics–F.E.) be replaced by the term *community* (*Gemeinwesen*), which corresponds to the French word *commune*.[39] This argument was complemented by Marx's rejection of the idea of "free state", a rejection formulated in *The Critique of the Gotha Programme* (1875), where he wrote that *freedom consisted in transforming the state from an agency that stands above society into an agency fully subordinated to society* (italics–S.E.).[40]

Engels returned to the forms specific to the state in the transition period in his criticism of the preliminary social democratic programme (currently called the Erfurt programme), voiced in June 1891. He brought up again the issue of democratic centralism, which requires a broad system of local government from bottom up, and pointed to the case of France in 1792–8, which took over the American schema of organization. He ranked that system higher than Swiss federalism, with appointed civil servants below the cantonal level.

In this connection it is imperative to mention that in this document Engels claimed that the working class could rise to power only in the form of a democratic republic, which is a specific form of the dictatorship of the proletariat.[41] This claim became for decades the subject-matter of vehement disputes in the international labour movement. All this suggests certain reflections.

First of all, it seems obvious that Engels did not mean a bourgeois republic, but a republic in which the parliament could in fact function as the highest authority in the state, an authority exercised on behalf of the people. With a simultaneously expanded local and self-government these two institutions could easily coalesce institutionally into a "communal system". This would be a–longer, it is true–path leading to the goal the Commune had in view.

Secondly, the problems under consideration here were closely linked to the hypothesis, advanced by Marx and Engels, that the future proletarian revolution would break out in the most strongly industrialized states in Western Europe. In these countries the parliament had been deeply rooted in the political tradition and in the consciousness of the masses as a progressive institution, which moreover underwent far-reaching transformations after the fall of the Paris Commune. This was due to the fact that European parliaments came to include numerous representatives of social-democratic parties, which–combined with other forms of extra-parliamentary class struggle–opened quite new prospects.

Engels reverted to these new prospects of a legal struggle within representative bodies in 1895, when writing his introduction to Marx's *Class Struggles in France, 1848–50*. He claimed there that making an effective use of universal suffrage means for the proletariat a new and constantly improving method of struggle; it turned out that those political institutions which the bourgeoisie used to consolidate its domination, offered the proletariat new tools with which it could combat those institutions.[42] In Engel's opinion, the new legal and political situation had many advantages:

(1) universal suffrage, won from the bourgeoisie as a concession resulted in a constant increase in the number of worker votes, thereby making the bourgeoisie cautious and making the masses realize their strength;

(2) it created broader opportunities for propaganda-making among those sections of the masses which were not yet covered directly by the agitation of the workers parties;

(3) it gave working class representatives access to the parliamentary platform, from which they could attack their opponents in the parliament and it addresses the masses outside the parliament with much more authority and freedom than had been possible in the press and at public meetings.

Engels linked this argument with a thorough knowledge of the prospects of the revolutions in his times. These had deteriorated radically both because of a new stratification of society, and also following the great advances in military technique and organization. In connection with the first issue, Engels wrote that there would probably be no new uprising with which all strata would be in solidarity; in the class struggle, all intermediate strata would probably never gather around the proletariat to make the reactionary party, grouped around the bourgeoisie, vanish almost completely; "the people" would thus always remain divided.

This was, on Engel's part, an unambiguous hypothesis stating that political pluralism was a regular and inevitable phenomenon.

When it came to the workers' armed clash with the police and/or the army, the times of unexpected assaults, the times of revolutions carried out by small, motivated minorities at the head of politically naive masses were over. When a total transformation of the social system is at stake the masses must participate consciously in the process, must comprehend themselves what the conflict is about and to what purpose they offer their blood and their lives. Winning over the masses, and hence the peasants, *previously* (italics–S.E.) would guarantee a permanent victory. This by no means was advice to renounce revolution: the right to revolt, Engels wrote, was the only *really* (italics–S.E.) historical right, the only one on which all modern states were based.[43]

It is significant that the revisionists and reformists who were making use of Engels' writings of 1891–5 to substantiate their antirevolutionary standpoint, disregarded his fundamental reservation (quoted above) concerning non-renunciation of revolution; they also included some Western students of the worker movement (for example Tormin[44]).

The critique of the Erfurt programme also included a new element, namely a more precisely formulated attitude towards the federal state, which Engels in some cases did not treat as the antithesis of democratic centralism, but considered it to be its progressive variety. He rejected federation as not useful for Germany (it would "Swissify" the country), but thought it justifiable in the United States in view of that country's enormous territory, and in those cases where a federation could solve a national issue (he gave the example of Britain, where such a solution would be progressive, because it comprises four nations living on two islands).

Decades later Engels' suggestion found confirmation, because many a state adopted a federal system as a solution to its national conflicts, and in Britain itself latest developments include a degree of autonomy for Scotland and Wales; Spain is following in its wake, and aspirations for local and/or national autonomy are nascent in France.

The general conclusion that imposes itself is that pluralism in the labour movement was, in a sense, a natural reaction to advanced centralism in bourgeois states, with its expanded bureaucracy, at that time still unknown in Britain and even more alien to the United States, which was then practically isolated from Europe. In particular, the broad scope of American local government was both little known in Europe and, to be truthful, difficult to understand. This was due to the fact that historically local and self-government in Europe had been following a quite different course.

Among the second-generation Marxists, Karl Kautsky held an exceptional position as a universally recognized authority, in particular after his criticism of revisionism, formulated at the turn of the nineteenth century. Later, he was valued by Lenin for his theoretical works. Nor can we disregard him when discussing the issues of pluralism. First of all, it must be borne in mind that the Erfurt programme was largely drawn up by him (and accepted without discussion at the party congress), and that he, too, ws the author of the comments to that programme.[45] This won him extremely wide popularity. Kautsky's standpoint was that of pluralism of the paths that lead to socialism: he accordingly considered both a peaceful parliamentary course and a variety of revolutionary measures. However, there is no need to go into the details of his varying assessments of revolutionary prospects in the various countries in this book, nor into his "gradual deviation towards opportunism", for which he was blamed by Lenin in *The State and Revolution*.

He was a social pluralist in his analysis of society, in which he perceived the plurality of groups and strata, and he accordingly opposed any post-revolutionary uniformization of society by stressing the thesis that some vocations and/or industries would require a centralized, bureaucratic organization (for. example, the railways), whilst other enterprises could be managed by vocational organizations and still others could have the form of associations. Great diversity of forms of democratic organization of enterprises is obviously possible, and it could not be expected that all vocations would be organized along one and the same schema. He reverted to this idea many times in one of his basic works on social revolution. Here is another characteristic statement of his: small enterprises could take on most varied forms as far as the legal aspect of ownership is concerned, they could complement large state-owned or commune-owned factories, take from them raw materials and tools and provide them with their own products, or else produce for private buyers or for the market. Another significant formulation is: most diverse types of property within the means of production, such as state ownership, communal ownership, ownership by an association (consumer or producer co-operative), private ownership, could co-exist in a socialist state. The same applies to the forms of enterprises; and their organization: bureaucratic, vocational, association-based (free associations), personal; and it applies also to the form of circulation of goods: on a contract basis, by purchase from state-owned and communal stores, by purchase from consumer associations and from producers themselves, and so on. He claimed that *the variety of economic mechanisms he saw in his society would be quite possible in a socialist society* (italics–S.E.).[46] This claim was the principal element of his conception of a democratic organization of production.

The transition to socialism does not require expropriation of peasants and small producers, either. Kautsky emphasized that their economic activity, based on small-scale property, can neither threaten social revolution nor perpetuate that form of property. Social revolution would be shaped by technological advances in industry, with ensuing new and more attractive forms of existence. He thus stressed the gradualism of expected changes, an opinion reflected especially in his studies on the agrarian question and on social revolution, and in minor contributions as well. What he wrote entitles us to say that Kautsky did not envisage expropriation of peasants by the working class ("small peasant holdings would probably remain private property") after the revolution because of the danger of a breakdown of agriculture.[47] He saw great difficulties in the socialization of small holdings and he accordingly suggested that appropriate conditions be met before such holdings are involved in the process of socialization.[48]

Kautsky's long polemic with the revisionist elements in Bernstein's theory should not blur the fact that their opinions were largely convergent on the issue under consideration here. Bernstein saw the specific feature of social development in an increasing, and not decreasing, social differentiation. Important also was his thesis that within the working class there would be a growing differentiation of interests and that that class itself would become largely stratified, even though its interests would be subordinated to the primary interest of opposing the pressure of capital.[49]

Bernstein's analysis followed a similar course when it came to the middle strata. He pointed, with exaggeration but on the whole correctly, as was shown by later events, to the economic resistance of small and medium-sized enterprises in industry and trade, and of analogous farms and holdings in agriculture. He correctly predicted the numerical growth, and their increased social importance, of the clerical group, that new "middle estate" which decades later would be described by C.W. Mills in *White Collar: The American Middle Classes.*

Bernstein was a pluralist in his view of political theory and practice, which was manifested in his opposition to the monism of parliamentary rule. The parliament should, in his opinion, complement democratic self-government which should take the form of both local government and vocational self-government (trade unions) and self-government in voluntary activities (cultural and sports associations)[50]

Kautsky's pluralistic view of capitalist society was combined with, or, rather due to, his making a strict distinction between the state as a system of coercion, i.e., the state marked by centralized bureaucracy, and highly differentiated capitalist society. Only the former can be abolished by a single political revolution: the latter requires a long process of patient transformation.[51]

He was also pluralistic in his approach to national issues. In his study on the emergence of nationalities he wrote that not only was there no necessary collision between the aspirations of the proletariat and those for national self-determination, but that the latter was a prerequisite for the development of class struggle; he accordingly declared himself in favour of the formation of nation states. Kautsky's standpoint on this issue was later used by Lenin in his great controversy with Rosa Luxemburg.[52]

Kautsky, however, was a uniformist in other matters. In his comment on the Erfurt programme he advanced the thesis that in the society of the future its members (primarily workers) would have *the same interests* (italics–S.E.). This formula later became one of the sources of the simplified interpretation, encountered in political literature published in socialist countries, which reduced the problem to the dichotomy of social interests versus individual interests, with the omission of group interests.

His view of the future socialist society as a unified one was also due to his utopian ethical views. He thought that the classless society could do without coercion and without penal sanctions, that acts aimed at the communist order would be so isolated that the pressure of public opinion which would then *speak out unanimously* (italics–S.E.) would suffice.[53]

This viewpoint also was not without effect upon the simplified interpretation of problems of socialist society, both in the East and in the West.

Kautsky reverted to the fundamental problems raised in the discussion of the Erfurt programme in his study on "the road to power" (*Der Weg zur Macht. Politische Betrachtungen über das Hineinwachsen in die Revolution*, Berlin, 1909), where he foresaw the advent of revolutionary conflicts.[54] At that time, however, he also advanced the risky thesis that the proletariat would probably be isolated in the struggle as it would not be in a position to win over the petty bourgeoisie and the peasantry. This was why in his subsequent studies he would write the petty bourgeoisie off. In his opinion this stratum (class) was almost insignificant from the point of view of the system of production, and any theorist who wanted to study the system could disregard it and concern himself solely with capitalists and proletarians. But a politician would, in his opinion, make a great mistake if, following the theorists of the capitalist mode of production, he treated the petty bourgeoisie as a negligible quantity.[55] A working-class politician must count on the possibility that the petty bourgeoisie will transform itself into a reactionary stratum. When it came to the peasantry, Kautsky saw merely the possibility, though not a very likely one, of the proletariat's winning over the stratum consisting of small-holders. Kautsky's standpoint differed clearly from that of Marx, who in his letter to Engels of 16 April 1856, wrote that it was imperative that a proletarian revolution be supported by a new version of the peasant war.[56]

Kautsky's standpoint, very briefly outlined above, must have been interpreted as one which would bring about isolation of the proletariat in decisive class struggles; it meant betting on the proletariat to win as the most numerous social class. We have to admit that Kautsky was consistent in extending his scepticism to include the intelligentsia.[57] In his mistrust of the latter he was close to anarchists and anarcho-syndicalists, and, like them, failed to notice the stratification of the intelligentsia and its differentiated group interests.

For all his vehement polemics with Rosa Luxemburg in 1910–12 on various issues, and in particular on her theory of the role of spontaneity in mass movements, to which he opposed the importance of organization, Kautsky was in agreement with Luxemburg on the point now under consideration. Both of them thought that the proletariat was isolated and could not count upon support by other social classes and strata. Kautsky did point to conflicts of interests between the petty bourgeoisie, on the one hand, and the big landowners and the big industrialists, on the other, but interpreted them merely as a factor which weakened the ruling classes. He was very consistent on that issue.[58] When it comes to party organization, Kautsky was far away from Marx's position in the First International. Kautsky did not accept democratic centralism; he was a centralist pure and simple. His standpoint, shared by the leaders of the German social-democratic party, was extended by Kautsky also to include the future socialist state.

Had Bakunin lived longer he would have probably readdressed his furious attacks against Marx and levelled them at Kautsky: the target could have been better chosen.

5.4 BOLSHEVISM VERSUS JACOBINISM AND ANARCHISM

The parallel between Jacobinism and Bolshevism has attracted many writers. As early as in 1920 A. Mathiez wrote a pamphlet on the issue; M. Duverger stressed the influence of the Jacobinic constitution of 1793 upon the Soviet system, while A. Hauriou even want so far as to maintain that communist institutions imitated the Western schema.[59] Some people even jumped to very emotional conclusions drawn from such facts as that some social democratic, mainly Menshevik, leaders who opposed Lenin accused him of extreme Jacobinic centralism (the accusers temporarily also included Trotsky), or, to give another example, that Lenin ordered in 1918 a monument of Robespierre to be erected in the Kremlin gardens. As if a monument dedicated to that man of indomitable courage indicated acceptance of the political opinions and practices of the Jacobins.

M. H. Fabre wrote that both *La Montagne* and the Soviet regime went in the same direction in their search for the unity of state power. He even called the Soviet system a parliamentary dictatorship (?!).[60]

But other authors were more balanced in their opinions. G. Vedel suggested that the example of the Jacobins provoked Soviet leaders to reflection and that they made use of the ideas underlying the revolution of 1792–4 to improve their tactics. A. Mestre, having analysed the discussion at the First Congress of the Social Democratic Party (London, 1903), spoke cautiously about an *indirect* (italics–S.E.) influence of the Jacobins upon the Bolsheviks.[61] This is correct: the Bolsheviks were, in fact, provoked by the writings of Marx and Engels to reflect on Jacobinism. Furthermore, between their own political experience, acquired in three revolutions in Russia, and the revolutionary experience of the Jacobins there were two intervening elements: post-Marxian writings on anarchism and new Bolshevik studies on the Paris Commune of 1871.

Lenin took up the problem of Jacobinism on several occasions, and a careful reading of his works can easily show which elements of Jacobinism he had accepted. Let us concentrate on the issues of primary importance. First, in the Jacobinic rule he saw first symptoms of a revolutionary democratic dictatorship of the lower classes, the dictatorship of the majority of all those at the bottom of the social scale, without which it would not be possible consistently to transform society into a democratic one; this is tantamount to a revolution within revolution.[62] In this context Lenin paraphrased Marx's paradox about radicalization of a bourgeois revolution by saying that power passes into the hands of the liberals only if democracy wins against the liberals. Lenin self-evidently thought of a situation in which the lowest classes are weak and not mature enough to stay in power, but, having been briefly the *raison d'être* of the revolution they determined to some extent *the degree of democratism* (italics by V. Lenin) over the next decades of quiet development.

Second, Lenin thought that the seizure of power by the previously oppressed class (he stressed this aspect many a time) was an essential feature of Jacobinism. The first and the second point are closely inter-connected and result in the requirement that revolutionary actions should be organized and guided from a single revolutionary centre.[63]

Third, in connection with Jacobinic terror it must be emphasized that Lenin treated it as the reply to "white terror"; he thought that it should never be directed against any groups of the people, and should always be combined with the movement of the masses. This was both a condemnation of the anarchist principle and practice of individual terror and of terror "within one's own ranks".[64] It is worth while comparing this with Lenin's statements on terror in the period of war communism.

Fourth, Bolshevism is inseparably connected with the class-conscious proletariat being *organized* by a revolutionary social-democratic party. This process of organization must be controlled by a revolutionary centre of decision-making.[65]

Fifth, and most important for the issues we are now concerned with, Lenin rejected the individualism of the Jacobins, and assessed favourably the growth of popular associations, a network of which developed during the French revolution.[66] In this connection, the principle of open debates both in the Jacobin club and in the Convention itself were a natural manifestation of the freedom of public opinion.

Lenin was far from considering the Bolsheviks to be ordinary and direct disciples of the Jacobins, and his opinions on the forerunners of the left in the French Revolution was very much differentiated. In his polemic with Rosa

Luxemburg he pointed to the fact that the parallel between the Jacobins and the Bolsheviks, on the one hand, and the Girondists and the Mensheviks, on the other, was intended not to identify the trends included in each pair, but to show what were the relations between the elements of each pair. This was what the parallel was to mean. Lenin also clearly cut himself off from the Jacobins when it came to their extremely harsh and biased assessment of the Girondists. Lenin did not consider the latter to have been traitors, but described them as inconsistent and opportunistic defenders of the revolution. This justified the necessity of their being attacked by the Jacobins, but did not justify their extermination.[67] All this shows what were the limits of Jacobinic inspiration.

It might perhaps be interesting–before closing the Jacobin problem–to mention that Gramsci, the Leninist, opposed the Jacobin tradition in the communist movement. Only in the last period of his life did he come to the conclusion that the Jacobins conceived dictatorship only as a temporary measure and not as an organizational principle in the reconstruction of society.[68]

When it comes to the assessment of anarchism by Lenin we shall concentrate on his *The State and Revolution*, where he followed Marx and Engels by rescuing from oblivion those of their texts which were of essential significance for the comprehension of the great controversy. His explanations and supplements went in two directions.

The first was concerned with the allegedly apolitical attitude of the anarchists and anarcho-syndicalists, their tendency to dismiss the issues of political forms which they pretended to solve by the immediate abolition of the state. Lenin on many occasions opposed that depolitization of the worker movement, which applied above all to the replacement of a separate party by a non-party organization of workers.[69] On the other hand, Lenin used to emphasize that on other essential issues the opinions of the communists converged with those of the anarchists. This convergence applied to self-government, that is, the communal system, but unlike the anarchists, the communists interpreted the formation of such a system as a political problem, the problem of power, which required the setting up of a centre of decision-making that would serve the working class. However, Lenin did not hide his high esteem for Kropotkin who spoke of co-operatives within the framework of the soviet system as a counter to growing Soviet bureaucracy.[70]

Another convergence is that of the goals, one of them being an immediate abolition of the machinery of the state, which the anarchists wanted to eliminate at once, while the communists held that the proletariat needed the state during the period of class struggle. Temporary preservation of *such* a state paves the way for its withering away.

The second trend in Lenin's reflections was to make use of his criticism of E. Bernstein's *Conditions of Socialism and Tasks of Social Democracy* (1899) and impart thereby the proper guidance to the polemic between social democrats and anarchists, for that was the path along which revisionism was penetrating the international labour movement and Marxism was being deprived of its revolutionary sense. It was only Bernstein who, in his study of 1899, accused Marxism of Blanquist elements. Lenin in particular criticized the identification by Proudhon of federalism with the communal system, also approved by Marx. The parallel between the two, based on a purely legal and institutional approach to the issue, disregarded the *revolutionary origin of the communal system*. The founder of revisionism must have misunderstood the sense and nature of democratic centralism.

As compared with Proudhon, Marx was a centralist, but his centralism was based on freely organized communes, united in their struggle against capitalism. Bernstein failed to grasp the idea of voluntary centralism, developing from the bottom upwards, because for him all centralism was a product of bureaucracy, which could only be imposed from above.

In this connection it is worth mentioning that Lenin explained the success of anarcho-syndicalism (greatly influenced by Proudhon's ideas) by the disappointment and disgust which the revisionism and opportunism of the social democrats at that time had evoked in the West European proletariat.

At this point we arrive at the third element in Lenin's analysis, an element based on the experience of the Russian revolutions of 1905 and of February 1917. In the spontaneously formed soviets Lenin saw the revival, under different historical conditions, of the communal system, which Marx had interpreted as an opposition to the bourgeois parliamentary system.

When analysing the experience of the soviets in 1905 (in an article "Our Tasks and the Soviets of Workers' Delegates" of November 1905), Lenin treated them as a nucleus of a provisional revolutionary government, because the political decisions made by those soviets were practically of such a nature. This was an activity of revolutionary bodies as instruments of a future reconstruction of society. But the said article came to be published only after Lenin's death and thus was then not known to broad circles of Bolshevik activists.[71] Note also that the soviet of factory delegates in St Petersburg emerged as a revolutionary committee, and not as an element of the future machinery of the socialist state. Trostky assigned that council fairly limited tasks: elections to the constituent assembly, elimination of absolutism, destruction of the apparatus of the police and the bureaucracy; he thus did not associate the St Petersburg soviet with the dictatorship of the proletariat, and *a fortiori* did not assign it the task of introducing it.[72] On the contrary, in his article "The Slogan of the United States of Europe", published in 1915, Lenin wrote that the system of the democratic republic would be that political form of social organization which would abolish the bourgeoisie and thus ensure the victory of the proletariat.[73] Such also was the opinion which prevailed in the Bolshevik party. Sticking (after 1905) to Engels' idea can be explained, on the one hand, by the scarcity of historical experience provided by the revolution of 1905, and, on the other, by the illusions the masses still had about the bourgeois parliamentary system, which in Russia had not yet been discredited at that time. Only the formation of soviets on a mass scale during the bourgeois-democratic revolution in February 1917 brought out the issue of the form of the proletarian state in a very acute manner. It was most closely connected with the Marxist theory of the bourgeois-democratic revolution evolving into a socialist one.

The vaccillations between the parliamentary republic as a form of the dictatorship of the proletariat and the system of soviets as an improved version of the communal system were terminated by Lenin immediately after his return from the exile: he did that by publishing his *April Theses* (1917), which recommended, as the programmatic goal of the Bolsheviks in the organization of the state in Russia, not a parliamentary republic, which in Lenin's opinion would then mean a step backwards, but "Soviets of delegates of workers, land labourers, and poor peasants", without which it was not possible to expect support for the revolution by the peasants and a democratic transformation of the agrarian structure.

Lenin saw in the soviets a flexible form of sociopolitical organization that offered opportunities for peaceful development and for a non-revolutionary transformation of society on socialist principles. Such a possibility existed until the massacre of workers in July 1917 by the troops sent by the bourgeois-democratic government. The *April Theses* did not mean any universal recipe for all revolutions to come, for Lenin they spoke explicitly about the situation in Russia at that time. Several months later, just before the revolution began, and hence before the first soviet state emerged, Lenin had managed to avoid assigning it an absolute value: he was correct in foreseeing that the period of transition from capitalism to communism would bring a great variety and diversity of political forms of the dictatorship of the proletariat. In this way he, as it were, made a reservation against treating the soviet system as the only model of the dictatorship of the proletariat, even though this was the only possible form under the conditions prevailing in Russia at that time. This idea of the diversity of revolutionary forms was formulated by him on many occasions. For instance, in his paper "On Our Revolution" (January 1923), he saw the possibility that Eastern countries could pass to socialism *without going through* the capitalist phase of development.

Recently, that is, after World War II, this Leninist formula of the variety of political forms, included in *The State and Revolution*, was confirmed in practice in socialist states which emerged at that time. This had been due to many causes. Without entering into details we can say that the Bolsheviks formed a minority in the soviets until the last few months before the revolution, and that there had been practically no Bolshevik cells in the peasant councils. Such cells had existed at the provincial level, but at the lower ones, and they had then been completely absent in communal soviets.

The peasants kept themselves at a distance from the soviets as they still did not see the local authority in them. Trotsky spoke of the astonishing coolness of the peasant masses toward the soviets.[74] Already, at the Stockholm congress of his party, when the experience of the revolution of 1905 and 1906 was discussed, Lenin noticed clearly that it was imperative to set up peasant organizations in the rural areas. Yet even at the First All-national Congress of Peasants (May 1917), called up by Social Revolutionaries in May 1917, no mention was made of the soviets as the future authorities. And Bolshevik cells were almost completely missing in the rural areas.[75] It was only in September 1917 that the peasant masses *began* to associate the agrarian programme with the soviets, and the final fusion of the workers' and soldiers' soviets with peasant ones took place only after the revolution, namely on 26 January 1918.[76]

The soviet system excluded from the process of politics those classes, strata, and professional groups which were a threat to the revolution (the so-called *lishentsi* were deprived of electoral rights), but it left much leeway to the masses in expressing their opinions and initiating various organizational activities. Those principles were formally included in the first Soviet Constitution of 10 July 1918. During the period of war communism the pluralistic principles under which the delegates' soviets functioned were confined within specified limits.

The soviets on the whole revealed remarkable political and organizational effectiveness. Manifestation of these possibilities of the Russian proletariat aroused hopes, after World War I, in war-tired soldiers and workers. The soviets were watched with fascination by the masses in Central and Western Europe.

5.5   ROSA LUXEMBURG AND KARL KAUTSKY ON THE SOVIET REVOLUTION IN RUSSIA

The first stage of the revolution in Russia was not favourably received by most labour leaders in Western Europe, among whom attention was focused on Rosa Luxemburg and Karl Kautsky. Their attitude was especially unfavourable towards the Soviet form of the dictatorship of the proletariat. In this connection we cannot disregard Rosa Luxemburg's well-known study *The Russian Revolution*, which she wrote in prison in October 1918.[77]

She did admit that the Bolsheviks had been the first to have courage enough to make the proletariat grasp political power, that Russia embodied the consequences of 100 years of evolution in Europe, and that the revolution of 1917 was the direct continuation of the revolution of 1905–7; she also accorded the Bolsheviks the historic merit of having, from the very beginning, proclaimed and used with iron-hard consistency the only tactics which could save democracy and promote the revolution.

Lenin's party was thus the only one in Russia which even in the first period grasped the true interests of the revolution and was the driving force of that revolution, being at that time the only party that pursued a truly socialist policy.

This explains the fact that the Bolsheviks, who originally formed the majority that had been cursed, slandered, and witch-hunted by all, quickly came to the fore of the revolutionary forces and could gather under their banner all truly popular masses: the urban proletariat, the army, the peasants, and also the revolutionary democratic elements, that is, the left-wing social-revolutionaries. All other aspects of the Russian revolution were viewed negatively by Rosa Luxemburg.

First of all, she criticized the Bolshevik agrarian policy, in particular the immediate division of land among peasants and their taking over the possession of that land, whereby she explained the change in the peasants' attitude towards the socialist revolution; she blamed the Soviet authority for having itself blocked the socialization of agriculture which thus became the arena of the conflict between the urban proletariat and the peasant masses.

The Leninist agrarian reform created, in her opinion, a new and powerful stratum of enemies within the people, enemies whose resistance would be much more dangerous and stubborn than that of the land-owning nobility and gentry.

The second point was concerned with national policy, that is, the formula that the nations had the right to self-determination, including the right of seceding politically from Russia. Rosa Luxemburg saw a glaring contradiction between the firmness and consistency with which Lenin defended that thesis, and the determined centralism in other Bolshevik policies and their attitudes towards other democratic principles. On this occasion she ridiculed the national aspirations of the Ukrainians in words which only our respect for the great revolutionary prevents us from quoting here. There can be no doubt who was a centralist in that controversy and who represented the approach which today is termed pluralism in national and ethnic issues.

Rosa Luxemburg believed that the defence by the Bolsheviks of the aspirations of oppressed people to independence within their own respective states threatened the international revolutionary movement. As she put it, the *cliché* (italics–S.E.) about self-determination and the entire national movement, which was then the greatest threat to international socialism, came to be greatly strengthened just by the Russian revolution and the negotiations at Brest Litovsk. Rosa Luxemburg did not seem embarrassed by being for that matter in the same rank as H. Cunow, the leading reformist, who had declared several years earlier that the emerging prospect had been *not national differentiation, but the integration of small nationalities within one large state in which one culture would prevail.*[78]

The third point of criticism referred to the Constituent Assembly, or rather its dispersion by the Bolsheviks. Rosa Luxemburg did not question the fact that the composition of that body had no longer been representative of the balance of power in the country, but she excluded any revolutionary removal of that assembly. She suggested *ex post facto* another solution: the Bolsheviks should have immediately called up another assembly, elected by renewed and more advanced Russia. The elections should have been held immediately. In this connection she criticized the Soviet electoral law; in particular, she attacked not so much the fact that some categories of citizens (the *lishentsi*) had been deprived of electoral rights, but that the scale of this exclusion had been too wide. She wrote with indignation that the electoral law which summarily deprived wide social strata of their voting rights and thus placed them outside society which, however, did not have any place for them in its economic system. Hence the deprivation of rights was not a definite measure intended to serve a definite purpose, but a general rule that would be *binding* permanently (italics–S.E.) was an unrealistic *ad hoc* solution, and not out of necessity resulting from dictatorship.[79]

Fourth, she condemned the dictatorial "red" terror, to which she opposed broadest democracy, public opinion, and broadest political freedom. She saw in them the framework within which only that life which can luxuriantly breed *ad hoc* thousands of new forms can have its own creative force and can itself correct all its own mistakes. She concluded by stating that the essential error in Lenin's and Trotsky's theory was that they opposed dictatorship to democracy.[80]

The ensuing polemic was about whether Rosa Luxemburg wished to have her work published (it was published posthumously by Paul Levi) in view of the fact that she wrote it under extremely disadvantageous conditions and in great haste, which was imperative in her situation. (The present writer considers this controversy, which at one time took place in Poland, too, to have been pointless because it did not go into the merits of the case.[81]) On the other hand, the publication itself was a fact which came to play a definite role in the international labour movement (both Lenin and Clara Zetkin took issue with the pamphlet in question), so that we have to adopt some attitude towards the issues raised by her from the point of view of those pluralistic aspects to which the present book has been dedicated.

The objection that the Bolshevik agrarian policy had to result in an opposition between the urban proletariat and the peasants, which in Rosa Luxemburg's opinion would end in permanent centralization and further repressions, was refuted shortly after her tragic death, when the "new economic policy" was put into effect. She wrote that small peasant holders should, of course, not be deprived of their plots, and the authorities could wait quietly until the advantages of the socialized economy win them over voluntarily to associate in co-operatives and later to join the fully nationalized economy. After seizing power the socialist government ought, in any case, to have taken measures that would have those fundamental elements of a future socialist reform of the agrarian conditions in view; and at least it should have avoided all that which could later block its path to such measures.[82] This sounds like a positive comment on the NEP agrarian policy, and at the same time as a warning against resorting to coercion in the process of collectivization of agriculture, collectivization interpreted as co-operativization in various forms.

It is self-evident that Rosa Luxemburg, when commenting on the steps taken during the first months of the revolution, could not have foreseen the turn marked in the Bolshevik policy by the initiation of the NEP. We can understand that the revolutionary author, writing in prison, jumped to conclusions, as she wanted to clarify some issues for herself. But nothing can justify the claim, made years later, that there had been political continuity between the period of war communism, with the various committees of poor peasants active in the rural areas, and the Stalinist policy of a sudden, mass-scale and compulsory collectivization of agriculture, that claim of continuity disregarding the several years of the NEP.

In the said pamphlet, Rosa Luxemburg vehemently criticized the Bolsheviks for their interpretation of the national question. There is no need to comment on that controversy, which is on the whole fairly well known. It suffices to say that this controversy, too, has been settled by history. Let us, however, pay attention to the claim that the Bolsheviks were inconsistent in that their programme on the national issue was in contradiction with their "firmly centralistic" attitude. Now the Bolsheviks were neither centralists in general, nor bureaucratic centralists, but based the Soviet system on the principle of democratic centralism (in the Marxian interpretation of the term), from which they had–as they believed–to depart during the period of war communism (see below). Lenin's theses on the resolution of the national problem lay at the foundation of the Soviet federation, which became a model for many countries. It suffices to say that Yugoslavia, separated for many years from the Soviet Union by constitutional or systemic controversies and which finally adopted a different form of its sociopolitical system, remained faithful to the Soviet model on one essential point: in Yugoslavia, too, the federal system is devised to solve the national question and is subordinated to the latter. Even some capitalist states have sought inspiration in the Soviet solution to the problem. In Canada, there are strong tendencies to reconstruct the federation so as to use it in resolving the controversies between the English-speaking provinces and French-speaking Quebec. Similar trends are noticeable even in Belgium, which formally is not a federal state. Even less important ethnic differences tend to find protection in constitutional solutions, to mention the United Kingdom, which went through a constitutional change creating the autonomy of Scotland and Wales. In post-colonial countries, federal institutions are used to protect the rights of the various ethnic and supra-tribal entities.[83] Thus treating federal institutions and autonomies as instruments in resolving national and ethnic conflicts has become a world-wide phenomenon.

Rosa Luxemburg criticized the Bolsheviks for their attitude towards the

Constituent Assembly, but when she left prison and engaged in political struggle in the controversy–the National Assembly versus the Soviet republic–she declared herself, like K. Liebknecht did, firmly in favour of the dictatorship of the soviets.[84]

This was what Lenin primarily had in mind when he wrote in his *Publicist's Comments* (March 1922) that Rosa Luxemburg after leaving prison corrected most of her errors.

When it comes to the electoral law she just lacked reliable information both on its provisions and on the general political situation of Russia, both at home and in the international arena. There is no other explanation of an experienced revolutionary worker demanding immediate elections in the country which is in a state of confusion due to the intensifying civil war and faces the mortal threat of Allied intervention in collusion with Germany. This was a demand which could result in Russia's repeating the errors of the Paris Commune. Rosa Luxemburg believed that only those employed in state-owned industrial enterprises enjoyed electoral rights and that the majority of the population, including some workers, was deprived of them.

Lenin made many statements on the *lishentsi* (people deprived of public rights); he maintained that depriving the exploiters of the electoral rights was a *purely Russian* (Lenin's italics) issue, and not a problem of the dictatorship of the proletariat in general;[85] depriving the bourgeoisie of their electoral rights was not an indispensable feature of the dictatorship of the proletariat, but merely a concomitant phenomenon; the institution of *lishentsi* had not been planned by any party, but emerged by itself in the course of the political struggle;[86] open participation by the bourgeoisie in the counter-revolutionary action organized by Gen. Kornilov paved the way for the formal elimination of the bourgeoisie from the soviets.[87] Lenin spoke in the same spirit at the 8th Congress of the Russian Communist Party (Bolsheviks); at that time he estimated that the number of the *lishentsi* amounted to 2–3 per cent of those who had voting rights.[88]

Rosa Luxemburg condemned the "red" terror as a reply to the "white" terror, initiated by the St Petersburg massacre in July. But the tragic irony of history had it that she herself fell a victim of counter-revolutionary terror ten weeks after having formulated that condemnation. Yet, what was essential was not her demand that full democracy be introduced immediately, nor her call for spontaneous action, but the warning against the distortions resulting from bureaucratic centralism, which would end in a degeneration of the dictatorship of the proletariat by making it abandon democracy and pluralism, which are specific to every popular system. The danger was also noticed by Lenin, as is proved by what he wrote on the subject shortly before his death, and in particular by his political testament, in which he warned against the bureaucratic and centralist tendencies represented by Stalin and intensified by the latter's personality.[89] It was, thus, not by chance that the essay by Rosa Luxemburg had not been published in print during her lifetime; she must have decided against the idea, being guided by her sense of responsibility as a revolutionary leader and theoretician, and her desire to be more rigorous in her writings.

Kautsky's attitude towards the October Revolution was marked by his retreat from the revolutionary ideas included in his earlier works, highly appreciated by the Bolsheviks, which was explicitly stated by Lenin on various occasions. A milestone in the development of his views was *Der Weg zur Macht* (1909), and the period from 1912 to the end of his life was a sequence of critical sallies against the Bolsheviks, and later against the Soviet system, which was in harmony with his coming closer to the theoretical standpoint of Bernstein, whom he had earlier opposed both vehemently and successfully.[90] This evolution of his views was not unnoticed by Lenin, whose controversies with Kautsky began in 1914, had their scope expanded, and were *first* firmly and comprehensively expounded in *The State and Revolution*.

Going into the details of that controversy would lead us away from the principal subject-matter of this book, and this is why we shall confine ourselves to those issues which are of direct interest to us.

(1) The pride of place in the controversy goes to Kautsky's thesis that Russia was not yet ready for the dictatorship of the proletariat, because material conditions for that were lacking in the country's socioeconomic development; in particular, the level of the productive forces was not high enough, and hence the October Revolution had to be a bourgeois revolution. This claim was elaborated by Kautsky in *Die Diktatur des Proletariats* (1918), but was also made by him in *The Proletarian Revolution and Its Programme*, where he maintained that the Russian revolution occurred too early and that the Bolsheviks tried to bypass historical phases. M. Waldenberg is right in emphasizing the fact that that meant Kautsky's retreat from the standpoint occupied by him previously and described by him in connection with the revolution of 1905.[91] To this change of standpoint was linked the consistent rejection of the Bolsheviks' claim that the imperialist war (that is, the war of 1914–18) could be transformed into a civil one, a possibility which at one moment turned into a necessity. This assessment of the nature of the revolution in Russia was linked to his wrong evaluation of the relations between the working class and the peasants. Influenced by the revolutionary situation in Germany Kautsky advanced the thesis (cf. his *Terrorismus und Kommunismus*, 1919) that the interests of the peasantry as a whole were in conflict with those of the urban proletariat.[92] He thus abandoned his earlier, not very firmly asserted, opinion that it would be possible to win the support of the peasants (*Die Diktatur des Proletariats*). Hence a high level of production would be the only way of transforming society without a revolution into a socialist one. This opinion was based on the assumption that there was an inevitable antagonism between the working class and the

peasantry; it was also an extrapolation onto Russian society of Kautsky's old claim concerning the self-isolation of the proletariat. At the time when revolution was a topical issue Kautsky assigned primary importance to non-obstruction of production, as if the war in Russia had not, be it by its long duration alone, disorganized production.

But other leading theorists of social democracy, people like Otto Bauer and R. Hilferding, were of a different opinion on the issue of the October Revolution: they did not conceal their friendly feelings for the revolutionary efforts undertaken by the Bolsheviks.[93]

Kautsky's writings, aimed directly at the first proletarian revolution, were accompanied by his attempts to eliminate revolutionary formulations from Engels' last works, written shortly before his death (see above) and to make them appear reformist in nature.[94]

(2) Kautsky earlier ascribed only limited significance to electoral campaigns and confrontations in the parliament: he saw in them merely an opportunity for consolidating the influence of the social democratic party in the working class, and the principal role was to be played by various forms of extra-parliamentary struggle. Now in the period of his controversy with other theorists the order was clearly reversed and Kautsky started ascribing the *primary* importance to electoral campaigning and parliamentary action. Yet previously, probably impressed by the great electoral victory of the social democrats in 1912, accompanied by a rapid increase in trade union ranks, he used to stress the priority of legal measures. His views came to crystallize clearly: the struggle of the masses was subordinated to parliamentary action so as to become its appendage, and finally the revolutionary strike on the mass scale was renounced by him as a tactical measure. The goal of the political struggle was now formulated by him in a way which meant a revision of Marx's recommendation that the machinery of the state be destroyed; in one of his works he wrote that the power should be won by winning a majority in the parliament and by raising the parliament above the government, and not by destroying the machinery of the state.[95]

This was why at that time Rosa Luxemburg blamed him for striving to confine the activity of the German social democratic party to the parliamentary arena, which precluded the possibility of making that party revolutionary.[96] In view of this evolution of opinion it cannot be wondered that Kautsky thought that the Soviet power should subordinate itself to the Constituent Assembly, which was the opposite of Lenin's view. The same attitude was adopted by Kautsky in connection with the revolution in Germany.[97]

(3) This aggressive criticism of the Soviet system was being extended by Kautsky over other fields. When taking up, in the work mentioned previously, the problem of "the red terror" and analysing anew the experience of the Paris Commune, he blamed the Bolsheviks for striving to solve by violence those economic problems for which they had no economic

solutions and he suggested parliamentary democracy instead of Soviet dictatorship. In his analyses he totally disregarded the origin of war communism and the conditions under which that system had to function, nor did he pay any attention to the motives behind the political decisions made by the Bolsheviks. He criticized severely the Soviet electoral law for having infringed the principle of universality and stigmatized the Soviet system for having deprived its opponents of the freedom of speech and association. In the first pages of *Die Diktatur des Proletariats* Kautsky–at the time when the civil war was raging in Russia–raised the pluralistic demand for economic freedom, freedom of opposition and freedom of political association. The same idea can be found, in various versions, in his *Terrorismus und Kommunismus*.[98]

Lenin often commented on the turn in Kautsky's views. We shall try here to grasp the most important elements in Lenin's replies, and shall also occasionally refer to the standpoints of other revolutionary leaders.

In the well-known polemic paper *On Our Revolution* (aimed at Sukhanov, Kautsky's follower in Russia) Lenin replied to the criticism that the revolution in Russia had been started too early. Lenin claimed that the level of production can be neither the only nor the principal criterion of appraisal of whether a country is ready for a revolution. The war of 1914 created a new situation, most unlikely to recur, a situation of which one should have availed oneself by taking a great and inevitable risk.[99] But a revolution is also a war, and this was why Lenin quoted Napoleon I: *"on s'engage et puis ... on voit"*. Lenin's standpoint took into account such factors as the experience of the working class, small in proportion to the total population of Russia, but availing itself of the experience in the organization of production, acquired in those industries which were marked by a high concentration of capital, and also availing itself of the political experience, acquired by the Russian proletariat as a result of having taken part in three revolutions within 12 years.[100]

To the criticism that the revolution was bourgeois in nature Lenin replied thus: it was such as long as the Bolsheviks went hand in hand with the peasantry as a whole; they realized that very clearly and after 1905 had never tried to skip over the inevitable level of historical development or to dismiss it by decrees. From April 1917 on, however, the revolution could not stop at that, because events in the country were going on, capitalism had made a step forward, everything had been ruined on an unprecedented scale, and would *require ...* steps towards socialism.[101]

Is it significant that those who so often availed themselves of Rosa Luxemburg's essay on the revolution in Russia in order to repeat Kautsky's criticism that might be formulated thus: "you should not have seized the power", as a rule disregarded or minimized two elements in her essay: all that which she had said in favour of the October Revolution and the Bolsheviks, and her sharp criticism of Kautsky's views. These statements of hers are worth recalling here.

On one occasion she wrote that when it comes to the war and the revolution in Russia the events had proved not the lack of political maturity of the Russians, but the lack of the maturity of the German proletariat necessary for discharging its historical duties; stressing that immaturity was the first task of a critical analysis of the Russian revolution, a revolution whose fortunes totally depended upon the international situation. And on another occasion we read: Kautsky and his Russian adherents, who wanted the Russian revolution to preserve the bourgeois character that marked its first stage, were exact copies of those German and English liberals in the nineteenth century who had distinguished two periods in the French revolution, the "good" revolution during the first, Girondist, stage, and the "bad" one from the Jacobins' seizure of power; shallow liberal historiography was naturally unable to grasp the fact that without that seizure of power by the "unrestrained" Jacobins the first shaky and partial successes of the Girondist stage would also soon be brought to ruin; "the golden mean" cannot be observed in any revolution, since the natural law of revolutions calls for rapid decisions.[102]

F. Mehring wrote on the Russian revolution even earlier; in his article "Die Bolschewiki und wir" (May–June 1918) he stressed, in referring to Marx, that every revolution must be assessed by its individual features–in the historical sense of that term–so that the fact that the Russian proletariat was not numerous could not be decisive.[103]

It is common knowledge that the role of the soviets had been a controversial issue in the Russian revolutionary movement until Lenin formulated his "April theses"; from that moment on the Bolsheviks were practically unanimous in their opinion that the proper role of the soviets was not confined to functioning as agencies of the revolutionary struggle, but consisted in being the organizational core of the nascent proletarian state. If Kautsky saw the source of the authority of the soviets in the fact that Russia did not have any tradition of other organizational forms of a democratic system, then this supported Lenin's opinion; Lenin, however–and this is worth emphasizing again–did not raise the soviets to the rank of the universally binding pattern. Mehring in his article also referred to the flexibility of the soviets, who used to leave room for action to all strata of the working classes without thereby losing their own freedom of action, so that they were superior to all earlier revolutionary governments by the reasonable firmness with which they were putting their revolutionary measures into effect.[104]

This was why Kautsky's thesis that the soviets should be subordinated to the parliament, which he upheld with reference to both Russia and Germany, could not be taken into account by the Bolsheviks.[105]

Lenin replied to Kautsky on this issue extensively in his paper *The Proletarian Revolution and the Renegade Kautsky*, where he formulated the problem and offered the solution: dictatorship against whom? and democracy for whom? Lenin claimed that these need not be antonyms, because a dictatorship might restrict the political rights of that class against which it had been organized, and protect the democratic rights of the class which had seized power. Kautsky introduced to the discussion of the Soviet system the concept of opposition, whose rights should be protected. Yet the concept of opposition is a parliamentary one, and hence is inapplicable to a period of revolution and civil war.[106]

When replying to accusations of terror Lenin stated that violence was adequate to the resistance offered by the exploiting classes. "But when it comes to the petty bourgeoisie our idea was that of an understanding, but we were forced to resort to terror."[107] War communism was a regime of rigid regulations, requisitions, and repression, a reply to the intervention of foreign armies, a result of the civil war and famine. Lenin stressed this aspect of the problem in his report submitted at the Fifth Congress of the Soviets.

Both Lenin and Trotsky treated war communism as an episode in the revolutionary struggle, whose violence accounted for the fact that only the nationalization of the disorganized bourgeois economy would make "consumers' communism" possible. It was imperative to bring that stage to an end as soon as possible, the more so as war communism delayed the reconstruction of the national economy.

In his work on Kautsky, Lenin repeated his opinion on the relationship between the parliamentary and the Soviet system, and wrote that the latter should become the core of the machinery of the state. In a revolutionary period it is not the majority of electoral votes which is decisive, but support by the majority of the masses. It is so because the bourgeoisie, even in revolutionary periods, has great possibilities of manipulating the vacillating masses of voters.

Lenin also reverted to the problem of the *lishentsi* and referred to the limitation of the electoral rights of specified groups of the population not as to any permanent institution, but as a temporary operation, dictated by the necessity of saving the revolution. In this connection he referred to Plekhanov who already in 1903 both foresaw and recommended (at the 2nd Congress of the Russian Social Democratic Revolutionary Party) such a temporary abandonment of democratic principles.[108]

Other revolutionary leaders also argued with Kautsky; next to Lenin it was Trotsky who was most active in this respect as in the paper mentioned above (cf. note 94). In it he took up a range of problems which were the subject-matter of the controversy between Kautsky and the Bolsheviks, namely the dictatorship of the proletariat and democracy (he in particular defended Engels against Kautsky's distorted interpretation, p. 20), the Constituent Assembly and the soviets, the use of terror (in which connection he recalled Marx's standpoint on the issue), war communism (which both social democratic and bourgeois writers usually associated with his, Trotsky's, name), and the peasant problem (p. 125).

It is significant that at the time of those controversies and resulting polemics, which pivoted on the problems of the dictatorship of the proletariat and democracy, Kautsky travelled to Georgia, at that time ruled by the Mensheviks. His analysis of their rule there appeared in book form. The next year saw the appearance of Trotsky's book on the Menshevik rule in Georgia, its leading idea being that the supposedly democratic rule in Georgia was manipulated by the imperialist interventionists.[109] Bukharin, too, in a separate book polemized with Kautsky's views.[110]

When we watch the discussions provoked by the evolution of Kautsky's opinions we can hardly resist the impression that we witness a double paradox. A great Marxist theorist, which he was, is replaced by a poor politician, lost in a revolutionary situation, and when the revolution does break out, the former campaigner against revisionism turns himself into a revisionist.[111]

We had to discuss this at some length because the system of opinions which marked Kautsky in the later period, and also the said essay by Rosa Luxemburg, came to lie at the foundation of all that which has been written about "red totalitarianism" as an immanent necessity of the system, and helped spread the belief in the alleged antinomy between democratic pluralism and socialism as a system to which pluralism is, and by definition must be, alien. This was also the basis for establishing the supposed necessary continuity between war communism and the period of Stalin's dictatorship, the basis for defining the essential and "inevitable" characteristics of all socialist systems.

Clarification of this issue is of primary importance, for otherwise all discussion of pluralism within Marxism would be meaningless. Disregard of historical continuity and an arbitrary choice of a certain period as the basis for characterizing the significant features of a system is at variance with the basic methodological recommendations.

5.6   BRIEF REMARKS ON ENDEAVOURS TO ORGANIZE THE SOVIET SYSTEM OUTSIDE RUSSIA

The concept of the Soviet system had various interpretations in the worker movement in Central Europe, despite the fact that the source of the inspiration was obvious. The system was set up primarily in Germany, where a revolution broke out in November 1918, preceded by the mutiny in the German navy in Kiel.[112] The organizational form of that revolution–concerning which a controversy had been going on for years over whether it was bourgeois-democratic or socialist (proletarian) in nature–was based on soviets. One of the principal controversial issues was the shape of the organization of the state: was it to be capped by a National Assembly or was it to be based on soviets (*Rätediktatur*) after the Russian pattern? One should not be misled by the large number of the workers' and soldiers' soviets in

Germany, even though the proletarian nature of the governments in Bremen, Braunschweig and Bavaria was indisputable. The majority of them was dominated by the reformist Social Democratic Party, assisted by the right wing of the Independent Socialist Party (USPD), that right wing representing "a revolution within the revolution" in Germany. Only few soviets were controlled by the left, consisting of the Spartacus Union and the "independent" left. The reformist majority did not intend to destroy the soviets from the inside: as it did not treat them as state agencies it wanted to make them solve local problems in the capacity of local government bodies that would remain as a complement to the parliament.

Some politicians saw in the soviets a democratic form of representation of workers' interests; this interpretation was favoured by some bourgeois parties and some authors (W. Rathenau), as they saw in them a safety-valve that would prevent a revolution from breaking out.[113] The left wing of the worker movement was a much weaker party in that confrontation, and the fact that it was not led by any organized centre (the Communist Party of Germany was set up only at the turn of 1918) contributed to a rapid collapse of the revolution, sealed by the elections to the National Assembly in January 1919, which gave the majority of seats to bourgeois parties. Events in Bavaria followed a different course.

The peculiarity of the Soviet Republic of Bavaria was the fact that it was assisted by a peasant uprising, during which peasant soviets were being established spontaneously. No active political alliance developed, however, between the peasantry and the working class, because the Bavarian Communists underestimated the importance of the peasant movement, and they themselves were setting up in Munich assemblies of factory committees which elected their delegates not on the strength of revolutionary consciousness and political experience, but on the strength of vocational competence: acquaintance with production and sales. The said committees were thus not bodies of any local government.[114] They were workers' soviets only by name and did not resemble in any way those forms of political organization which had been worked out by the Bolshevik Party. The lack of any clear-cut programme on the part of the Soviet Government of Bavaria, its inability to channel the revolutionary vigour of the masses, and the said underestimation of the non-revolutionary peasant movement resulted in that government succumbing to military force after a civil war of brief duration.[115]

At the time in Germany when the attempt to set up a soviet republic had been ultimately defeated, Hungary saw in March 1919 the emergence of a soviet republic which replaced the bourgeois democratic republic set up in October 1918. Its specific feature was that the power was taken over by the soviets in a *peaceful* manner, both in Budapest and in the provinces. This attracted Lenin's attention, who saw in that an unprecedented development, revealing that which was blurred by the events in Russia; namely that communism was linked to a new proletarian democracy, which replaces the old parliamentary system. At the Meeting of Delegates in Moscow in March 1918 Lenin drew attention to the role of a peaceful taking over of power ("the bourgeoisie ... resigns of its own will") as a specific precedent.[116] The soviet government in Hungary was a coalition government which included communists, left-wing social democrats, centrists, and right-wing social democrats. The Soviet Republic of Hungary survived for over 4 months to be abolished as a result of external military intervention. Its fall was speeded up by the sectarian errors of its leaders. The imprudent nationalization of small enterprises (contrary to the decree of 26 March 1919, which excluded enterprises that employed not more than twenty workers) estranged the petty bourgeoisie. Even greater mistakes were made in the rural areas. On the one hand, peasant farms of less than 57 hectares (100 holds) were not socialized. On the other, on the remaining land so far held by great land-owners (55 per cent of the total) no agrarian reform was carried out, but co-operative farms were being organized on a mass scale, which in turn disappointed and estranged the rural proletariat and poor peasants.[117] Under such circumstances organizing the soviets as the agencies of a local government ended in a failure.

The picture of the revolutionary situation in Europe would remain incomplete if we did not mention the tendency, prevailing in 1918–19, to set up soviets (or councils of a similar nature) in those countries where their scope was much smaller. This was the case of England, where shop stewards' committees were being set up. In Poland in 1918–19 soviets of workers' delegates were set up in Warsaw, Lublin, Lódź, the Dąbrowa Coal Basin, and in some 80 other localities. In the Lublin area soviets of delegates of workers and farm labourers were established, in the south of Poland a peasant republic was set up in the Tarnobrzeg region, but except the Dąbrowa Coal Basin, where the soviets succeeded in organizing their Red Guard, they did not function as organs of power that enjoyed sufficient authority.[118] The situation in China was quite different: the formation of the Communist Party of China preceded the first worker movements; the party led the Canton Commune in 1927 and held its first congress in 1931, when the Soviet Republic of China was established; it survived until 1934.[119]

It is interesting to note Lenin's response to the first wave of formation of the soviets outside Russia. In his article "Conquered and Registered" (1919) he concluded that the soviet form of state had become an international property.[120] He took the problem up at the Eighth Russian Congress of the Party (March 1919) and stated that the idea of peasant soviets became victorious at Bukhara, in Azerbaijan and also in Armenia. He reverted to the issue at the Second Congress of the Komintern (1920), where he stressed the plasticity and simplicity of the structure of the soviets. He also pointed to the fact that this form of political organization can be used in countries with a predominantly peasant population still not delivered from feudalism. Those countries, which have not passed through the capitalist stage of development, can skip over it owing to the peasant soviets and the soviet form of the state. Lenin's idea came to be reflected in the Comintern Programme which envisaged the possibility of skipping over the capitalist stage of development in the case of certain countries. The same idea was advanced by Lenin in his talks with the Mongolian delegation in the autumn of 1921.

Yet, although the soviets at that time became an international phenomenon without any direct political or military intervention by the Bolsheviks, Lenin never assigned an absolute significance to them and never abandoned the thesis on the plurality of paths toward socialism, as formulated in *The State and Revolution.*

In the light of the pluralistic elements which characterize Marxism the ill-conceived tendencies to standardise society are false conclusions drawn from the theory of the dictatorship of the proletariat; they are the false consciousness of socialist society.

Fetishizing certain terms and *a priori* condemning others is a characteristic feature of the dogmatic trend in Marxism. The use of a term which having been quoted for many years usually leads to its debasement. The same applies to certain names in the history of sociopolitical thought, for which there can be no positive context.

Pluralism evokes such derogatory associations in certain Marxist circles, but if one sees in it a lively intellectual trend, capable of conveying new ideas, one cannot approve of such primitive practices and will subject these ideas to critical verification.

NOTES AND REFERENCES

1. J. L. Talmon, *The Rise of Totalitarian Democracy* (New York, 1960), p. 44; see also R. A. Nisbet, *The Quest for Community* (New York, 1953), p. 147.
2. M. L. Goldschmidt, "Rousseau on Intermediate Associations", in: J. R. Pennock and J. W. Chapman (eds.), *op. cit.*, chap. 8.
3. K. Marx and F. Engels, quoted after the Russian-language version of their collected works, vol. 4, p. 299; vol. 23, p. 162.
4. K. Marx and F. Engels, *op. cit.*, vol. 5, pp. 508 ff; vol. 28, p. 81.
5. K. Marx and F. Engels, quoted after the Polish-language version of their selected works. vol. 2, p. 112; G. Lefebvre, *La Révolution française* (Paris, 1968), pp. 62 ff. See also R. Garaudy, *Les Sources françaises du socialisme scientifique* (Paris, 1949), pp. 51 ff; he quotes the protests of "The Furious" against the freedom of one class to starve another. Cf. M. Bouloiseau, *La République Jacobine (10 auguste 1792 to 9 thermidor an II)* (Paris, 1972), pp. 15 ff, who says that the play of opposing forces destroyed the republic before it had time to consolidate (p. 252). Consult also J. R. Suratteau, *La Révolution française* (Paris, 1973), *passim* and the bibliography quoted there.
6. K. Marx and F. Engels, Russian edn, vol. 19, p. 193.
7. *Ibid.*, vol. 4, p. 299; vol. 6, p. 114.
8. *Ibid.*, vol. 3.
9. Quoted after *Iz istorii yakobinskoy diktatury 1793–4 (History of the Jacobinic Dictatorship, 1793–4)* (Odessa, 1962), p. 82.
10. Quoted after A. Mestre and Ph. Guttinger, *Constitutionalisme Jacobin et Constitutionalisme soviétique* (Paris, 1971), pp. 12, 32.
11. Quoted after H. Arendt, *On Revolution* (New York, 1965), pp. 244 ff., cf. A. Soboul, *Les*

Sans-Culottes parisiens (Paris, 1957) and *idem.*, *Robespierre und die Volksgesellschaften in Maxilien Robespierre, Beitraege zu seinem 200 Geburtstag*, ed. Walter Markow (Berlin, 1958).
12. *Ibid.*, pp. 41 ff.
13. K. Marx and F. Engels, Russian edn, vol. 1, p. 89.
14. *Ibid.*, vol. 23, p. 752.
15. K. Marx and F. Engels, *Selected Works*, Polish edn, vol. 1, p. 583 ff.
16. *Ibid.*, p. 224.
17. *Ibid.*, pp. 101, 105.
18. *Ibid.*, p. 108.
19. *Ibid.*, p. 132.
20. *Ibid.*, pp. 145, 172, 176.
21. *Ibid.*, pp. 253 ff., 292.
22. *Ibid.*, p. 510.
23. K. Marx, *Capital* (Moscow, 1962), vol. III, p. 863.
24. K. Marx and F. Engels, *Selected Works*, Polish edn, vol. 1, pp. 491, 495.
25. *Ibid.*, p. 452.
26. *Ibid.*, p. 490.
27. *Ibid.*, p. 488.
28. *Ibid.*, p. 490.
29. *Ibid.*, p. 494.
30. Cf. *La Première Internationale* (Genève, 1962), preface by J. Freymond, pp. v–xxxi.
31. K. Marx and F. Engels, *Selected Works*, Polish edn, vol. 2, pp. 18, 33.
32. *Ibid.*, vol. 1, p. 576.
33. M. Bakunin, "Die Commune von Paris und der Staatsbegriff", in: *Gesammelte Werke* (Berlin, 1923), vol. II, pp. 269, 274.
34. *Ibid.*, pp. 269–70.
35. K. Marx and F. Engels, *Selected Works*, Polish edn, vol. 2, pp. 447 ff.
36. K. Marx and F. Engels, Russian edn, vol. 13, part 2, p. 432.
37. *Ibid.*, vol. 26, p. 196.
38. K. Marx and F. Engels, *Selected Works*, Polish ed., vol. 1, p. 599.
39. *Ibid.*, vol. 2, pp. 32–3.
40. *Ibid.*, p. 22.
41. K. Marx and F. Engels, Russian edn, vol. 16, part 2, p. 109. This was a critique of the *draft* programme. But the programme in its adopted version was approved of by Engels.
42. *Ibid.*, vol. 1, pp. 122 ff.
43. *Ibid.*, pp. 126 ff.
44. W. Tormin, *Zwischen Rätediktatur und sozialer Demokratie* (Düsseldorf, 1954), p. 22.
45. The case of the Erfurt programme is explained in detail by M. Waldenberg in his *Wzlot i upadek Karol Kautsky'ego (The Rise and Fall of Karl Kautsky)* (Kraków, 1972), vol. 1, pp. 88 ff. The title of Kautsky's commentary: Das Erfurter Programm in seinem grundsätzlichen Teil erläutert, (Stuttgart, 1892), is quoted after Waldenberg, too.
46. *Die Soziale Revolution* (Berlin, 1902), *passim*.
47. *Die Agrarfrage...* (Stuttgart, 1899).
48. K. Kautsky, *Die Proletarische Revolution und sein Programm...*
49. E. Bernstein, *Die Voraussetzungen des Sozialismus und die Aufgaben der Sozialdemokratie* (Stuttgart, 1899) *passim*.
50. *Ibid.*
51. This distinction is clearly shown by Waldenberg, *op. cit.*, vol. 1, p. 524.
52. On Kautsky's standpoint on the self-determination of nations see Waldenberg, *op. cit.*, vol. 1, p. 307. On the assessment by Lenin of Kautsky's stand see W. Markiewicz, *Socjologia a służba społeczna (Sociology and Social Service)* (Poznań, 1972), especially the essay on the problems of nation in Lenin's works.
53. K. Kautsky, *Ethik im Lichte der materialistischen Geschichtsauffassung...*
54. *Der Weg zur Macht. Politische Betrachtungen über des Hineinwachsen in die Revolution* (1st edn, Berlin, 1909).
55. M. Waldenberg, *op. cit.*, vol. 1, p. 501.
56. K. Marx and F. Engels, *Selected Works*, Polish edn, vol. 2, p. 433.
57. *Die Soziale Revolution.*

58. M. Waldenberg, *op. cit.*, vol. 2, pp. 50, 70, 161.
59. A. Mathiez, *Jacobinisme et bolchévisme* (Paris, 1920); M. Duverger, *Sociologie politique* (Paris, 1966), p. 10; A. Hauriou, *Droit constitutionnel et institutions politiques* (Paris, 1966), p. 466.
60. M. H. Fabre, *Principes républicains de droit constitutionnel* (Paris, 1967), p. 204.
61. A. Mestre and Ph. Guttinger, *op. cit.*, p. 95.
62. V. Lenin, *Collected Works*, Polish edn, vol. 8, pp. 196, 255, 258; vol. 9, p. 45; vol. 10, p. 365; vol. 11, pp. 41 ff.
63. *Ibid.*, vol. 25, p. 117.
64. *Ibid.*, vol. 8, pp. 176–7. Lenin considered it a cardinal error that the Jacobins directed their terror against the leaders of the masses, the Hébertists and "the Furious", so that they had cut themselves off from the Sansculotte masses (cf. vol. 8, p. 297).
65. *Ibid.*, Polish edn, vol. 7, p. 150.
66. Cf. J. Monnerot *Sociologie du communisme* (Paris, 1963), p. 42.
67. V. Lenin, *Collected Works*, Polish edn, vol. 7, p. 442; vol. 8, p. 196.
68. M.L. Salvadori, *Gramsci e il problema storico della democrazia* (Torino, 1973), pp. 148 ff.
69. This was the standpoint taken by Lenin at the Fifth Congress of the Russian Social Democratic Party in February 1917, cf. vol. 12, pp. 126 ff. He reverted to the issue in November 1917, when he quoted the preface A. Lunacharskiy's (Voinov's) unpublished (and lost?) pamphlet on the party's attitude toward the trade unions, in which he blamed syndicalism for (i) anarchical weakness of their organization, (ii) exciting the workers instead of turning the trade unions into a fortress of a class-based organization, (iii) following Proudhon's individualistic theory, (iv) unreasonable abhorrence of politics. Cf. Vol. 13, pp. 159 ff. and also A. Losovski, *Anarchosinohkalism i kommunism* (Moskva, 1924).
70. Testimony of V.D. Bonch-Bruevich (Lenin's close collaborator): Meeting with Kropotkin, in I. Deutscher: *Not by Politics Alone…the Other Lenin* (London 1973), pp. 75 ff.
71. V. Lenin, Polish edn, vol. 10, pp. 1–2.
72. Quoted after W. Tormin, *op cit*, p. 14.
73. V. Lenin, *Selected Works*, Polish edn, vol. 1, p. 765.
74. L. Trotsky, *Geschichte der russischen Revolution* (Berlin, 1933), pp. 335, 347–50.
75. *Ibid.*, p. 282.
76. Quoted after A. Ciołkosz, *Róża Luksemburg a rewolucja rosyjska* (*Rosa Luxemburg and the Russian Revolution*) (Paris, 1961).
77. *Ibid.*, pp. 196–8.
78. *Ibid.*, pp. 199–204. H. Cunow considered the nations' right to self-determination as incompatible with the Marxist theory. Cf. his *Partei Zusammenbruch? Ein offenes Wort zum inneren Parteistreit* (Berlin, 1915), pp. 33 ff.
79. A. Ciołkosz, *op. cit.*, pp. 206, 210–11.
80. *Ibid.*, pp. 212, 215.
81. The discussion was between J. Hochfeld and R. Werfel, cf. *Po prostu*, issues of 17 Feb., 3 Mar., 24 Mar., 1957.
82. A. Ciołkosz, *op. cit.*, pp. 195–6.
83. On this issue see Crawford Young, *The Politics of Cultural Pluralism*, (Madison (Wisc.) 1976), in particular chaps. 1 to 3.
84. R. Luxemburg, *Selected Works*, Polish edn, vol. 2, pp. 142 ff, 453.
85. V. Lenin, *Selected Works*, Polish edn, vol. 2, p. 399.
86. *Ibid.*, p. 413.
87. *Ibid.*, p. 414.
88. V. Lenin, *Collected Works*, Russian edn, vol. 29, pp. 162 ff.
89. From this period on, the differences btween Lenin's and Stalin's views became more evident.
90. His coming closer to Bernstein's standpoint was ambivalent. He nevertheless tried to bring out the differences between himself and Bernstein. In a letter of July 1919 he wrote that one of the differences of opinion between them pertained to revolution, which Bernstein *always* (italics–S.E.) considered to be useless or detrimental. "I opposed that very vigorously and was right about that. But people never know how to tell a social from a political revolution. The latter can only be a sudden act and was indispensable in Eastern Europe. The military monarchy could not be overcome in any other way. But that took place now, and the task now is a social revolution only–except for Asia and the colonies.

That revolution can take place only step by step, so that it may not be diagnosed as a revolution from the outside. One cannot tell with precision, where and when capitalism began; accordingly, one cannot say that now capitalism comes to an end and socialism begins." Quoted after M. Waldenberg, *op. cit.*, vol. 2, p. 529; see also that author's comments on those differences, *ibid.*, p. 530.

91. K. Kautsky, *Die Diktatur des Proletariats* (Wien, 1918); *idem.*, *Die proletarische Revolution und sein Programm* (Berlin and Stuttgart, 1922); M. Waldenberg, *op. cit.*, vol. 2, pp. 299, 339, 496.

92. K. Kautsky, *Terrorismus und Kommunismus. Ein Beitrag zur Naturgeschichte der Revolution* (Berlin, 1919).

93. Cf. Otto Bauer, *Bolschewismus oder Sozialdemokratie?* (Wien, 1920). On Hilfersing's standpoint see M. Waldenberg, *op. cit.*, vol. 2, p. 338.

94. K. Kautsky, *Von der Demokratie zur Staatssklaverei. Eine Auseinandersetzung mit Trotski* (Berlin, 1921).

95. K. Kautsky, *Die prolaterische Revolution...*, pp. 82 ff., quoted in M. Waldenberg, *op cit.*, p. 98.

96. R. Luxemburg, "Das Offiziösentum der Theorie", quoted in M. Waldenberg, *op. cit.*, p. 156.

97. K. Kautsky, *Nationalversammlung und Räteversammlung* (Berlin, 1918).

98. To Kautsky's *Terrorismus und Kommunismus* Trotsky replied with "Terrorismus und Kommunismus. Anti-Kautsky", 1920, included in *Grundfragen der Revolution* (Hamburg, 1923), to which Kautsky in turn replied with *Von der Demokratie...* and *Die proletarische Revolution...* In the former of the two he predicted a quick collapse of the Soviet system (pp. 74 ff).

99. From the very beginning of the war Lenin thought that the imperialist war had to be transformed into a civil one; he followed that path of thought till the outbreak of the revolution, whereas Kautsky had abandoned that idea. Cf. V. Lenin, *Collected Works*, Polish edn, vol. 21, pp. 20 ff. and vol. 35, pp. 139 ff.

100. *Ibid.*, vol. 33, pp. 493 ff.

101. V. Lenin, "The proletarian revolution and the renegade Kautsky", in: *ibid.*, vol. 28, p. 303.

102. R. Luxemburg, *op. cit.*, pp. 187, 193.

103. Quoted after M. Waldenberg, *op. cit.*, p. 354.

104. *Ibid.*, p. 355.

105. In March 1919 Lenin explained at the First Congress of the Communist International that the Bolsheviks were guided by revolutionary pragmatism. That was why at first they had not declared that they would not recognize the National Assembly, but when the soviets had become popular and won power, they had concluded it was time to disperse the Constituent Assembly. See also his "Elections to the Legislative Assembly and the Dictatorship of the Proletariat", *Collected Works*, Polish edn, vol. 30, pp. 252 ff.

106. V. Lenin, *Rewohicja proletariackon...*, pp. 236 and *passim*.

107. V. Lenin, *Collected Works*, Polish edn, vol. 28, p. 214.

108. *Ibid.*, p. 275.

109. K. Kautsky, *Georgien. Eine sozialdemokratische Bauernpolitik. Eindrücke und Beobachtungen* (Wien, 1921); L. Trotsky, *Zwischen Imperialismus und Revolution. Die Grundfragen der Revolution an dem Einzelbeispiel Georgiens* (Hamburg, (2nd edn) 1923), in particular chap. IX: "Das Recht der nationalen Selbstbestimmung und die proleterische Revolution". The book was included in *Grundfragen der Revolution*.

110. N. Bukharin, *Karl Kautsky und Sowjetrussland* (Wien, 1925).

111. This duality, which also marked other leaders of the Second International (including O. Bauer), and its sources were pointed to by Lenin in his essay on the infantile disease of "leftism" in communism (cf. his *Collected Works*, Polish edn, vol. 31, pp. 98 ff). On pluralistic elements in Marxism see N. Geras Classical and Proletarian Representation in *New Left Review* Jan–Feb, 1981 pp. 83 ff.

112. W. Tormin, *op cit.*, E. Kolb, *Die Arbeiterräte in der deutschen Innenpolitik 1918–1919* (Düsseldorf, 1962).

113. Lenin called combining the soviets with the National Assembly a nonsense (cf. his paper read at the First Congress of the Comintern in March 1915, *Collected Works* Polish edn, vol. 28). But that nonsense was advocated by the then two largest left-wing parties, SPD

and USPD. Cf. W. Tormin, *op. cit.*, pp. 71 ff. Inclusion in the Weimar Constitution of the provision concerning shop councils was commented on by Lenin as a concession due to the fact that German workers called for a soviet rule. (Lenin in Sept. 1919.)

114. It is significant that Lenin in his message to the Bavarian Republic asked to be informed whether a council of workers' delegates had been set up. *Collected Works*, Russian edn, vol. 29, p. 238.

115. G. Werner: *Bavarskaia Sowietskaia Respoublika* (Moskva, 1934); N. Zastienker *Bavarskaia Sowietskaia Respoublika* (Moskva, 1934).

116. V. Lenin, *Collected Works*, Russian edn, vol. 29, pp. 203, 246, 260 ff.

117. Bela Kun, *La République Hongroise des Conseils* (Budapest, 1962). Other data have been drawn from M.F. Lebovitch's paper Sovety v Vengriyi (The Soviets in Hungary), *Voprosy Filosofii*, No. 2 (1958).

118. Cf. B. Bicz, *Rady Delegatów Robotniczych w Polsce 1918–19 (Councils of Workers' Delegates in Poland, 1918–19)*, (Moscow 1934); M. Misko (ed.), *Z historii ruchu rewolucyjnego w Polsce, 1918–19 (History of the Revolutionary Movement in Poland, 1918–19)* (Warszawa, 1950).

119. Cf. G. Yefimov's writings (in Russian) concerned with modern Chinese history *Soviety w Kitaie*, (Moskva, 1933); *Programmyje dokumenty kitaiskich sovietow* (Moskva, 1935).

120. V. Lenin, *Selected Works*, Polish edn, vol. II, pp. 458 ff.; *Collected Works*, Russian edn, vol. 31, pp. 217 ff. See also the *Programme and Statute of the Communist International* (in Russian) (Moskva, 1936), pp. 111 ff.

CHAPTER 6

Pluralistic Elements in the Socialist Reconstruction of Society

6.1 THE NEW ECONOMIC POLICY (NEP) AS SEEN AGAINST THE BACKGROUND OF THE EVOLUTION OF SOVIET SOCIETY

Departure from war communism, a policy dictated by higher necessity and a policy the victims of which must have been the soviets together with the nascent system of proletarian democracy, required not just a return to the previous condition, but the working-out of an alternative policy based on new principles. It was to the consolidation of such a policy that Lenin dedicated the last two years of his life. In this study, we shall disregard the wide range of economic and social problems discussed by Lenin in his last programmatic article,[1] and shall confine ourselves to the issue most germane to our purpose. The New Economic Policy (NEP) meant renunciation of extra-economic measures of coercion in the sphere of the national economy, measures which were not suitable in a period of peaceful development for the socialist system; it meant renunciation of the system of restrictions and controls, and restoration, in a sense, of the market conditions. NEP reflected the collapse of the illusion that the development of the national economy can be guided by decrees without regard to economic laws.[2]

One of the basic trends of the new policy was setting store by the economic enterprise of the peasants, which could stimulate industry; it was also setting store by home trade as a basis of economic and political bonds between the proletariat and the peasantry. Lenin made it a point that the policy concerned with the peasants should above all take their interests into account, that the authorities should reconstruct and modernize agriculture without hurrying and without resorting to pressure. Changes should be brought about by a system of co-operatives, which were to be the meeting places of individual enterprise and the leadership of the government agencies. These changes started with the introduction of a tax in kind (later changed into a tax in specie, which after the period of requisitions was accepted by the peasants with great relief), and this was followed by the legalization of trade in land and in surplus produce from peasant holdings.

The expanded and differentiated network of co-operatives, which under war communism had been transformed into the state system of apportionment of goods, regained in its autonomy. Restoration of these co-operatives' right to make their own economic decisions enabled them to gain control of ever larger spheres of wholesale and retail trade. That did not take place without competition: NEP also opened possibilities to private enterprise in wholesale and retail trade, but the consolidating co-operative system was gradually driving NEP-men out of that field.

In Lenin's opinion, 10 to 20 years should be enough to set up a "civilized" co-operative system in the rural areas, which would mean a marked turn towards socialism. Expansion of the co-operative system under the Soviet conditions, that is after a political revolution, was for Lenin tantamount to an expansion of the socialist system itself.[3] The reservation is to be made here (even though we shall revert to the problem) that Lenin did not mean producer co-operatives (*kolkhozes*), but co-operatives concerned with distribution and sale, and also other co-operative organizations, that is those forms with which the peasants had been acquainted before 1914. But those forms, traditional in a sense, were to, and did, perform new functions in a new social system. The *NEP did mean a decisive departure from authoritarian methods of solving economic problems and running the national economy*; it meant the fundamental decision of preserving, next to the nationalized (state) sector of the national economy (which included heavy industry, all large enterprises in light and processing industry, transportation, banking, and foreign trade), the co-operative and the private sector. In the last one, the greatest role was, of course, played by small peasant holdings (25 million), while in industry the small enterprises, which numerically formed an overwhelming majority, employed little more than 12 per cent of the manpower.[4]

In this mixed socialist economy, the first in the world, the weight of the nationalized sector was so great that, in Lenin's opinion, it secured to that sector the position of control in the national economy as a whole. This fact made it possible both to denationalize small enterprises and craftsmen's workshops (which mostly turned out goods for immediate consumption) and to decentralize state enterprises.

NEP thus meant transferring economic decisions, within specified limits, to the co-operative and the private sector, it meant a policy of winning over and activating, both economically and socially, the intermediate strata–especially in the rural areas, but also in towns.

This established economic bonds between town and country, which was a peace-time analogue of the revolutionary alliance between the revolutionary proletariat and the peasantry.

Lenin saw in NEP the only path from patriarchalism to modernity. Political action should be assisted by cultural activity, which was to concentrate on the elimination of illiteracy. Lenin thought that this would help the socialist reconstruction of society, whereas obtrusive insistence on spreading communism in the rural areas could only harm the cause of socialism. He thus shifted the centre of gravity to the peace-time organizational work in the sphere of the national economy and culture.[5]

There is an excellent observation on Lenin's plans of reviving and expanding the co-operative system under socialism in Oskar Lange's reflections on the subject concerning the conditions in Poland:

> there is already a co-operative movement, which was born under capitalism as a movement of classes and strata which were predominantly non-capitalistic ... it is a form of self-defence of those classes and strata .... When that movement is covered by the process of building socialism it changes its form, too, because a part of the socialist economy and the co-operative property are transformed into a kind of socialist property. The socialist revolution faces not only the problem of socializing the capitalist property by expropriating the capitalists, but also the problem of a socialist transformation of the property of small producers. These ... are not enemies of the working class, ... on the contrary, they are its allies. Hence it is obvious that there is no problem of expropriating these small producers, allies of the working class, and that they must be brought into the orbit of the socialist economy in another way, namely through the co-operative movement.

The latter is described by him thus:

> the co-operative movement is the only socially possible way of socializing the small producers and the small-scale services, for it can activate certain economic incentives which the economy based on social property is not in a position to activate on the same scale. ... The effects of the co-operative economy are more directly linked to a given group of co-operative members, and hence their economic interest in their work is more direct.

When referring to the co-operative self-government Lange wrote:

> the co-operative movement, in view of the group character of co-operative property, has produced a fine tradition of a democratic management of socialized economic enterprises [and further] co-operative management is socialist management if the managers are responsible to society as a whole, and not only to members of a given co-operative.[6]

In politics, the period under consideration was marked by the campaign, which fully developed only after Lenin's death, to revive the soviets. This was a natural sequel to the replacement of administrative pressure by increased political freedom, reflected for a number of years in a legal activity of opposition parties. Those parties vanished some years later because of a lack of any prospects of undermining the well-consolidated one-party system and returning to a multi-party system, which had existed after the revolution until the period of war communism. The process was sealed by the emigration of eminent leaders of those opposition parties. That new period was also marked by the laying of institutional foundations of a federal, multi-national Soviet state, which was paralleled by Lenin's vehement condemnation of Great Russian chauvinism.[7]

When the NEP period is assessed, one of the most controversial issues is the proper interpretation of the Tenth Party Congress (March 1921) and its decisions, which were made at the very beginning of the NEP period and applied to relations within, and the unity of, the ruling Communist Party. This is essential, because the Congress preceded by a mere couple of months the publication of Lenin's article "On the Tax in Kind". Growing economic and political problems made the Congress adopt the decision on the unity of political *action*. The well-known prohibition to form factions applied to *discipline in carrying out a policy,* but was *not intended to hinder the freedom of* political *discussion before a decision was made, nor the freedom of* theoretical *discussion after a political decision was adopted.* The concept of deviation was for the first time formulated at that Congress. Lenin referred to deviations not as any articulated trends (the discussion then focused on the anarchist and syndicalist Worker Opposition,[8] but as a group of people who strayed "a little" (Lenin's formulation) off course. In his interpretation, a deviation is something which can be remedied, and not an anti-party heresy to be rooted out. While criticizing the opponents he also mentioned their services in those matters which were not at issue; that is, the democratization of the Soviet state, and pointing to the necessity of combating bureaucracy, in which the Worker Opposition could be a valuable ally. He reminded the audience that the opponents were given the opportunity to lay down their arguments in the central party organ (which at that time had a circulation of 250,000 copies), and stressed many times that the decisions adopted at the Congress did not prohibit further theoretical discussion in books and special publications. But if differences of opinion on essential issues recurred, nothing could prevent them from representing their views to the party as a whole.[9]

The fact that representatives of the Worker Opposition, supported in this respect by Lenin, were elected to the Central Committee despite the general atmosphere created by the Kronstadt Uprising, is of essential significance for the appraisal of the political atmosphere prevailing at the Tenth Congress. There is no reason to treat Lenin's speeches and the decisions adopted at the Congress as the foundation on which, a few years later, Stalin's policy of party monolithism could be based. On the contrary, everything seems to indicate that those documents were a preparation for the new economic policy, and Lenin took the Jeffersonian stance that the defence of minority rights to present its views is the essence of democracy.

As seen by Lenin, this new economic policy was threatened most by bureaucratic centralism, which could annihilate what had already been done and block the further correct development of that policy.[10]

In Lenin's view, NEP was not reduced to a plan of expanding the co-operative movement, even though co-operatives were to cover the whole of society and even, as it were automatically, to lead it to socialism. NEP was an *integrated plan of transforming society and democratizing the machinery of the state*. Hence Lenin's numerous (especially in the last period of his life) castigations of bureaucracy: his reference to "a workers' state with a bureaucratic distortion"; the formulation about the communist bureaucrat as the greatest enemy holding a high position in the machinery of the state; his appeal that the trade unions should defend workers against their proletarian state; his stigmatizing the Asiatic methods of production, to which he opposed the European forms in public life.[11]

The NEP was a general plan of reconstructing society on socialist principles, outlined to cover an epoch, or at least a number of decades. It was an idea of a–as we would put it today–systemic change

Bukharin, who after Lenin's death was, of all party leaders, most engaged in the implementation of the NEP policy (which brought him into a sharp conflict with Trotsky) saw the best antidote to bureaucracy in thousands of small and large associations, clubs, and other organizations, which would make it possible to reach the broadest masses on matters of direct interest to them and to work on them by persuasion. Bukharin also saw in the soviets a block to bureaucracy, and after Lenin's death he accordingly took a vigorous part in the drive to revive them. In his opinion, local soviets should become schools of management for non-party activists. At the Twelfth Party Congress Bukharin continued Lenin's policy of criticising Great Russian chauvinism and called for understanding of the aspirations of small nations.

The NEP period was marked by a lively cultural life. Acceptance of the principles of the new system served as the meeting place of the various trends, which was accompanied by novel achievements in art and literature. NEP was not merely an economic phenomenon, but it made a deep imprint upon the inner life of the party, leaving no sphere of life untouched.

S. F. Cohen, the author of a monograph on Bukharin, is right in stating that the NEP atmosphere won the co-operation of the masses, including numerous groups of intellectuals and technologists. He describes that period as co-existence of the monopoly of political power with pluralism and variety in other fields. But even he, animated by good will and probably one of the first American authors to question so comprehensively the antinomy between a one-party system and pluralism, failed to grasp everything: in Lenin's view he saw his coming closer to Bernstein. It turns out that grasping the difference between reforms *instead of* a revolution and reforms *after* a revolution was too difficult for Cohen.[12]

It is worth while recalling the attitude adopted towards the NEP by Kautsky. It would seem that since he saw the limits of the socialization of production and properly estimated the importance of the co-operative movement he was particularly well prepared for an understanding of the idea behind the introduction of NEP. But it turned out to have been otherwise. His total appraisal of NEP sounded like a sentence: an immense step backwards, capitulation to capitalism, resulting in the fall of the Bolshevik dictatorship in Russia.[13] Kautsky saw in NEP a confirmation of his claim that the Russian proletariat was not ready to carry out socialist economic transformations, and that such transformations should be made gradually under a system of parliamentary democracy.

NEP, together with unquestionable economic progress, brought with it a number of undesirable phenomena both in the economic sphere (where a wave of speculation that affected the lively interests of the working class was most acutely felt of all) and in the sphere of habits. Many party workers believed that the economic status of licensed capitalists, combined with nascent elements of speculative capital which emerged during the NEP period, could become the starting point for the restoration of capitalism.

The arrogant counterculture of the NEP-men was a challenge to the egalitarian ethos of the younger generation of communists. This led to a great discussion within the Bolshevik party in the late 1920s. Bukharin stood for the continuation of the NEP policy. He conceded that it had to be corrected, and that it was necessary more strictly to supervise the economic activity of the NEP-men, but he thought–in accordance with Lenin's view–that NEP was a long-term matter, a policy for a whole generation. But the leaders of the Bolshevik Party followed Stalin, who initially backed this policy for tactical reasons but after having defeated separately Kamenev and Zinoviev and last but not least Trotsky, he was out for Bukharin who eventually had to perish, and Stalin announced NEP as a tactical manoeuvre and as a temporary retreat. He thought that NEP had already played its role. While Lenin had planned NEP for a generation, Stalin delcared that, the reconstruction of the national economy completed, the pre-war production level achieved, and industrialization being on the way, the NEP was to be terminated. He announced that circumstances favoured a complete reversal of the policy. This marked the period of compulsory collectivization on a mass scale, carried out with a ruthlessness that reminded one of the period of war communism. Some authors wrote about collectivization *en masse* as an October Revolution in the rural areas, but it was in fact a return to the methods used under war communism, which ousted Lenin's civilized co-operative system.[14]

This put an end to Lenin's dream of making an alliance between revolutionary enthusiasm and the cleverness of an intelligent businessman. The turn made by Stalin meant the end of mixed structures. As M. Waldenberg put it:

The classical Marxist theory of social development accepted the

existence of mixed structures in the base and in the superstructure as a
regularity which marks *transformation of one* socioeconomic *formation
into another* [italics–S.E.] The classical Marxist interpretation of the
process of transition from capitalism to socialism also assumed the
existence of mixed structure during the transitional period.[15]

The "turn" did not apply to economy alone. Methods typical of war
communism were for the first time used within the party. That started a
period of repressions and restrictions in the various fields of public life. The
concept of deviation was given a new and, as the political trials in the late
1930s were to show, ominous sense.

In this context it is worthwhile to point to the stance taken by E. Varga,
who claimed that the capitalist danger called for an economic leap forward,
and hence for centralization of many spheres of social life and collectivization
on a mass scale. "From this point of view", he wrote, "Stalin was right in
having revised Lenin's and Bukharin's plans and having so quickly put an
end to NEP."

It was only after Stalin's death that the 20th and the 22nd Congress of the
Communist Party of the Soviet Union initiated a return to Lenin's position
and passed a verdict on bureaucratic centralism. This opened prospects for
reference to those pluralistic elements which should be the proper sense of
the Soviet system. In the programmatic documents adopted at those
Congresses two ideas came to the fore: (1) rejection of the Stalinist thesis
concerning the incessantly exacerbating class struggle resulting in replacing
the conception of the dictatorship of the proletariat by that of the Soviet
all-national state as better complying with the stage of social development
achieved; (2) this in turn gave rise to the idea of communist social
self-government. This must have necessarily led to the revaluation of the
Soviet representative system, an increased role for social organizations, the
proper functioning of the federal institutions, and the rule of law in the
sphere of civic rights.

Empirical verification would be required to show how far these tendencies
are winning ground. We shall discuss later the decentralization tendencies
observed in the Soviet Union by Western authors. At this moment we have to
stress that the opinion that social differentiation reduces class differentiation
(which can, in fact, only be the rudimentary differentiation that conditions
the other ones), belongs to the past. A collective study of social differentiation in the Soviet Union reads: "The fact that the most lively interests of all
groups are common to them does not preclude specific and individual
interests." But in the next sentence this is restricted to the first level of the
development of the communist formation, until "such a level of maturity is
attained which would eliminate all basis for divergences between individual
interests, group interests (specific interests of the various social groups etc.),
and interests of society as a whole."[16] The authors thus claim that an

advanced socialist society would be marked by a uniformity of interests. There are no reasons why such forecasts should be made, because the observable trend is that of a growing differentiation of interests, especially the vocational ones, which means a growing differentiation of both formal and informal groups, a growing complexity of society and the processes which are taking place in it. This is a general law of development, both in biological and societal life.

It is remarkable that no such restriction is found in the report submitted by the CPSU Central Committee to the 24th Congress, where we find the following formulation:

> When posing and solving problems of a *further* [italics–S.E.] development of our political system, which is an ideological issue, the Central Committee started from the assumption that the policy of the party yields desired results if it takes into account both the interests of the whole nation and those of the social classes and groups within the nation, and if it guides them so as to form a single common tendency.[17]

In the Soviet literature concerned with the social sciences more and more authors oppose a simplified interpretation of the structure of socialist society. The opinions of G. Shakhnazarov seem representative in that respect. In criticizing Western authors' views concerning social stratification he opposes the tendency to identify social classes and social groups, but treats these concepts as complementary. While claiming that in Soviet society there are no class antagonisms in the sense of class stratification, he stresses that:

> a lack of antagonism does not mean a lack of all contradictions. Interests, whenever they exist and are specific in nature, can and do bear various relations to one another. Such relations take on the three basic forms: convergence of interests, their mutual neutrality, and the various shades of contradiction among them. Even though these contradictions are not antagonistic, they may become very acute. ...[18]

Contrary to the opinions current in the West, the views of Soviet authors on the issue of one-party and multi-party systems are formulated in a similar spirit (see below the digression from the analysis of the Polish political system). But even now it is worth while dwelling on two issues: democracy within the party, and the leading role of the party relative to the machinery of the state. Vigorous enforcement of democracy within the party is postulated by party documents of the highest rank, issued in the post-Stalinist period, but it is also significant that endeavours are made to revive the Leninist tradition in that respect.[19]

When it comes to the other issue there is also the common trend, which refers to the Leninist practice, that the leading role of the party should not be interpreted as the replacement by it of the machinery of the state through interfering with the process of administration, or, worse still, through issuing orders. "It is common knowledge that the dictatorship of the proletariat was conceived by the founders of Marxism and practised after October 1917 as a system of power based on a broad representation with the Communist Party as the leading ideological and political force.[20] Both the new Soviet constitution and the ratification of both covenants on human rights point to the normative acceptance of the pluralistic elements inherent in Marxism. These tendencies expressed in political documents inspired by Medvedev's hope that progressive reforms in the Soviet Union may be achieved by legal measures.[21]

It is obvious that the efforts tend to revive an *autonomous* (italics–S.E.) sphere of decision-making of the Soviet representative bodies and social organizations. Looking for significant features of elements of pluralism in Soviet society is natural when it comes to the antithesis of bureaucratic centralism.

6.2 PLURALISTIC ELEMENTS IN SOCIALIST TRANSFORMATIONS AFTER WORLD WAR II: POLAND

(a)   *Class structure and structure of interests* (Some comments on
the discussion of the relations among the concepts: class,
stratum, group.)

Choosing Poland as an example is due not only to the present writer's better knowledge of sociopolitical conditions in Poland as compared with other countries which turned to socialism after World War II, but also to the strongest continuity in the emergence and revival of pluralistic elements in the sociopolitical structure of Poland. No such continuity can be found in other socialist countries which emerged after World War II,[22] except for Yugoslavia, whose case will be discussed later.

In Poland, opinions on class structure were for a long time a subject of controversy which is not yet over. Linked to them were certain unclarified issues concerning changes in class consciousness. Common acceptance of Lenin's well-known definition according to which classes are:

> large groups of people which differ from one another by their respective positions in a historically determined system of social production, by their relationship (usually fixed and established by law) to the means of production, by their role in the social organization of labour and hence by the way of acquiring and the size of that part of social wealth which each of them has at its disposal,[23]

could serve as the point of departure, but did not suffice to solve problems of socialist societies, and in particular the problem whether in a given society class stratification remains or not, and if it vanishes, then what the stage of that process is at a given time and how it manifests itself. The emerging doubts seem natural in view of the fact that neither Marx nor Engels had left in their works any elaborated theory of classes,[24] and the discussion over the problems of classes, summed up by Lenin's definition quoted above, pertained to class structure in bourgeois societies, so that its conclusions cannot mechanically be applied to socialist societies.

The problem of class and social structure in Polish society was an object of controversy in the mid-1960s and the early 1970s. But these controversies over class division should not veil the real contradictions within both classes and strata. The contradiction which marks the basic status of workers in socialist society consists in the fact that the workers are co-owners of the nationalized means of production and members of the dominant class, but at the same time they perform subordinate functions in the factories. This controversy may give rise to a lasting problem, especially if we consider the fact that in Poland after 1945 the most politically conscious workers, capable of thinking in terms of society as a whole, were promoted to high ranks in the machinery of the state and in economic administration, and assigned important social and political functions. On the other hand, the number of workers with almost no social and political experience increased enormously.[25]

W. Wesołowski speaks forthrightly about the process of decomposition of class features in socialist societies. The role of differentiating features is accordingly being taken over by the features of social status themselves, such as the nature of work done, income, education, prestige, and so on. Such features, separated from the determining effect of their relationship to means of production, exist under socialism as it were autonomously. In this connection, even though classes tend to disappear in an advanced socialist society, there remains a form of social differentiation which might be termed *stratification* (italics–W.W.).[26] In a word, new problems come to the fore: they are linked to the inner differentiation of the working class, the peasantry, and the intelligentsia by income and privileges, by participation in the process of government, vocational and professional qualifications, level of social consciousness, and social prestige. This makes the three basic categories of people split into groups and strata, the division following different lines from that of class division.[27]

The centre of gravity must be shifted from definitional and classificational issues to the dynamic forces working in socialist society and to the development trends of that society, which has been pointedly shown by W. Wesołowski.[28] *If we follow after Marx's view that the proletarian revolution marks the beginning of the end of class structure, then we cannot claim, more than thirty years after a fundamental transformation of our society, that the class structure is still the only basic characteristic of socialist society.* Class society is *polarized* and has the basic antagonism, born of exploitation, as the driving force of its development. That model of society has obviously started losing its validity, and the old class division is losing its *raison d'être*: the element of antagonism has vanished. This disappearance of objective class characteristics has often been pointed to in both economic and sociological literature on the subject.

This is why Polish industrial sociologists have studied formal and informal group differentiation within socialist enterprises.[29] The consumption fund, including the wage fund, and the level of wages are no longer determined by conflicts of antagonistic interests of the owners of the means of production on the one hand, and the workers on the other. These matters are settled by plans, which various vocational groups try to modify and even, once a decision has been made, to distort according to their own interests.

In rural sociology we have to take note of the standpoint of B. Gałęski, who in 1963 concluded his monograph thus:

> ... class division ... is of marginal importance, and class conflicts based on that division cannot be taken today as the main line along which social forces in the rural areas are concentrated. ... In the Polish rural areas today the most numerous social categories are peasants who own family holdings and so-called peasant workers, owners of small holdings who commute to local factories where they work. ... This differentiation of the stratum of peasants, which in view of the changes in class structure in town and country is not linked to class division, has become the dominant one.[30]

These socioeconomic changes have been followed by changes in social consciousness. Little more than one half of the population is of the opinion that class division survives in Poland.[31] In towns, it is the division into skilled and unskilled workers which is coming to the fore, with a marked differentiation of the former category into vocational groups. The intellectuals form a separate group, while the professionals, who form the bulk of the intelligentsia, are divided into professional groups, among whom technologists and the managerial and administrative groups deserve to be singled out. The mass of little-qualified clerical personnel has become separated from the old intelligentsia, to which they belonged when secondary education was much less common, and has come to exist as a distinct group.[32]

In towns, sociologists single out a petty bourgeoisie as a separate class, which must give rise to objections if we consider the present stage of development of Polish society. If the owners of the means of small-scale production be treated as petty bourgeois, then their status will be greatly differentiated within the vocational groups of which they are members. In those cases in which their own labour dominates they can hardly be called petty bourgeois. On the other hand, in some cases (monopoly position on the market, production for export, and so on) small and even middle-size capitalists may emerge from the petty bourgeoisie.[33]

Peasant workers are that stratum which on the account of its being bi-vocational links town and country.[34] In the post-1945 period it has been marked by a great differentiation and constantly growing ranks, which is due to advances in industrialization. It is worth noting that there are much more such bi-vocational groups, especially in small towns.

Social structure in the rural areas also reveals far-reaching changes. Both rural capitalists (analogous to the *kulaks*) and the rural proletariat and land labourers (officially defined by the Institute of Rural Economy as owners of dwarf holdings who worked at least 150 days a year as labourers on their neighbours' farms) have vanished.[35] *This means the disappearance of the two poles of antagonism.* On the one hand, there is a marked differentiation into the peasants who work on their own holdings, the agricultural workers on state farms, tractor drivers, mechanics and so on, employed by agricultural organizations, and members of farming co-operatives. Disproportions within the first category are markedly growing smaller (on the other hand the limit of 20 hectares per farm is rarely exceeded, and on the other the weakest dwarf holdings are being eliminated in various ways), which indicates that moderately egalitarian conditions will prevail in the rural areas, too.

The blurring of class differences and the fluid boundaries of the new strata account for *an increased importance of membership in definite vocational groups.* The process has been extremely complicated in the rural areas, where the path from a peasant to a farmer means replacing a largely self-supporting holding by a market-oriented farm. This process will be reinforced by both the growing division of labour in the rural areas (differentiation of vocational groups) and administrative reforms (which stress the role of *communes* as administrative units). It is obvious that only small towns as vocational and cultural centres can bring town dwellers and country people together. In large towns, absorption of country people by town dwellers is the only possible outcome.

Over ten years ago B. Gałęski wrote that, under socialist industrialization, the determining system would be not that which forms a social class, but that which shapes a vocational group.[36] In the late 1970s this was no longer a mere hypothesis: *transformation of the class structure into a strato-vocational one is on the way.*

The vanishing of class differences covers objective economic processes (disappearance of social polarization), but it is not to say that the consciousness of the working class is vanishing, too. On the contrary, it is spreading: it covers some groups of the intelligentsia, and penetrates the rural areas, where outposts of the working class in the form of skilled workers, tractor drivers, mechanics, etc., have appeared. It is significant that members of the intelligentsia who are of working-class origin continue to feel their bonds with the working class.[37] This spreading of working-class consciousness sometimes finds formal reflection in documents adopted by vocational organizations. The Congress of Engineers and Mechanicians adopted in 1957 the resolution in which technologists as a vocational group are referred to as a *component part* (italics–S.E.) of the working class.[38] As S. Widerszpil put it, here we have to do with the formation of ideological bonds, as reflected in the adoption by the members of a group of an ideology common to that of another class.[39]

The crafts *en masse* consider themselves workers, and the new legal status which grants them the privileges of workers is most likely to strengthen the process. All these changes have minimized mutual dislikes which divided large blocks of society.[40] Such dislikes have been reduced to conflicts which sometimes arise among vocational groups. The source of such conflicts is fairly easy to eliminate, because the diagnosis has been made.

> As has been found, the system of salaries and wages does not in every case take the hierarchy of qualifications and prerogatives into account; by being at variance with the accepted hierarchy of prestige and equitable payment it results in a malfunctioning of the factory system, insufficient use made of the qualifications and abilities of individuals and vocations and in stresses and conflicts among both individuals and groups.[41]

Polish people are opposed to radical egalitarianism but on the other hand are very sensitive to suspected origins of wealth. The majority is in favour of moderate egalitarianism acknowledging higher incomes justified by knowledge, talent and skill. Changes within socialist society in Poland and its new stratification and clearly marked vocational structure give rise to very intricate problems; one of them would be the assigning of the proper place to social organizations as spokesmen of definite, greatly diversified, interests.

This analysis, which I wrote only two years ago, before the outbreak of the present crisis, seems to be in striking contradiction to the 1980–1 events. They shattered the social and political structure of this country which witnessed a sudden awakening of workers' class-consciousness internalized in a few months by the overwhelming majority of the intelligentsia and peasants. In the wake of the Solidarity-Movement all over the country new organizations mushroomed. New ties developed giving the nation a new integrity.

From what I said above it follows that class-consciousness is related to rudimentary cleavages of society, of a deeply polarized society. And this harmful polarization (in a certain sense artificial because it could be avoided) was triggered off by an inept, highly bureaucratic policy which nurtured conflicts unseen before. The stubborn blocking of all kind of reforms made the conflicts extremely acute, and brought about the self-mobilization of the working class.

It turned out very soon that this was the consciousness of the bulk of the nation too. This new brand of unity explains the relentless activity of so many.

It is quite natural that in a period of severe crisis this reborn class-consciousness is overshadowing group interests and their particular consciousness. But this trend should be considered as a temporary phenomenon and with the overcoming of the cleavage between the masses and the ossified bureaucracy (partly by dismantling and partly by controlling it) the unavoidable process of superimposing on the rudimentary class-consciousness the consciousness of a whole spectrum of vocational groups will take its course. And this is warranted exactly by the new, rebellious pluralism.

(b)   The problem of one-party and multi-party systems

The popular democracies had not passed through the period of revolutionary mobilization that would reveal, to the very bottom, the new differentiations and diversified trends, nor had they experienced war communism. It was only after a couple of years that they adopted the regime of bureaucratic centralism, shaped during the many years of Stalin's leadership. The decisive period was that of 1948–9, which in its political structure–though not in that field alone–corresponded to the turn achieved by Stalin in the Soviet Union in the 1930s. This does not apply to Yugoslavia, which in the said period started evolving in the opposite direction. The period between the end of World War II and that political turning point should not be compared to NEP, not only because of the complete difference in historical conditions, but also because of the tasks faced by the political leaders in the Soviet Union and in the popular democracies, respectively.

But the parallel is justified on two points: in both cases the situation was marked by a sharp political struggle over the choice of ways to achieve the socialist transformation of society; in both cases the newly emerging structures were characterized by some elements of a new social and political pluralism. An additional parallel can be seen in the premature termination of these processes: in both cases a turn was made under the pressure of the official and obviously dogmatic, wrong doctrine of the incessantly exacerbating class struggle–despite the decisive victory of the masses.

Any comparative treatment of the problem would disrupt the composition of the present book, and would also face considerable methodological obstacles in view of the far-reaching differences among the various states in their respective political and social structures. The range of sociopolitical systems varied from semi-feudal Albania to highly industrialized Czechoslovakia. Yugoslavia, Rumania and Albania adopted the one-party system, while the other countries did not; Rumania remained a monarchy for a couple of years after the fall of Nazism–all these facts would excessively complicate the course of reasoning.

This is why the problem of political and social pluralism is illustrated by the case of Poland.

The emergence, after World War II, of states which adopted the socialist system but not the one-party one was treated in the West as a tactical move, and often as just a camouflage of the one-party system, because the latter was treated as an indispensable feature of the Soviet model. That belief was due to an insufficient knowledge of facts: not only had a coalition government been formed by the Bolsheviks together with left-wing Socialist Revolutionaries (an alliance which came to an end only in June and July of 1918 after the latter rose against the Bolsheviks), but the Bolshevik Party was ready further to co-operate with other parties and political groups on the condition of their being loyal to the revolutionary cause. There were many statements made by Lenin on that subject; note also that, significantly enough, despite the said uprising that could be interpreted solely as a counter-revolutionary act, neither the Mensheviks nor the left-wing Socialist Revolutionaries had their parties delegalized. More significant still, their temporary removal from territorial soviets was withdrawn after their declaration of readiness to fight the intervention armies and their representatives after the elections returned to local and even provincial soviets. That period witnessed legal activity by such groups as the anarchists, the revolutionary communists, the international social-democrats, the Bund (party of Jewish social democrats), the Poalei-Zionists, etc. All these groups had their own press and enjoyed the freedom of public activity. The relationships between the Bolsheviks and the said groups differed from case to case, according to the political oscillations of the groups, oscillations depending on the changing situation during the civil war. The one-party system emerged *only* towards the close of the civil war, that is, in 1920–1, largely because some of these groups had joined the Bolshevik party *en bloc*.[42]

From the point of view of political principles it cannot be claimed that the dictatorship of the proletariat is incompatible with a multi-party system; there are no reasons to treat the one-party system as the political principle of the period under consideration, even though today the one-party system has become deeply rooted in the Soviet political tradition. So has it in Yugoslavia and Rumania.

The controversies over one-party and multi-party systems under socialism are no longer topical because both systems can be found in socialist countries. Yet it must be borne in mind that there were reasons to engage in them: there was a strong tendency to standardize party systems and to treat the multi-party ones as manifestations of a certain tactical measure. Such tendencies can be seen in an article by Hilary Minc (in 1949), which announced the political unification of Poland. The matter was at issue for a fairly long time, and it was only Stalin's sudden death which struck it off from the agenda.[43]

When we come to the "tripartite" alliance, as it existed in Poland until the hot summer of 1980, we have to reflect on the recruitment base of the three parties and of other political groups.[44] Following the fusion of two worker parties, the Polish Worker Party and the Polish Socialist Party, in December 1948 the Polish United Worker Party became the sole representative of the working class and, in varying degrees, of all other classes and strata.

Of the two remaining parties, the United Peasant Party recruits its members primarily from among peasants who own private holdings (4.9 per cent of holding owners are its members) and from among white-collar workers (approximately 20 per cent of its members are in that category).[45]

The Democratic Party draws its members from the various categories of white collar workers (approximately 48.5 per cent), the rest coming from among craftsmen (both owners of private workshops and members of co-operatives) and some private merchants.[46]

Members and friends of the three Roman Catholic groups, the Znak Poalei-Zionists, the Pax, and the Christian Social Association, are to be sought in the same strata and groups which form the recruitment base of the United Peasant Party and the Democratic Party.[47]

Comprehension of the differences in the social composition of the various elements of the multi-party system is essential for grasping the argument that the guiding role is being played by the Polish United Workers' Party.[48]

The question arises as to what importance should be attached to the Polish multi-party system. It would obviously make no sense to compare it to the multi-party systems in the West, since those function on different political principles and are based on the existence of opposition parties. Nevertheless the Polish party system must be treated as some kind of political pluralism.[49] It seems that the most adequate explanation would be to treat the allied parties as *organized interest groups which act as political parties* to be able to participate in the process of politics on behalf of the groups they represent. Their participation in that process is subordinated to two goals: acceptance of the strategy of social development worked out by the Polish United Workers' Party (and in that sense it means implementation of the decisions made by that party and its leaders), but also representation and defence of the special interests of their respective recruitment bases. The latter goal indicates what autonomy the United Peasant Party and the Democratic Party have within the tripartite alliance and sheds light upon the nature of the membership of its representatives in the supreme governmental and political bodies.

We have to point in this connection to the formulations to be found in the new Polish Constitution, which, when referring to the Front of National Unity, mentions co-operation between the Polish United Workers' Party, on the one hand, and the United Peasant Party and the Democratic Party, on the other. Thus a certain political principle has been given constitutional rank, which obviously stabilizes the position of the allied parties and after 1980 enhances their strength. Note also that the Roman Catholic groups, while represented in the Polish Diet, have not been classed in the same way, and their role in the political life of the country has not yet been defined by the political decision-making body, and is still being discussed in those groups themselves. In these discussions, at one end of the range of opinions we notice the tendency to form a broad Roman Catholic loose political grouping, and at the other, the tendency to confine activities to the social level. The Roman Catholic movement is in fact differentiated and, except for the Pax Association, we may speak about programmatic pluralism, which draws inspiration from both the Catholic personalistic philosophy, whether Maritain's or Mounier's, and the basic documents adopted by the Second Vatican Council and also the encyclicals and political statements made by Popes John XXIII, Paul VI, and John Paul II.

In view of the differentiation of the Roman Catholic movement in Poland, and also for doctrinal reasons, the Church hierarchy in this country does not identify itself with any of these groups, even though in the past the Znak has enjoyed some preferential treatment. On those matters which directly concern the Church, its hierarchy is in direct contacts with the highest political authorities, without the intermediary of the lay associations. As a result of these contacts the Church hierarchy in Poland has in recent years become a *factor of political influence*.

The relationships between the Polish United Workers' Party and its two allied parties, on the one hand, and the Roman Catholics, on the other, leaves out only those who are organized in separate associations and institutions. Those relationships also cover a definite policy towards the masses of non-organized Roman Catholics and towards the Roman Catholics within those parties. It seems obvious that the striking social and political activation of Roman Catholics in Poland is becoming a permanent element of the country's political culture.

The term adopted in the Polish literature on the subject is that of the system of a hegemonic party (a term which I consider inappropriate).[50] If this term is to be adequate for defining Polish conditions (it has been drawn from descriptions of Western parliamentary systems in those states where elections have in practice resulted in a permanent hegemony of one and the same party), it must be accompanied by some qualifications, because it does not in itself reflect the said differences in the recruitment base of the various parties, differences which condition the functioning of the multi-party system in Poland. When using that term we have to bear in mind that it raises to the status of the permanent principle the fact that the key posts in the machinery of the state are held by members of the Polish United Workers' Party. On the other hand, it does not suggest that the PUWP has a monopoly of initiatives in social matters, because, that would be at variance with the principles of the socialist political system. This is why the political practice should be interpreted in accordance with the formulation, to be found in the new Constitution, that the PUWP plays the leading role, which cannot mean its hegemony. The hegemonic position of the PUWP does not mean that it is the same in all social strata and groups and in all public organizations. It suffices to recall the fact that more farmers are members of the United Peasant Party than of the PUWP (4.9 and 4.0 per cent, respectively); the same applies, by analogy, to the craftsmen as members of the Democratic Party and the PUWP, respectively, especially in small towns. Thus the system of hegemony looks different at the central and provincial levels than it does in the lowest administrative units.

The hegemonic position of the PUWP in the Polish multi-party system certainly ought to be differentiated into historical periods. In some of them the allied parties were treated as political partners; those periods were marked by the functioning of committees for the co-operation of the allied parties, and by the fact that the allied parties participated in political decision-making and the autonomy of the interests they represented was respected.

Such periods also were marked by the co-operative attitude of the political organizations of Roman Catholics. After the reforms made in October 1956 the then leader of the Znak Association in his programmatic article advanced the thesis that there was an unwritten covenant between the nation and the PUWP: 'the nation has conceded political leadership to the PUWP, but, of course, not unconditionally, the condition being that the October pro-gramme be put into effect.'[51]

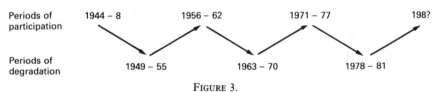

Periods of participation	1944 – 8	1956 – 62	1971 – 77	198?
Periods of degradation	1949 – 55	1963 – 70	1978 – 81	

FIGURE 3.

Periods of co-operation alternated with those during which the allied parties were deprived of any role in decision-making; their political status was degraded, and at one time even their very existence was threatened. These oscillations are illustrated by Figure 3. This polygonal line also illustrates (some corrections being necessary in this respect) the policy towards social organizations and certain strata and vocational groups, and the economic policy as well. The years 1949–50 opened a period of the degradation of the role of the trade unions, which should have counteracted the bureaucratic distortions originating in a sudden intensification of centralism; a period of destruction or etatization of co-operative self-government, destruction or atrophizing of public associations, and degraded relations with the Church.

The official opinion then, very characteristic of bureaucratic centralism, was that all intermediate bodies should only transmit political decisions to the masses, without functioning as autonomous elements of social initiative. Note that the years 1950–3 saw in Poland marked tendencies towards uniformity, a regression of organizational processes which not only prevented new associations from being set up, but even destroyed existing ones. With few exceptions, the membership of those surviving associations decreased, and associations themselves became less active. Organizational activity increased anew in 1955–7 to be subdued by a recurrence of bureaucratic rigidity as shown in Figure 3.

The said period was also one of greatly reduced democracy within the PUWP, and of a decline of the rule of law in the sphere of civic rights.[52]

It seems, however, that the 1980–81 *rebellion in the framework of the system and legality* has a chance to stop the harmful swing, due to the profound changes which are on the way. The bureaucratic equilibrium leaving the upper hand to executives, topped by an uncontrolled and hence irresponsible centre of decision-making (renewed only by appointment and co-optation) seems definitely upset. The emergence of an independent, broad, trade union movement quickly transformed into a powerful organization led to the imposition of a new principle: of solving conflicts through negotiations. This outburst of political activity was triggered off by years of bureaucratic inertia, by the incapacity of the state and party apparatus to solve vital problems, by the incredible economic and social mess into which the country was driven.[53]

In these turbulent months the Catholic Church rose to a new status. It strengthened its moral authority as well as its political influence. It assumed the double role: of moderator in a prolonged bitter social conflict and simultaneously of the defender and supporter of all projects aiming at the democratization of the system. Tamara Deutscher is right in her picture of the latest events: the party's former monopoly over economic policy is now shared with Solidarity while the Church has extended its access to the media and its privileges within the educational system.[54] The mounting tide of criticisms, unrest and spontaneous changes could not leave the party apparatus unruffled. Cracks within the party, in spite of secrecy and monolithic declarations, could be observed in the last years without difficulty. Under the pressure of events, as general dissatisfaction was gaining momentum, the cracks developed into a split–at the top, too: the leadership emerged divided into those who favour sweeping reforms and those who would prefer to minimize them. To complete the picture, a mutiny of the rank-and-file in the party followed. In order to back the reformers they started organizing informal, horizontal party contacts, a pre-Congress activity which is a challenge to the *vertical*, traditional organization of the party apparatus.

This trend did not, of course, stop at the threshold of the apparatuses of the allied parties. In fact they were deeply affected by the restless, vehement tug-of-war within the Party. A spectacular turn was taken by the last Congress of the Democratic Party (Spring 1981): the former leadership–with one exception–was literally wiped out. In the meantime the Catholic political groupings and clubs, unaffected by the internal tensions of the allied parties, doubled their activity. In summary, the rapidly growing expansion of pluralist elements in the Polish political structure is now a matter of fact. However, their durability, the chance to stop the unfortunate "swing", will be tested by history.

When it comes to the structure of interests we can single out the following organizations which had to undergo a process of democratization unexpected by their leaders:

(1) mass organizations, intended to integrate interests of broad groups;
(2) organizations representing particular interests;
(3) organizations which serve small-scale and highly specialized interests (micro-organizations).

The role of mass organizations is sometimes exaggerated in the literature on the subject published in socialist countries. All problems of social organizations are thereby restricted to mass organizations. Of course, these organizations are the most important of all, but it is a pity that they are all heavily bureaucratized as the massive workers' protest dramatically brought to light.

Organizations with a limited membership are not to be underestimated. As Jan Szczepański writes, 'The most durable and closest relationships link people in small groups. In small groups, in microstructures, the social bonds are the strongest, and the forms of subjective relationships are a result of forms of personal contacts and those relationships in which an important role is played by emotional factors.'[55] Mass organizations, being very complex, may always make their members feel anonymous and helpless, the latter feeling being due to their merely apparent social activity. In a word, they may breed alienation. This can be counteracted only by being diversified internally into comparatively small subsystems. A very large number of smaller organizations makes it possible to take care of the vital interests of the members, ultimately also on a mass scale. This opinion is far from being isolated in the literature published in popular democracies, and has also been expressed in recent items in the Soviet literature on the subject.[56]

(c) On mixed socioeconomic structures

The ebb and flow of pluralism in Polish politics, by which we have characterized the relationships within the party system (cf. the polygonal line, Figure 3) and oscillations in the position of social organizations, are also applicable to socio-economic conditions.

The said polygonal line can also illustrate the conflicting trends within both the state and the co-operative sector. If decentralization of decision-making is treated as a manifestation of pluralism, then the ebb and flow of bureaucratic centralism must be interpreted as conflicts within those sectors, conflicts which are still far from being settled, even though the pressure of decentralization trends, dictated by obvious requirements of economic life, is constantly increasing.

The leading Polish economists, Michał Kalecki, Oskar Lange, and Edward Lipiński, declared themselves on various occasions in favour of such a decentralization (democratic centralism). They often emphasized the great importance of workers' self-government which, combined with proper economic incentives, rouses the indispensable spirit of enterprise in the workers.

Decentralization assumes the autonomy of units of the socialized economy (economic subsystems) and, at the lower levels, an expansion of workers' self-government and a genuine self-government of all co-operatives. A decentralized system must have a "controlled market mechanism". Such is the interpretation of democratic centralism in the national economy, if its interpretation is not distorted, that is, if the role of the modifying adjective is not forgotten.

Without going into detail it is worth while discussing the intricate problems of the private sector which bring out the specific features of sociopolitical pluralism in the Polish system.

Shortly after 1945 Poland was marked by a typical mixed structure, with dominant private agriculture and a large role played by private craftsmen and tradesmen. As has been said, the years 1949–50 opened a period of bureaucratic centralism, marked by attempts compulsorily to collectivize agriculture and to restrict the private sub-sector in towns by administrative measures (the tendency being to put an end completely to private crafts and trade).

When that policy broke down in 1955–56 a number of decisions were made. Bureaucratic centralism could not favour the autonomy of economic units, especially those which had a non-socialist title to ownership of the means of production. The ideological prejudice, which made some people find it extremely difficult to drop the concepts of class enemies and "relics" of capitalism (treated ahistorically), was combined with the impatience of bureaucratic centralists who favoured the state sector as based on nationalized property and run by the government. The gross product turned out by that sector is in all socialist countries incomparably larger than that of the co-operative sector which, moreover, being based on group property, represents socialism of an inferior kind. It even seemed that group property (representing perhaps more egoistic interests) would be absorbed by the nationalized property. But specialists in social services and in the economics of consumption, sociologists and lawyers view the problem differently as they take consumers into account as well.

The issue of which form of property should be preferred in specified branches of production and under specified circumstances should be settled by reference to socioeconomic, and not merely economic *goals*. Roughly speaking, large enterprises are, and should be, state-owned, while small-scale producers should form co-operatives of various kinds. There seems little purpose in state enterprises covering that field, too.[57] On the other hand we can easily imagine co-operatives which produce precision instruments, small numbers of other specialized products, and commodities intended for immediate consumption.

The lowest place in that hierarchy was occupied by the private sector, which even several years ago was considered "the red-lamp quarter" of socialism.

Following its further development individual property became engaged not only in the production of durable goods, but also in the production of those means of production which require mainly human labour to turn them out. This evolution is explained by the fact that under the Polish system of planning the individual sector is, though in a different way than the state and co-operative sectors are, linked to the national economy as a whole primarily by distribution and sales co-operatives, contracts of various kinds, by the state-controlled policy of distribution of raw materials, and the price, credits and taxation policies.

This diversified individual sector has an importance of its own. If to over one million peasants working on individual farms we add some 370 000 craftsmen who provide nearly 60 per cent of the services (that is, nearly one million people living from crafts) and a number, difficult to estimate, of vegetable- and fruit-growers, carriers, tradesmen, restaurant-owners and people who provide services to tourists (those who rent rooms and run motels and small hotels), then it is clear that regardless of the viewpoint adopted it would be groundless to exclude from the socialist economy a large number of gainfully employed persons and their families who earn their living, directly or indirectly, from those trades. Such exclusion would have to be based purely on the formal criterion of the title of ownership of the means of production.

The position of that sector within the national economy as a whole is shown in Figure 4. The expansion of the genuinely self-governing co-operative sector and the stabilization of the private sector mean, in economic terms, a decentralization of decision-making in the national economy, a decentralization justified by the local nature of small-scale production and services.[58]

This nature of the property of means of production must sharply restrict the possibility of the state authorities issuing direct orders. The authorities must strive to make the individual sector carry out its share of the national plan by such indirect measures as contracts falling under civil law, by supervision, and by resorting to adequate economic incentives. Direct micro-economic decisions must be made within the private sector itself.[59]

The suspicion with which the continuing functioning of the market was eyed as a remnant of capitalism, to be driven out when the centralized planned economy proves successful, may slowly disappear.[60] And this would

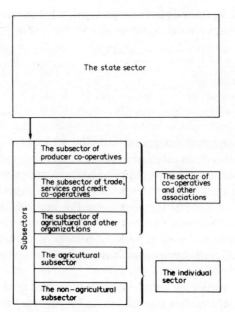

FIGURE 4. The present socioeconomic system in Poland.

mean a large amount of autonomy for state enterprises on the home market and abroad.

Figure 4, before Summer 1980, had a purely normative meaning. In fact, the co-operative system was under such heavy bureaucratic pressure that it lost completely its autonomy of decisions and should have been considered as another branch of nationalized economy. The individual sector for the same reason fought hard for survival. Perhaps the coming years will give the Figure another meaning–a descriptive value.

The idea of a sector of individual economy means that that sector must be built into the system *as an autonomous one,* in the socialist system. That "building in" can be achieved only through the intermediary of self-governing co-operatives of various kinds and with assistance on the part of the state. This also means abandoning the primitive schema of thinking according to which employment in one of the two forms of socialist economy, state-owned or co-operative, guarantees the socialist attitude of the employees. This primitive way of thinking disregards the fact that in the two sectors there are also petty bourgeois cliques (which sometimes border on organized crime), while assuming that those employed in the private sector must by definition be hostile, or at best indifferent, to socialism, the system under which they live or may even have been born. Note also that in Poland the individual sector is the main recruitment base of the United Peasant Party and the Democratic Party, or, to put it more precisely that their base consists of its corresponding subsectors in town and country.

In many quarters it was argued that the Polish system–like similar ones in the East–is not to be reformed. This seems ridiculous when confronted with a wave of deep-going reforms on the way.

6.3 SYMPTOMS OF ABANDONMENT OF THE TOTALITARIAN MODEL OF SOCIALIST SOCIETIES IN WESTERN POLITICAL SOCIOLOGY

It does not seem necessary to discuss what in the West is meant by totalitarianism, and even less so to discuss the various shades of that opinion. It will suffice briefly to recall the origin and the evolution of the concept. At first, the term *totalitarianism* was applied to Fascism, probably as a result of statements made by Mussolini and other Fascist leaders on the nature of the totalitarian state. Probably *The Times* was the first, in 1929, to apply that term to both Fascism and Communism.[61] E. Heimann put the term *red Fascism* in circulation in his book *Communism, Fascism or Democracy*, published in 1938. The superficial analogy came to be insisted upon more and more strongly.[62]

The misdeeds of bureaucratic socialism provided food for stressing that analogy. A special role was played in that respect by the writings of C. J. Friedrich, who refined his description of totalitarianism over many years, while consistently bringing Italian Fascism, German Nazism, and what he called communism, to a common denominator.[63] Friedrich's works on totalitarianism are marked by ahistoricism and a lack of any comparison between the Fascist and Nazist ideology with the sociopolitical theory of Marxism and between the policies of the two systems. It is significant that neither the abandonment of terror applied *en masse* nor the reforms undertaken in the Soviet Union after Stalin's death, nor the differentiated policies of East European socialist states have resulted in a revision of the totalitarian model used to explain the processes that take place in socialist countries. True, in a collective publication which appeared in 1969 Friedrich made some corrections of his views, but he nevertheless retained the totalitarian model of socialist societies *in toto*. He recalls in the Introduction to have always claimed that neither Fascism nor Communism had been totalitarian from the very beginning, but became such when putting their respective ideological principles into effect. In conclusion he concedes that there have been temporary disturbances in the model, but it would be questionable to mitigate the conception as a whole. In his opinion it is also obvious that by making efforts to cope with the various social and political difficulties totalitarianism matures, the process giving rise to various maladjustments which threaten its stability.[64] This reasoning resembles that of K. W. Deutsch, who in 1954 analysed the possibility of the disintegration of the monolith. It is to be noted, however, that Deutsch's analyses were so abstract that they could be applied to any excessively centralized state.[65]

The diverse varieties of application to socialist countries of the totalitarian conception were to be encountered till about 1970.[66] Their authors were as astonishingly carefree as, for example, A. B. Ulam, who drew a parallel between Khruschev and Boccaccio.[67] Furthermore, in 1972, Leonard Schapiro in his book *Totalitarianism* used mainly examples taken from the period of Stalin's rule and presented that period as significant, and in that connection drew the parallel between Lenin, Mussolini, and Hitler (cf. p. 23 of the book). And yet both documents and reliable testimonies indicate Lenin's style of handling matters. If we want to give an example of collective political leadership, then we have to mention the periods of Lenin's leadership, both before and after the revolution. The reader of Schapiro's book, with all good intentions, can only say that it is not quite clear whether Schapiro is informing us about other people's (mainly Friedrich's) opinions on the interpretation of processes taking place in socialist countries, or whether he is offering his own views as well.[68]

Many attempts have been made to cover extra-European political systems by the totalitarian conception. H. Arendt extended the idea to India and China as representatives of traditional Oriental despotism. Other authors have extended the totalitarian model to pre-industrial societies.[69] In this connection we have to point to another argument (put forward by K. W. Wittfogel) which is supposed to support the application of the totalitarian model to socialist societies. Results of long studies of "hydraulic" civilizations (the term corresponds to the Asiatic mode of production and to Oriental despotism) are compared by him with the Marxist theory and the policies of the Soviet state. He blames Marx (and Engels) for having later mitigated the criticism of Oriental despotic empires when he realized that the dictatorship of the proletariat would result in such a system. In this way Marx is supposed to have betrayed scholarly truth, whose importance he often used to extol. Lenin is blamed by Wittfogel for having changed his opinion of Oriental despotism when he came to face the possibility of rising to power (as if such a possibility existed already in 1905).

Wittfogel, who is an authority on Chinese and Indian history, does not seem to think that certain discrepancies in formulations on that matter in Marx's and Engels' works were due to their lack of any profound knowledge of the problem, and were not any proof of their tactical ruse on the issue of scholarly and scientific truth. Hence the fragmentary and circumstantial nature of their statements on the issue concerning which they could only formulate some hypotheses.

In all those diatribes against the Marxist ideology and socialist society, against the theory and policies of the modern "hydraulic society" the only point which agrees with facts is that in the Stalinist period, beginning with the 1930s, discussion on the Asiatic mode of production was blocked from above because analogies with what was going on in the Soviet Union were evident.

In the conclusion to his book, which has the significant subtitle referring to a comparative study of totalitarian power, Wittfogel defined socialist society as an industrialized system of state-imposed slavery.[70] This shows that scholarly competence does not make one immune to ideological fanaticism which readily absolves one from a lack of sufficient competence in fields which one has not studied so thoroughly as the Asiatic mode of production in Antiquity and the Middle Ages.

Let us briefly describe the totalitarian model of socialist societies as it is found in Western literature, bringing out those points which are common to all the varieties of that model.

Now, all totalitarian trends deny the possibility of democratic processes in socialist countries because they exclude the possibility of emergence of social and political pluralism. By social pluralism is meant here such a differentiation into groups which makes it possible to present their interests and to influence political decisions. By political pluralism is meant the differentiation which consists either in a socialist multi-party or in a possibility of suggesting alternate political decisions within a one-party system, the latter solution being closely connected with democracy within the party. Further, all pluralism, if it is to be recognized as such in a modern society, assumes the existence of public opinion. The totalitarian model denies the existence of public opinion in the socialist system and excludes the possibility of its emergence in the course of time and of respect for constitutionally guaranteed civic rights. This is linked in turn to a distorted presentation of the problem of the one-party system: on the one hand, the various forms of multi-party system in Central Europe are presented as just a façade of a one-party system, comparing it with the multi-party systems in Western Europe, instead of comparing it with the one-party systems in socialist countries, which would be methodologically more correct. Further, the problem of one-party systems in Yugoslavia was disregarded. The totalitarian model is thus the antithesis of all pluralism.

Second, the totalitarian model is ahistorical, it is of necessity static, and fails to take into account the development of socialist societies, their dynamic evolution full of meandering and making use of their reserves so, periods of regression were followed by democratic tendencies. The ahistoricism of that model also found expression in the extrapolation of the bureaucratic degeneration both into the past, that is, the period shortly before and after the revolution of 1917, and into the future: it denied the possibility of democratization, i.e., extended participation in making political decisions and putting them into effect. That ahistoricism was also manifested in extrapolations in space, in the form of the claim that all states formed after the Soviet pattern "must", or "have to", replicate the policies of the Soviet original.

This takes us to the third feature of the model. Describing sociopolitical practice in terms of that model made it possible to assign specified features to

Marxism. Has the ideology of class struggle not resulted in the dictatorship of the proletariat, best illustrated by the period of Stalin's power? Is it not to be expected that the said ideology will bring about a return of Stalinism? In this way the period of the worst political practices, the period during which human rights and the rule of law were trampled upon, was used to question the humanism of Marxist thought. The ethics of hatred, which was claimed to mark the class struggle, was said to have resulted in Stalinism, the inevitable and the most characteristic product of that ideology.

This extrapolation was greatly facilitated by the way in which the term *communism* was handled. If every period of development, both that following the revolution of 1917, and the times of Stalinism, and the period when Stalinism was being overcome means communism, then there are no prospects of evolution other than disintegration. The totalitarian model suggests the existence of a closed system for ever incapable of any democratic evolution.

Fourth, the totalitarian model is marked by the fact that analysis is focused on the summit of the political structure, namely on the struggle for power. In that model such struggle must inevitably end in putting forward a leader, which some authors hold to be the most characteristic feature of "communist totalitarianism". The one-sidedness of this interpretation enables one to disregard both the lower levels of the political structure and the process taking place in society at large. Atomization of society under communism is shown as its most significant feature (H. Arendt). This selection of problems to be studied must have resulted in identifying the machinery of the state with the whole of society, which marks totalitarianism.

The superficiality and the time-serving nature of the said model was becoming visible as changes were taking place within socialist countries and differences among them were growing, too. The model was useful in explaining neither the first period of the Soviet system, namely that between the revolution of 1917 and the advent of war communism, nor the NEP period, nor the period of World War II, when the Soviet state was fighting, together with its Western allies, against the aggressive totalitarian states. It is obvious that the Soviet Union was struggling for its own existence, but also for certain fundamental principles common to mankind, against the humiliation of peoples and in defence of human rights. Some years later those ideas came to be embodied in the basic documents adopted by the United Nations.

The totalitarian model explained neither the inner contradictions and changes in the various societies which had moved away from capitalism, nor the conflicts between their states. On the other hand, that model suited perfectly that period of international relations which was marked by the polarization of hostile blocs of states, eyeing one another with suspicion. This was why the 1960s saw the tendency towards a more balanced analysis of socialist societies, a tendency which was at first manifested in certain corrections to that totalitarian model. For instance, M. Fainsod discussed "rationalized" or "enlightened" totalitarianism.[71] Z. Brzeziński at first became more reserved, which can be seen in the second (1967) edition of the book written by him jointly with C. J. Friedrich (*Totalitarianism and Dictatorship*), that second edition having been prepared for the press by the latter author alone. Brzeziński's other study, published in the same year, carries a mitigated version of totalitarianism,[72] and in the book prepared by him together with P. Huntington, which was a comparative study of the United States and the Soviet Union, no use was made of the totalitarian model here under consideration. The authors paid much attention to both interest groups in the Soviet Union and non-organized social forces there.[73] The term *totalitarianism* has disappeared from Brzeziński's later works altogether. The development of polycentric ideas in West and East, and particularly the emergence of the so-called Eurocommunism, did not remain without influence on his views. In the course of these political developments new vistas opened for pluralism in the East.

H. Arendt considerably modified the text of the third edition of this monograph. She realized, as she put it, that the official "counterideology", that is, anticommunism, inherited from the cold war period, facilitated neither research nor practical activity, and in part three of that volume she restricted the application of the totalitarian model to the period of Stalin's authoritarian rule.[74] Another author points to the fact that under socialist systems interest groups are something like pluralistic brakes imposed upon the omnipotent executive power and serve as the basis on which the criticism of political practices rests.[75] G. Almond and G. P. Powell described party secretaries as pragmatists who solve problems instrumentally.[76]

M. Curtis went much further. He did that in the tripartite discussion organized by C. J. Friedrich, which goes to the credit of the latter. Curtis wrote that if the communist countries were automatically labelled as totalitarian, with all the negative connotations associated with totalitarianism, then those countries would emerge not only as an inevitable enemy, but also as the embodiment of evil and heresy, which must be isolated. But the danger of basing one's foreign policy on rigid ideological formulas is obvious, and endeavours to put them into effect result in endless conflicts and moral crusades against those who oppose such formulas. Curtis thought that obliterating the boundary between the state and society is typical of the writings of totalitarians, and stressed that such ideas, if automatically applied to all communist states, would make one disregard not only the changes taking place in the Soviet Union itself, but also the differences among the other regimes, in which changes had taken place to a varying extent. In his polemic with Friedrich he questioned the monolithic character of one-party systems and pointed to the role of the opinions of the various groups upon decision-making in the Soviet Union, opposed the Nazi ideology to the Marxist one, and predicted that the totalitarian model (discussed above in the present book) would no longer be used in analyses of socialist societies.[77]

The list of authors and the new subjects they have taken up could be continued, but the present writer would like to formulate here his opinion that the change described above had been influenced by I. Deutscher, who was one of the few to outline the tendency to democratize the socialist system from within once Stalin's political heritage was dismissed. He drew also the conclusion from the fact that the Soviet Union has been pushed into World War II, that the concept of two totalitarian systems waging war against each other could not be maintained; he saw in this war elements of class struggle on an international level and this assumption could explain the position adopted towards the Soviet Union in those times by the working class in the West.[78]

Retreat from the totalitarian interpretation intensified with the appearance of studies of group differentiation in socialist countries, studies which analysed elements of pluralism. Their authors did not confine themselves to making the totalitarian model more flexible, but simply rejected it and proceeded to construct a pluralistic model of socialist society. G. H. Skilling was one of the first to do so. In 1966 he published an article on *Interest Groups and Communist Politics*,[79] which, after having been reprinted twice, was next included as the opening chapter in the collected papers on *Interest Groups in Soviet Politics*, (eds G. H. Skilling and A. F. Griffith).[80] That book deserves attention despite the fact the late 1960s saw many publications written in an entirely new spirit.

J. C. Hough, as if expanding the said description by G. Almond and G. P. Powell, wrote a monograph on regional party secretaries in the Soviet Union.[81] As he saw it, the local party authorities were not interpreted as intrusions which disturbed an effective functioning of the administrative system, but as its integral part which contributed signally to its effectiveness. The study aroused much interest and came to be often discussed in the literature on the subject. The same category of works whose authors dissociated themselves from the traditional totalitarian interpretation includes writings by H. J. Berman, H. W. Ehrmann, J. N. Hazard, W. Leonhard, D. Lane and M. Lodge, S. I. Ploss, the said monograph by S. P. Cohen and other works by Skilling.[82]

When reading these papers edited by Skilling and Griffith one has no doubt that nearly all contributors were firm in rejecting the totalitarian image of socialist society. In one of the items we find the statement that the conception of a totalitarian system in which the only party, free from internal conflicts, imposes its will upon society and upon all social groups was challenged by another approach, which took into account conflicts among groups, conflicts which affected the policy-making by the party.[83] The authors noticed the various aspects of the differentiation of Soviet society both in the sphere of interests and in the very political structure, and concluded that that society was not free from conflicts. Skilling claimed that the state monopoly of the mass media did not exclude sharp confrontations of opinion, even in an open way.[84] He drew attention to the fact that in the Soviet Union organized groups were not necessarily spokesmen for certain attitudes, but sometimes loosely knit groups of individuals could suggest certain decisions to state and party authorities.[85]

It is worth emphasizing that the authors did not mechanically apply the group analysis, as practised in the West, to Soviet society, as they were aware that such an analysis had to refer to such realities of Soviet life as the position of the Communist Party in the socialist system, and that politics under that system cannot be treated as an automatic result of pressures and counter-pressures of rival groups.[86] Some contributors noticed the possibility of social initiatives and of criticizing and discussing bills. They also pointed to the role of experts, in which they saw a characteristic manifestation of the process of removing the remnants of the Stalinist period.[87]

The volume under consideration includes papers which are remarkable by their intention to present the problem in an unbiased way. J. P. Hardt and Th. Frankel describe the efforts made by managers of state enterprises to obtain such freedom of action which is indispensable in economic management.[88] P. Judy draws the picture of differences of opinion of Soviet economists on political economy and the process of planning in particular.[89] The paper on Soviet lawyers analyses the various aspects of their activity, and the authors seem to understand that abiding by the Marxist ideology does not preclude necessary autonomy, based on the principles of the socialist rule of law. The thesis is illustrated with two examples: the attitude of progressive Soviet lawyers towards the introduction of the death penalty for offences against the socialized economy (in 1961–2), and towards the act on the parasitic way of life, the authors' approval being extended not only to the various Soviet lawyers who wrote on the subject, but also to the Soviet Supreme Court, which at its plenary meetings of 12 September 1961 and 18 March 1962, signally limited the applicability of the act.[90]

The contributors reveal an interesting difference of opinion on the fundamental issue, namely that of the significance of group analysis in the study of socialist societies. P. S. Griffith does not share the opinion of G. H. Skilling, and claims that it is more fruitful to study the "tendencies of articulation" which emerge from social activity as a whole and effectively formulate alternative policies.[91] Yet stressing the analysis of the "tendencies of articulation" does not preclude the study of formal and informal groups. As could be expected, Skilling in the concluding chapter points to the complementary nature of both approaches.

The book which we have just discussed marks an important step forward in the study of socialist society. Yet–in the interest of the further obstacle-ridden dialogue–it seems necessary to point to the shortcomings of these collected papers. We shall refer to the most important problems only.

(1) The book obscures the difference between social and the political structures by treating certain parts of the state and/or party machinery as autonomous interest groups. The blurring of that basic distinction can even be seen from the contents list. The authors make the mistake, quite common in American political-science literature concerned with interest groups ("pressure groups"), which has been pointed out by the present writer on another occasion.[92]

(2) As announced in the title, these collected papers are on interest groups in Soviet politics, but the frequent use of the terms *communism* and *communist* suggests, wrongly, as was the case amongst the authors of the totalitarian model, that the conclusions are also applicable to other socialist societies in Eastern Europe. This obliterates the differences among those societies and in a sense also is a relic of the former mode of thinking.

(3) Not all the authors notice the eufunctional factors of social differentiation, factors born of the basic acceptance of the foundations of the new system and the limitations of criticism to the ways in which the social goals are to be attained, to the priorities to be given to specified goals, and to the criticism of certain leaders; nor do they notice that the various groups and strata of socialist society tend to co-operate yet exaggerate conflicts. Should those conflicts really have priority, general dysfunction would ensue.

The items mentioned above do not seem to mark an episode which could, in political science, give place to a return to the totalitarian model. This is indicated by the various studies of selected problems characteristic of socialist states,[93] by the literature concerned with workers' self-government in Yugoslavia, by studies of interest groups in Poland, and by studies which strive for a deepened pluralistic analysis of socialist societies in general.[94]

Some unpublished works, which the present writer, by courtesy of their authors, was able to read during his stay in Canada in 1973–4, are marked by a competent analysis and restrained criticism.[95]

In periodicals, we notice an increasingly factual approach in articles which appeared in the *Revue d'études comparatives Est–Ouest* in Paris. In this connection it must be explained that it is not by coincidence that we have disregarded the literature on political sociology published in Western Europe, because it did not resort to the totalitarian model discussed above. In this respect mention should be made of matter-of-fact studies by K. von Beyme.[96] Papers edited by D. Lane and G. Kolankiewicz also deserve attention: their contributors, making use of a critical analysis of Polish sources, shed light upon social differentiation in Poland. Their studies cover class differentiation (with interesting comments on changes within the working class), on differentiation into strata (mainly the peasantry), and on differentiation into groups (primarily informal ones). They explicitly reject the possibility of using the totalitarian model as a research instrument. For instance, they criticize F. C. Barghorn (as a contributor to *Political Culture and Political Development*, by W. L. Pye and S. Verba (eds), 1968) for having written about inhabitants of socialist countries as robots. Without negating the value of the papers edited by G. Almond and S. Verba they criticize them for their tendentiousness, the ideological commitment to "Western democracies", and for the condescending undertones in the description of "totalitarian" states (both sets of quotation marks used by D. Lane).[97]

Even earlier the sterility of adopting the monolithic nature of socialist societies as the point of departure of analyses was emphasized by G. Ionescu, who wrote that in no modern society can the state carry out its complex political, cultural, social, and economic activity only through the intermediary of its omnipresent and omniscient officials without co-operation with interest groups and without restraining actions on the part of those groups.[98]

For these reasons no marked retreat from the previous opinions was necessary in Western Europe. The difference, as compared with the United States, was probably due to the experience which Western European countries acquired when occupied by the totalitarian states, which gave them an unlucky opportunity for participant observation. The said difference must have also been due to much easier contacts with European socialist states and the resulting better knowledge of those countries. Mention must also be made of Roman Catholic personalism, for years engaged in a dialogue with Marxism. This is why our discussion can be limited, with a few exceptions, to the American literature on the subject.

A definitive abandonment of the totalitarian model seems a preliminary condition for any serious international dialogue in the social sciences.

The propagators of the totalitarian model failed, or were unwilling, to notice certain phenomena marked with a specific regularity. They were recording and emphasizing the distortions, but were not in a position to explain the resistance in defence of the humanistic values of Marxism. They failed to notice that every new generation in socialist countries poses anew the two most essential questions:

(1) What are the causes of the discrepancies between the political practice and the Marxist system of values?
(2) How can the distortions of those officially accepted values be remedied?

The problem was seen with great clarity by Oskar Lange, who wrote about the dialectics of the process of building socialism. Centralist methods are effective when it comes to a rapid industrialization, and as a result they cause a quick growth of the ranks of the working class. The number of the workers increases and their political consciousness and maturity rise. That development of the working class is parallelled by another important sociological factor, namely the emergence of a new intelligentsia, largely of worker and peasant origin. When it becomes obvious that the highly centralized and bureaucratic methods of management block further progress, part of the political machinery of the state becomes convinced that it is necessary to change the methods of management and public administration. Thus new social forces emerge, which both call for and facilitate a change in those methods.[99]

The socialist system has certain built-in mechanisms which provide an objective opportunity to oppose distortions, for correcting those practices which deform the system. One of the important factors which favours renewals consists in the indoctrination of a right to popular power in the broad sense of the term. The ethical and democratic values of Marxism also work in favour of this fight. When the political practice is at variance with them, this breeds a contradiction, very fruitful in its consequences.

An interesting light upon the nascent tendencies that promote further democratization of socialist systems has been shed by the research (headed by Stefan Nowak) on "continuity and change in cultural traditions". The studies have shown that Polish people feel an acute urge to commit themselves to public causes. On the whole, in Polish society the intensity of those needs is very strong. Most people are firm in their opinion that one should be committed to issues other than one's personal affairs. Note that such tendencies can materialize if there is a large number of both informal groups and various social organizations.

As has been shown by Nowak's studies, the need to commit oneself is based on the acceptance of the principles of the socialist system and its fundamental institutions, and its humanistic values above all. Such acceptance is even more important by being common to all generations, to the young and to adults alike.

In the summing up of these studies we read that as the status of the family was growing the frequency of stressing such characteristics of a good system as vast opportunities for criticism and enterprise of the masses, increased influence of the citizens upon the process of government, and increased independence of specialists, was increasing, while the frequency of approval of a strong central authority was decreasing.

The clear correlation between the standard of education and the choice of the characteristics of a good system suggests a certain long-term forecast: if it is assumed that the average standard of education in Poland increases, then it is to be supposed that the citizens' expectations concerning the democratization of the Polish system in its various fields will intensify.[100]

The results of those studies confirm E. Lipinski's reasoning:

> Like the model of socialist culture, the system of socialist economy is not a ready-made product and will never become one. Systems "come into being" and develop in contradictions, in struggle, in efforts.

Socialism won not only because it means a more rational economy, or can certainly become such, but also because it has become part of a *new system of values* [italics–S.E.]. Marx, while he could not imagine how the socialist economy would function–even today, after half-a-century of its existence new forms of its functioning are being tried–proved correctly the necessity of capitalism being overcome by socialism.'[101]

These potentialities inherent in the socialist system have also been noticed by certain Western authors. I. Deutscher wrote in connection with the fiftieth anniversary of the October revolution that it was beyond doubt that the system of education always kept in the Russian people the consciousness of its revolutionary heritage and calling. And Klaus von Beyme saw the socialist system's best tool for overcoming crises in the coherence of the ideological base and the ability to regenerate, shown by the Marxist theory, which makes an extremely coherent whole.[102]

The new generations grown up under the socialist system, better educated and at a higher level of culture, expect not declarations and paternalism on the part of the authorities, but opportunities for actively participating in social life in accordance with the spirit of socialism, in which they have been raised. In a totalitarian system no such mechanisms exist: the system can only be abolished by force.

Comprehension of these facts is essential for grasping the difference between the totalitarian systems and distortions, even glaring ones, within socialist systems. The former ones function in agreement with their respective ideologies, whereas the latter ones draw inspiration for their democratization from the system of values that is opposed to the ideologies of Fascism and racialism.

This is the foundation of the dialogue which the publications mentioned above by way of example seem to announce. The conclusion in H. Spiro's entry on totalitarianism in *The International Encyclopaedia of the Social Sciences*[103] is characteristic in this respect: he questions the usefulness of the concept as an instrument of analysis and expresses his hope that the entry will disappear from the next edition.[104]

6.4   ELEMENTS OF PLURALISM IN YUGOSLAVIA

Pluralism in Yugoslavia has two aspects: self-governmental and ethnic. But the system of values on which both the worker self-government and the local government are based is fundamentally relative to the system of those values which determine the functioning of the institutions that safeguard the separate interests of nations and ethnic and religious groups. The two aspects did not develop in parallel. The present system of self-government originated from the workers' self-government, and the idea took full shape only during the conflict within the international worker movement, marked by the

Yugoslav communists' withdrawal from the Comintern. At that time the workers' self-government identified itself as the alternative solution to bureaucratic centralism (which in Yugoslavia often used to be termed *administrative socialism*), which precludes, or limits, participation in decision-making and in management. On Yugoslavia's part that step was a rejection of the attempts to standardize the international worker movement, attempts inspired and ordered by Stalin personally.

The Yugoslav doctrine interprets participation as a joint conscious activity; that is, in Marxian terms, as cognition and organization by the individual as a social force of his own possibilities. This breeds associations with *Capital*, vol. 1, where Marx refers to a union of free people working as a single social force, as manpower. The signal to tackle fundamental reforms was given as early as June 1950 by Tito himself when he delivered to the National Assembly a speech on the worker's management in economic enterprises. The basic ideas of the address were elaborated in the programme of the League of Yugoslav Communists (1958)[109] which formulated the problem so that socialism was treated as a system based on the socialization of means of production. In that system the producers, who *form* associations, directly control social production. The socialization of the means of production did not identify it with their nationalization, and thus meant a gradual driving-out of the state from all spheres of socioeconomic and cultural life by a system based on self-government. The expansion of self-government was promoted at the Ninth Congress of the Union of Yugoslav Communists. The constitution of 1974 states that Yugoslavia's social system is based on the power of the working class and all working people, and on relations among people as free producers and intellectuals, who enjoy equal rights.[106] This is a conception of socialization as a complex process of long duration, and not as a single act of nationalization of the means of production.[107]

W. Brus, when describing the Yugoslav system, remarked that the growth of workers' self-government resulted in complications and inevitable tensions, but it would not have to become a "pole of incompetence", opposed to experts (as it occurs to managerial solutions), on the condition that a consistent distinction is made between operational and strategic decisions.[108]

The said programme referred to a mutual restriction: of the independence of producers by central social and state institutions, and of these in turn by the independence and self-government of producers. Thus the development trend is to increase the direct influence of producers not only upon economic processes, but upon other social processes as well, and to restrict the political power of the state in the sphere of direct production.[109]

In connection with this thesis on mutual restriction let it be recalled that its need in Yugoslavia was perceived by Oskar Lange as early as in 1957: he stressed that if the danger of an anarcho-syndicalist degradation is to be avoided, then both in co-operatives and in state enterprises groups of producers should act as *trustees of social interest* (italics–S.E.).[110] Only such a self-government would be eufunctional in the socialist system.

In connection with those programmatic principles the new constitution refers to social, and not state-owned, property (p. iii of the basic principles of that constitution).[111]

The need for an adequate balancing of demands of the self-government and of a sufficient central control of affairs by the state, especially in the socioeconomic sphere, are being voiced with increasing frequency by leading Yugoslav theorists and politicians.[112] They claim that if that had been done earlier certain negative effects (lack of co-ordination) observable in social processes in Yugoslavia would have been avoided. This means abandoning a certain idealization of the system based on self-government, which implied that such a system would automatically solve its own problems. That idealization must have necessarily depreciated the co-ordinating role of the central authorities. In this connection one should note E. Kardelj's warning against technocratic distortions within a system based on self-government[113].

Some authors make a clear distinction between participation and self-government.

(1) Participation can exist without self-government, but not vice-versa.

(2) Participation can be enforced or free in various proportions (note that this may lead to manipulated participation), whereas self-government by definition can be neither enforced nor manipulated. This means that the stronger the pressure, the weaker the self-government.

(3) Thus participation as a system is narrower than social self-government. It is narrower also in the sense that people can participate in putting into effect decisions which they have not made–a situation that could hardly be termed self-government.. In the case of self-government people participate in all stages of decision-making.

(4) In the case of participation its subject-matter and scope is determined by someone else, so that individuals and groups enter a ready-made framework of social life, whereas in the case of self-government its participants create for themselves their social situation.[114]

Following the experience of 25 years, the principles of worker self-government were extended so as to cover all branches of public administration, thus completing and reinforcing local government. Hence the constitution of 1974 offers a picture of an integrated social self-government.[115] This is reflected in the sphere of individual rights, where the basic political right is that to social self-government; that right ensues from new socioeconomic conditions and differs radically from the classical rights to freedom, inherited from bourgeois revolutions.

As envisaged by the constitution, the right to social self-government is an inalienable right to participate in the process of decision-making concerning all the states of social reproduction. The right to work is thus combined with the right to social self-government. The latter includes the right to direct participation in decision-making in all social matters, and the right to all-sided information, in which Yugoslav theorists of the self-government system see an effective barrier against attempts to manipulate the working masses in a technocratic and bureaucratic manner. J. Djordjević defines the right to self-government as a new form of active freedom, as the individual's liberation from the state of being governed and from political alienation. O. Lange formulated that earlier in a similar way. In his Belgrade lecture mentioned above, he said that a lack of an effective worker self-government results in a bureaucratic degeneration, and hence in alienation.[116]

The extended system of self-government is intended to replace the traditional system of representation, which inevitably leads to the supremacy of executive power. This widespread social self-government is supposed to be the specific feature of the Yugoslav path of socialist development. In this way the new constitution puts into effect the depolitization of the system, postulated in the programme of the Union of Yugoslav Communists.

W. Brus criticized the idea of depolitization of the self-government structure by arguing that basic macro-economic decisions are by their very nature political ones since they identify and assess the goals of economic activity, and provide the general criteria and framework of economic calculations, which do not thereby lose their importance; his conclusion was that the objective would be not to depolitize the national economy, which is impossible to attain, but to democratize politics.[117]

The programmatic formulations characteristic of the Yugoslav system have their institutional analogies at all levels, from the communal assemblies, treated as the elementary self-governing sociopolitical communities, to the Federal Assembly.

The communal assemblies consist of three chambers each: that of collective work, that of local communities, and the sociopolitical one.

The self-governing representative system has at its lowest level delegations elected by the basic "organizations of collective work", by private farmers and craftsmen, by employees of state institutions and sociopolitical organizations, and by local communities. One and the same person can serve for a maximum period of eight years, that is, two terms of office. Note that those who (like managers) cannot be elected to workers' councils are not eligible. Delegations elected in this manner form, through indirect elections, assemblies at higher levels.[118]

As is claimed by Yugoslav theorists, this system has many advantages: it puts an end to the traditional primacy of the executive power, observable in both capitalist and socialist countries; guarantees the initiative of the masses; makes it possible to merge political and functional representation into a single body; eliminates the phenomenon of professional politicians. It would thus mean the end of the political man (*homo politicus*) in the sense of an élitist group, but at the same time spread politicians to the various forms of self-government, which are to embody public life. It is believed, as a matter of principle, that the system now under consideration abandons the idea that takes an individual abstract citizen as the point of departure. The Yugoslav system is based on work associations, which unequivocally settles the dilemma of individual versus group participation. The key to the issue is the organic bonds between the various levels of the self-governmental system.

Yugoslav theorists often refer to the heritage of the Paris Commune, which the new system is to implement. In doing so they compare the new Yugoslav constitution with the Soviet constitution of 1918. For them, the self-governmental system is syncnymous with both the dictatorship of the proletariat and self-governing democracy. The Yugoslav system of self-government differs radically from participation in bourgeois state parliamentary systems.[119] Not only is its scope incomparably wider, but it is not guided by the idea of social solidarity. On the contrary, its basic assumption is that social conflicts are inevitable and that they do not reduce to class conflicts, but manifest themselves as group conflicts or conflicts of particular interests.

Only further empirical research could verify the functioning of the constitution effective only as of 1974. These studies should pay special attention to two issues: how the delegates' system functions in fact, and whether it really reduces the still considerable importance of the executive power, mentioned by some authors (for example, M. Ribarić). Further, such studies would have to explain how the Yugoslav one-party system, with its standing of over thirty years, combines with the new and freshly formed self-governmental system; how democracy within the party functions in a one-party system. The importance of these problems is enhanced by the fact that the self-governmental system has become the main field of the party's activity.

The picture is different when we approach national and ethnic pluralism in Yugoslavia. In that field the reception of the institutional solutions of the Soviet federation, which was expressed in the constitution of 1946, has not undergone any major changes. This means the idea of Yugoslavia as a multi-national state, which was seen as a solution to age-old conflicts on the basis of self-determination by nations and smaller ethnic groups, and on the basis of their equality. These conflicts were both ethnic and religious, and, to make matters worse, they were combined with great differences in the national income (seven to one in the case of Slovenia and Macedonia), which added fuel to traditional animosities.

But in the course of time it was concluded that the hierarchical federation with decisions made at various levels did not suffice to solve the intricate problems of multi-national Yugoslavia. A solution was found in the conception of a *self-governmental federation*, which would complement the "statal" structure. That self-governmental federation was to be a barrier against bureaucratic centralism, which tended to feed the chauvinism of stronger nations (Kardelj's formula, to be found in his book on the national issue in Slovenia, where he opposed the tendencies to form a single artificial Yugoslav nation),[120] and at the same time as a barrier against centrifugal tendencies and the chauvinism of weaker groups. In a multi-national state the leading role of the working class must assume the full freedom and equality of every nation and smaller ethnic group.[121] This self-governmental federation was to be supported by the principle of direct co-operation among republics and provinces, which in the Yugoslav political doctrine is termed *co-operational federalism*.

The idea of a self-governmental and co-operational federation was certainly a novelty. One of the authors lists its following advantages:

(1) while the Union Council is the chamber of delegates of self-governing organizations, communities, and sociopolitical organizations, the Council of Republics and Provinces is, in the two-chamber structure of the National Assembly of federal Yugoslavia, supposed to protect the special interests of those republics and provinces;

(2) republics and provinces must be represented in the major federal executive bodies;

(3) those decisions made by federal authorities which pertain to the vital interests of republics and provinces must be *approved* by the republic or province concerned;

(4) uniform economic development is the basis of the equality of nations and smaller ethnic groups.[122]

The Yugoslav system tries in this way to solve the problem of double allegiance, which emerges in every federation. But in this field too, an empirical verification is necessary especially as the April 1981 riots in the Korsova autonomous region were a serious challenge to the federal system as a whole. The issues especially to be examined would be: how does the Communists' League, based on the organizational principle of democratic centralism, function within the self-governmental federation. Co-ordination of the one-party system and the actual role of the League of Yugoslav Communists with the pluralistic foundations of the system is still an unsolved problem, and leading Yugoslav politicians realize the difficulties. Foreign researchers usually regard the system in some way as pluralistic; one of them defined it as a polycentric polyarchy involving a network of élites to which access was usually open–with some minor exceptions.[123] And how can these two above-mentioned principles, which differ in both origin and tradition, be brought in practice into harmony? How does the self-governmental co-operational federation combine with the federation of republics and provinces, which are statal entities?

It can be said in conclusion that both aspects of Yugoslav federalism, when examined together, and confirmed and developed during the XI Congress of the League of Yugoslav Communists, mean *rejection of the principle of territorial political representation* and a trend towards a gradual transformation of the centre of political decision-making into an arbitrator, who, however, being supplied with comprehensive information, can always take the lead by his own initiatives. But, as has often been stressed by Yugoslav political theorists, this formula does not mean an end of evolution. They treat the system of their country as an open one and subject to further changes, whose direction cannot be determined now. The Yugoslav variety of pluralism can be defined as a system–this can now be seen clearly based on the idea of an intertwining of social and political self-government. This is a conception which serves both the interests of producers and the aspirations of the nations and nationalities of Yugoslavia.[124] Its asset is its ability to reach compromise in both fields.

6.5 PLURALISM REPRESENTED BY COMMUNIST PARTIES IN LATIN EUROPE

Recent years have seen the emergence of pluralistic social and political Communist parties in Western Europe (Italian, French, and Spanish), formulated in a number of party documents. That pluralistic programme of reforms[125] has been accepted, with small modifications, by the Communist parties in Britain and Japan. The programmatic principles worked out by those parties provoked numerous controversies both in the West and in the East. Some Western ideologists interpreted them as a mere tactical manoeuvre intended to help those parties rise to power in their respective countries, and also questioned the autonomy of those parties relative to the governing Communist parties in Eastern Europe. On the other hand, the latter parties often raised the objection (varying in timing and intensity) of revisionism, the Spanish Communist Party being subject to the sharpest criticism.

Before we analyse the pluralistic elements in those programmes it is worthwhile recalling certain facts, because those programmes had been *preceded by periods of important political experience*. There were three such periods. The first was the Popular Front in France, discussed briefly in Chapter 1.

The second was the period of republican governments in Spain, in the later stage with the participation of communists. That period was one of especial importance. In the socioeconomic sphere the communists opposed the nationalization of small industrial enterprises and small and middle-sized farms, nationalization carried out by more radical parties. In the political sphere they defended parliamentarism as the proper way of restructuring society and declared themselves in favour of a political institutionalization of the national separateness of the Basques and the Catalans. Finally, in the case of Catalonia they agreed to include the Trotskyists in the Popular Front, despite the essential differences which separated the Communists and the Trotskyists.

The Spanish communists must have been affected in these respects by the governing Popular Front, but Santiago Carillo, from whose book *Euro-communisme et Etat* these data are drawn, refers to an extremely interesting and important fact, previously known only to a few. A letter to Largo Caballero, signed by Stalin, Molotov, and Voroshilov on 21 December 1936, took up the issue of various paths to socialism, taken up again only at the 20th Congress of the Communist Party of the Soviet Union. The letter states that "it is very likely that the parliamentary path would prove a more effective path of revolutionary development than it had been in Russia". This is followed by advice suggesting legislation that would satisfy the peasants, especially in matters of taxation, and would attract small and middle bourgeoisie by protecting it against expropriations. Close co-operation with other republican parties is recommended, too.

While this letter must *ex post facto* be assessed as a tactical move, at the time of its writing, Carillo says, many leading Spanish communists accepted it *bona fide*.[126]

The third period is that of the participation of the Communist parties in French and Italian cabinets after World War II.[127]

The said three Communist parties in Latin Europe drew inspiration for their programmes from the experience acquired in various states and in various periods.

There are sometimes essential differences among the standpoints of these three parties, but in discussing their struggle for power we shall try to bring out that which is common to them. The Italian Communist Party, which has for years co-governed in six out of the 22 regions, has the greatest experience in the exercise of power. This experience was broadened in the last period which although it did not bring the Italian communists to power, nevertheless they participated three years in the majority. The experience of the French Communist Party is limited to the municipalities it has administered solely or in co-operation with the socialists. In the case of the Spanish Communist Party, the Franco regime with that party's resulting delegalization for many years, deprived it of such experience after World War II but the last municipal elections (Spring 1979) opened new vistas to get experienced also in the running of public affairs.

In politics, the said Communist parties in Western Europe evidently try to expand in their home countries their social base and also their coalitions with other parties, in order to increase the chances of an electoral victory and the chances, once the elections are won, of staying in power and ensuring stability to left-wing governments with the participation of communists. By starting from the assumption that the potential of these strata and groups whose support could be won is large, these parties try to attract not only the professionals (especially those with a technological training), except for the highest-salaried ones, directly connected with the capitalists, but also the mass of white-collar workers, the "desk proletarians and semiproletarians", who are growing radical *en masse*. The same language, which outlines prospects of stabilization, is used to address the middle class in towns (craftsmen, traders, and small and medium entrepreneurs), the intellectuals, and the mass of farmers, owners of small holdings, and land labourers.

The range of allies envisaged by Italian and Spanish communists is broader than that envisaged by the French Communist Party. The Italian communists have long seen a possibility of co-operation (and have even put such co-operation into effect during 1976–9) with the Christian democrats ("the historic compromise") if these approve changes in the social and political structures in Italy and abandon their policy of immobility. The "historic compromise" is a conditional programme, depending on the acceptance of broad reforms.[128]

The reader who does not known Gramsci's ideas well could associate "the historic compromise" with the latter's "historic bloc".[129] An explanation may accordingly be to the point. Gramsci, referring to the experience of factory councils in Turin, strove to work out the principles of immediate revolutionary activity of the masses, aimed at Fascism, but also at bourgeois parliamentarism, whose regeneration he did not expect. His "historic bloc" was *the antithesis* of that existing historic bloc which *de facto* linked the industrialists in the North with the big landowners in the South followed by the middle bourgeoisie, the professionals, the middle strata, and backward peasants. In Gramsci's conception, "the historic bloc" was to strive for a revolutionary abolition of Fascism. The driving power of that bloc was seen by him in the alliance of the working class and the rural proletariat (the peasants in the South and in Sicily and Sardinia). In that bloc *hegemony* was to go to the working class. By hegemony Gramsci meant both the dictatorship of the proletariat in the Leninist sense of the term, and the ideological guidance of the proletariat. The latter issue pointed to the special role of the intelligentsia, without whose participation in the revolutionary worker movement no decomposition of the dominant bourgeois ideology would be possible. As seen by Gramsci, the intelligentsia was an indispensable factor that would hold "the historic bloc" together.[130]

Thus "the historic bloc", as Macciochi is right in pointing out, was not meant to be a shapeless amalgam of the various social classes, nor a simple system of alliance: it assumed the hegemony of the working class which was to guide its allied classes in economy, politics, and culture.[131] Gramsci's revolutionary conception was thus aimed not only at Fascism, but at the parliamentary system as well.

The adoption by the Italian Communist Party and by other communist parties in Latin Europe, in a quite different situation in 1960, of the prejudicial decision concerning the peaceful and gradual evolution of bourgeois society towards the socialist system (in which the achievements of bourgeois democracy would be exploited and the growing role of the communist parties would be taken into account) must have resulted in their working out a new strategic plan. It was prepared by the first steps made by the Italian Communist Party after World War II. Togliatti, drawing conclusions from the failed attempts at a revolution on the part of the Greek communists, from the very moment of his return to Italy (1944) continued Gramsci's ideas, but adapted them to a completely new situation. A special role in that policy was to be played by the tolerant attitude towards the Roman Catholics and by a dialogue with them, intended to define forms of political co-operation.[132] That policy took into consideration the role of the intermediate strata in Italian society and the strength of the religious tradition in that country, reinforced by the power of the papacy.

When the overturning of Allende's legitimate popular government shook the international worker movement, an urgent need arose to work out an alternative policy, which Berlinguer termed the "historic compromise". At the time when Berlinguer advanced his proposal in 1973[133] the "historic compromise" included the socialists, the communists, and the Christian democrats, but during the electoral campaign of 1976 it came to cover other parties, leaving only the Neo-Fascists (MSI) out.

The Italian Communist Party considers the majority "of 51 per cent" to be unstable and insufficient for the exercise of power.[134] An alliance with the Christian democrats was supposed to guarantee the stability of structural reforms and to serve as a barrier against a reactionary coup that could come from both the Neo-Fascists and the army and/or the police. Neutralization of those forces which could effect an antidemocratic coup is believed to be a preliminary condition of the drive for structural reforms.

The Spanish Communist Party, when legalized, came to co-operate not only with leftist parties, but even with democratic anarchists. It co-operated in putting an end to the Franco regime, and its programme was instrumental in effecting deep-reaching structural reforms which changed Spain into a largely decentralized parliamentarian democracy. The autonomy of ethnic- ally distinct regions, especially Catalonia and the land of the Basques, has become a fact. Spanish communists claim that this is a path to a gradual debureaucratization of the machinery of the state.

They have also advanced a new idea of the historic bloc, which replaces the old idea of the worker–peasant alliance by an alliance of the world of labour and the world of culture, which would make it possible to solve problems concerning the whole of Spanish society.[135]

The French Communist Party has not only the narrowest range of political allies or co-operators, namely one limited to socialists and left-wing radicals, but also the most shaky alliance. A different standpoint is characteristic of Roger Garaudy, former member of that party's Political Bureau, who for years has seen a "new historic bloc" as an alliance of the working class and the new strata of technologists, executives (*cadres*), and certain groups of intellectuals, a bloc which would have the consciousness of its unity instilled into it.[136]

Let us now try to analyse the main trend of the changes taking place in those three parties.

(1) All the three parties not only accept the fact that the working class in their respective countries is represented by other parties too, but solemnly declare the acceptance of existing multi-party systems (in the case of Spain this is still only postulated) and respect for the results of general elections, even if they should later be voted out of power.

In this connection mention is due to the Italian formula, which can, however, be referred to the parties now under consideration: the Italian Communist Party is not outside but inside the system of parliamentary democracy, of which it is one of the major factors. L. Gruppi, whom we are quoting now, says that the formula of the dictatorship of the working class and the peasantry is not applicable to the present-day economic and social situation in Italy.[137] This means, on the one hand, an expansion of parliamentary democracy, and on the other, a staggering of gradual reforms over a long period. They begin by putting the national economy in order and in modernizing social and political structures. But in the long run the cumulation of gradual reforms should result in reforms of revolutionary significance.[138] This also means a clear opposition to syndicalist tendencies and an unambiguous path to further development.

Unlike in Yugoslavia, communists in Latin Europe assume the system of political representation to be the basis of their policies. All the three parties treat the liberties won by bourgeois revolutions as a minimum that must be expanded so as to serve as fully as possible the broadest masses. These liberties, "democracy brought to completion", are treated as a necesary complement to political pluralism. P. Birnbaum believes that the Euro-communist strategy has its basis in the acceptance without reservations of the principle of democratic parliamentary representation which considerably brings these parties nearer to the German social-democratic party in the period of Kautsky's decisive influence. This may be open to doubt but surely does not relate to French communists.[139]

(2) In the socioeconomic field the three parties postulate the nationaliza-tion of banks and the principal means of production. The Italian Communist Party often used to come up against a further extension of the scope of nationalization. Considering the large public sectors of the national economy

in both Italy and France, these demands cannot estrange the middle classes. Furthermore, socialization itself is interpreted pluralistically as it includes nationalization, municipalization, and various co-operative forms which would replace capitalist property in many branches of the national economy. This refers to elements of socioeconomic pluralism in the Marxist theory. The planned economy constructed on this base should be democratic, i.e. the plans should be made with the active participation of factory workers, agricultural producers, and consumers. Not only personal property, which could be inherited, but also the private property of craftsmen's workshops and small and middle-sized industrial and commercial enterprises would remain outside the scope of socialization. The policy of these parties is thus focused on the socialization of large private enterprises. The private sector should co-exist with the public one and should include small and middle-sized enterprises.[140] The protection extended to that type of property is explained by the fact that those enterprises have suffered much under monopolistic state captialism. A similar attitude was adopted in the programmes of the three parties towards agriculture, in which small holdings and middle-sized family-owned farms should be protected by the state. This is thus a programme of mixed economy, which should be the basis for further economic, political, and cultural changes.

In this connection it is worthwhile recalling Oskar Lange's reflections on the subject: "... the working class can, and as a rule does, have as its allies peasants and petty bourgeoisie, and under certain conditions also part of the bourgeoisie, namely that part of it which has been in conflict with monopoly capital". "Under conditions other than those in the Soviet Union there is no need to transform so rapidly the small market economy into a socialist one." "If the Italian road to socialism consists in an alliance with the middle strata in town and country, if the popular power abstains from the policy of forcing them to adopt socialist forms of production, then the issue remains open whether small industrialists, small craftsmen and the remaining traders want to form co-operatives or to run their enterprises on a private basis."[141]

(3) In the field of culture the standpoints of the three parties are convergent too: they reject commercialized culture and declare themselves for the freedom of literary and artistic production, thus precluding the monopoly of any single trend in that sphere. Freedom in literary and artistic production inevitably results in its variety.

It may thus be said that these three communist parties closely link political pluralism to socioeconomic pluralism, the latter being mainly connected with democratic planning, that is, with guaranteeing the producers' say in the formulation of the plan at its various levels.

The three parties in the first period thus envisage an expansion of democratic institutions within the capitalist system, to be followed by a transformation of such a democratized system into a socialist one. The second period could probably be labelled that of revolutionary reforms, of a peaceful evolution towards socialism.

This would explain the reasons why the formula of the dictatorship of the proletariat was dropped at the 22nd Congress of the French Communist Party. The results of that congress must have been astonishing for those French political sociologists who saw in the French Communist Party mainly a tight political texture that restrains the life and thought of its political activists. On the other hand, those who saw the continuity of development from the Popular Front on, and the increasingly determined adoption, after World War II, of a peaceful evolution towards socialism, must have considered the process as natural.[142]

The formula of the dictatorship of the proletariat was, in the international worker movement, traditionally connected with the idea of a political revolution by the working class. The dictatorship of the proletariat always meant a revolutionary seizure of power and a revolutionary organization of a proletarian state, and this fact determined the limits of its democratism. It is self-evident that choosing a peaceful evolution towards socialism and including in that process the intermediate strata must have resulted in a reversal of priorities. In the revolutionary variant the seizure of power and organization and defence of a proletarian state, which is the main instrument of a socialist reconstruction, of society come to the fore, while democratization of public life is to be a result of changes in the socioeconomic base.

The priorities look otherwise when communist parties assume a long peaceful evolution toward socialism. This means raising the rank of democratic freedoms, but also assumes acquiring the control of the centre of decision-making by democratic methods alone, with the co-operation of other progressive forces such as other allied political parties.

A digression seems to the point here, to bring out the historical relativity of the conception of the dictatorship of the proletariat, a conception linked to the revolutionary situation and the problem of staying in power once it has been seized as a result of a victorious revolution. The dictatorship of the proletariat was favoured not by communists alone. It suffices to recall the socialist left, namely the Austro-Marxists (Max Adler above all),[143] and the Polish Austro-Marxists, who at that time included Oskar Lange. The latter wrote in 1930 (jointly with M. Breit) that "When striving for a planned economy the labour movement must realize that socialism cannot be attained by a slow and gradual transforming of the capitalist system into a socialist one. The advent of socialism is possible *only* [italics–S.E.] as a result of a revolution, both political and economic."[144]

On the other hand, the vanishing of class antagonisms and external threats to the system, combined with a certain ceiling of economic changes, have resulted in the replacement, in the Soviet Union, of the formula "dictatorship of the proletariat" by the formula "all-national state", which, by the way, drew–in the Mao-period–charges of "Soviet revisionism" on the part of Chinese communists.

But let us now return to communist parties in Latin Europe.

The opinion of the three parties, which instead of a civil war recommend a peaceful road to socialism, is a tentative optimization of the process of politics, and a lowering of its social and moral costs. But it cannot be treated as a final abandonment of the revolution. This depends on the line of policy adopted by the parties and groups which act on behalf of capitalist interests. Attempts to block the process by counterrevolutionary coups, acts of terror, and constant encroachments on the rule of law may force the communist parties to revert to the idea of a political revolution. In a political struggle decisions are dictated not only by one's own intentions, but also by the moves of the opponent. This brings us to an interesting parallel with the pluralistic elements in the popular fronts of the 1930s, but that is a subject to be left to the historians of the international worker movement.

All the three parties in Latin Europe are making use of the formulation "programme of a pluralistic social development" or similar ones, in which the term *pluralism* invariably occurs.

Yet attention must be drawn to the fact that the debate over pluralism and related issues has been rather shallow. In particular, lack of connections in theoretical and programmatic statements and, to make matters worse, in everyday political practice, between political pluralism and democracy within the party have resulted in France, after the last elections of March 1978, in sharp critical statements by intellectuals and certain party leaders. The same issue was raised by the opposition at the congress of the Spanish Communist Party in April 1978. Similar criticism is not lacking when it comes to the Italian Communist Party, and outside its ranks they are formulated publicly by the dissident group named Il Manifesto.[145]

The issue is of essential significance: the critics claim that decisions made "at the top" and alliances concluded by party leaderships perhaps comply with the parliamentary usage and ordinary electoral manouevring, but not with the interests of the mass of voters at the end of the twentieth century. Those masses want actively to participate in working out the new principles of the socioeconomic system and policital leadership, and not to have just to carry out the decisions made by a narrow group of political leaders. The dialogue at the top should have its counterpart in a dialogue among the lower levels of those political parties which have decided to co-operate.

It may be added that the underdevelopment of democracy within communist parties undermines the credibility of their most solemn declarations. Other participants in "blocs", "alliances" and "compromises" do not need to have the political perspicacity of a Machiavelli or a Talleyrand to pose to themselves the question: "if this is the way they treat the members of their own parties, how will they treat us if they rise to power?"

The hypothesis suggests itself that without a convincing democratic practice in their own ranks from top to bottom the communist parties in Latin Europe cannot expect a breakthrough that would enable them to enter the cabinets. Note that in this democratic practice the pride of place goes to supervision and subordination of the executive bodies and the whole party machinery to elected bodies, and that in accordance with the spirit and letter of party regulations and the doctrine of democratic centralism. This was exactly the focus of the inner-party struggle in Poland in 1980–81.

The programme of the three communist parties is not so much a programme that is to enable them to give greater participation in power, but a programme of stabilization of a definite form of sociopolitical evolution after they rise to power; that is to be achieved by a combination of alliances with other worker parties and a simultaneous coalition with bourgeois-democratic parties. This is a programme not only of action within their respective countries, but of a *dialogue with social democratic parties* in those European countries in which the importance of communist parties is small or minimal (United Kingdom, Austria, Federal Republic of Germany). This is a programme of exploiting to the utmost the opportunities offered by bourgeois parliamentary democracy for a gradual preparation for the transition to a socialist reconstruction of society.

One can conclude this by saying that the polycentrism predicted and recommended by Togliatti in his "political testament" of 1964, has become a fact, that it complies with Lenin's forecast of a pluralistic evolution of the international worker movement. It also seems reasonable to advance the hypothesis that the communist parties in Latin Europe will sooner or later find themselves in a situation in which the point will be–to paraphrase Marx's thesis on Feuerbach–not to interpret society, but to transform it.

NOTES AND REFERENCES

1. V. Lenin, *Collected Works*, Russian edn, vol. 27, pp. 387 ff.
2. The term used by Bukharin in 1924.
3. V. Lenin, *Collected Works*, Vol. 26, p. 336; vol. 27, pp. 391, 396.
4. For the data see A. Baikov, *The Development of the Soviet Economic System* (New York, 1947).
5. V. Lenin, *Collected Works*, vol. 27, pp. 387 ff, 396 ff, 401, 405, 414 ff.
6. O. Lange, *Pisma ekonomiczne i społeczne, 1930–1960 (Writings on Economic and Social Issues, 1930-1960* (Warszawa, 1961), pp. 419 ff.
7. These opinions were formulated by Lenin in a number of notes concerned with the 12th Party Congress, in which he did not participate, for health reasons.
8. Lenin, who treated on a par the worker opposition and anarcho-syndicalism (he also blamed Bukharin for syndicalism, cf. *Collected Works*, vol. 32, pp. 75 ff), firmly opposed convening an All-Russian congress of producers, but his opposition was not based on ideological grounds: it was due to the immaturity of the working masses and the acute class struggle then taking place in Russia (cf. *ibid.*, p. 215).
9. The interpretation of the documents relating to the 10th Party Congress and Lenin's opinion, expressed on various occasions, do not justify blaming Trotsky for being an advocate of factionalism and for radically differing on that matter from Lenin. The documents published in *The Third International After Lenin* (New York, 1957), do not

substantiate that criticism of Trotsky, whose image as a vehement factionalist forms part of the Stalinist legacy.

10. R. Medvedev *Kriga a socialistitcheskoi democratic.* (Amsterdam-Paris, 1972) p. 71.
11. See Lenin's statements on the functioning of the Soviet machinery of the state (quoted after the Polish-language version, Warszawa, 1956. See also the analysis of bureaucracy offered by E. Varga, in *Le Testament de Varga*, with a preface by R. Garaudy (Paris, 1970).
12. S. F. Cohen, *Bukharin and the Bolshevik Revolution. A Political Biography, 1888–1938* (London, 1974), pp. 133, 270 ff.
13. Cf. K. Kautsky, *Von der Demokratie zur Staatssklaverei*, and *Die proletarische Revolution und sein Programm.*
14. I. Deutscher, *Stalin: A political Biography* (London, 1949) pp. 301 ff.
15. M. Waldenberg, "Problematyka struktur mieszanych w dziejach myśli socjalistycznej (Problems of Mixed Structures in the History of Socialist Thought), *Państwo i Prawo*, No. 11 (1973), p. 11.
16. *Classes, Social Strata and Groups in the Soviet Union* (in Russian) (Moscow, 1968), p. 221.
17. *The 24th Congress of the Communist Party of the Soviet Union*, (in Polish) (Warszawa, 1971), p. 113.
18. G. Shakhnazarov, *Socialist Democracy* (in Russian quoted after the Polish-language version (Warszawa, 1974), pp. 51–5).
19. Cf. the Statute of the Communist Party of the Soviet Union, Art. 3, Sec. b. See also the Report submitted at the 23rd CPSU Congress (quoted after the Polish-language version (Warszawa, 1966), p. 111). Y. Shakhnazarov points out that while under Lenin the highest party authorities used to meet even during the civil war, thus offering their members an opportunity for criticism and presentation of their own proposals; under Stalin no party congress was convened during the 14 years between the 18th and the 19th Party Congress (*op. cit.*, p. 64).
20. See the programme of the RCP(b) adopted at the 7th Congress, the resolutions of the 11th party congress, and various statements by Lenin. Cf. Shakhnazarov, *op. cit.*, p. 88.
21. R. Medevev, *op. cit.*, p. 374.
22. On the endeavours to democratize the socialist system in Czechoslovakia see H. G. Skilling, *Czechoslovakia's Interrupted Revolution* (Princeton, 1976). See also O. Šik: *The Third Way, The Marxist–Leninist Society and Modern Industrial Society* (London, 1976), especially on Czechoslovakia.
23. V. Lenin, *Selected Works*, Polish edn, vol. II (Warszawa, 1951), article on Great Initiative, p. 520.
24. Cf. J. Hochfeld, *Studia z marksistowskiej teorii społeczeństwa (Studies on the Marxist Theory of Society)* (Warszawa, 1963), especially his article on Marx's general theory of social classes (Warszawa, 1963), p. 149 ff.
25. S. Widerszpil, *Skład polskiej klasy robotniczej (The Composition of the Polish Working Class)* (Warszawa, 1965), p. 181.
26. W. Wesołowski, *Klasy, warstwy i władza (Classes, Strata and Power)* (Warszawa, 1974), pp. 185 ff.
27. S. Widerszpil, *op. cit.*, p. 208.
28. W. Wesołowski, "Proces zanikania różnic klasowych (The Vanishing of Class Differences), *Studia Socjologiczne*, No. 2 (1964), pp. 31 ff.
29. Cf. the papers prepared for the 3rd Congress of Polish Sociologists, M. Hirszowicz (ed.), (Warszawa, 1967), in particular those on the sociological aspects of the formation of socialist enterprises. See also A, Matejsko, *Socjologia zakładu pracy (The Sociology of Factories)* (Warszawa, 1969), chaps. IV–VIII.
30. B. Gałęski, "Chłopi i zawód rolnika (The Peasants and the Farmer's Occupation). *Studies in Rural Sociology*, (Warszawa, 1963), pp. 33, 150.
31. The exact figure was 52.1 per cent, while 38.5 per cent were of the opposite opinion, and 8 per cent had no opinion on the issue. Cf. J. Malanowski, *Stosunki klasowe i różnice społeczne w mieście (Class Relations and Social Differentiation in Towns)*, (Warszawa, 1967), p. 256. In the light of the analyses quoted, and of the results obtained by Malanowski himself, his final conclusion seems excessively cautious: he claims that social membership plays the principal role in determining a person's position, but divisions other than class-based, namely vocational ones, let themselves be known. This situation is probably not finally crystallized.

32. It is characteristic of changes in consciousness that only 14 per cent of the respondents replied to the question "How do you intend to increase your income?" by stating that they wanted to increase the acreage of their farms. Cf. B. Gałęski, *op. cit.*, p. 65. A. Sarapata's research shows that the discrepancy between actual income and that postulated by the various vocational groups was moderate. Cf. his *Studia nad ruchliwością społeczną w Polsce (Studies in Social Mobility in Poland)*, (Warszawa, 1965), pp. 109 ff.

33. A. Sarapata, *op. cit.*, p. 398.

34. In the Polish literature on the subject the term was introduced by J. Tepicht in 1952. It is estimated that the number of peasant–workers in Poland amounts to about one million.

35. B. Gałęski, *op. cit.*, p. 31.

36. *Ibid.*, p. 42 and *passim*.

37. S. Widerszpil and J. Janicki, "Do jakiej klasy należysz? (What Class Are You In?)", *Zycie Gospodarcze*, No. 25 (1959).

38. Quoted after E. Lipiński, *Rewizje (Revisions)* (Warszawa, 1958), p. 93. He treats workers, engineers and technicians as "complex workers" (cf. p. 136). On the expansion of the ideology of a non-institutionalized group (in this case, and working class) upon other groups see S. Ossowski, O osobliwościach nauk społecznych (The Peculiarities of the Social Sciences), (Warszawa, 1962), p. 63.

39. S. Widerszpil, *op. cit.*, p. 198.

40. J. Malanowski, *op. cit.*, p. 300.

41. A. Sarapata, *op. cit.*, p. 406.

42. This is based, among others, on M. Waldenberg, "Rozwój poglądów Lenina na system partyjny w warunkach dyktatury proletariatu (The Development of Lenin's Views upon the Party System under the Dictatorship of the Proletariat)", *Studia Socjologiczno-polityczne*, No. 13 (1962).

43. Hilary Minc, "Some Problems of Popular Democracy" (Polish), *Nowe Drogi*, No. 6 (1949).

44. P. Winczorek, "Funkcje stronnictw sojuszniczych w systemie politycznym z perspektywy 30–lecia PRL (The Functions of Allied Parties in the Polish Political System as seen in the Perspective of 30 years)" *Państwo i Prawo*, No. 7 (1974), pp. 67 ff. In view of the three Roman Catholic groups which function outside the tripartite alliance we speak about a multi-party system. On the Polish party system see W. Skrzydło, "Podstawowe zasady ustroju politycznego (The Basic Principles of the Polish Political System), in: *Studia z zakresu konstytucjonalizmu socjalistycznego (Studies in Socialist Constitutionalism)*, (Wrocław, 1969), pp. 101 ff.

45. On the United Peasant Party see Z. Mikołajczyk, "Próba opisu i klasyfikacji członków Zjednoczonego Stronnictwa Ludowego (A Tentative Description and Classification of members of the United Peasant Party)", *Wieś Współczesna*, No. 4" (1966); Z. Mikołajczyk and E. Patryn, *Struktura i funkcje partii chłopskiej (na przykładzie ZSL) (The Structure and Functions of a Peasant Party—as exemplified by the United Peasant Party)*, (Warszawa, 1968).

46. Cf. P. Winczorek, *Miejsce i rola SD w structure politycznej PRL (The Position and Role of the Democratic Party in Poland's Political Structure)*, (Warszawa, 1975).

47. Note that the small group of Roman Catholic deputies to the Seym enjoys the support of the Church of Rome and of para-ecclesiastical organizations. In 1973, the Roman Catholic Church had 27 dioceses in Poland, with 6470 parishes, 14,300 secular priests, 45 male orders with 8000 monks, and 101 female orders with 28,000 nuns. Religious schools include 45 seminaries and two schools of university rank: the Catholic University of Lublin, and the Academy of Roman Catholic theology. The Church can also influence public opinion through 60 periodicals and about a dozen publishing houses.

48. The term 'guiding role' was carried by the 1976 constitution–it was less provocative than the term 'leader-role' used in party documents.

49. R. Kothari and J. J. Wiatr, "Systemy partyjne a pluralizm polityczny: porównanie między Indią a Polską (Party Systems and Political Pluralism: a Comparison of India and Poland)", *Studia Socjologiczno-polityczne* (1968), No. 25, pp. 178 ff.

50. J. J. Wiatr, "Kształtowanie się i rola systemu partyjnego PRL (The Formation and Role of the Party System in Poland)", in: W. Wesołowski (ed.), *Struktura i dynamika społeczeństwa polskiego (The Structure and Dynamics of Polish Society)*, (Warszawa, 1970), p. 44. The formulation has been adopted by other authors.

51. Cf. the editorial in *Tygodnik Powszechny* of 3 Feb. 1957.

52. S. Ehrlich, *Praworządność, Sejm (The Rule of Law and the Diet)*, (Warszawa, 1956).
53. S. Ehrlich, "La Ribellione all'interno del sistema, Polonia, 1980", *Democrazia e Diritto*, 6 (1981).
54. I. Deutscher: "Poland—Hopes and Fears", *New Left Review*, Jan–Feb. 1981, p. 61.
55. J. Szczepański, *op. cit.*, p. 289.
56. Cf. C. A. Jampolska, *op. cit.*, pp. 13ff.
57. It follows from Y. Kvasha's analysis that the state-owned industry should avoid organizing enterprises which employ less than 50 persons. Cf. his article in *Voprosy Ekonomiki*, no. 5 (1967), p. 31.
58. The schema is drawn from the present writer's article "Trzeci Sektor (The Third Sector)", *Bulletin of the Democratic Party*, No. 2 (1977).
59. The tendency to form the private sector was discussed by the present writer in "Secteur privé ou secteur de l'économie individuelle", *Revue d'études comparatives*, vol. 6, no. 2 (1975). The tendency was reflected in Polish constitutions (both that of 1952 and the one now in force) and in a number of acts. A press communiqué of 5 Nov. 1976, for the first time referred to the state-owned, the co-operative, and the individual sector.
60. In the Polish literature on the subject such a standpoint was also consistently adopted by W. Brus. See also O. Šik, *Plan and Market under Socialism* (1967).
61. H. Spiro, "Totalitarianism", in: *International Encyclopaedia of Social Sciences* (New York, 1968), vol. 16, p. 106.
62. F. Borkenau, *The Totalitarian Enemy* (London, 1940); H. Arendt, *The Origins of Totalitarianism* (New York, 1951); E. Barker treats every one-party system as a totalitarian one, cf. *Reflections on Government* (Oxford, 1942), pp. 284 ff.
63. Cf. C. J. Friedrich (ed.), *Totalitarianism:* Proceedings of a Conference held at the American Academy of Arts and Sciences, Cambridge (Mass.), 1954; C. J. Friedrich and Z. Brzeziński, *Totalitarian Dictatorship and Autocracy* (New York, 1956).
64. C. J. Friedrich, M. Curtis and B. J. Barber, *Totalitarianism in Perspective—Three Views*, (London, 1969), Introduction, pp. 153–4.
65. K. W. Deutsch, "Cracks in the Monolith: Possibilities and Patterns of Disintegration in Totalitarian Systems", in: C. J. Friedrich (ed.), *Totalitarianism*.
66. J. A. Armstrong, *The Politics of Totalitarianism. The Communist Party of the Soviet Union from 1934 to the Present*, (New York, 1961); R. J. Liften, *Thought Reform and the Psychology of Totalitarianism. A Study of Brainwashing in China* (New York, 1961); B. B. Burhc (ed.), *Dictatorship and Totalitarianism* (Princeton, 1964); R. Aron, *Démocratie et totalitarisme* (Paris, 1963); (there is an American edition of 1969); P. T. Mason, *Totalitarianism—Temporary Madness or Permanent Danger?* (Boston, 1967); H. Buchheim, *Totalitarian Rule, Its Nature and Characteristics* (Middletown, 1968).
67. B. A. Ulam, *The New Face of Soviet Totalitarianism* (Cambridge (Mass.), 1967), chap. 7.
68. L. Schapiro, *Totalitarianism* (London, 1972).
69. H. Arendt, *The Origins of Totalitarianism* (new ed.) (New York, 1966), p. 311; B. Moore, Jr, *Political Power and Social Theory: Six Studies* (Cambridge (Mass.), 1958), p. 75; J. H. Kautsky, *Political Change in Underdeveloped Countries: Nationalism and Communism* (New York, 1962).
70. K. W. Wittfogel, *Oriental Despotism* (New Haven, 1957).
71. M. Fainsod, " 'Rationalized' Totalitarianism", in: H. R. Swearer and R. Longaker (eds), *Contemporary Communism* (Belmont, 1963), pp. 88–92.
72. Z. Brzeziński, *Ideology and Power in Soviet Politics* (New York, 1967), chap. 1.
73. Z. Brzeziński and S. P. Huntington, *Political Power USA/USSR* (New York, 1964), pp. 195 ff.
74. H. Arendt, *op. cit.*, p. xi and Part Three: Totalitarianism.
75. G. Ionescu, *The Politics of the European Communist States* (New York, 1967).
76. G. Almond and C. P. Powell, *Comparative Politics. A Developmental Approach* (Boston and Toronto, 1966), pp. 24, 61, 87, 312.
77. *Ibid.*, pp. 55, 59, 94, 105–7, 112 ff., 126.
78. I. Deutscher, *Russia What Next?* (London, 1953), and his later articles: La Révolution inachevée Paris, 1967 and in *New Left Review* (Nov.–Dec. (1980), vol. 124.
79. G. H. Skilling in *World Politics*, vol. XVIII, no. 5, (April 1966).
80. Princeton, 1975 (first published in 1971).
81. J. P. Hough, *The Soviet Prefects: The Local Party Organs in Industrial Decision-Making*

(Cambridge (Mass.), 1969); and *idem.*, "The Soviet System. Petrification or Pluralism?", *Problems of Communism*, no. 2 (1972).

82. N. J. Berman, "The Struggle of Soviet Jurists against a Return to Stalinist Terror", *Slavic Review*, **XXII** (2) (June 1963), pp. 314 ff; *idem.*, *Justice in the USSR* (New York, 1963); and *idem.*, "Legality Versus Terror: The Post-Stalin Law Reform", in: C. M. Carter and A. F. Westin (eds), *Politics in Europe* (New York, 1965), pp. 184 ff. H. W. Ehrmann was one of the first to point to the universality of pluralism. See H. W. Ehrmann (ed.), *Interest Groups on Four Continents* (Pittsburgh, 1958), which for the first time included a presentation of the views of socialist authors (J. D. Djordjević, *Interest Groups and the Political System of Yugoslavia*); J. N. Hazard, "Social Control Through Law", in: A. Dallin and A. Westin (eds), *Politics in the Soviet Union: Seven Cases* (New York, 1966); D. Lane, "Socialist Pluralism", *Political Studies*, **XVI** (Feb. 1968), 102 ff; W. Leonhardt, "Politics and Ideology", in: A. Dallin and T. B. Larson (eds), *Soviet Politics since Krushchev*, (Englewood Cliffs, 1968), chap. 3; M. Lodge, "Groupism in the post-Stalin Period", *Midwest Journal of Political Science*, **XII** (3) (Aug. 1968), 827 ff; I. Ploss, *Conflict and Decision-making in Soviet Russia: A Case Study of Agricultural Policy, 1953–63* (Princeton, 1965); G. H. Skilling, "Group Conflict and Political Change", In: Ch. Johnson (ed.), *Change in Communist Systems*, (Stanford, 1970).

83. *Ibid.*, p. 17.

84. *Ibid.*, p. 43.

85. *Ibid.*, p. 90. He polemizes with M. Olson cf. *The Logic of Collective Action* (Cambridge (Mass.), 1965), pp. 5–17, 132–67, who, on the strength of American data, incorrectly assigned general validity to the statement that groups organize in situations in which the decisive factor is the members' inability to make their interests materialize in any other way.

86. *Ibid.*, p. 39.

87. *Ibid.*, pp. 249, 317 ff., 320 ff., 403. The importance of experts in the process of politics had been stressed earlier. See D. D. Barry, "The Specialist in Soviet Policy-Making", *Soviet Studies*, **XVI** (1964), 152 ff; J. F. Hough, "Reforms in Government and Administration", in: A. Dallin and Th. B. Larson (eds), *op. cit.*, pp. 37 ff.

88. *Ibid.*, chap. VI, "Industrial Managers".

89. *Ibid.*, chap. VII, "The Economists".

90. D. D. Barry and H. J. Berman, *op. cit.*, chap. IX, "The Jurists". See also M. Armstrong, "The Campaign Against the Parasites", in: P. H. Juviler and H. W. Morton (eds), *Soviet Policy-Making: Studies of Communism in Transition* (New York, 1967).

91. *Ibid.*

92. S. Ehrlich, Le pouvoir et les groupes de pression (Paris and The Hague, 1971). Note two case studies concerned with education in the Soviet Union: J. J. Schwartz and W. R. Reech, "Group Influence and Policy Process in the Soviet Union", *American Political Science Review*, **LXII**, (3) (1968), 840 ff; Ph. D. Stewart, "Soviet Interest Groups and the Policy Process: The Repeal of Production Education", *World Politics*, **XXII**, (1) (1969), 29 ff.

94. D. Lane and G. Kolankiewicz (eds), *Social Groups in Polish Society* (London, 1975); G. Ionescu, *The Politics of the European Communist States* (New York, 1967).

95. Cf. R. B. Day, *Preobrazhensky and the Theory of Transition Period*; R. F. Griffiths, *Images, Politics, Arms Control: Aspects and Implications of Past Soviet Policy Toward the United States*, who tries to establish relationships between the Soviet foreign policy and conflicts of opinion among Soviet researchers concerning the sociopolitical structure of capitalism. D. V. Schwartz prepared a monograph on the theoretical assumption underlying the Soviet system of management, two parts of which have appeared in print: "Recent Soviet Adaptations of Systems Theory to Administrative Theory", *Journal of Comparative Administration*, 5, (2) (Aug. 1973); "Information and Administration in the Soviet Union: Some Theoretical Considerations", *Canadian Journal of Political Science* (June 1974). P. Salomon dedicated his monograph to the study of the influence of Soviet criminologists and jurists upon penal legislation.

96. K. von Beyme, Neuere Ansätze zur Theorie des Gruppenpluralismus, in: *Geschichte und Politische Wissenschaft. Festschrift für Erich Gruner* (Bern, 1975), p. 122. See also his discussion in *Oekonomie und Politik im Sozialismus* (München, 1975), p. 335.

97. D. Lane and G. Kolankiewicz (eds), *op. cit.*,; D. Lane, *The Role of Social Groups*, pp. 318

ff. See also the comprehensive criticism of the totalitarian model in the same author's monograph on The Socialist Industrial State, *Towards a Political Sociology of State Socialism* (London, 1976), *passim*.

98. G. Ionescu, *op. cit.*, pp. 3 ff.

99. O. Lange, "Pisma ekonomiczne i społeczne, 1930–60", *op. cit.*, p. 140.

100. Ciągłość i zmiana tradycji kulturowej (Continuity and Change in Cultural Tradition), an unpublished report prepared under the guidance of S. Nowak at the Warsaw University Research Centre for the Methodology of Sociological Research. Owing to Professor Nowak's courtesy the present writer had an opportunity of reading the text and has obtained permission to quote it. Cf. chap. XXII, "The Summing Up of Major Results", pp. 588–611.

101. I. Deutscher, *La Révolution inachevée. Cinquante années de révolution en Union Soviétique, 1917–67* (Paris, 1967), p. 67.

102. K. von Beyme, *Oekonomie und Politik im Sozialismus* (München, 1975), p. 348; D. Lane, *The Socialist Industrial State*, pp. 64, 67.

103. H. Spiro, *Totalitarianism*.

104. In conformity with H. Spiro's views is the conclusion drawn by G. Blazynski in: *Flashpoint Poland*, (New York and Oxford, 1979).

105. Béograd, 1958; see in particular pp. 112, 123, 174. The Programme of the League of Yugoslav Communists. See also: *The Essential Tito*: Introduction by H. Christman (New York, 1970), p. 79.

106. See in particular the resolutions of the 9th Congress, "The Socialist Development of Yugoslavia on the Principle of Self-Government and the Tasks of the Union of Yugoslav Communists" and "The Political Ideology Underlying the Development of the Union of Yugoslav Communists" (in Serbian) (Beograd, 1959). Consult also the Yugoslav constitution, The Basic Principles, II. The evolution of the Yugoslav system from centralization to expanding self-government is described in: J. Djordjević, "A Contribution to the Theory of Social Property", *Yugoslav Thought and Practice*, No. 24 (1968). See also, by the same author, "Le Concept du système politique autogestionnaire", in: *Le Socialisme dans la théorie et la pratique yougoslave* (Dec. 1974).

107. The broader aspect of the issue is discussed in W. Brus, *Uspołecznienie a ustrój polityczny (Socialization and the Political System)* (Uppsala, 1975). The Yugoslav model is discussed in chap. II, pp. 91 ff.

108. W. Brus, *op. cit.*, pp. 102 ff.

109. The programme of the Union of Yugoslav Communists, *op. cit.*, pp. 125 ff., 141.

110. O. Lange's lecture in Belgrade on 18 November 1957. Cf. his Pismalekonomiczne i społeczne, 1930–1960, *op. cit.*, pp. 134 ff.

111. See also Part II, Chapter I, Art. 18 and following ones.

112. Quoted after B. Zawadzka, "Jugosłowiański system delegacji (The Yugoslav System of Delegation of Power)", *Państwo i Prawo*, No. 3 (1976), p. 99, who is right in stating that "The state does not have to be a force that is alien and hostile to society; it can also be interpreted as the central spokesman of all-national interest, and such a function is indispensable even in a completely decentralized and self-governing society".

113. E. Kardelj, *op. cit.*, no. 42/1973.

114. S. Tomic, *Revolucija, politicka participacija i samoupravlanie* (Saraievo, 1975).

115. On the doctrine which underlies the Yugoslav system of self-government and its evolution see J. Djordjević's paper on interest groups in Yugoslavia in: H. Ehrmann (ed.), *Interest Groups on Four Continents* (Pittsburgh, 1958); E. Kardelj: "Problemi noise socialisticne graditstve", *Liubliomoi 1956–1974*, v. I–IX; N. Poisic: *Kluse i politika* (Beograd, 1974); A. Bibić, "The Direct Articulation of Interests in the Self-management System of Yugoslav Society", paper circulated at the IPSA Round Table Conference at Dubrovnik, September 1975.

116. See his "The Yugoslav Constitution and New Individual Rights and Freedom", in: *Scritti in Onore di Caspare Ambrosini*, (Milan, 1970), Vol. I, p. 599; O. Lange, *op. cit.*, p. 136.

117. W. Brus, *op. cit.*, pp. 131 ff.

118. See the Yugoslav constitution, Part II, Chap. II; P. Nikoloć, *Le Système socio-politique yougoslave* (Beograd, 1974); and B. Zawadzka, *op. cit.*, and the literature of the subject she quotes.

119. Cf. J. Djordjević, *Teorija socializma i samoupravna "empiria"* in *Teorija i praksa samouprav-*

lanija w Jugoslawii (Beograd, 1972).
120. Introduction to *Razwoj Slovenskago narodnego uprawnja*, (Ljbljana, 1975).
121. A. Bibić, *The Direct Articulation...*; N. Pasić, *Nacjonalno pitanije u sowremenoj epoki* (Beograd, 1973).
122. A. Bibić, *op. cit.*
123. The Conclusion of D. Rusinov's monograph: *The Yugoslav Experiment 1948–1974*, (London, 1977).
124. E. Kardelj: *Democracy and Socialism...*, p. 68 ff. and his: *Self-management and the Political System* (Belgrade, 1980).
125. Some of these documents are of special importance; the common programme of a future left-wing government in France, worked out by the communists and the socialists and later accepted by left-wing radicals (June 1972), the 14th Congress of the Italian Communist Party (March 1975) the agreement between the Italian and the Spanish Communist Party (11 July 1975), and that between the Italian and the French Communist Party (11 November 1975), and finally the 22nd Congress of the French Communist Party (February 1976). The data are available from the press for 1972–7. See also the separate publications: *Programme commun du parti communiste et du parti socialiste pour la France*, (Paris, 1975), the documents pertaining to the 22nd Congress of the French Communist Party in *Le socialisme pour la France* (Paris, 1976). Consider also the data relating to the Congress of the Spanish Communist Party (April, 1978).
126. S. Carillo, *Eurocommunisme et Etat* (Paris, 1977), pp. 183 ff.
127. In 1981–1982 The French communists are again in government and the Italian communists are firmly established in several regional governments.
128. S. Tarrow: Historic Compromise as Popular Front: Italian Communism in the Majority 1976–1979 in *The End of Eurocommunism?* (London, 1981).
129. L. Graziano: In *Political Compromise: Italy after the 1979 Elections, Government and Opposition*, vol. 15 (1980) p. 190 ff; and his: "The Historic Compromise and Associational Democracy. Toward a New Democracy?", *Inter. Pol. Science Rev.*, vol. 1 (1980), p. 345 ff; M. Azcarate and I. Claudin: *L'Europe de l'Atlantiqué à l'Oural* (Paris, 1979), p. 42.
130. For Gramsci's views of the state revolution, and those social forces which could join it, see *L'Ordine nuovo*, (Torino, 1935); *Note sul Machiavelli, sulla Politica e sulla Stato Moderno*, (Torino, 1955, first published in 1949); *La Costruzione del Partito communista*, (Torino, 1971; first published in 1949). For comments on his ideas see P. Togliatti, *Gramsci* (Roma, 1967); G. Bonomi, *Partito e rivoluzione in Gramsci*, (Milano, 1973).
131. M. A. Macciochi, *Pour Gramsci* (Paris, 1974; first published in 1948), p. 162; Ch. Buci-Olucksman, *Gramsci et l'Etat*. (Paris, 1975), p. 317; F. Bon et M. A. Burnier: *Les nouveaux intellectuels*, (Paris, 1966), ch. 7, who reflect in an interesting way on Gramsci's concept of the organic intellectual; see also J. M. Commett, *A. Gramsci and the Origins of Italian Communism*, (Stanford, 1967); J. M. Piotte, *La Pensée politique de Gramsci*, (Paris, 1970) p. 104 ff.; H. Portelli, *Gramsci et le bloc historique*, (Paris, 1972).
132. Cf. Exchange of open letters between bishop L. Betazzi and E. Berlinguer, *Rinascità*, 14 Oct. 1977.
133. Cf. *Rinascità* of 23 Sept, 5 Nov. and 9 Nov. 1973.
134. E. Berlinguer's formulation at the congress of the Roman federation, 9 March 1975. He said that the left-wing alternative, i.e. an alliance of the communists and the socialists only, would not make it possible to solve the vital issues which Italy faced (*Unità* of 10 March 1975). On changes within the Italian Communist Party see *Sociologie du communisme en Italie* (Paris, 1974).
135. In this connection S. Carillo, when speaking about the vanguard nature of the Communist Party, emphasizes that such a role of that party is not something that can be decreed, but is a status that must be won in a political struggle. *Op. cit.*, pp. 59, 61, 149.
136. R. Garaudy again formulated his standpoint in the article "Pour un Avenir à visage humain". *Le Monde* of 20 April 1978.
137. L. Gruppi in *Rinascità* of 17 Oct. 1975. A few days later E. Berlinguer stated on the same subject, when speaking at the meeting of the Italian Communist Party Central Committee, that "It is unrealistic to present the strategy and tactics of the Russian revolution of 1917 or even 1905 as the schemata of the political campaign to be waged in the West. This is so not only because several decades have elapsed since that time, but also because it is inconceivable that socialism could be built in the West in the forms and by the methods

once used in the Soviet Union and other Eastern European and Asian countries". Cf. *Unità* of 30 Oct. 1975.

138. Note in this connection the remarkable statement by Waldeck-Rochet, that a peaceful transition to socialism should not be confused with parliamentary methods (cf. *L'Avenir du Parti communiste* (Paris, 1970), pp. 112 ff). The range of possible legal actions to be taken within the bourgeois-democratic system is broader.

139. P. Birnbaum: *Le Peuple et le gros. Histoire d'un mythe* (Paris, 1979) p. 218.

140. Statistical data show that 80 per cent of Italian workers are with enterprises which employ less than 500 persons each. On the role of the private sector see F. Ferri at a colloquium organized by the Italian Communist Party in November 1974 (quoted after *Études*, Paris, April 1976, p. 525).

141. O. Lange, "Pisma ekonomiczne i społeczne," *ed. cit.*, pp. 47 ff, 60.

142. The former include A. Kriegel, *Les Communistes français*, (Paris, 1968), p. 213; the latter, G. Lavau, "Le Parti communiste français dans le système politique français", in: *Le Communisme en France*, (Paris, 1969). See also (in this same collection of papers): Le P. C. F.: "Structures, composition, moyens d'action", pp. 183 ff.

143. Max Adler, when analysing the concept of the dictatorship of the proletariat and proletarian democracy, treated them as very closely linked to one another. See his *Die Staatsauffassung des Marxismus* (Wien, 1922), p. 191, and his popular paper on political and social democracy (quoted after the French-language version, *Démocratie politique et démocratie sociale* (Paris, 1970), pp. xi, xiii). See also A. Donneur, *Histoire de l'union des partis socialistes pour l'action internationale, 1920–23* (Génève, 1967); N. Leser, "Der Austromarxismus als Theoriem und Praxis", *Kölnische Zeitschrift für Soziologie und soziale Psychologie*, **20** (3), (Sept. 1968), 471 ff. A good selection of Austro-Marxist texts was presented by T. B. Bottomore *et al.*, *Austromarxism* (Oxford, 1978).

144. O. Lange, *op. cit.*, p. 33.

145. Analysis of processes within the parties of Latin Europe and their policies in: D. L. M. Blackmer and S. Tarrow: *Communism in Italy and France* (Princeton (N.J.), 1975); M. Basi and H. Portelli (eds), *Les P.C. espagnol, français et italien face au pouvoir* (Paris, 1976); P. Lange and S. Tarrow (eds), *Italy in Transition: Conflict and Consensus* (London, 1979).

Conclusion: The Rationality of Pluralism

Any concluding remarks are meant neither to be a summary of the book nor to be limited to conclusions that can be drawn directly from the text, even though we begin with such conclusions.

(1) We have labelled as pluralistic every present-day trend in socio-political thought that opposes bureaucratic centralism, because the latter bars from participation in decision-making those to whom such decisions apply, and imposes the implementation of decisions regardless of whether these are accepted by those directly concerned. Every trend which opposes standardization of public life is pluralistic. Pluralism is not a feature of any single sociopolitical system or form of government which distinguishes it from the remaining ones. On the contrary, the antinomy of degenerated uniformistic centralism and pluralism recurs in every historical epoch, or, to use the Marxist terminology, in every formation. The phenomenon of pluralism should be the object of research on the level of political structure, economic structure and in the field of cultural life. This book was limited to the first two levels.

Even patriarchal centralism is not acceptable from the pluralistic point of view, because that system–under the cover of approving democracy and an humanistic patronizing approach on the part of the leading political authorities–precludes all possibility of joint decision-making, and even influencing the decisions. This reflects the song of the Nile oarsmen reproduced by Alan Moorehead from *The Blue Nile*:

Steersman: My sons, you are men, row away stoutly.
Oarsmen (in chorus): God and Muhammad.
Steersman: God strengthen you.
Oarsmen: God and Muhammad.
Steersman: The moon shines brightly.
Oarsmen: God and Muhammed.
Steersman: The smooth river runs swiftly.
Oarsmen: God and Muhammad.
Steersman: The wind is against us but God is for us.

Oarsmen: God and Muhammad.
Steersman: Row on, my sons, the supper is cooking.
Oarsmen: God and Muhammad.

It must accordingly recur in the history of sociopolitical and socio-economic thought. One trend goes from Confucius and Plato to Hobbes to all advocates of authoritarianism in the recent period. The other goes from Aristotle to Locke, de Montesquieu, and de Tocqueville to the present-day varieties of pluralism. Between these two trends the works of Rousseau and Hegel are a subject of endless controversies. De Montesquieu opposed absolutism and saw the way of humanizing it in an improved and moder-nized monarchy based on estates; that is, in the version of pluralism characteristic of his times. After de Montesquieu we note a long sequence of tendencies to oppose uniformization of social life, namely authoritarian rule, bureaucratic centralism, totalitarianism, technocratic ideology, and all tendencies towards monolithism. In a word, endeavours to monopolize social initiative are opposed by respective forms of pluralism. For pluralism is an historical concept. Pluralistic trends emerge whenever in a given epoch there is a need to counteract the tendencies, or established institutions, which block the further evolution of the social system.

(2) Hence the attitude of pluralism toward revolution is of special importance. Every revolutionary upheaval brings a new social differentia-tion to the surface. New spontaneous forces are then only seeking new organizational forms. This is why all the three now co-existing types of systems: capitalist, socialist, and post-colonial, must be analysed from the point of view of pluralism.

The old pluralism of social and political forms is thus replaced by a new one[1]: revolutionary pluralism has its say. Its temporary restriction, or even brutal suppression, should not make one jump to conclusions. We have tried to explain, by referring to the case of the Jacobinic and the Bolshevik revolution, that restrictions of freedom should be considered as transient features of the new system, and not a matter of principles. It is a matter of practice, subject to change provided that history leaves enough time for such a return to principles, to lasting revolutionary values. Phenomena which we assess negatively from the moral point of view were due to the fact that revolution was threatened. This threat being removed a directive emerges: the return to pluralistic principles inherent in revolutions.

The thesis that socialist societies can, and even are bound to develop along pluralistic lines is not a concession to the theory of convergence, for the differences between the capitalist and the socialist system are still dominant and will remain so in the foreseeable future. These two systems differ in:

(a)   the set of fundamental values (strategic goals):
(b)   political structure;

(c)   structure of interests;
(d)   the type of the interaction between the two structures—that is, the nature of the processes of decision-making;
(e)   political culture—that is, values and institutions which condition one's behaviour in the process of making political decisions.

But no one who is sane would claim that the adjectives *capitalist* or *socialist* are applicable to atomic piles, space vehicles, computers, electronic devices, the PERT system, ergonomy, certain principles of labour organization in industry, agriculture, transportation systems, and so on. If so, then analogies in those fields are irrelevant to the issue of convergence.

(3)   The pluralism of pluralisms, discussed in the present book relates not only to society within a given state, but also to opinions and adequate institutions in international relations. Acceptance and comprehension of different roads to socialism has been recently striking in the international labour movement and in relations among communist parties.

(4)   Moreover, pluralism pertains not only to formal groups, but to informal ones as well. This distinction is particularly applicable to élites, which can take on the form of formal and informal groups. R. Aron claims that in a stabilized democratic society we can see a pluralism of heterogeneous élites, in relations among which co-operation prevails.[2] But our analysis should begin with the pluralism of social movements. As their self-consciousness increases they form informal groups out of which, or next to which, organizations emerge and strive to dominate the centre of decision-making. Such groups sometimes come ahead of, and inspire, social movements. The point is that the process should take place in accordance with pre-established rules of the game.

Pluralism thus can and should be examined at various levels and confronted with certain sequences of events (always bearing in mind the difference between normative and descriptive pluralism). This can be visualized by the schema shown in Figure 5, which can have two variations.

One point more. Only some trends can be unambiguously described as

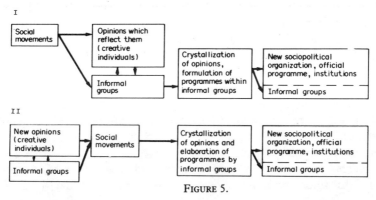

FIGURE 5.

pluralistic, the anarchists being extreme pluralists. The antithesis of pluralism is to be seen in totalitarian ideology and society. The anarchists deny the need of any centre of political decision-making, which they identify with "the oppressive state", whereas the advocates of totalitarianism reduce all sociopolitical facts to the functioning of that centre which they identify with the state, and in turn identify the state with society. When it comes to other ways of thinking and sociopolitical systems, it would be more prudent to class them as more or less pluralistic. One could try to graduate them on a certain scale within given historical periods. Today, pluralism in the democratic system is being eroded by the concentration of capital in industry, agriculture, and culture (commercialization of the press, publications, and certain branches of art) and by the tradition of bureaucratic centralism, the classical example of which is France, (hence the resistance at the top level to regional reforms, and especially to autonomy for Basques and Brittany).

In socialist systems, the distortions due to bureaucratic centralism (the danger clearly sensed by Lenin) are the strongest uniformizing force as it occurs in nearly all vertical lines of economic, social and political structure. Under bureaucratic centralism, its representatives consider it quite natural to concentrate all social initiative at the top level of the political structure, and since that is not possible, they either assimilate it as their own if it suits their purposes, or thwart it. In this way they create the appearances of omnisciences, they pretend that all new ideas in the sphere of social reforms are born in the centre of political decision-making. The striving to eliminate manifestations of pluralism and/or to block all trends towards pluralism is intended to prevent independent authority from emerging within society, because the existence of such authorities would hinder the self-reproduction of that authoritarian system. To conclude, we have to eliminate from our analysis all arbitrary value judgements.

(5) Pluralism of pluralism–the object of this book–is not a matter of arithmetic. It is the autonomy of the subsystems and the voluntariness of emerging organizations which determines how far a certain system can be considered pluralistic. The Soviet state under NEP was in many respects pluralistic and under Stalin's dogmatism it had totalitarian features, even though Stalin in 1920 declared himself an adherent of pluralism in national, ethnic, and religious issues and in manners,[3] and in *Problems of Leninism* included certain declarations which by our criteria we would qualify as pluralistic, because he wrote about the soviets around which various social organizations should swarm, and about the party that in the course of evolution will ... wither away. This was his lip service to Lenin's vision of the soviets, and to his critical approach to the party apparatus. Lenin's vision was pluralistic and antibureaucratic.

A digression is necessary here. Developed and correctly functioning institutions whose task is to examine the legality of decisions of the administration do protect the individuals against the self-will of the bureaucracy, but that guarantee of the rule of law cannot be the antidote to the monopoly of official initiatives. If bureaucracy is to be overcome effectively, autonomous intermediate bodies must function under socialism, too. Their differentiation should correspond to the differentiation of social interests under that system. It is only within that organizational framework that the individual can take initiative, and the system as a whole can function in accordance with its principles. Putting an end to the abuses and structural distortions that marked the many years of Stalin's authoritarian regime added vigour to decentralization tendencies, opened new vistas to Soviet federalism, and to the path of the country's pluralistic development.

The "arithmetical" simplification manifests itself in a glaring form when we proceed to analyse the Yugoslav and the Mexican system, which are one-party ones. How far the two systems are pluralistic can be judged only when the processes taking place in the subsystems have been examined, and in particular when it is known what influence they have upon the centre of political decision-making. But this is not all. The procedure by which that centre is established and supervised (in fact, of course, and not merely in terms of legal provisions), including the possibility of making personal changes in it, would also have to be examined.

(6) Pluralism does not mean a sphere of arbitrary decisions. Organizationalpluralism of a given society, if it is to function without major upheaval or even cataclysms, *must* function on democratic principles. N. Rashevsky's thesis that excessive uniformity threatens the stability of systems[4] is directly applicable to the subject-matter of the present book (for example, values protected by a ramified system of legal guarantees, shielded by the rule of law).

Technocrats imagined that the impact of cybernetics upon science and that of rapid computers upon social transactions would provide additional arguments in favour of a centralized control of society. This is a misunderstanding due to a mechanical transfer of what we know about control of the production line and the knowledge of the possibility of controlling certain biological processes upon social processes. Yet the latter are governed by special laws, typical of highly organized beings. In social and political processes the feedback can be neither mechanical nor, *a fortiori*, automatic (with a few exceptions); in these processes the decisive role is played by the autonomy of decision-making by subsystems, by emergence of social movements which are difficult to foresee (note the sudden eruption of students' riots in 1968 and the spontaneous turn of events in Poland's hot summer of 1980), the behaviour of informal groups, which is difficult to observe and more so to control, and the initiative and resourcefulness of individuals. Technocrats see in social and political processes only the problem of *management*, but fail to notice that of *self-government*.

David Easton, writing about the process of politics, points out that systemic feedback makes it possible to obtain unity from heterogeneity.[5]

The correct interpretation of the scientific metaphor of self-regulating society can only mean control from the bottom to the top to the centre of political decision-making. Perhaps in a not too remote future every citizen will have his registration number, and all essential data concerning his person will be fed into computer memory by skilled programmers. This would open two opposite prospects. One would be a specific disfranchisement or manipulation of individuals thus reduced to the role of data items. The other would mean a more efficient and a more just society—on the condition of an effective from-the-bottom-up control of the use made of those data by the centre of political decision-making. The use made by society of technological progress is ultimately determined by the scale of values adopted as the binding one.

Pluralism is thus an inseparable element of democracy, under socialism too. For what is the alternative solution? As has been emphasized often, it reduces to bureaucratic centralism, with totalitarianism as its extreme variety. While disregarding its other features, we may say, from the point of view of the problem discussed at this moment, that it means a system in which the machinery of the state (or, to put it more rigorously, the political structure) is deprived of its social milieu. It means a situation in which voluntary and other social organizations are dissolved formally or in fact, through erosion of their prerogatives and authority, though with observance of legal appearances. The social environment ceases to exist once it has been subordinated to the machinery which depends solely on the centre of political decision-making.

In the case of the totalitarian state we know, from recent history, that it devoured its social environment by monopolizing all initiative and raising coercion to the rank of the principal regulator of social processes. Such tendencies yield situations in which a given society must be defined as a "closed system". It is controlled by the centre of political decision-making (the central regulating system) in which personal changes take place through co-optation from among people at the next lower level or through shifts at the top level. In such a system, the process of politics as a rule takes place within the bureaucratic apparatus.

I am using here the term "closed system" strictly in the Weberian sense—as elaborated in his fundamental work, *Economy and Society*—where by the process of "closing" a social system he means conscious efforts of social collectivities to maximize rewards by restricting access to rewards and opportunities by barring it according to a preconceived selection. F. Parkin writes that strategies of exclusion may be regarded as the predominant mode of closure in all stratification systems, which he calls *"power of exclusion"*. The excluded challenge this power using their own *power of solidarism*, which directs pressure upwards.[6] The phenomenon of a closed system has its counterpart in psychology. Closed systems tend to be run by closed minds.[7] A closed system models them according to its internal logic. It needs authoritarian personalities.

On the contrary, an open system is marked by not being isolated from its social environment, whence (that is, from the outside) it incessantly receives information, impulses, initiative, influences, and so on, which makes it possible better to define goals and to increase the probability of attaining them, and above all to "renovate" the centre of decision-making personally. In a closed system the information inputs are either blocked or function incorrectly, because their number has been reduced to a minimum, which is inevitably linked to arbitrariness in selecting sources of information. This results in an overloading of information channels, because the selection mechanisms (the autonomous decision-making centres in subsystems) have been eliminated. This yields a kind of information vacuum; in a milder case we have to do with a *sui generis* information anaemia.

Decisions made on the basis of incomplete or distorted information must be wrong. With such inputs optimal decisions are impossible. Decisions must be wrong not only because of a narrowing down of the basis of information, but also as a result of the elimination of correcting elements.

In the case of the totalitarian state this has necessarily resulted in a catastrophe of the system. Under bureaucratic centralism, degradation of the quality of decisions is inevitable so that the attainment of the fundamental goals becomes questionable, and the attainment of partial goals is unavoidably delayed while the costs of reforms increase immeasurably. Parkinsonian controversies over prerogatives and the resulting successive reorganizations drive out controversies over the attainment of strategic goals, over ideas and values.[8]

This is accompanied by a specific shifting of goals, so that autonomous objectives are pursued by the various sections of the state and party machinery in order to achieve their particular interests. K. von Beyme points to the fact that in the socialist system close links between the state and society account for the fact that the various sections of the state and party machinery largely function as separate interest groups.[9] As we know, this cannot contribute to the success of the whole.

The system of bureaucratic centralism has ceased to be a learning system. Dysfunctional phenomena; to use Merton's expression, or, to put it plainly, pathological ones, tend to dominate. Such a dysfunction ends in recurrent crises of the system, which not only prove that the remedies applied earlier were just palliatives, but also show that both the centre of decision-making and its subsystems have developed false consciousness, which is a characteristic feature of all closed systems.

The founders of cybernetics treated information, however we interpret the concept, and its circulation as the element of cohesion of every organization.[10] Of course, in society treated as a self-regulating macro-system the quality of information and the speed of its circulation are of essential importance for its functioning, and even its survival. The same applies to every social organization taken separately. Circulation of information (the key issue being the constant process of transforming information into decisions) means that the centre of decision-making responds to information coming from the outside by making adequate decisions, which are next corrected in socially useful time on the basis of new information on how these decisions were implemented (feedback). Such corrections serve the proper functioning of organizational evolution, which is to say that they should bring the system closer to its set target.

Thus in a closed system there can be no feedback. K. W. Deutsch says that a society or a community, if it is to regulate itself, must have information of three kinds coming in all the time: first, information *about the external world* (italics–S.E.); second, information about its own past; third, information about itself and its component parts. If one of these three information flows is broken either by a direct act of violence or coercion, or comes to be kept secret (which is a form of coercion), society turns into an automaton. It loses control of its own behaviour, not only by some of its own parts, but ultimately also of the centre of decision-making.[11]

That continuous cyclical exchange of information and social (group) decisions (i.e., transformed information) between a system and its social environment can be presented as the following formula, where i stands for information and d for decision:

$$i\text{--}d\text{--}i_1 \ \ldots \ d\text{--}i\text{--}d_2 \ \ldots \ i\text{--}d\text{--}i_n$$

This phenomenon might be termed social metabolism. This idea served as the foundation of the present writer's two books, in which a distinction is made between interaction of two structures: the structure of interests, that is, influences (which generates information), and the political structure (which generates decisions), intertwined by chains of feedbacks.[12]

Such processes require the existence and functioning of diversified social groups. Lack of such diversification is conducive to even those interests which are socially eufunctional with a given social system being lost or disregarded.

(7) Pluralism obviously does not guarantee that optimal decisions be made by the decision-making centre of the system, but elimination of pluralism in a sense guarantees that much worse decisions will be made, which sometimes threatens the integrity of the whole system. Briefly speaking, pluralism makes it possible to improve the process of decision-making and better to foresee the course of events under uncertainty that is characteristic of all social processes, and thus better to put decisions into effect once they have been made. A functioning pluralist system enlarges the probability of better, more effective decisions.

(8) Such a concept as a political culture is hardly imaginable without pluralism: it cannot be made solely by the centre of decision-making, and *a fortiori* cannot be dictated by it. It emerges from a certain differentiation of opinions and organizational forms, which assume toleration, and from a

combination of co-operation and conflicts. Simmel treated the number of groups with which an individual is connected as a measure of culture.[13] If we disregard the problem of subculture, within the framework of a social system political culture means:

(a) internalization of the goals of the system and the hierarchy of basic values by the individuals and groups who make up that system;
(b) stable (and hence well-functioning) principles of co-operation;
(c) stable (and hence well-functioning) principles of conflict solving;
     (Principles (b) and (c) apply to individuals, institutions (formal groups) and informal groups)
(d) unambiguous and well-functioning rules whereby the centre of decision-making is elected and supervised.

This interpretation of political culture intentionally emphasizes its normative nature, because the rule of law is an inseparable element.

(9) Historical variations of centralism and uniformism have their counterparts in variations of pluralism. The conflict of these two opposing principles and trends takes on different forms in every period and in every state. Hierarchical bureaucratic centralism disrupts existing social bonds or at least reduces them and makes them insipid, while uniformism results in isolating the individuals and in atomizing society. Ideologists of centralism conceived in this way start from the assumption that the content of what we call public interest is given and that its sense is mysteriously discovered by a talented statesman who is the only one called to make it materialize.[14]

This viewpoint comes very close to that of C. Schmitt, an ideologist of Nazism, who claimed that the essential, or rather necessary, feature of democracy consists in its homogeneity and elimination of heterogeneity.[15] This was why in his book *Die Hüter der Verfassung* (1931) he saw the cause of the fall "of the Weimer republic in pluralism, polyocracy, and federalism".

In a socialist system, tendencies towards bureaucratic centralism threaten the very existence of that system,

> "because the methods of highly centralized administrative planning and management, which largely resort to extra-economic forms of coercion, are not characteristic of socialism, but are rather a certain technique of war economy. Difficulties emerge when those methods of war economy are identified with the essence of socialism and taken to be its essential component.[16]

This idea is well complemented by one of Lukács' last statements: no reform can be carried out by a bureaucracy, because putting it into effect requires participation of the masses.[17] Lange used to speak about *active planning of/by an organized society.*[18]

(10) All this does not mean assigning an absolute value to social and

political pluralism; nor may one–to confine oneself to a narrower issue–assign any such absolute value to decentralization. In some epochs centralization is unavoidable when such sociological factors as weakness of the working class in an underdeveloped country intervene.

> The policy of building socialism in general, and in particular in underdeveloped countries, where additional tasks of socialist industrialization emerge and a rapid modernization of agriculture takes place, requires a *large degree of centralization* [italics–S.E.] in the management of the national economy.[19]

But these are problems characteristic only of the *first period* of reconstruction of society on socialist principles.

Further, the problem is not: centralization versus decentralization, because facts demand answers to definite questions: which spheres should be centralized, and which decentralized, and possibly also: to what extent? Decisions of which kind are to be decentralized? This is a problem of *social purposefulness*.[20] This purposefulness can be appreciated not in abstract but within a given historical context which sets *limits to pluralism too*. They are decisive for the maintenance and the survival of the system.

Then totalitarianism is being abandoned in favour of democracy, a *pluralism of bureaucratic élites* (which as a rule develop in complex organizations) *may be to the point temporarily*. As compared with the preceding period it will be a partly open system, but aspirations of society, once aroused, will not rest satisfied with that for a long time. This is an important question, because *in the process of politics time is a factor* which no centre of political decision making can afford to disregard. It is an illusion of authoritarian personalities in power that they can make decisions any time. However, in a political process (waging war included) time is a very precious commodity.

(11) *Integration of a pluralistic society* requires a great intellectual and organizational effort on the part of the main centre of decision-making and by such centres at lower levels, an effort which is needed to convince members of the system that the policy to be carried out is a correct one. This is so because decisions concerning the use to be made of material and intellectual means evoke different reactions in different subsystems. Thus in a pluralistic sociopolitical system we have to do with *integration by levels*, which is a kind of *indirect integration*.[21] In a long process élites emerge which acquire increasing experience in making decisions of public importance. In such a system élites of subsystems can become the recruitment base for the centre of political decision-making.

In standardized (unidimensional, to refer to the title of the well-known book by H. Marcuse) societies the centre of decision-making issues numerous declarations and passes numerous decisions, but listens little. Little wonder it proves difficult to put such decisions into practice.

Alternatively, in pluralistic societies the centre of decision-making listens more and is more restrained in issuing declarations, which increases the probability of its decisions being put into effect. In the former case the information flow resembles a one-way street, with the movement from top to bottom. In the latter, it resembles a two-way street, with the movement from bottom to top and from top to bottom. Another analogy is that with a monologue and a dialogue, respectively.

(12) It is easy to notice the contradiction between the growing complexity of social facts and the growing social differentiation (which Simmel treated as the problem of conservation of psychosocial energy)[22] on the one hand, and the tendencies towards uniformity, on the other. These tendencies also have an adverse effect below the level we are concerned with here, namely in the sphere of individual psychology. This is so because they raise *additional* obstacles to the initiatives by individuals to introduce novelties in the fields of intellectual creativity, organization and technology. When it comes to public activity, standardization, which deprives individuals of their initiative and possibility to participate in public life, drives them into apathy.

Participation in the implementation of the decisions made at the top can neither satisfy individuals nor favour the attainment of social goals. The decisive factor is the possibility of displaying social initiatives on the part of individuals and autonomous groups, of participating in making such initiatives materialize, of controlling from the bottom the centre of political decision-making and its executive apparatus. To be a man means to participate in the life of the community.[23] Note that we mean participation in the sense outlined above. This is why the Yugoslav doctrine, as has been said, is correct in not identifying participation with self-government or self-rule (*autogestion* in French), for the latter is a higher kind of participation. Active participation is conducive, as some American authors stress, to an increased sense of responsibility.[24]

In a standardized society apathy is a positive value from the point of view of that conception, since it contributes to its further uniformity, and does work on the positive feedback principle. Apathy in the sphere of public activity finds compensation in the striving to grow rich at any price, in aspirations to conspicuous consumption, which becomes a very high value, sometimes the highest of all. In such a situation tendencies to moderate egalitarianism are discredited as naive and utopian—but they are nevertheless deeply rooted in the masses. Striving for moderate egalitarianism is also rational objectively, from the point of view of the system itself.

On the basis of the studies carried out by J. Reykowski we can advance the hypothesis that blocking social initiatives, hampering creative and innovative work develops an egocentric attitude in individuals, and suppresses the prosocial one.[25]

Artificial, bureaucratic obstacles on the road to the satisfaction of individuals' aspirations hamper socioeconomic development very seriously.

R. Presthus is right in saying that man is not born with a predisposition to political apathy and disappointment, but learns them from his bitter experience.[26]

The conservatism built into the system of bureaucratic centralism, that depersonalized barrier against the pluralism of hierarchies, and the sharp break between the various levels all block the *sui generis* social system of capillary vessels and paralyse the initiative of individuals and groups. It is primarily creative people who collide with these obstacles. Social inactivity imposed from above, activity confined to that which is controlled from the top and limited to the vocational sphere, restrict creative abilities, breed stress and often alienation, political first and social next.

Public activity of individuals and groups has instrumental goals in view. It is inspired by individual and group interests which are resultants of individual interests, but at the same time has certain non-instrumental or extra-instrumental goals, too. As Aristotle wrote, the very participation in public life may be for many a goal in itself and satisfy the natural need of social activeness and the resulting prestige.[27] E. E. Schattenschneider said wittily, members of an abolitionists association fighting against capital punishment do not necessarily face the danger of being hanged ...

By pointing to the bridge that takes us to individual and social psychology, and even psychiatry, we wish to emphasize that pluralism must be investigated at three levels:

(a) macrosocial,
(b) microsocial,
(c) in connection with the personality of the individual, who is a biosocial entity.

(13) Pluralism is a necessary, but not sufficient, condition of democracy. In order to activate autonomous elements as generators of information it is not enough to decentralize the machinery of the state and to make autonomous decisions relative to the main political centre; that machinery must function democratically at all levels with respect to the citizens who should have at their disposal institutional possibility of supervising it, such as control of public administration by courts, such as an electoral system under which lower centres of decision-making are responsible to representative bodies, or a system of incessant consultations with the population concerning the key issues because *ad hoc* consultations in precarious economic situations do not serve their purpose. Hence complex organizations, which represent interests of large sections of the population not only should be autonomous in relation to the machinery of the state, but also decentralized like that machinery, that is, supervised by their members, because every complex organization tends to become bureau-

cratic. Hence also there should be a mass of small organizations representing interests of small groups.

Further, the basic requirement is that certain mechanisms should guarantee in a routine way personal changes in the main centre of political decision-making, or even a total exchange of that personnel. It is self-evident that such insititutional changes cannot be carried out without a genuine system of public opinion. In present-day highly industrialized society an important role is played by independent experts, and also by experts who are spokesmen for group interests.[28] They cannot be replaced by official or appointed experts because these depend on the bureaucratic machinery. All this is necessary for the emergence of alternate proposals to most comprehensive decisions. In a word, what is necessary is not only the discharge of civic duties (at all levels), but also the full use made of constitutionally guaranteed civic rights. It is only then that the generators of information will operate at full capacity and corrective mechanisms will start functioning effectively.

Pluralism thus cannot be identified with democracy, but on the other hand it cannot be analysed in isolation from the totality of problems that relate to democracy.

Socialist society cannot and should not be identified, or even associated, with Zamyatin's "only state", with Huxley's "brave new world", with Orwell's ubiquitous and omniscient state. Socialist society needs a state in which coercion on the macrostructural scale disappears and interference with the individual's personal rights is reduced (within the limits of the rule of law) to minimum a state in which the centre of decision-making selects and reduces the number of the decisions it makes to strategic ones and transfers the making of tactical decisions to government and social subsystems.

This forms the framework within which prospects are open for creative initiatives and social activity, a framework that cannot allow decisions to be made only at the top without an active participation of the various systems at the grass-roots level.

POSTSCRIPT

At the end of chapter 6.2 (p.200–201) I wrote: "In many quarters it was argued that the Polish system like the others in the East, is not to be reformed. This seems ridiculous when confronted with a wave of deep-going reforms on the way". Since 13 December 1981 there is in Poland a military state of emergency. Does not the author of these words seem ridiculous himself? However, I maintain my stance: in spite of the military regime deep-going economic, social and political reforms, one after another are enacted, as settled in the 1980 agreements signed in Gdańsk, Szczecin and in other towns.

In spite of dramatic events which flare up suddenly, the thorny carpet of restrictions and prohibitions is slowly rolling back. The steady, relentless push towards pluralism may be slowed down, but it cannot be frozen or "abolished", when backed by the bulk of the nation.

Warsaw, 5 May 1982.

NOTES AND REFERENCES

1. In American political sociology the problem was noticed by G. McConnell, "The Public Values of Private Associations", in: J. R. Pennock and J. W. Chapman (eds), *Voluntary Associations*, p. 110: "The shape of pluralism is changing and with this will come new explanations and participations".
2. R. Aron, "Social Structure and the Ruling Class", *British Journal of Sociology*, 1 (March) 1950; see also *L'Opium des intellectuels* (Paris, 1955), by the same author. On the issue of co-operation between the élites Aron's views come close to those of C. W. Mills, who stressed the co-operation of the three groups of élites: industrial, military, and political. For the criticism of the various élitist theories see T. Bottomore, *Elites and Society* (London, 1964).
3. At the meeting of the people of Daghestan in 1920 Stalin stressed the necessity of respecting the local customary law and other customs.
4. N. Rshevsky in P. F. Lazarsfeld (ed.), *Mathematical Thinking in the Social Sciences* (Glencoe, 1954), pp. 67 ff. (quoted after K. W. Deutsch, *The Nerves of Government* (New York and London, 1966), pp. 40 ff).
5. D. Easton, *A Systems Analysis of Political Life* (New York, 1965), p. 376: "The Systemic Feedback Loop achieves 'Unity out of Multiplicity'."
6. F. Parkin, "Strategies of Social Closure in Class Formation" in: F. Parkin (ed.), *The Social Analysis of Class Structure* (London, 1974) p. 4.
7. M. Rokeach *et al.*, *The Open and Closed Mind?* (New York, 1960).
8. Apart from C. N. Parkinson's well-known satirical essays see R. Goodwin, *The American Condition* (New York, 1974), p. 104.
9. K. von Beyme, *Interessengruppedn in der Demokratie* (München, 1969), p. 79.
10. Cf. N. Wiener, *The Human Use of Human Beings* (Boston, 1950), *passim*, and *idem.*, *Cybernetics* (New York, 1948), *passim*; C. E. Shannon and W. Weaver, *The Mathematical Theory of Communiction* (Urbana, 1949), pp. 99 ff.
11. K. W. Deutsch, *op. cit.*, p. 129.
12. Grupy nacisku (1962), in its later version entitled *Władza i interesy* French transl. *Le pouvoir et les groupes de pression*, (Warszawa, 1974), and *Wstęp do nauki o państwie i prawie* (*Introduction to Politics and Law*) (Warszawa, 1973).
13. G. Simmel, *Ueber soziale Differenzierung* (Leipzig, 1890), pp. 103 ff.
14. E. Fraenkel, *Der Pluralismus als Strukturelement der freicheitlich-rechtsstaatlichen Demokratie* (Berlin, 1964), p. 28.
15. C. Schmitt, *Die geistesgeschichtliche Lage des Parlamentarismus* (Berlin and Leipzig, 1926), p. 14.
16. O. Lange, "Rola planowania w gospodarce socjalistycznej (The Role of Planning in the Socialist Economy)", in: *Pisme ekonomiczne i społeczne*, p. 139.
17. "Entretien avec G. Lukàcs", *L'Homme et la Société*, No. 20 (1971).
18. O. Lange, *op. cit.*, p. 141.
19. *Ibid.*, pp. 57, 140.
20. S. Ehrlich, *Wstęp* ... (Introduction to Politics ...), *ed. cit.*, chap. VI, sec. 4.
21. S. Ehrlich, *Władza i interesy*, (Power and Interests) *ed. cit.*, chap. XII, sec. 3.
22. G. Simmel, *op. cit.*, chap. 6, "Die Differenzierung und das Prinzip der Krafterpasrnis".
23. D. W. Keim, "Participation in Contemporary Democratic Theories", in: J. R. Pennock and J. W. Chapman (eds), *Participation in Politics* (New York, 1975), p. 26.
24. Cf. W. L. McBride, "Voluntary Associations", in J. R. Pennock and J. W. Chapman (eds), *op. cit.*, p 214.

25. J. Reykowski, *Osobowość a społeczne zachowanie się ludzie (Personality and Social Behaviour)* (Warszawa, 1976), p. 229.
26. R. Presthus, "Toward a Post-Pluralist Theory of Democratic Stability", paper presented at the 10th Congress of the International Association of Political Science, Edinburgh, August, 1976.
27. I. Berlin, *Two Concepts of Liberty* (Oxford, 1958), p. 43, refers to "desire for status and recognition".
28. S. Ehrlich, "Ekspert–zagadnienie polityczne (Experts–A Political Issue)", *Państwo i Prawo*, No. 6 (1973).

Index